FLORIDA STATE
UNIVERSITY LIBRARIES

FEB 9 1999

TALLAHASSEE, FLORIDA

THE DOMINION BUREAU OF STATISTICS

CANADIAN PUBLIC ADMINISTRATION SERIES

Iain Gow, A. Paul Pross,
Co-editors

J.E. Hodgetts
Editor Emeritus

This series is copublished by the Institute of Public Administration of Canada as part of its commitment to encourage research on contemporary issues in Canadian public administration, public sector management, and public policy. The Institute also seeks to foster wider knowledge and understanding among practitioners, academics, and the general public.

McGill-Queen's University Press

CANADIAN PUBLIC ADMINISTRATION SERIES

THE BIOGRAPHY OF AN INSTITUTION:
The Civil Service Commission of Canada, 1908–1967
J.E. Hodgetts, William McCloskey, Reginald Whitaker, and V. Seymour Wilson

OLD AGE PENSIONS AND POLICY-MAKING IN CANADA
Kenneth Bryden

PROVINCIAL GOVERNMENTS AS EMPLOYERS:
A Survey of Public Personnel Administration in Canada's Provinces
J.E. Hodgetts and O.P. Dwivedi

TRANSPORT IN TRANSITION:
The Reorganization of the Federal Transport Portfolio
John W. Langford

INITIATIVE AND RESPONSE:
The Adaptation of Canadian Federalism to Regional Economic Development
Anthony G.S. Careless

CANADA'S SALESMAN TO THE WORLD:
The Department of Trade and Commerce, 1892–1939
O. Mary Hill

CONFLICT OVER THE COLUMBIA:
The Canadian Background to an Historic Treaty
Neil A. Swainson

FEDERALISM, BUREAUCRACY, AND PUBLIC POLICY:
The Politics of Highway Transport Regulation
Richard J. Schultz

FEDERAL-PROVINCIAL COLLABORATION:
The Canada-New Brunswick General Development Agreement
Donald J. Savoie

JUDICIAL ADMINISTRATION IN CANADA
Perry C. Millar and Carl Baar

THE LANGUAGE OF THE SKIES:
The Bilingual Air Traffic Control Conflict in Canada
Sandford F. Borins

CANADIAN SOCIAL WELFARE POLICY:
Federal and Provincial Dimensions
Jacqueline S. Ismael

MATURING IN HARD TIMES:
Canada's Department of Finance through the Great Depression
Robert R. Bryce

HEALTH INSURANCE AND CANADIAN PUBLIC POLICY:
The Seven Decisions that Created the Canadian Health Insurance System and Their Outcomes, Revised Edition
Malcolm G. Taylor

CANADA AND IMMIGRATION:
Public Policy and Public Concern
Second Edition
Freda Hawkins

CANADA'S DEPARTMENT OF EXTERNAL AFFAIRS
The Early Years, 1909–1946
John Hilliker

GETTING IT RIGHT:
Regional Development in Canada
R. Harley McGee

CORPORATE AUTONOMY AND INSTITUTIONAL CONTROL:
The Crown Corporation as a Problem in Organization Design
Douglas F. Stevens

SHIFTING SANDS:
Government-Group Relationships in the Health Care Sector
Joan Price Boase

CANADA'S DEPARTMENT OF EXTERNAL AFFAIRS
Coming of Age, 1946–1968
John Hilliker and Donald Barry

THE INSTITUTIONALIZED CABINET:
Governing the Western Provinces
Christopher Dunn

THE DOMINION BUREAU OF STATISTICS:
A History of Canada's Central Statistical Office and Its Antecedents, 1841–1972
David A. Worton

The Dominion Bureau of Statistics

A History of Canada's Central Statistical Office and Its Antecedents, 1841-1972

David A. Worton

The Institute of Public Administration of Canada

McGill-Queen's University Press
Montreal & Kingston • London • Buffalo

HA
37
.C26
W67
1998

© McGill-Queen's University Press 1998

ISBN 0-7735-1660-3

Legal deposit first quarter 1998
Bibliothèque nationale du Québec

Printed in Canada on acid-free paper

McGill-Queen's University Press acknowledges the support of the Canada Council for the Arts for our publishing program.

Canadian Cataloguing in Publication Data

Worton, David A. (David Albert), 1924–
The Dominion Bureau of Statistics: a history of Canada's Central Statistics Office and its antecedents, 1841–1972

(Canadian public administration series; 22)
Co-published by the Institute of Public Administration of Canada.
Includes bibliographical references and index.
ISBN 0-7735-1660-3

1. Canada. Dominion Bureau of Statistics—History.
I. Institute of Public Administration of Canada.
II. Title. III. Series.

HA37.C22W67 1998 352.7'5'0971 C97–901075–6

This book is affectionately
dedicated to the memory of my
long time mentor and friend, the late
Simon A. Goldberg, 1914–85

Contents

PREFACE

The suggestion that I should write a history of official statistics in Canada was made by the then chief statistician of Canada, Martin Wilk, at a meeting of the agency's Policy Committee early in 1984. Before I had a chance to think or say much, there were almost instantaneous murmurs of approval from my colleagues around the table, and so I seemed to have got the job.

Intuition suggested that the story should start in pre-Confederation days and be told against the background of Canada's growth from a staple economy with a population of barely two million, mostly living in what is now eastern Canada, to a mature industrial economy with a population ten times larger in a domain stretching almost five thousand miles east to west, *a mari usque ad mare*. The political, economic, and social developments that brought about this transformation would in turn trigger the need for statistics, a need at first satisfied by demographic and agricultural statistics. As Canada industrialized and became a trader in the world economy, more extensive and complex needs would emerge. Finally, the advent of the Second World War and the reconstruction that followed it would demonstrate indisputably the key role of statistics in public and private decision making. Paralleling the emergence of these needs would be the development of organizational arrangements and the successive revolutions in the technology by which they could be satisfied.

This would have been a fascinating challenge for any historian, but for me it had a special attraction. Since coming to what was then the Dominion Bureau of Statistics in mid-1962, I had become progressively more fascinated with what I felt was not just a department of government like any other, but rather one with a unique mission, requiring unique skills and aptitudes to carry it out. I thought of the professional ranks of the bureau as a kind of secular priesthood – one, moreover, in which women could stand on equal terms with men. Most of the senior staff had spent their entire careers in the bureau, and of those who, like myself, had entered in the late 1950s and early 1960s, almost all stayed for the long haul.

Many people in other parts of the public service would, I think, be hard pressed to recall the name of their department's first deputy head. This was not so with the bureau. R.H. Coats, who founded it in 1918 and guided its development over the next quarter century, was a legendary figure in 1962 and remains so today. From the beginning, his prime objective was to demonstrate to the Ottawa establishment that statistics was not just the mechanical counting of numbers.

Rather, as he continually strove to show, the statistician had a responsibility to develop numbers in the context of a considered analysis of needs, and to render the finished product relevant and helpful for decision making in all areas of society. This was uphill work during the 1920s, but, as the Depression developed and persisted, an awareness that statistics could assist in the identification and resolution of social and economic problems began to emerge. The great breakthrough in the recognition of the statistician's role came with the fashioning of the System of National Accounts to meet the needs of postwar reconstruction. Coats had clearly envisaged the spirit, if not the substance, of the system, and his perception, and that of his successors, continue to inspire the modern generation of statisticians.

Closely related to Coats's quest for professional recognition was the issue of his reporting relationship. As long as he was accountable to the nonprofessional deputy head of the Department of Trade and Commerce, rather than directly to the minister, he felt that his ability objectively to serve other government departments, and indeed the public at large, was prejudiced. This situation was a source of friction and even despondency throughout Coats's tenure, and it is to his great credit that it did not impair the professional achievements just referred to.

Coats did not, of course, start with a clean slate. He always generously acknowledged the contributions of those who had laid the foundations on which he built Canada's centralized statistical system. I was therefore obliged to explore, with no small degree of fascination, the work of his nineteenth- century predecessors, notably Joseph Charles Taché and George Johnson, as well as Archibald Blue, whose mantle Coats assumed in 1915.

I chose to start my story with the formation of the Province of Canada in 1841, and more particularly with the enactments of 1847 and 1852, which *inter alia* authorized the censuses of 1851-52 and 1861. Despite their weaknesses, these latter are generally regarded as being in direct continuity with the post-Confederation censuses. The legislation was recognizably a precursor of the statistics acts that followed Confederation, and it also established the administrative arrangements that were carried over intact into the Dominion of Canada.

Statistical activity in British North America did not begin in the Province of Canada. Statistics had been collected for almost two centuries before, beginning with the census of population and agriculture of 1665 in New France. There were twenty-one subsequent censuses before the 1840s in what became, after the conquest, Canada and then Lower Canada. During the same period, some thirty censuses were conducted under both British and French auspices in what are now the four Atlantic provinces. These activities were splendidly documented in Volume four of the 1871 Census of Canada and later, on the basis of revised and extended source material, in volume one of the 1931 Census of Canada.

I have frequently been asked why I chose to end the history at 1972 rather than bringing it completely up to date. My reply is that a great deal of dust must settle before there can be a balanced perspective on developments at Statistics Canada during the past two decades or so. The 1970s in particular were difficult and controversial years. Many of the people involved, of whom I was myself one, are still around – some indeed are still with the bureau – and almost certainly have different perceptions of the events they lived through. In any case, the story would have to be told without benefit of archival records. Nevertheless, I have prepared an epilogue that looks briefly at the issues of the 1970s, suggests how they came to be resolved, and offers a snapshot of the bureau of the mid-1990s.

In the spring of 1984, I organized a dinner colloquium for all the old bureau hands I could track down. I was fortunate enough to get Nathan Keyfitz and Simon Goldberg who, although no longer resident in Canada, were in Ottawa at the time. Others present included N.L. McKellar, C.D. Blyth, E.B. Carty, Jenny Podoluk, V.R. Berlinguette, W.D. Porter, H.J. Adler, A.D. Holmes, I.P. Fellegi, and L.E. Rowebottom. I had also hoped to get A.H. Le Neveu, who had served longer than any of the others, but illness at the last moment kept him away. My objective was not to compile reminiscences, for I subsequently used oral evidence very sparingly, but rather to get a feel for what it had been like to work in the bureau during the two or three decades prior to my own appointment. I subsequently taped follow-up interviews with Keyfitz, Goldberg, and McKellar, and much later I talked in Toronto with C.M. Isbister, who preceded Goldberg as the key figure in the full development of the System of National Accounts, building on the foundations put in place by the late George Luxton.

This verbal exposure to the personalities of Coats and his successors, Cudmore and Marshall, made them larger-than-life figures for me and added considerable zest to the subsequent archival research. In the case of Coats, I discovered in 1986 that the house of my second daughter's prospective parents-in-law, on Manor Avenue in Rockliffe Park, had been bought by them from Coats's widow soon after his death. Thus I had the near-awesome pleasure of sitting at Coats's hearth on several occasions. Unfortunately, the house was sold some years later and subsequently demolished.

A few words about sources. The National Archives provided most of the material. For the Department of Agriculture both before and after Confederation, I could find nothing relevant to statistics – understandably perhaps, since statistics were demonstrably very low on its scale of priorities. My nineteenth-century sources were therefore mainly the annual reports of the ministers of Agriculture, the various items of statistical legislation, the proceedings of the House of Commons, and the published reports of successive decennial censuses. Indeed, these latter, particularly as they described the evolution of census methodology, were invaluable right through to modern times. Other helpful nineteenth-century sources were the annual reports of the ministers of Trade and Commerce and those of the Province of Ontario's Bureau of Industries.

The statistical operations of the Department of Labour during its first decade or so are well documented by both the King papers and departmental archives. British command papers describe the involvement in the Dominions royal commission of Sir George Foster, the minister responsible for statistics after the Department of Trade and Commerce took over the Census and Statistics Office from the Department of Agriculture in 1912. The period from Coats's appointment as Dominion statistician in 1915 right up to the mid-1960s, after which I could no longer use archival material, is extensively, if somewhat haphazardly, documented.

Record-keeping practices and archival policy during most of this period appear to have been at the discretion of the Dominion statisticians' secretaries. At one point in my research, I came across a fascinating but quite unprintable letter written by George Johnson shortly before his retirement in 1905; Miss Gertrude Kehoe, who looked after Coats's files, had found it in the course of a periodic housecleaning and salvaged it for him as a curiosity item. This sort of tidiness perhaps explains why there are no records left from the old Census and Statistics Office and its forerunners. On the other hand, the National Archives contain an abundance of material relating to the administrative minutiae of later censuses and many publications that should more properly have been in the bureau's library.

In 1987 a records management officer at Statistics Canada, Denis Gelineau, brought to my attention a cache of historical records going back to Coats's time that had been sitting in a corner somewhere for at least thirty years. Mr Gelineau very kindly gave me the run of these files before shipping them off to the National Archives. But the casual approach to record keeping extended beyond the secretarial and administrative staff. Often the written material I scrutinized was undated and bore no identification of authorship. And letters, both in and out, that had also transmitted some document were frequently notated to indicate that the document in question had not been sent to file (or "fyle," as Coats spelt it).

In closing with acknowledgments, I would first like to thank Martin Wilk for his early vote of confidence. Soon after his retirement, serious illness on my part brought the fledgling project to a standstill for almost a year, and its recurrence from time to time following my own retirement in 1988 delayed completion still further. I am therefore grateful to Ivan Fellegi, Martin Wilk's successor, for his continuing patience. In 1993, on the occasion of the seventy-fifth anniversary of the establishment of the Dominion Bureau of Statistics, a popular history of those years was published, but Ivan never lost sight of the need for a scholarly treatment going back before Confederation.

Administrative support was provided by Guy Labossière, Assistant Chief Statistician, Management Services, until his retirement a few years ago, and subsequently by his successor, Yvon Fortin. Transcription services were provided successively by my former secretary, Grace Lackey, Margaret Richardson, Diane Levesque and, most recently, by Nancy Bryerton and Caroline Joly. I am very thankful that they had computer technology to assist them in coping with what would otherwise have been a nightmare of successive rewrites. I would also like to thank Susan Feeney and Fred Baker of Statistics Canada's library, and Rita Groulx of the Communications Division, for their assistance in identifying suitable photographic illustrations. Danielle Baum, also of Statistics Canada, was responsible for transforming the manuscript into camera-ready copy.

Bureau colleagues, past and present, offered helpful comments on the draft manuscript as it developed, but for editorial guidance, I am overwhelmingly indebted to Professor J.E. (Ted) Hodgetts. At the time when the Institute of Public Administration first expressed an interest in the project, Ted was general editor of the institute's publication program. My long gestation period overlapped his formal retirement from this function, but he very generously offered to see my manuscript through to the stage of submission to external readers. I know he spent a great many hours with my drafts and, to the extent that I have been successful in my task, considerable credit must go to him. Needless to say, I claim exclusive responsibility for the history's shortcomings. Ted's successors as joint editors, Paul Pross and Iain Gow, have been similarly helpful.

Above all, I would like to thank my wife, Joyce, who literally had to live with the project. She cheerfully endured my untidy working habits for far too long and was always there with gentle but effective encouragement whenever my creative muse seemed to be faltering.

Joseph Charles Taché *was the first to outline the requirements of a comprehensive statistical system. He served as deputy minister of Agriculture, first with the Province of Canada and then in the Dominion government, from 1865 to 1888. He planned and conducted the decennial censuses of 1871 and 1881. (Courtesy of Statistics Canada.)*

George Johnson*, appointed in 1887, was the first officer of the post-Confederation Department of Agriculture with a full-time responsibility for statistics. His achievements included the planning and conduct of the 1891 census and the development of the Canada Year Book. He served until 1905. (Courtesy of Statistics Canada.)*

Archibald Blue *was appointed special census commissioner in the Department of Agriculture in 1900 and conducted the decennial censuses of 1901 and 1911. He was the prime mover behind the new statistical legislation of 1905, which established a permanent Census and Statistics Office with a mandate for the collection of intercensal statistics. He served as chief of this office until his death in 1914. (Courtesy of National Archives of Canada, Neg. no. PA 197036.)*

Robert Hamilton Coats *was the Department of Labour's principal statistician from 1902 to 1915. In the latter year, he was appointed Dominion statistician and controller of the census on the basis of his research for the Department of Labour and his contribution to the work of the Departmental Commission on Official Statistics of 1912, which recommended a centralized statistical system for Canada. He laid the groundwork for the establishment of the Dominion Bureau of Statistics in 1918, which he headed until his retirement in 1942. (Courtesy of Statistics Canada.)*

Delegates to the Conference of Commonwealth Statisticians held in Ottawa, September- October 1935. ***R.H. Coats*** *(front row, fourth from left) served as chairman and* ***H. Marshall*** *(back row, extreme right) as secretary.* ***S.A. Cudmore*** *was also a delegate (back row, extreme left). To the right of Coats is the UK high commissioner to Canada,* ***Sir Francis Floud****. (Courtesy of Statistics Canada.)*

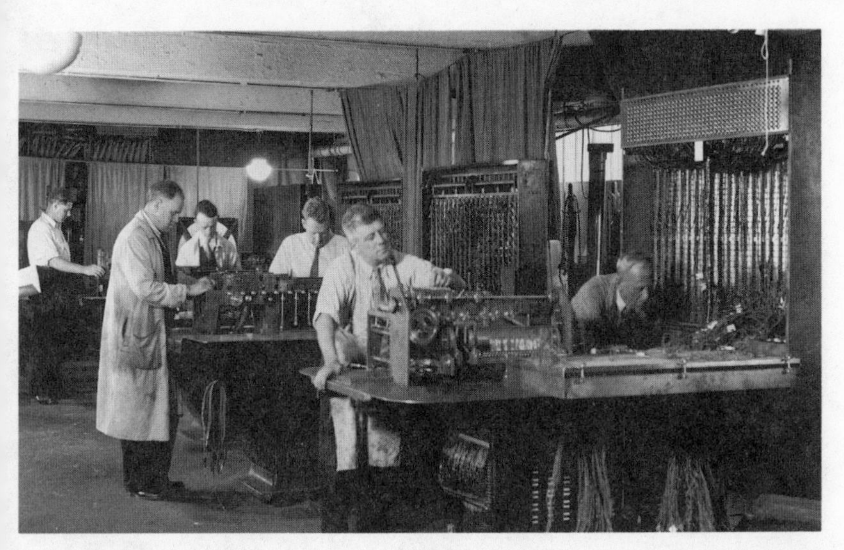

The machinery used for tabulating census records from 1911 through 1941 was largely custom built by ***A.E. Thornton*** *and* ***Fernand Bélisle*** *(foreground centre) of the bureau's Mechanical Tabulation staff. (Courtesy of Statistics Canada.)*

***Coats** makes his retirement speech on 25 January 1942 in the utilitarian surroundings of the **Edwards Mill**. On the table behind him are the thirteen volumes of the dictionary he had received from his staff as a retirement gift. (Courtesy of Statistics Canada.)*

*Between 1927 and 1952, the bureau was accomodated in the makeshift premises of the former **Edwards Mill** on Green Island. The location and view were excellent, but working conditions left much to be desired. (Courtesy of Statistics Canada.)*

As wartime demands upon the bureau grew, the increased staff literally had to work elbow to elbow. (Courtesy of Statistics Canada.)

***Sedley Anthony Cudmore** was recruited by Coats from the University of Toronto in the early days of the new Dominion Bureau of Statistics. He succeeded Coats as Dominion statistician in 1942 but served for less than four years before his sudden death in 1945. (Courtesy of Statistics Canada.)*

Herbert Marshall, *another early recruit from the University of Toronto, developed the bureau's programs of price and balance of payments statistics during the 1920s and 1930s. He succeeded Cudmore as Dominion statistician in 1945 and served until 1956. (Courtesy of Statistics Canada.)*

In 1952 the bureau was finally rewarded with what was then a spacious new home in Tunney's Pasture. Just visible on the pillars at the front of the building are the name plaques that annoyed John Diefenbaker by their omission of the word "Dominion." (Courtesy of Statistics Canada.)

The 1951 census management team Rear (left to right): ***G. Anderson, F. Boardman, M. Waddell, L. Forsyth, C. Scott, D. Ralston, R. Ziola.*** *Front (left to right.):* ***N. Keyfitz, O. Lemieux, H. Marshall, J.T. Marshall, A. McMorran.*** *(Courtesy of Statistics Canada.)*

Walter Elliott Duffett *served with the Bank of Canada and the Department of Labour before succeeding* ***Herbert Marshall*** *as Dominion statistician at the beginning of 1957. He took the bureau through its period of greatest expansion before retiring in 1972. (Courtesy of Statistics Canada.)*

Simon Aaron Goldberg *was effectively Duffett's second in command throughout the latter's tenure. Building upon the earlier work of Luxton and Isbister, he was responsible for the full development and articulation of the System of National Accounts. In 1972 he was appointed director of the United Nations Statistical Office. (Courtesy of Statistics Canada.)*

It cannot, I think, be denied that those who cultivate the branch of knowledge which this Society was established to foster and promote, are held in less estimation than men who devote the same labour and similar talents to many other pursuits. This is partly due to the common mistake of confounding the laborious collection of facts which constitutes the second process of every sound statistical inquiry with the whole procedure, overlooking alike the judgment and scientific insight which planned the inquiry, and the critical and analytical talent employed in discovering and displaying the truth.

> Dr William A. Guy, "On the Original and Acquired Meaning of the term 'Statistics' and on the Proper Functions of a Statistical Society: also on the Question whether there be a Science of Statistics; and, if so, what are its Nature and Objects, and what is its Relation to Political Economy and 'Social Science'". *Journal of the Statistical Society*, London, vol. 28 (December 1865): 478-93.

THE DOMINION BUREAU OF STATISTICS

CHAPTER ONE

1841–1867
Statistics in the Province of Canada

INTRODUCTION

In 1841, following the Durham Report, the Province of Canada was formed by the union of the provinces of Upper and Lower Canada, which were subsequently known as Canada West and Canada East until, after Confederation in 1867, they became Ontario and Quebec. The new province was in the process of transformation from a staple economy, based on the fur trade, to an agricultural economy using European immigrants to settle virgin lands. During the 1840s, however, there were no public departments with responsibility for these and related functions, and consequently no obvious locus for the collection and analysis of the statistics that could monitor economic and social development.

This chapter reviews the legislation enacted by the province to establish a statistical function – in the first instance, largely centred around the conduct of censuses and the collection of vital statistics. Curiously, one census, that of 1851-52, had already been conducted before the need for organizational continuity was addressed. The arrangements that resulted were inadequate, and some six decades passed before effective remedial action was taken. Concerns over the poor quality of the province's first two censuses prompted the inspired appointment of a statistical "new broom" in the person of Joseph Charles Taché. Taché subsequently took the statistical function into Confederation, conducting the censuses of 1871 and 1881, and he must be recognized as one of the fathers of Canadian statistics.

THE CENSUSES OF 1851-52 AND 1861

In 1847, under the Act for taking the Census of this Province and Obtaining Statistical Information therein,[1] a Board of Registration and Statistics was set up consisting of the receiver general, the secretary of the province, and the inspector general. There was provision for a secretary to the board but it had no departmental affiliation, and, beyond specific references to censuses and to vital and criminal statistics, its mandate was vague. The board's prescribed annual report to the legislature was, for example, required to contain "all such information relative to the Trade, Manufactures, Agriculture and Population of the Province as they may be able to obtain."[2]

A census of Upper Canada for 1848 and a general census of the province covering 1851 were carried out under the provisions of the 1847 act. The model for the content of the 1851 census was the decennial census of the United States, which had begun in 1790 as a vehicle for the collection of purely demographic data but had subsequently been extended to cover various kinds of economic and public institutions and activities – manufacturing in 1810, agriculture and the mineral industries in 1840, as well as a census of governments in 1850.[3]

This practice of "piggybacking" on the constitutional standing and funding authority of the demographic censuses was frequently challenged in the United States Congress by so-called "constructionists" who argued that the census should be restricted to its narrower constitutional purposes.[4] Nevertheless, the practice continued for most of the nineteenth century and was also embraced in Canada, which took it even further. Thus, the 1851 census of the Province of Canada had both a personal and an agricultural component, the former covering not only purely demographic data but information on trades and occupations, housing, public buildings, and places of worship. It also required a listing of "every shop, store, mill and manufactory, with their returns of capital produce, rent, number of hands employed, etc."[5]

Census commissioners and, through them, enumerators were appointed barely a month before the date of the census. No training was provided; the census schedules were thought to be self-explanatory. The census was conducted in January 1852, but no reference was made in the subsequent report to difficulties that might have ensued from the winter weather. The report, which appeared in August 1853, was euphoric in tone, asserting that the census findings had clearly laid to rest any notion that, in its growth and prosperity, the province had been lagging behind the United States. In support of this claim, a number of specific comparisons were made with the agricultural production of Ohio, as shown in the US census of 1850.

But a sombre note was struck in the report's caution that "a very general feeling was found to prevail throughout the Colony, that the Census had some direct or indirect reference to taxation – and in this belief the Enumerators were frequently received most ungraciously, and the information sought was, not only partially, but, in some cases, altogether withheld." And there were other factors that cast doubt on the results: "On the whole the Census of Lower Canada has been taken with greater care than that of the Upper Province, where, unfortunately, many of the Enumerators proved themselves wholly unfit for the duties assigned to them."[6] These comments provided a foretaste of the extremely harsh assessment of the quality and analytical usefulness of the 1851 and 1861 censuses made some dozen years later by J.C. Taché shortly after he assumed responsibility for statistics as the province's first deputy minister of Agriculture.

But even before the first 1851 census report had been published, the 1847 legislation had been amended in a manner that would provide the definitive framework for statistical activities during the remaining years of the province's existence and effectively determine the post-Confederation approach to statistics until the end of the century. A Bureau of Agriculture was formally established,[7] and provision made for the appointment of a minister of Agriculture, who was also given the continuing responsibility for census and statistics. The minister replaced the inspector general on the Board of Registration and Statistics and was appointed its chairman. By comparison with the corresponding statement in the 1847 legislation, the statistical provisions of the new act were much more positive, requiring the minister to "institute inquiries and collect useful facts and statistics relating to the Agricultural, Mechanical and Manufacturing interests of the Province, and to adopt measures for disseminating or publishing the same in such manner as he finds best adapted to promote improvements within the Province, and to encourage immigration from other Countries."[8]

But the act provided no operational arrangements for carrying out the minister's statistical responsibilities. This problem was resolved before long, however, through an initiative on the part of William Hutton, secretary of the Board of Registration and Statistics, who steered through cabinet an Order in Council, dated 20 February 1855, integrating the work of the board with that of the Bureau of Agriculture under a common secretariat.

The reference in the new act to the encouragement of immigration is indicative of the way one related function after another was gradually absorbed into the mandate of the minister of Agriculture. Immigration and colonization were always the most important of these since a majority of immigrants found employment on farms. In turn, the connection with immigration led to responsibility for the enforcement of quarantine regulations and, when epidemics occurred, for public health generally. Again, the majority of new inventions were related to farming methods, so that the registration of patents became a departmental responsibility. And, since agricultural products constituted Canada's major exports, Canadian participation in international exhibitions was also organized by the department.

These all became major program activities. In 1861, for instance, even the peak expenditures for the census of that year ($118, 393. 77) were modest relative to the amounts being spent regularly on the support of agricultural societies ($102, 620. 21) and emigration [*sic*] and quarantine ($48, 435. 57).[9] Such programs, moreover, had an immediacy that, because of the limited complement of managerial and staff resources in the Bureau of Agriculture,inevitably pushed statistics into the background. There was a clear indication of this tendency in the low priority given to the conduct, compilation, and analysis of the 1860–61 census, authorized by the new act, which was simply a repeat of that taken nine years earlier.[10]

Concerns about the poor functioning of the statistical service soon became a recurring theme in the annual reports of the ministers of Agriculture. In that of 1862, for instance, the Honourable F. Evanturel noted that "of late years, the [reporting] duty ... imposed upon the Board ... as well as the general objects for which the Board was constituted, have been completely lost sight of, or laid aside. There is no executive machinery in the Department for the collection of statistical information. No records exist of the labors of the Board, or of the results of any statistical investigations or compilations, and, except as far as the Census is concerned, the general functions of the Board of Registration and Statistics appear to have been suffered to become a complete dead letter."[11]

Evanturel went on to argue "the great value of a systematic collection of facts in figures – or statistics – in the administration of the affairs of the State, for the furtherance of political science, and for the general information of the country." He urged upon the executive "the necessity of an immediate and permanent resuscitation of the Board of Registration and Statistics, as an entirely separate and distinct Branch of the Department, unconnected altogether with the general or miscellaneous duties of the Bureau."[12] Writing a year later, Evanturel's successor, the Honourable L. Letellier, saw the neglect of purely statistical responsibilities as part of a more general malaise. He therefore proposed a more radical solution, namely; the appointment of a permanent deputy head. "I am convinced that the faulty organization which has been so prejudicial to the efficiency of the service, is to be mainly attributed to the absence of a functionary of this kind, and that the adoption of my suggestion would be a certain and permanent remedy for the evil."[13] By the time of the next report, Letellier had been succeeded by the Honourable T. D'Arcy McGee, who made a similar assessment, arguing that "the political head of a Department cannot enter into the minutiae of its management, nor oversee its working other than in a very general way."[14]

Joseph Charles Taché – The First Deputy Minister

In September of 1864 McGee did in fact appoint a deputy minister,Joseph Charles Taché, whom he described as having "long acquaintance with every part of the country, and tried administrative experience."[15] These restrained comments gave only the barest hint of Taché's impressive credentials, which included a medical qualification as well as legislative, journalistic, and academic experience. Taché's family was at the forefront of public service in Canada in the nineteenth century. His uncle, Sir Etienne Paschall Taché, was twice joint premier of the province and presided at the Quebec conference on Confederation before his death in July 1865. Taché held the position of deputy minister of Agriculture through Confederation until 1 July 1888.

Taché's initial impact as deputy head perhaps owed something to his immediately preceding position as chairman of the province's Board of Prison Inspectors. "Discipline was firmly restored," reported McGee, "and regular attendance during office hours enforced. Abuses which had grown up insensibly, especially with regard to franking of letters and telegraphic dispatches, and in connection with the consumption of articles of stationery, were immediately checked." And, more pertinently to the substantive responsibilities of the department, "the labor of rescuing all the records from a state of promiscuousness, and from the constant danger of destruction they were in, commenced."[16]

But perhaps the greatest significance of the Taché appointment lay in its recognition not only of the need for better administration but also of the increasingly technical nature of government. As McGee observed: "It is apparent that some of the attributions committed by law to this Department have reference to subjects not only administrative, but also in a greater or less degree scientific in their character, necessitating the presence of at least a few men of thorough education, and more than ordinary aptitudes, among its permanent staff."[17]

The minister's report for 1865 included a memorandum, or "Memorial," providing Taché's assessment of the statistical system that he had just inherited. In reviewing the performance of the Board of Registration and Statistics, Taché repeated Evanturel's earlier criticism: "There have been no statistics worthy of the name ever collected, and none at all published, except such as are contained in the Reports of the two Censuses of 1851 and 1860, of which I shall speak by and by. During the period of the existence of the Board[18] ... only very few meetings have taken place at Census time; no regular minutes of even such meetings have been kept ... The law, virtually, has remained from the time of its adoption a dead letter." In turning to the census statistics themselves, Taché was not just severe, but devastating: "What is today called our statistics – I mean the Census Reports of 1851 and 1860 – are fallacious statements, and not to be relied upon in any essential point ... Not to speak of the deficiency in form, of the gross errors of calculation, of the want of indexes, the four Volumes produced on the two last Censuses can be said, a priori, to be nearly worthless, for they give as facts figures which express absolute impossibilities."[19]

Taché provided numerous examples of these impossibilities, or "absurdities of the most ridiculous character," as he called them at one point:

- The number of living children under one year of age, in the Census of 1851, is stated to be by many thousands greater than the total number of births of the whole of the then last twelve months.
- In the Census of 1860, all the births are made a part of the living population, as if there had been no stillborn, or no deaths accruing from that very number of births.

- Twelve mills in the County of Norfolk are said to have manufactured only 5,100 barrels of flour out of 139,000 bushels of grain; but, on the other side, 15 mills in the County of Middlesex have manufactured 23,775 barrels of flour out of only 35,000 bushels of grain.
- In Lower Canada, the whole amount estimated as the value of the manufactured flour is less than the value of the raw material said to have passed through the mills; so the 440 flour and grist mills that are said to have been in operation during the year 1860 have not only worked in vain, but have lessened the annual product of the county [*sic*] of more than $100,000 in value.
- The shipyards of Upper Canada are represented as having built no ship, but that 0 of ship is valued at $74,700.
- The City of Hamilton is represented as containing only one place of worship, which is a Wesleyan Methodist Church; and the City of Three Rivers is said to possess no place of worship for the Catholics.[20]

Taché's comments on the methodology used in compiling census data shed some light on these curious results: "The addition of the columns do not always agree; but they do sometimes agree in totals, while they quite disagree in the details forming the elements of the calculation. I have learned, by consulting the traditions of the office, that such a wonderful result was obtained by a high-handling of figures, called at the time – *to make them correspond*."[21]

In considering how to rectify the system "which [had] brought forth such lamentable results," Taché saw no need to change the arrangements for "a superior ordering and controlling authority," namely, the Board of Registration and Statistics, together with provision for the office of Secretary of the Board, "on whom depends the practical working system in the greatest measure."[22] Rather, in Taché's view, the solution lay in taking certain necessary steps at the actual working level, without which any tinkering with the organizational superstructure could not be effective.

The first of these was the requirement for a regular, permanent, well-chosen, and properly paid staff of statistical clerks. Taché's recommendations with respect to staff had as much to do with better training and work organization as with numbers, where his plans called for only "two permanent first-class clerks, already well qualified" to be recruited. He contrasted this modest outlay with the larger savings that would result from "no longer employing at Census time a host of untrained, undisciplined, and for the most part totally unfit clerks, at salaries never less than $2.00 a day." He noted that such expenditures had amounted to over $50,000 for the census of 1860 alone, "without anything else in compensation than two worthless volumes of disgraceful statistics."[23]

Secondly, Taché proposed "the affiliation of the head permanent officers of different Departments as consulting auxiliaries in Statistical matters connected with their respective offices." This was no more than the notion of holding periodic meetings between these officers and the secretary of the Board of

Registration and Statistics, "either singly, or collectively," to discuss, as Taché put it, "the best mode of collecting, analyzing and arranging statistics connected with the matters of their respective Departments." It must, however, have seemed a difficult idea at the time, as perhaps also did Taché's third recommendation, namely: "the temporary and occasional employment of men of science for the collection and arrangement of Special Statistics, and the adoption, as official documents, of well-executed statistical labors, obtained from public associations, corporate bodies, and important companies."[24]

But these proposals could not have stimulated much interest or enthusiasm without reference to the grand purpose for which they were required. The highlight of Taché's memorial was therefore his vision of the substantive content of a rehabilitated statistical system. As a prerequisite for what might be possible in the future, the work of methodically assembling and assessing the existing body of "shapeless and disjointed" statistical documentation had to be undertaken:

> The idea of creating the Statistics of a Country cannot be logically conceived without the desire of going back to the remotest period of its history; for, the Statistical science is, above all, a science of comparisons and proportions, and the longer the time, and the larger the figures, the more accurate the inferences and conclusions. My project, then, would be to gather carefully all such information as is to be found in old and recent Censuses, in the printed and manuscript documents of all sorts collected in our libraries, in our religious, judicial, and administrative archives, to complete them at the light of statistical intrinsic and extrinsic criticism, and to arrange them in the shape of abstracts, with indexes, notes and indications of the sources from which they are drawn. Necessarily, such a work would require time, and a great amount of care and labor; but I am confident that, with such an organization as the one I have proposed, it would be possible to regulate the work in such a way as to publish every year a handsome volume of most interesting and valuable information.
>
> The volumes to be published before the taking of the next Census to form the first of a regular series, and to be a complete résumé of the Statistics of the Province from its discovery to the year 1870, such series to be continued afterwards in a more extensive form, by the publication, every year of each decade, of Miscellaneous Statistics, ending by the decennial Census reports.[25]

Taché concluded this landmark report sombrely but hopefully: "Such is the summary of the project of creating real Canadian Statistics, which I lay before your Board: it is the product, the result, and the conclusion of long, tiresome and considerate thoughts, and many laborious nights of conscientious labor; no wonder, then, Gentlemen, that I should feel sanguine, and express my earnest hopes that it will meet with your approval."[26]

These "earnest hopes" were not misplaced, for the Board of Registration and Statistics[27] approved Taché's grand project on 18 January 1865, the day after it was submitted. His request for extra staff was also acted upon promptly.[28] Thus, McGee's report for 1865 told of "a satisfactory degree of progress during the first year" on Taché's work program. In particular, "a very useful revision of the published Census of 1861 and that of 1852, by comparison with the original documents in our possession, has been made."[29]

Vital Statistics

McGee's 1866 report indicated continuing progress but noted that this would have been even greater were it not for the difficulties of persuading local sources to provide vital statistics returns. Taché's memorial had not touched upon such difficulties directly, although he could not have been unaware of them. In any case, they were the subject of study by a select committee of the Legislative Assembly during 1865. The committee addressed the situation in Upper Canada only rather than in the province as a whole, for as Taché explained in his 8 September 1865 submission to the committee, "the system of Registration of Births, Marriages and Deaths among the French population of Lower Canada is so perfect, that, notwithstanding all other changes and perils of destruction, vital statistics of every family and mostly every individual buried or living in the country can be ascertained, from the beginning of the establishment of the country in the commencement of the seventeenth century to this very day."[30]

The committee's report appeared as an appendix to the minister's 1866 report and its main finding was that the older Upper Canada legislation requiring reports to county registrars of marriages solemnized had apparently worked well, but that the more recent comprehensive approach covering births, marriages, and deaths adopted in the 1847 legislation relating to census and statistics was "a dead letter," in that "the Returns required to be supplied under the Census Act are so irregularly given as to be utterly worthless." Accordingly, it was recommended – on the advice of such witnesses as Taché himself and W.H. Johnson – that, while the present system of relying on the clergy for records of marriages need not be changed, this was not sufficient in the case of births and deaths where a system of civil registration was required.[31] The model in view here was clearly that of England and Wales, where a formalized civil registration system for births, marriages, and deaths, under the supervision of a registrar general, had come into effect in 1837.

Nevertheless, as Taché pointed out, the adoption of such a system had by no means been plain sailing in England and Wales, and it could not be assumed to be directly applicable to Canadian circumstances. "For a quarter of a century this question has been the subject of constant enquiries, attempted enactments, laws and amendments in England, and no sooner than in 1836 had a law been passed for the adoption of a definite system; still, the following year (1837) it was found necessary to suspend its operation, and afterwards to adopt material amendments." Taché argued that the details of the system would require a great deal of additional study and consideration, but was confident that a special office of registrar general would not be needed. "The actual Board of Registration and Statistics could, with its Secretary, perform the task imposed upon the Registrar General in England; again, the local registrars and superintendents could be selected by the Board of Registration and Statistics from the better qualified judicial, municipal or educational officers of each County or Registration District." He noted that "some time again will elapse before I have given the matter all the thoughts and enquiries it needs, having besides many other things to do."[32] One of these distractions was his service during much of 1865 as Canada's commissioner at the Universal Exhibition in Paris.

The Blue Book

Another obstacle to the more rapid progress of Taché's statistical reforms was undoubtedly the drain imposed upon the Bureau of Agriculture's small staff by the requirement to produce the annual Blue Book, or "Statement of the Offices, Names of Incumbents, Salaries and Other Information concerning the Public Service of the Province of Canada."[33] McGee's report for 1864 had commented: "The Blue Book for the year 1863, having been returned for addition and correction, by Your Excellency's command, it was found absolutely necessary to make it almost anew; this arrear of labor, although proceeded in with all possible dispatch could not be finished before the end of the year. Defects of many kinds will unavoidably still be found in this second edition of the Blue Book of 1863, executed after time and in the midst of the multiferous occupations of re-organizing everything in the Department, but I hope your Excellency will not take it as a criterion to judge of what is intended for [the] future."[34]

The Blue Book had not up to that time been a public document, but the 1864 and subsequent editions were published. In his report for 1866, McGee recommended "that future editions embrace a much wider field of information so as to make this publication a complete repertory of the official statistics of the Dominion of Canada."[35] This was a curious recommendation, since the Blue Book, by virtue of being essentially a listing of names, salaries, etc., lacked any obvious potential for internal or comparative analysis and could hardly have been a very promising foundation for Taché's "general system of official Canadian Statistics." It is not even clear why it should have been assigned to the minister of Agriculture, rather than, say, to the Department of Finance.

In fact, the Department of Finance was already publishing annually a volume of miscellaneous statistics,[36] most of which derived from the administrative operations of other government departments and the reporting obligations of institutions operating under government charter. Neither Taché's memorial nor any of the ministerial reports of the mid-1860s make any mention of this publication, but its elements were no doubt earmarked for Taché's "mass of well-prepared information on the territorial, vital, religious, educational, administrative, military, judicial, agricultural, commercial, industrial, and financial Statistics of our country."[37]

Conclusion

McGee continued as minister of Agriculture for the Province of Canada right up to Confederation, but did not take office in the new Dominion government, so that the final reporting of stewardship for the province's statistics was formally provided by his federal successor, the Honourable J.C. Chapais. The report[38] reaffirmed the basic thesis of Taché's memorial, that "before publishing the first series of general official statistics, it is first necessarily requisite to enter upon a preparation of retrospective statistics, to serve as a foundation on which to base statements of the numerical position of the country." It described continuing, if spotty, progress on the "vast and magnificent" project of "a general system of official Canadian statistics" but warned against expectations of a speedy conclusion to the undertaking: "The experience of all countries proves that it is only by dint of patience, labor and time, constantly asking and incessantly correcting for years in succession, that it is possible to produce anything worthy of being offered to the public under the authority of the state."[39]

The groundwork thus appeared to have been laid for a viable system of post-Confederation statistics. Statistical activities had begun unpromisingly and had proceeded in like fashion through most of the quarter century of the Province of Canada's existence, producing only two population/agricultural censuses of uncertain quality. Almost in the province's dying days, however, a messiah had appeared in the person of Joseph Charles Taché, and the brisk approach to future statistical work that he sketched out in his celebrated memorial augured well for the new Dominion.

As the next chapter will demonstrate, the assembly and preparation of abstracts of the historical censuses for all of British North America, and in particular the revisions to the 1851 and 1860 censuses of the Province of Canada, were completed in time to form a brilliant backdrop for the published findings of the 1871 census.[40] But the parallel promise of the regular annual publication of a varied range of intercensal statistics was not to be honoured by Taché and his colleagues until 1886,[41] by which time it was quite evident that, in some areas like vital statistics, where there had been such a strong commitment to improvement, very little had really been achieved.

As a final pre-Confederation flourish, there may be mentioned a fleeting appearance by Canada among the developing international statistical community. In 1860 the Fourth International Statistical Congress was held in London under the patronage of HRH Prince Albert. The first of these had been organized in

Brussels in 1853 by the Belgian astronomer and statistician Adolphe Quételet, and a further eight took place over the next quarter century before their functions were assumed by a new organization, the International Statistical Institute, formed in 1885.

The fourth was the biggest and most successful of the congresses, due again to the organizing skills and diplomatic leverage of Quételet, who had been the mathematics tutor of Prince Albert during the 1830s. There were 586 delegates from all over the world, including seven from the United States and three from Canada.[42] Of the latter, only one had official credentials – the Honourable A.T. Galt, minister of Finance for the Province of Canada.[43]

CHAPTER TWO

1867–1905
Dominion Statistics after Confederation

INTRODUCTION

In the division of functions between the Dominion and the provinces, the British North America Act of 1867 allocated "the Census and statistics" to the Dominion.[1] The draft of the act considered at the Quebec conference on Confederation in October 1864 had mentioned only "the Census." R.H. Coats, architect of Canada's present-day statistical system, speculated that the addition of "statistics" was most probably due to the influence of Taché.[2] Both the timing and impact of Taché's 1865 memorial support this view. In any case, the Act was unambiguous as regards the census, for it specified that a general census of the population of Canada be taken in 1871 and subsequently at ten-year intervals, distinguishing "the respective populations of the four provinces," and further directed that the findings of these censuses be used as the basis for the future adjustment of parliamentary representation among them.

But it was less clear what, other than censuses, was being allocated to the Dominion with respect to statistics. As regards those substantive matters falling within Dominion jurisdiction, each of the responsible departments would be in a position to assemble and analyze statistics relating to its own operations. But in most of the fields where the provinces enjoyed exclusive or concurrent jurisdiction, there was similar statistical potential. The view therefore emerged that, while the act could not be read as precluding the assembly and publication of statistics by the provinces, statistics were nevertheless a matter of national concern and should be considered as coming under the general coordinating authority of the Dominion government.[3]

As to how this might be achieved, it could not be expected that a constitutional enactment would address the minutiae of administration. So it is hardly surprising that the pre-Confederation model should have been thought adequate, for the time being at least. Thus, when the Department of Agriculture of the Province of Canada was transformed into a Dominion department, bringing with it most of its former portmanteau of responsibilities and personnel, these continued to include statistics. The exact wording in the enabling act[4] was "The Census, Statistics, and the Registration of Statistics," the latter apparently serving notice of an intent to readdress the difficult problem of vital statistics that the Select Committee of the Province of Canada had reported on in 1865.

But the new Dominion minister of Agriculture, Chapais, in his first post-Confederation report, was cautious about the prospects of any imminent major statistical initiative: "I refrain from entering into any proposition as regards a measure for the carrying out of the Statistical Office of the Dominion for the reason that I think that the beginning should date from the taking of the next census as a base, the preparation for which and the requisite labor relating thereto, being more than can be performed by the small staff of officers now employed at Statistics."[5]

Chapais's comment on the meagre resources available for statistics reflected a situation that barely improved until the turn of the century. The problem was that statistics were essentially being treated as an afterthought in a department with what it saw as more important primary responsibilities, such as immigration and land settlement. The post-Confederation years were by no means a period of unrelieved inaction and failure in statistics, but the will and the means addressed to statistics were inadequate to the growing needs of that era. This can be demonstrated by a review of the major successes and failures in the implementation of the Department of Agriculture's statistical mandate during the period 1871 to 1905, and by reference to some directly related developments elsewhere. The story begins with the census – the basket into which most of the statistical eggs of this period were put. The department's work with other elements of the "general system of official Canadian statistics" – vital statistics, criminal and insolvency statistics, the yearbook, labour and agricultural statistics – are then considered in turn. The story of the yearbook's development is a happy one, but apart from censuses and criminal statistics, the department's other efforts were generally unproductive.

The First Four Censuses of Canada

As Chapais had stressed in the report referred to earlier, the goal of a general system of official Canadian statistics had to be synonymous, for the time being at least, with diligent preparation for the 1871 census, authority for the conduct of which was given in May 1870.[6] For the next two or three years, the minister's reports gave predominant attention to this work. The report of Hon. Christopher Dunkin for 1870, for instance, stressed the unprecedented nature of the task, noting that "there was no previous machinery of any kind for taking the Census. Everything had to be created."[7]

Taché had continued as deputy minister of the Dominion department, and the careful planning, recruitment, and training procedures described reflected his determination to avoid repetition of the problems highlighted in his 1865 memorial, concerning the calibre of enumerators and the wasteful "host of untrained, undisciplined, and for the most part totally unfit clerks" who had been responsible for compilation and analysis in the previous censuses of the Province of Canada. Apart from any other considerations, the purely logistic difficulties of this enlarged census operation, now covering New Brunswick and Nova Scotia, as well as Ontario and Quebec, were much greater.

Taché's memorial had visualized the publication of the 1871 census as including a résumé of all previous censuses, and progress to this end was satisfactorily reported on in the minister's reports for 1867-68, 1869, and 1870. The 1867-68 report also claimed considerable progress on the more general tasks of historical compilation that Taché's successive ministers had constantly emphasized as the necessary foundation for the system eventually to be put in place: "35 works of Memoirs, printed or in manuscript, have been carefully studied, line by line, for the purpose of extracting from them all the information susceptible of numerical analysis; besides which, notes of interest were in the meantime taken of valuable data applicable to the Statistical science. These 35 works comprise altogether 91 volumes, and over 20,000 pages, every one of which was minutely examined."[8]

The report went on to detail the prospective outputs from this process – tables and statements classified under the headings of navigation, immigration, emigration, population, commerce, customs, finances, medical statistics, judicial statistics, education, administration, military and war statistics, and Indians, going back in some instances as far as 1763. In retrospect, however, the hopes expressed by the minister appear to have been far too optimistic; with limited exceptions, this material turned out to be too sketchy and incomplete to warrant publication.

The model for the content of the 1871 census – as indeed for its Province of Canada predecessors of 1861 and 1851 – was the United States census, which, since its inception, had extended its content far beyond purely demographic data. Another important similarity with the US census was the use of the *de jure* system of enumeration by which the population was enumerated according to habitual place of residence. This was argued as being better fitted to "the circumstances of special difficulties of organization, of immense extent of territory, and of federal political institutions."[9]

The *de jure* method caused no noticeable problems in 1871, but when the bill to authorize a mid-decade census of Manitoba and the North-West was debated in the House of Commons in 1885, its use in the 1881 census was severely criticized for distortions and overcounting in the less permanently settled parts of the country. Sir Richard Cartwright charged the government with manipulating the allocation of parliamentary seats: "It may have been for the purpose of depriving the Province of Ontario of a large share of the representation to which it is entitled."[10] This criticism must have struck home, for in taking the 1891 census, a time limit was introduced with respect to the determination of place of residence. Enumerators were instructed that, unless a very clear reason could be given for continued absence, e.g., children going abroad for their education, persons absent for more than twelve months were not to be counted.[11]

The 1871 census had nine schedules and 211 questions covering: nominal return of the living; nominal return of deaths; return of public institutions, real and personal estate; return of cultivated land and products; return of livestock, animal products, home-made fabrics and furs; return of industrial establishments; return of products of the forest; return of shipping and fisheries; and return of mineral products. It can be judged to have satisfied the expectations held out for it in Taché's 1865 memorial. More information had been simultaneously gathered about more people than ever before in British North America, and it was all compiled, analyzed, and published more or less on target.[12] In addition, there was a bonus in the form of volumes four and five, the first containing Taché's promised résumé of previous censuses, and the second a very extensive compilation of statistics of marriages, births, and deaths culled from parish records of the province of Quebec, together with a partial offering of similar information from Nova Scotia – the first fruits of a new registration system begun in 1866. Volume five also provided a comparative analysis of the 1871 and the two previous censuses. In his formal letter of transmittal for the census as a whole, Taché gave credit for the two volumes to the team of Drapeau, Johnson and the Abbé Tanguay that had been appointed for this work immediately after approval of the 1865 memorial.

Of the two volumes, it is four that has retained its lustre. It contained, in addition to the tabular material, a chronological narrative that stands as a unique work of scholarship, covering, among other topics, the tragic history of the uprooting and expulsion of the Acadians, as well as the counterpoint story of the resettlement in Canada of the United Empire Loyalists after the revolutionary war. Volume four also attempted to piece together the fragmentary evidence on the size, dispersion, and way of life of the aboriginal population.[13]

In the case of volume five, on the other hand, performance fell short of promise. After all the diverse material gathered by the three researchers had been assembled and assessed, only the vital records of Quebec could stand scrutiny as an integrated historical data base. One memorable feature of volume five, however, was the report of an investigation of 421 reputed centenarians enumerated at various times in earlier censuses. This appears to have been the first quality check in modern census taking, occasioned by the seeming implausibility of some of the returns. The findings were intriguing: "By examining the schedules of the censuses of 1851, 1861, and of 1871, it has been discovered that many of these centenarians, having continued to live in the same locality, whose identity could be ascertained, have become 15, 20 and even, in one case, 31 years older, in the interval of ten years between one census and the other."[14] Only eighty-two of the 421 cases were authenticated, and thus a harmless cottage industry was ruined:

> A recent case is well known in Canada of an old man still alive, who, like many of his predecessor macrobites, was deriving revenue, dinners, and feasting from his profession of centenarianism. He was armed with the authentic copy of registration of his birth, but in which the last two figures of the date had been altered. The parish priest who had certified the copy, having seen reproduced in the newspapers that copy of registration thus falsified, protested against such a use of his signature, and the so-called centenarian, whose stomach was the stronger that it had not lasted one hundred years by a good many, had to desist from a trade which he was prosecuting by deceit practised on his customers and victims.[15]

By contrast with the 1871 census, which was authorized by an *ad hoc* enactment, that of 1881 was conducted under the authority of the Census and Statistics Act, 1879 (42 Vict., cap.21), which first regularized the decennial census by making provision for a census in 1881 and in every tenth year thereafter. A second feature of the new act, discussed below, was an explicit statement of the minister's broader responsibilities with respect to statistics – in fulfilment, apparently, of the earlier ministerial commitment to "a measure for the carrying out of the Statistical Office of the Dominion" once the 1871 census was out of the way.[16]

The 1881 census was for the most part an uneventful undertaking. It was similar in structure to that of 1871 but a little leaner in content, with eight schedules and 172 questions. As an administrative operation, it was considerably more complex than its predecessor since, in addition to the four founding provinces, it also covered Prince Edward Island, Manitoba, and British Columbia, together with the North-West Territories as then defined. The results were, however, published faster than those of the 1871 census, and the total cost was about fifty thousand dollars less than the half million spent on the latter.

But it was not all plain sailing. Taché found it necessary to write in the introduction to the final volume of the census of 1881 that:

> the third volume of the Census of 1881 ... is the subject of attacks from some newspapers. I have thought it my duty ... to show the fallacies and the unfairness of the attacks. ... Men at all acquainted with the subject will not take notice of such errors, apparent or real, unless they materially affect the general results of the investigation; they know that when the returns give 32,350,269 bushels of wheat, it means about 32,000,000, and that such errors or inaccuracies of details, whether they are of enumeration, or compilation, of posting or printing, some being of overrating and others of underrating, generally balance each other; the only question

> is to see if they are not such as to notably influence the grand result and its proportionate deductions.[17]

Anticipating future problems of industrial classification, he also noted that "many errors of the critics have their source in the fact that several known industries are mixed in various establishments which must be recorded under one title, because it is impossible to discriminate between them and make up accounts for each separate element of the joint undertaking."[18]

The year 1885 saw the introduction of legislation authorizing a mid-decade census in "the Province of Manitoba, the North-West Territories and the District of Keewatin" for the purpose of monitoring population change in these areas of active settlement and rapid growth.[19] The assistant commissioner for the North-West census was the famous western missionary, Father Lacombe. The mid-decade census became a constitutional requirement in 1905 when the provinces of Saskatchewan and Alberta were created.

In 1888 Taché retired, his mantle as deputy minister falling upon John Lowe, secretary of the department. Lowe was no stranger to statistical work. He had taken part in all the post-Confederation censuses, as well as having been the Canadian protagonist in the extended dispute concerning US statistics on the alleged exodus of population during the early 1880s from Canada to the United States.[20] But Lowe was able to leave statistics in other hands, for in 1887 the first senior full-time statistician, George Johnson, had been appointed.[21]

At this time, dissatisfaction was beginning to surface in the United States with the efficacy of the omnibus census. This was a technical issue, unrelated to the purely legal concerns of the "constructionists" referred to in the preceding chapter. Writing in 1888,[22] Francis A. Walker, superintendent of the US censuses of 1870 and 1880, condemned industrial statistics produced in conjunction with demographic information as intrinsically inadequate and too infrequent. The census, he argued, should be confined to the enumeration of population and the collection of agricultural information, with other statistical inquiries being conducted intercensally. These views had no immediate impact in the United States or Canada.

In 1891 George Johnson, now designated as Dominion statistician, conducted the Dominion's third decennial census, consisting of nine schedules and 216 questions. The minister's report for 1890 stated that "great care has been exercised to preserve the essential features of previous census-taking, while at the same time introducing new features in order to bring the statistics obtained up to the most modern views of what a census should be as a national stocktaking."[23] One unusual feature of the 1891 census related not to its content but rather to its experimental use of electrical tabulating equipment. Such equipment had been successfully used in the US census of 1890, bringing instant fame to its designer, Herman Hollerith. The minister subsequently reported that: "In order to expedite the compilation of the immense mass of material, machinery has been employed and a considerable portion of schedule No. 1 has been compiled and the facts sorted by electrical appliances."[24]

The census of 1901 was perhaps the most remarkable statistical undertaking before or since that time, in that its content ballooned from nine schedules and 216 questions in 1891 to eleven schedules and 561 questions. And the total cost of the census, at $1.2 million, was more than double that of the 1891 census.[25] The minister, Hon. Sydney A. Fisher, commented as follows in his 1901 report: "During the current year the work of organizing for the taking of the decennial census has exacted a great deal of attention and labour. It was felt important that a good deal of information which had not been before gathered in Canadian censuses should be obtained. The elaboration of the schedules for this purpose required the attention of an expert who could devote his whole time and attention to this particular labour. Mr Archibald Blue was therefore appointed Special Census Commissioner, and has been able to carry out most satisfactorily the taking of the Canadian census."[26]

The new appointment effectively sidelined Johnson, who spent the rest of his career working on the new yearbook.[27] Blue's expert standing derived from some sixteen years of service with the Province of Ontario, first as assistant commissioner of Agriculture and secretary of the Bureau of Industries, and then as head of the Ontario Bureau of Mines. Because of this latter connection, he is almost certainly the only statistician ever to have been honoured by having a mineral, "Blueite," named after him. His qualifications had been very persuasively urged upon Fisher by mutual acquaintances. John Cameron, president and manager of the *London Advertiser*, wrote: "I have known Blue intimately for 30 years, and regard him as one of the most able men in the Dominion ... If you can get hold of Blue, the appointment would reflect much credit on yourself and your department, and would strike the imagination of the public."[28]

Blue asked for, and got, a salary of $4,000. In making the formal offer, Fisher wrote: "I must tell you frankly that several of my colleagues thought it a very difficult thing for us to offer you a greater sum than that granted to a Deputy Head of a Department."[29] It was, however, paid from the "Outside Votes" appropriation and not from "Civil Government" and, for this reason perhaps, was not regarded as creating an unacceptable precedent.

The conviction that "a good deal of information which had not been before gathered in Canadian censuses" should now be obtained was almost certainly a consequence of the more optimistic view of economic prospects that began to prevail in the final years of the century. A major factor in this optimism was the conviction that, with the settlement of the American West completed, the Canadian West – "the last, best West" – would come into its own, its settlement serving as the engine of generalized economic growth. This in fact happened. Between 1901 and 1911, Canada benefited from a net migration of 715,000, whereas in the three comparable decades from 1871 on, there had been negative net migration of 85,000, 205,000, and 181,000 respectively. And between 1901 and 1911 gross national product in constant dollars increased by seventy-nine percent, by far the highest increase for any single decade since 1871.[30]

The 1901 census therefore sought information on the characteristics of the immigrants now pouring into Canada – place of birth, year of immigration, racial origin or nationality, mother tongue, etc. The need for such information, in conjunction with the more general requirement for extended and improved economic statistics, inspired the new Census and Statistics Act of 1905, which not only elaborated and extended the authorized range of statistical activities, both census and non-census, but also provided a new instrument for carrying them out, namely, a separate Census and Statistics Office within the Department of Agriculture. The effectiveness of this legislation and of the arrangements for implementing it are an important theme of the following chapter.

Vital Statistics

The preoccupation with censuses in 1871 and later did not completely distract attention from other issues. During the immediate post-Confederation years the most obvious statistical expectations, other than those vested in the 1871 census, stemmed from the Department of Agriculture's responsibility for "the Registration of Statistics." There was a fair measure of potential momentum here since the area of vital statistics had been the subject of recurring attention in the Province of Canada.

Vital statistics were seen by Taché as important mainly in the context of a comprehensive scheme of population statistics, in which the results of periodic censuses would be kept up to date through attempts at the current measurement of migration and natural increase. The relevance of vital statistics to pubic health was a different and apparently neglected issue. The Central Board of Health, which in 1866 was preparing contingency plans against a threatened cholera epidemic[31] had authorized some statistical work, although only to the extent, and for the duration, of the epidemic.[32]

The role of the censuses themselves in the provision of vital statistics must first be reviewed before considering the attempts at current measurement. The Province of Canada's censuses for 1851 and 1861 had sought, through the inclusion of questions relating to births and deaths during the preceding year, to provide benchmarks for the current measurement of the natural increase. The quality of this information had prompted some of the most scathing criticisms in Taché's 1865 memorial, but he nevertheless went ahead with the same approach in 1871, seeking to remedy the faults of his predecessors by improved enumerator training and by asking more questions.[33] A similar procedure was followed in 1881, a year for which the quality of census results gave rise to extensive press criticism. But this had related mainly to agricultural and industrial information rather than to the characteristics of the population and the returns of births and deaths.

How effective, then, were Taché's efforts to collect mortality information in 1871 and 1881? This is not the place for a professional assessment of this work, but it can be noted that the 1851 and 1861 censuses generated for Ontario crude death rates of 8.8 and 7.3 respectively per thousand – levels that were not in fact achieved until a century later. The corresponding rates for 1871 and 1881 were perhaps closer to reality at 11.1 and 11.8 per thousand but still indicative of the underreporting of deaths on such a scale as to render them unfit for use in their intended purposes of benchmarking current registrations, which were fragmentary anyway. It was as late as 1901 before this point was officially conceded: "It is well recognized that the mortality returns are never full. They are often ten per cent or more below the actual deaths, as verified by local registration and other sources of information."[34] This was a clear acknowledgment that the benchmarking function of census death returns could never be effective, but there was nevertheless one final round of collection in 1911, the results of which were never published, before the 1912 Departmental Commission on the Official Statistics of Canada recommended the elimination of the mortality schedule from the census.

As regards current statistics of vital events, the Province of Canada's select committee had, in 1865, recommended for Ontario a system of civil registration, based on the English model, that would bring it up to the standards prevailing in Quebec for the Roman Catholic population. In his report for 1871, the minister of Agriculture summarized the situation as it then stood in each of the provinces: "In the Province of Québec a system of registration which has been in operation from the beginning of the colony, has succeeded well for a large portion of the population, but has failed for the rest. New Brunswick has no regular registration system. In the Province of Nova Scotia there is a Dominion Registration of Births, Marriages and Deaths by an outside Branch of this Department. In Ontario, the duty of such registration is attempted by the Provincial Government."[35]

The minister then quoted the blunt assessment of Peter Gow, registrar general of Ontario, of the work done in that province: "At present it is only the striking inaccuracy exhibited in the returns that calls for remark. No facts whatever of a statistical nature can be deduced from them." Gow made a more telling point by drawing attention to the anomaly of work being done in one province at the expense of the Dominion and, in another, at the expense of the province. He argued the benefits of a system of general registration applicable to the entire Dominion: "It is scarcely to be expected that the Provinces, if left to themselves, will simultaneously pass uniform laws upon this or any other subject, and for all useful purposes there is none more strenuously requiring identity of method and schedule. General satisfaction would be secured by the centralization of all statistical work in a Department specially devoted to that object, and established at Ottawa. In future years it may become a matter for regret that such a step was not taken on the birthday of the new Dominion of Canada."[36]

This reproach appears to have prompted the rather cautious reference in the minister's report for 1872 to the prospect of corrective action: "The subject of General Statistics has occupied that attention during the year which its importance demands, having in view to mature a system for obtaining a registration of births, marriages and deaths, and also for collecting agricultural and other returns."[37]

In April 1873 the minister, Hon. J.H. Pope, introduced legislation in the House of Commons as follows: "Resolved that it is expedient to provide a system of Registration of Marriages, Births and Deaths, throughout the Dominion, and for that purpose to attach to the Department of Agriculture an office to be called 'The General Registry and Public Archives Office'; and that the Minister of Agriculture shall be the Registrar General, and his Deputy the Deputy Registrar of Statistics; with power to make regulations (subject to the power of the Act to be passed in that behalf and the approval of the Governor-in-Council for attaining the objects aforesaid) and to employ the necessary officers and clerks."[38]

The summary style of Hansard reporting at the time omits the customary explanation of the government's reasons for introducing such a bill, and the details of what was to be done and how. Neither was there any explanation of why the bill was withdrawn a few weeks later in the session after second reading. There would presumably have had to be cooperative arrangements with those provinces like Ontario and Quebec where systems of vital registration were already in place, and the establishment and direct operation of such systems by the Dominion (on the Nova Scotia model) where they were not. It is difficult to see how such a scheme could have been planned without extensive consultation, and there is no evidence of this having taken place.

As it turned out, the provinces were left to shift for themselves. British Columbia had enacted civil registration in 1872; Manitoba followed suit in 1881, but it was later in the 1880s before anything was done in New Brunswick and the North-West Territories. In the meantime, Ottawa demonstrated its evenhandedness by withdrawing financial support for the registration of vital statistics in Nova Scotia in 1877.

Successive minister's reports during the 1870s demonstrated that the issues of health registration and vital statistics still rested heavily upon the Dominion conscience. The action that was eventually taken was made possible by sections 28, 29, and 31 of the Census and Statistics Act of 1879 (42 Vict., cap. 21), which, in its provisions for statistics other than those of the census, authorized the collection and publication of "vital, agricultural, commercial, criminal and other statistics" and provided that such work be carried out in conjunction with the provinces whenever appropriate provincial systems were already in place. At that time, municipal records appeared to be the most feasible source of vital statistics, and, after extensive consultation with the medical profession and local boards of health followed by a Dominion/provincial conference, a plan was agreed upon that the minister's report for 1882 described as follows: "The collection, compilation, tabulation and publication of mortuary statistics, including the causes of deaths, and the gathering of collateral information on the state of public health.[39] The working of that scheme is based on the organization of Local Boards, and their subsequent appointment of sanitary local officers, who are to be the statistical officers for the collection of the said mortuary statistics. It was found to be absolute necessary to limit the trial of such difficult statistical labour to eleven cities, viz. the capitals of the various Provinces, and such other cities as are possessed of a population of 25,000 inhabitants and over."[40]

The restriction of scope was necessary not only for statistical reasons but also on budgetary grounds, since the initial parliamentary grant was only $10,000. Out of this had to come a lump sum of $400 for each participating city and a per capita subsidy of one cent per head of population, with twenty-five percent of the total allotment constituting the salary of the statistical officer. For each mortuary certificate supplied, fifteen cents was to be paid, and the remainder of the allotment was meant to cover "a medical statement of health, and subjects connected with it, in each of these cities and neighbourhoods."[41] The first report on the workings of the program came in the minister's report for 1883. "Statistical Officers" had been appointed for ten cities, but complete returns had come in from only six of them (Montreal, Ottawa, Saint John, Hamilton, Toronto, and Halifax).

Subsequent ministerial reports gave the impression that the program was gathering momentum. Publication of a monthly bulletin was begun in the mid-1880s, improvements were made in the classification of diseases, and by 1891 25 cities were taking part. But quite out of the blue, the report of 1891 pronounced as follows: "The system of collecting mortuary statistics, carried on for some years, has been found, on examination by the statistician, to be so incomplete as to be practically useless, besides involving considerable expenditure of public money. The returns have been completed to the end of the year 1891, and the work of collecting these statistics ended, pending further examination with a view to obtaining fuller returns in connection with this important branch, by a better plan, if such can be provided."[42]

The way to such a "better plan" was mapped out in a Dominion/provincial agreement reached in 1893, shortly after the demise of the mortuary statistics program: "The Federal and Provincial authorities [should] co-operate in the work of collecting, compiling and publishing the vital statistics for the Dominion." And it was further recognized that "for obtaining the best results, it is desirable that the schedules and forms for collecting returns be as nearly uniform as possible for every province."[43]

Within a decade or so most of the provinces were collecting vital statistics, but, to paraphrase the comment made by Peter Gow twenty years earlier, they could not be expected to adopt, of their own volition, the kinds of uniform procedures that would result in comparable statistics. This had to be a Dominion initiative, and – notwithstanding the apparent willingness of the provinces to cooperate and the unambiguous authority provided by the Census and Statistics Act of 1879 – it was not until 1916 that it was launched.[44]

Criminal and Insolvency Statistics

Criminal statistics were the subject of Taché's first intercensal initiative towards the "general system of official Canadian statistics" outlined in his 1865 memorial. In the absence of the general enabling framework that was to be set out in the Census and Statistics Act of 1879, the work was authorized in 1876 by "An Act to make provision for the Collection and Registration of the Criminal Statistics of Canada" (39 Vict., cap. 13). At about the same time, "An Act to amend the Insolvency Act of 1875" (39 Vict., cap. 30) made provision for the collection and publication of statistics relating to insolvency proceedings throughout Canada, and the two programs were treated as operationally parallel by the Department of Agriculture.

The act dealing with criminal statistics required that the minister of Agriculture be given annual returns of information relating to the administration of criminal justice and the custody of prisoners in penitentiaries, reformatories, and goals, as well as returns under earlier legislation specifying the duties of justices of the peace. The innovative feature of this act was its provision for the remuneration of the persons filling up and transmitting the schedules. In addition to this incentive, however, the act also provided penalties for noncompliance.

The provision for statistics of insolvency was a more modest initiative that may have been viewed as a potential indicator of business conditions. The act stipulated penalties for noncompliance but, unlike that relating to criminal statistics, did not provide for remuneration of the assignees who were responsible for reporting. Some 1876 data on insolvencies were published in the minister's report for 1877, but the report's main emphasis was on the problems that were being encountered in carrying out the new responsibilities: "The labour of gathering reports from the numerous officers required by law to furnish Statistics of Insolvency and Criminal Statistics, and that for the first time, has been accompanied with enormous difficulties. The mere procuring of the Reports, and their correction, owing to the insufficiency of hundreds of the first documents furnished, has been a most arduous undertaking, although, as a rule, the officers have evinced their willingness to comply with the law, and to render the work of collating as expeditious as possible ... The publication of the Report of the Criminal Statistics will have to be delayed ... this will also be the case with the Insolvency Statistics of the year 1877."[45]

In the event, two years passed before it could be proclaimed that "the heavy work of inaugurating the publication of general criminal statistics ... has been brought to a first result." Insolvency statistics must have been easier to deal with, for, by this time, three successive sets had been published. Nevertheless the minister complained that "the difficulties of procuring the proper information of these two heads of statistical investigation are almost disheartening."[46]

Unfortunately, the government came to the conclusion in 1880 that the Insolvency Act, although only five years old, had outlived its usefulness and that public opinion favoured its repeal. It was argued in debate on the Insolvency Act repeal bill that the act had become "rather a means of escape for the dishonest and designing debtor than a mere means of relief for the honest and unfortunate debtor," and that "the rapacity of assignees, the dishonesty of debtors, the greed of some creditors ... have thwarted the beneficent intentions of the law."[47] Thus, the statistics of its operation might not, after all, have been very useful, but a substantial effort on the part of the Department of Agriculture had gone for nothing. As regards criminal statistics, references in the minister's reports very soon became no more than formal notices of their now quite timely tabling.

Statistical Yearbooks

In addition to revitalized census statistics, Taché's 1865 memorial had also promised "the publication, every year of each decade, of Miscellaneous Statistics." This was to be the means of displaying not only such new statistics as Taché had in mind – notably vital statistics – but also those existing statistics resulting from the activities of the various departments. These latter had in fact been published for a few years during the early 1860s at the initiative of Arthur Harvey of the Department of Finance of the Province of Canada.[48] It again turned out to be Arthur Harvey, rather than Taché, who was responsible for the first post-Confederation statistical yearbook, and he must be given credit for the sensible anticipation of a new statistical need. As the preface of the first edition put it: "In view of the approaching Confederation of the British Provinces in North America, and the prospect of their extending their commercial relations with each other and with foreign parts, a hand-book of common information respecting them seems to be required."[49]

The publication, which appeared continuously from 1867 until 1879, enjoyed a number of titles during its early years, eventually becoming known as the *Year Book and Almanac of Canada – An Annual Statistical Abstract of the Dominion and a Register of Legislation and of Public Men in British North America*. It was commercially published, and statistics took second place to almanac-type material, but it has to be regarded as quasi-official on account of Harvey's editorship.

In 1879 the Census and Statistics Act had finally given the Department of Agriculture an explicit statistical mandate, Section 33 providing that "the

Minister of Agriculture may cause to be abstracted and tabulated in a concise form, for easy reference, such information on various subjects susceptible of being represented by figures, as is contained in the departmental or other public reports and documents."

As Coats indicated later,[50] this legislation in effect gave the almanac venture "notice to quit," leaving a clear field into which the department could move. But the 1881 census was on the horizon, and it was several years before the statutory authority to publish a yearbook was exercised. The department's first compendium-type product was a one-time handbook prepared specially for the Colonial and Indian Exhibition,[51] which took place in London in 1886. It was written by George Johnson, at that time Ottawa correspondent of the Toronto *Mail*, who was appointed in the following year as the Department of Agriculture's first full-time statistician.

Johnson had a distinctive style that was later reflected in the annual yearbooks, as well as in a number of other works published under his own name.[52] His introduction to the London exhibition volume was a gem of imperialist sentiment: "Canada presents herself in the great metropolis of the Empire in friendly rivalry with her sisters who, with her and the Mother Isles, form that Greater Britain which Professor Seely has aptly described as 'a World-Venice, with the sea for streets' ... She aims at showing that her progress in arts, manufactures, commerce, wealth, education, government and general development is such as is rightly anticipated from every community sprung from the loins of Great Britain or influenced directly by the spirit of British enterprise." Johnson also noted that "the Exhibition is intended to be a family display, in which each participant, while presenting its own characteristics, remembers that it has also a place in the great British Empire."[53] He adroitly combined both these purposes through the inclusion with the handbook of a "Chart of the World Showing New Route Through Canada[54] Between England, China, Japan, Australia and the East."

The first edition of what started out as the *Statistical Abstract and Record* made its appearance in 1886. Although Johnson was formally appointed to the department in 1887, there were no immediate indications of his influence on the publication's format; in fact, the fourth edition, which appeared in mid-1889, credited a Mr S.C.D. Roper as "Compiler of the Abstract." In any case, this new venture seems to have proceeded cautiously at first, for there was no mention of it in the minister's reports until 1891.

The statistical content of the early abstracts was mainly material on finance, trade, post office and telegraphs, marine and fisheries, railways and canals, banking and insurance, etc. Coats said of this miscellaneous assembly of administrative data that "the figures, what there were of them, went in much as their makers made them ... in simple collocation, most of their imperfections on their head."[55] He nevertheless acknowledged the abstract as the "germ" of a comprehensive and systematized statistical system. The department's own primary responsibilities were covered under headings like population and vital statistics, which were rehashes of census data admixed with the new urban "mortuary statistics"; arts, agriculture, and immigration, where the "arts" component referred to patents of invention; as well as what was by then the soundly established program of criminal statistics.

For the fifth edition, relating to 1889, the title of the abstract was changed to the *Statistical Yearbook of Canada*, although there was no change in format and no explanation of the change in title. Some years later it became known as the *Canada Year Book*, a title it has retained to the present time. The 1893 edition contained an introduction signed by George Johnson, and his influence was demonstrated by a fifty percent increase in the number of pages from the previous year's edition. Johnson indicated that the yearbook contained many new features and had been remodelled in two parts, the "Record" and the "Abstract," which he explained as follows:

> The "Record" contains historical matter: the constitution and government of the country; results of the census of 1891; statements of the managers of our banking institutions; short presentations of important events of the year, such as the Behring Sea Settlement, the French Treaty, and other subjects respecting which public men require occasionally to refresh their memories; and concise biographic notices of prominent public men of Canada who have died during the year. It also contains a chapter on the forests of Canada, the first of a proposed series of monographs on subjects of importance to Canadians; and an account of Newfoundland – the first of a series on "Countries with which Canada does business."
>
> ... The "Abstract" is, as its name implies, a digest of the Bluebooks issued by the several departments, with such explanations as seemed necessary to meet a very general demand for something more than strings of statistical tables.[56]

But this approach was too ambitious to be sustained. Since 1891 the yearbook had been the subject of regular comments in the minister's reports, where the main emphasis was on the difficulties of keeping up with the demand, which increasingly had an international character. The 1896 report, for instance, noted that "requests for the book of 1895 from the governments, public libraries and chambers of commerce of France, Germany, the United States, Italy and other foreign countries have been received in greater numbers than in any previous years."[57] So Johnson retreated to a more utilitarian concept. The introduction to the 1896 edition commented that "in order to increase the number of copies available for the general distribution, compression has been the primary principle adopted in the preparation. The result is a larger issue and a smaller book."[58] This tactic was successful. For the years 1892-95 combined, a total of 9,600 copies had been produced, but for 1896 alone the figure was 4,000 and for 1897 5,500.[59]

Testimonials to the yearbook started to appear in the minister's reports. To call it "a credit to Canada and an example to the statisticians of other British colonies, and even in some of its features, to the statisticians of the mother land"[60] would today seem patronizing, but it was said with evident pride. Under Johnson's simpler format, the yearbook continued to prosper to the point where the 1904 edition had a circulation of more than ten thousand. This was, in effect, Johnson's last official undertaking, for he retired in 1906. The yearbook was almost immediately to undergo a major change in concept and style under Johnson's successor, Archibald Blue, but it stands as a monument to his creative imagination and – unusually for the era – his marketing sense.

The British Association Meeting of 1884

Canadian statisticians had their first exposure to the international scientific community when, in 1884, the British Association for the Advancement of Science held its first meeting outside the United Kingdom in Montreal. This came about largely through the urgings of the then governor general of Canada, the marquis of Lorne. Prospects for its success were ridiculed by the *Times* of London, which declared that "the proposal to hold a meeting in Canada and not in any part of Great Britain is really a proposition to suspend the work of the Association for a year. The year 1884 is to be a blank."[61]

However, the president of the association, in his opening address at the meeting of the following year declared that "our meeting in Montréal was a notable event in the life of the British Association, and even marked a distinct epoch in the history of civilization ... The inhabitants of Canada received us with open arms, and the science of the Dominion and that of the United Kingdom were welded."[62] This success led to a second meeting in Canada, held in Toronto in 1897. More than twenty papers were presented by Canadian authors at the 1884 meeting for consideration by the Economic Science and Statistics Section, and one of these, "Population, Immigration and Pauperism in the Dominion of Canada,." was by John Lowe, secretary to the Department of Agriculture.[63]

Labour Statistics

The persistent, although ultimately unsuccessful, attention addressed by Taché and his colleagues to vital statistics always acknowledged the connection between current records of vital events and those provided, directly or indirectly, by periodic censuses of population. These two sources, together with statistics on migration, were seen as the essential elements of a population model that could monitor progress in the settlement of the new Dominion. The Department of Agriculture's responsibility for immigration was taken over by the Department of the Interior in 1892, but both before and after that date statistics of immigration were a by-product of the administrative procedures for the selection and transportation of immigrants and their reception at ports of entry. As such, their quality during the nineteenth century and, indeed, well into the twentieth must be regarded as questionable. And, of course, there were no statistics of emigration.

In the early years of Confederation at least, no consideration was given to how the parallel development of the working population might have been monitored. But this is hardly surprising, given the prevailing stage of economic development and the consequent lack of any serious pressure for the government to concern itself with the detailed workings of the labour market.

Even so, the labour statistics that were collected in decennial censuses from 1871 forward were deemed sufficiently useful in later years to be included in quasi-official compilations of historical statistics.[64] These mainly covered the occupational and industrial distribution of the labour force. For example, the 1871 census publications included a tabulation, "Occupations of the People," derived from the personal schedule; it showed some 135 occupations from accountant to wheelwright, summarized under broad headings such as agricultural, commercial, domestic, and so on.[65]

The schedules addressed to employers provided employment information by industry and sex, with simple age breakdowns (under and over 16) as well as related yearly wages. This latter information was progressively refined, eventually showing breakdowns of owners and firm members, salaried officers and managers, salesmen, hourly rated employees, piece workers, and so on. A question on unemployment was asked in 1891,[66] but the resultant information was never published.

Day-to-day interest in the labour market tended to focus on working conditions in the various industries and localities, as might be indicated by statistics on wage rates, hours of work, earnings, and the cost of living. The Department of Agriculture's minimal efforts in this area during the first twenty years of Confederation were made not through its mainstream statistical capability but through the reports of immigration agents in various parts of the country. These became a regular feature of the annual minister's reports and consisted of a "Return of the Average Wages paid to Labourers, Mechanics, etc. (Per Diem and by Month with Board)," covering some dozen trades, and a "List of Retail Prices (Ordinary Articles of Food and Raiment Required by the Working Classes)." Up to 1891, when the department relinquished its responsibility for immigration, the quality and range of this rather primitive information was never elaborated, but it was eventually offered for some eighteen agencies and grouped together as a special appendix to the minister's report with, on one occasion at least, a reference in the report proper.[67]

By that time, however, far more comprehensive and better-quality labour statistics were being produced by the Province of Ontario under 1882 legislation that established a new "Bureau of Industries" within the Department of Agriculture, whose commissioner was required, *inter alia*, "to institute inquiries and collect useful facts relating to the agricultural, mechanical, and manufacturing interests of the Province, and to adopt measures for disseminating or publishing the same in such manner and form as he finds best adapted to promote improvement within the Province, and to encourage immigration from other countries."[68] The secretary of the new bureau was Archibald Blue,[69] who, as noted earlier, became a major figure on the Dominion statistical scene two decades later. His responsibilities were vigorously addressed from the start; particularly those pertaining to agriculture, but the bureau's first annual report showed that a survey of the production, capital, employment, etc. of manufacturing establishments, similar to that conducted by the Dominion census, had also been attempted in 1882.[70]

Subsequently, however, the question of statistics on labour market conditions was addressed directly, and the bureau's second annual report noted that "the Trade Unions and other organizations of the working classes were asked to make returns showing for the several trades and occupations they represent the rate of wages, cost of living, time employed, etc., at the chief industrial centres."[71] A year later, similar information covering some 22,000 employees was collected from establishment and household sources and tabulated over sixteen pages of the third annual report.

This work continued intermittently for a number of years, reaching a peak in 1892 when Part VI of the eleventh annual report presented "a report dealing with Labour Organizations in the Province of Ontario, together with an appendix containing information in regard to Labor Bureaus, Labor Statistics in various countries, and Legislation affecting Labor in this and other lands" – some 330 pages of material in all. But little further was done with respect to labour statistics, and the report of the Bureau of Industries eventually became a vehicle for the publication of agricultural and municipal statistics, together with information on chattel mortgages.[72]

The first demonstration of a serious interest in intercensal labour statistics on the part of the Dominion government originated from the work of the Royal Commission on the Relations of Labor and Capital, which had been set up in 1886, probably as a consequence of the unemployment brought about by the acute depression then prevalent. The commission's report, published three years later, argued that "the interests of working people will be promoted if all matters relating to them be placed under the administration of one of the Ministers of the Crown, so that a labor bureau may be established, statistics collected, information disseminated, and working people find readier means of making known their needs and their desires to the Government."[73]

The supporting arguments drew heavily on the perceived success of such bureaus in the United States, where, it was reported; "the first to be established was that connected with the Government of the State of Massachusetts. Following this, at intervals, bureaus of labor or industrial statistics have been formed in twenty-one other States, and in 1884 the National Bureau was established at Washington by Act of Congress. The Acts whereby the bureaus are established are very similar in their terms, nearly all providing that the work to be done shall consist of the collecting of information upon the subject of labor, its relation to capital, the earnings of laboring men and women, their educational, moral and financial condition and sanitary surroundings."

The government responded with legislation that established a Bureau of Labor Statistics within the Department of Agriculture. The minister was designated as commissioner of labor statistics, with the duties of collecting, classifying, arranging, and presenting in periodic reports to Parliament "statistics relating to all kinds of labor in Canada." These principally included:

- The number, age, sex and condition of persons employed; the nature of their employment; the extent to which the apprenticeship system prevails in the various industries requiring skilled labor; the number of hours of labor per day; the average time of employment per annum, and the net wages received in each of the industries and employments in Canada;
- The number and condition of the unemployed, and their age, sex, and nationality, together with the cause of their idleness;
- The sanitary condition of lands, workshops and dwellings; the number and size of rooms occupied by workers, etc.; the cost of fuel, rent, food, clothing and water in each locality in Canada; also the extent to which labor-saving processes are employed, the extent to which they displace hard labor, and their effect on the wages of adult laborers.[74]

Also included, in what was at the time an unremarkable expression of popular and official sentiment,[75] were: "The number and condition of the Chinese in Canada; their social and sanitary habits; the number of married and of single; the number employed, and the nature of their employment; the average wages per day in each employment, and the gross amount yearly; the amount expended by them in rent, food and clothing, and in what proportion such amounts are expended for foreign and home productions respectively; to what extent their labor comes into competition with the other industrial classes of Canada."

The opposition criticized this measure as superfluous on the grounds that the power to do what was being proposed already existed under the general-purpose statistical legislation of 1879, but the government argued the symbolic value of a statutory enactment. The collection and analytical requirements of the new act were, however, formidable to say the least, and it is difficult to see what could have been done with the $10,000 of annual funding provided. In the event, nothing was done, in spite of opposition pressures over a period of four years. The legislation lingered on the statute books until 1906, when it was finally repealed. By then there had been a fresh and more certain initiative with regard to labour statistics through the creation of a separate department, the mandate and activities of which will be described in the next chapter.

Agricultural Statistics

As noted earlier, the 1871 and subsequent decennial censuses included questions on agricultural activities and products. But in the minister of Agriculture's report for 1871, an unequivocal commitment was made to develop intercensal statistics on agriculture: "I propose to commence, as soon as practicable, the important work of gathering Agricultural Statistics to be periodically published in the same way as in other countries, by means of a system which is now being devised with due regard to reliability and economy."[76] Given the conjoint jurisdiction of the provincial and Dominion governments, this presumably meant through Dominion/provincial collaboration. As with census statistics, the inspiration here was probably the system in force in the United States, which since the late 1860s had been publishing annual statistics covering crops and livestock, based chiefly on reports from a network of volunteer farm correspondents.[77]

It was in fact more than a decade before there was any sign of action. In 1883 the minister described arrangements for crop reporting in Manitoba and the North-West, undertaken in cooperation with the provincial government of Manitoba. "The design is, by establishing a system of efficient and prompt collection of current statistics, to be able to present accurately the changes in crop conditions, and in the production of agricultural products, and of the results of agricultural labour."[78] The first fruits of this initiative were published as an appendix to the report. Similar figures were presented with the minister's report of 1884, which also made reference to the initiation "in those Provinces in which crop statistics are not already taken, of a system of obtaining returns of agricultural products by means of schedules circulated through the Postmasters in those Provinces, from which I hope to produce satisfactory results."[79]

But for several years subsequently the ministers' reports were silent on the subject, and no further agricultural statistics were published. Although there was no direct explanation of this, the department's appropriation accounts throw some light on the matter. A grant of $20,000 per annum was provided in each of the fiscal years 1883 to 1886, but only a little more than a third of the cumulative four-year appropriation was spent. Technically, the weak link in the system was probably the use of postmasters for collecting statistics, since Manitoba's own efforts were continued without Dominion assistance.

Since 1882, however, the Province of Ontario had collected agricultural statistics on an annual basis under the authority of the 1882 Bureau of Industries legislation. Thus, when the *Statistical Abstract and Record* began publication in 1886, its agricultural statistics were based on Dominion records of imports and exports of agricultural products, together with production figures provided by Ontario and Manitoba. However, these somewhat limited Canadian data were supplemented with statistics from the UK, the US, Australia, and elsewhere to show Canadian agriculture in a global context. For example, the division of the large and rapidly growing UK market for imported foodstuffs among various supplying countries was regularly analyzed, and parallel developments in other major agricultural economies were monitored.

After several years of silence on the question of Dominion agricultural statistics, the minister's report for 1890, commenting on the work of what it called the Commercial Division of the Statistics Branch, which was responsible for yearbooks, referred to "the number of applications for information on agricultural subjects to which no answers could be returned, owing to the absence of any system of collecting agricultural statistics for the Dominion. A quantity of information concerning the various systems for collecting these returns, in force in different countries, has been obtained, and if some similar plan was adopted in this country, the value to the farmers and the commercial community of the information thus obtained can hardly be overestimated."[80] This pious hope was repeated almost verbatim in the ministers' reports for the next twelve years. But no Dominionwide program was put in hand during the period under review in this chapter, although crop reporting was initiated in New Brunswick in 1897 and in the territories of Saskatchewan and Alberta in 1898.

CONCLUSION

For its work with censuses during the three decades or so following Confederation, the Department of Agriculture certainly merits a passing grade. The time was not yet ripe to heed the warnings of such authorities as Francis A. Walker as to the undesirability of collecting demographic and industrial information through the same vehicle. At any rate, as the following chapter will demonstrate, at least one authority considered the Department of Agriculture's later censuses to be of acceptable quality.

However, little progress was made towards Taché's dream of a general system of official Canadian statistics, which clearly implied a vigorous body of intercensal statistics to keep up to date the principal benchmark data provided by the decennial censuses. The enabling legislation was not in place until more than a decade after Confederation, but in any case, the necessary political and operational commitment appeared to be lacking. Honourable exceptions were the yearbook, which effectively pulled together the statistics derived as by-products from the administrative operations of other departments, and also criminal statistics. Not a little effort was expended in the area of insolvency statistics, but these were precipitately abandoned. And, in spite of much public muscle flexing, the department's Bureau of "Labor" Statistics never got off the ground.

The department's most signal disappointments were in the areas of vital statistics and agricultural statistics where successive ministers had persistently held out high hopes. Both, of course, depended crucially for success on effective Dominion/provincial cooperation, which was an underdeveloped art in the late

1800s. What efforts there were to make a start in the area of vital statistics ultimately foundered. Meanwhile, given the spectacular growth of the agricultural economy during the four decades after Confederation, the inability to generate a systematic approach to the production of intercensal agricultural statistics must be reckoned as a major failure on the part of the Department of Agriculture.

CHAPTER THREE

1892–1912
New Statistical Mandates and New Players

Introduction

Canadian economic development flourished for a few years after Confederation, but by the mid 1870s the country was in the grip of a depression that persisted for more than two decades, with only temporary relief in the early 1880s. The climate of budgetary restraint that the depression engendered was not conducive to new government initiatives, and this was no doubt an important reason for the reluctance or inability of the Department of Agriculture to undertake statistical work other than the conduct of decennial censuses.

In the mid-1890s, however, the economic barometer began to look more favourable, and the first decade of the twentieth century witnessed unprecedented economic growth. In parallel with these developments, the government was coming to recognize that relevant, accurate, and timely statistics could be used to monitor economic progress, and even to influence its scale and composition. As early as 1887 the MacDonald government had enacted legislation to create a Department of Trade and Commerce that would give full-time attention to the development and maintenance of both foreign and domestic trade – a responsibility hitherto belonging to the Department of Finance. The act was not proclaimed until 1892, but from a very early date the new department was publishing and analyzing trade statistics. A Trade Statistics Branch was eventually established under W.A. Warne, who reappears at several points later in this history.

Chronologically, the next major locus of new statistical activity to appear was the Department of Labour. Its primary purpose, the establishment of machinery to promote the settlement of what were called "trade disputes," was a direct consequence of the growing industrialization of the Canadian economy. A secondary but hardly less important purpose was the collection and regular publication of information on the workings of the labour market. This latter function was the means by which Robert Hamilton Coats made his first appearance on the statistical stage.

A final development, at which this chapter will look in detail, was the strengthening of the Department of Agriculture's statistical mandate by the Census and Statistics Act of 1905 (4-5 Edw. VII, cap. 5). By authorizing additional staff resources and establishing what was to be called the Census and Statistics Office as a separate entity within the department, the act sought to give continuity and a higher profile to the statistical function and provide the muscle with which to develop a program of intercensal statistics.

There were, of course, other pockets of statistical activity within the Dominion government and within the provinces also, where the jurisdiction was shared. These were not really part of the pattern of growing statistical awareness that this chapter describes but rather statistics such as those of railways, banking, mining, and fisheries, where the responsible department had a regulatory or administrative role. They were by no means insignificant in their collective impact, but they shall be looked at later in this history when a broader vision of Canada's statistical needs had taken hold and it had become clear that they should be incorporated into some overall framework.

Rather than dealing in chronological order with the developments heralded above, it will be more convenient to address the new statistical mandate of the Department of Agriculture first and then present an account of the statistical work of the Departments of Trade and Commerce and of Labour respectively.

The Census and Statistics Office

Robert Hamilton Coats, writing in 1946 from the vantage point of the centralized statistical system that had been his life work, described the half century of official statistics after Confederation as "a period of *volkerwanderung*, often ... down side lines if not in circles."[1] This may have been a reasonable characterization of most of the period reviewed in the preceding chapter, but it seems harsh as regards the first decade of the new century, which demonstrated encouraging signs of the government's growing realization of the need to put in place statistical arrangements better fitted to serve the national interest.

One such sign was the attempt to strengthen the Department of Agriculture's statistical mandate through the legislation of 1905.[2] In the House of Commons on 7 February 1905, the minister, Hon. Sydney Fisher, explained its twofold purpose. First, it provided for the establishment of a permanent Census and Statistics Office under the minister of Agriculture: "One of the greatest difficulties always found in the taking of the Census is the necessity of organizing a staff, almost on the spur of the moment, of inexperienced people who have never had much of this kind of work before. The difficult consequences on this hasty manner of operation would be avoided if there were a permanent census office."[3]

Secondly, continued Fisher, "what I consider quite as important is the necessity, in the present stage of our development, of obtaining accurate statistics during the ten years that intervene between the taking of the censuses." He then explained how this was going to be done:

> While [the new permanent office] takes a census of the population and obtains detailed information on all the different subjects which have been contained in our census once in ten years, [it] should also have the duty of taking information at first hand on a portion of those subjects every year. I do not propose that a whole census be taken every year ... I do not propose that on any one subject statistics should be taken every year, but I do think that between the two censuses, there should be a periodic taking of information along various lines and include each year a portion of the census information. For instance, certain agricultural statistics might be taken every second year, and certain other agricultural statistics in the alternate years. Certain industrial statistics might also be taken in the same way ... the work would not be done by enumeration but from the office here and done through the mails to a very large extent.[4]

By contrast with previous legislation, in which the power to require compulsory response applied only to the census, that power now applied to all statistical inquiries.

Under an Order in Council of 13 December 1905, Archibald Blue, who had hitherto held the position of special census commissioner, was confirmed as chief officer of the new Census and Statistics Office at his existing salary of $4,000. To clear the way for this appointment, George Johnson was compulsorily retired. On 24 August 1905, the minister wrote to him as follows: "After the pressure of business at the close of Parliament I took up the matter of the organization of the Census and Statistics Branch of my Department consequent upon the passage of the Census and Statistics Act of last session. Carefully considering the necessities of the service, I have come to the conclusion that there is no longer room in the Department for the office of Statistician, and I have therefore decided to abolish the office. As you have been the incumbent of this office, this will involve your retirement."[5]

Johnson responded graciously on the same day, stating that "I have never stood, nor will I now stand, in the way of any reform in the service calculated to benefit the people"[6] and acknowledging that for him to continue to serve would deny Blue the free hand he would require for his new responsibilities. It was, nevertheless, an anticlimactic end to a career that, largely through his work on the Yearbook, had made an important contribution to the development of official statistics in Canada. The blow would perhaps have been softened if Fisher had acceded to Johnson's request that ten years be added to his pensionable service, as Sir John A. MacDonald had verbally promised to do given Johnson's age at the time of his appointment. Fisher, although sympathetic, felt unable to accommodate him on the ground that his party had severely criticized this practice while in opposition and had avoided it since taking office.

The act retained the provision of the 1879 legislation for collaboration with the provinces in accessing their "vital, agricultural, commercial, criminal or other statistics," where appropriate systems for their collection already existed. But during the remaining years of the Department of Agriculture's statistical mandate, this authority was left unused, just as it had been during the previous quarter century. However, the new act made no provision for cooperative arrangements with other federal departments. In a note written in 1917 when, as Dominion statistician, he was drawing up plans for a centralized statistical system, Coats was critical of this missed opportunity to address the broader problem:

> The fact that statistics are so decentralized at the present moment in Canada is due in part to the policy deliberately adopted by the Census Office when it was organized on a permanent basis in 1905, namely to feel no responsibility for statistics in general but to throw back responsibility on the Departments. The old coordinating work in connection with provincial statistics was entirely abandoned, and the object of the Office seems to have been to interest itself primarily, if not solely, in work which it alone was carrying out. I understand that when the present statistics of the Mines Branch were inaugurated it was largely because the Census Office showed a disinclination to take up the work.[7]

New Statistical Initiatives

Nevertheless, the initiative of 1905 soon yielded tangible results with respect to its declared purpose of instituting intercensal statistical collection. The new Census and Statistics Office, strengthened not only in prestige but also in resources,[8] conducted a census of manufactures in 1906, a census of dairy production in 1907, and an agricultural census of Ontario, Quebec, and the Maritime provinces in the same year.[9] By this time the three Maritime provinces, as well as Saskatchewan and Alberta, had followed the lead of Ontario and Manitoba in the production of annual agricultural statistics including crop reports. But, as Coats later noted, "the figures were at all but complete cross purposes, coinciding neither as to time, definitions, nor general methods."[10]

In 1908 the Census and Statistics Office instituted a Dominionwide system of agricultural statistics that, in addition to providing monthly crop reports, also yielded annual estimates of many of the variables in the decennial census of agriculture.[11] These initiatives were an important first step in rectifying the Department of Agriculture's long neglect of agricultural statistics but, because they were carried out independently of the provinces, did nothing to clear up the confusion referred to by Coats.

A year of two earlier, the Dominion government had become involved with the new International Institute of Agriculture (IIA). The moving spirit behind the institute had been an American, David Lubin, who was perhaps the first to appreciate that the internationalization of trade in food and agricultural products was being severely hampered by the tardiness, or lack, of objective information on stocks, crop prospects, and related aspects of agricultural production and distribution. Lubin argued that this need would be satisfied by an international clearing-house of agricultural information and managed to secure the patronage of King Victor Emmanuel III of Italy, who invited the great states of the world to a conference in Rome in 1905 to pursue the idea further. Some thirty states formulated a scheme for an international institute that was submitted to the various governments with an invitation to join. The British government accepted and also asked that the "Dominions beyond the seas" be included. Thus, the government of Canada was invited to join in 1906 and duly accepted early in 1907.

As a major figure in world agriculture, Canada welcomed an international forum in which she could make an independent contribution. In 1909 Archibald Blue served on the Canadian delegation to the second general assembly of the institute as adviser on agricultural statistics and was thus the first Canadian official statistician to attend a meeting of an international organization. The Census and Statistics Office's new body of agricultural statistics provided the basis for satisfying the IIA reporting requirements, which became operative in 1910. The information was published in the *Census and Statistics Monthly*, which made its appearance in July 1908. At first, the publication was also a vehicle for nonagricultural statistics, but in April 1917 it was renamed the *Monthly Bulletin of Agricultural Statistics* and its contents correspondingly restricted.

The legislation of 1905 had been almost immediately amended to put the newly established provinces of Saskatchewan and Alberta on the same basis as Manitoba for the conduct of mid-decade censuses of population and agriculture. Thus, a quinquennial census of agriculture and population of the Prairie provinces was conducted in 1906. Its findings demonstrated how very rapidly the Canadian West was being settled. The combined population of the three provinces had gone up from 419,512 in 1901 to 808,863 in 1906 – an increase of ninety-three percent. Saskatchewan had both the highest absolute and proportionate increases of the three provinces, rising by 182 percent from 91,279 in 1901 to 257,763 in 1906. The Census and Statistics Office was also now in a position to devote resources to a more careful analysis of census findings than had hitherto been possible. Thus, at various times after 1905 there appeared in the new bulletin series studies on "Wage Earners by Occupation" (Bulletin I), "Occupations of the People" (Bulletin XI), and "Real Estate Owned in Canada" (Bulletin X) – all based on 1901 census data – as well as a study of "Immigrants of the Agricultural Class in the Northwest Provinces" (Bulletin VI), which utilized 1906 census data. These studies were the forerunners of the modern census monograph tradition. The only blemish on this impressive record of publication occurred with the revamping of the yearbook, which had been the department's principal contribution to "general statistics" during the previous decade. The "second series," as it was called, starting with the 1905 edition, was starker and briefer than ever before since, among other changes, it now provided only Dominion statistics and, except for an introductory section by E.H. Godfrey recounting "Events of the Year," contained no textual matter.

As the decade drew to a close, attention focused on the 1911 census. The 1905 legislation had provided for an elaboration of content, so that the 1911 census reflected the same omnibus approach as the 1901 census, with thirteen schedules made up of 549 questions. Content aside, it was also remarkable in that its processing depended heavily on the use of mechanical tabulating equipment, for which two full-time specialists were employed.[12] The timely publication of results was also facilitated by the use of bulletins to provide information on specific topics in advance of its formal release in the traditional census volumes. This census turned out to be the professional swansong of Archibald Blue, who died while in office in 1914 at the age of seventy-four. He had been appointed at a time when there was beginning to be a much better understanding of the need for good official statistics, so that his was far from the uphill task of his predecessors, but he must be given unreserved credit for the impressive, if somewhat narrowly focused, burst of creative energy displayed by the new Census and Statistics Office.

An Assessment of the Department of Agriculture's Statistical Work

The 1911 census was the last conducted under the auspices of the Department of Agriculture, since the Census and Statistics Office was transferred to the Department of Trade and Commerce in April 1912. Before looking at the circumstances underlying this transfer and subsequent developments, it is appropriate to make some assessment of the Department of Agriculture's forty-five-year-long custody of Canada's statistical mandate.

It would be unfair to attempt any such assessment with the benefit of hindsight. Even when, years later, there was a full understanding of, and purposeful commitment to, Taché's grand statistical design, substantial progress was slow to come. In fact, for more than a decade after Confederation, the goal had been purely a notional one. A tacit policy of statistical decentralization was followed. As Coats put it: "The provinces were severely let alone. Dominion government statistics were departmentalized. When the administrative motions of a Dominion department yielded statistics, well and good. If further statistics were needed as a guide to policy, the department went after them, if it had the powers; if it had not the powers, it sought them. The government as a whole considered that it was doing its duty if such figures got published, and if on top of that it took the census decennially and as inclusively as possible."[13]

The Department of Agriculture did indeed see that "such figures got published" in the yearbook from the mid-1880s on, but little effective use was made of the authority given by the legislation of 1879 to institute a program of general statistics. As noted above, the strengthened mandate of 1905 quickly yielded some impressive outputs, but new economic and political imperatives were by then beginning to indicate the need for even more forceful action.

The primary mandate during the nineteenth century, however, was the conduct of decennial censuses, and this is therefore the area in which judgments are most appropriate. Coats put his view on this matter very simply with comments such as "Taché laid too much on the back of the census" and "our old census bit off more than it could chew"; he went on to explain that "enumerators trained primarily for the comparatively simple task involved in population and agriculture cannot be trained over so wide an area for the vastly more complex inquiries involved in an industrial or institutional census."[14] Speaking more particularly of the great expansion of census content between 1891 and 1911, the 1912 departmental commission report, to which this history will return later, commented as follows:

> This complexity, by unduly increasing the demands made upon enumerators and the public, involves risk of confusion and inaccuracy ... The origin of the difficulty would seem to be this: As the work of enumerating and classifying the population originally assigned to the Census Office is carried out, opportunity appears for the collection of other data, notably facts relating to industrial conditions. By degrees the amount of this second and essentially different class of matter is multiplied, with the final result that the task of the Census becomes greatly enlarged, and the point of view with regard to it altered, while the new matter remains inadequate from the new industrial point of view.[15]

Such criticisms made no real distinction between the substantive merits of the various post-Confederation censuses. It has since been argued, however, that the censuses conducted by Blue were much better than those of his predecessors, Taché and Johnson. Urquhart, writing in 1987, stated that "the census of 1901 ... was a clear cut better than its predecessors," and that "by 1911 ... there had been time for a further refinement and improvement of the census in nearly all its parts."[16] He was referring to the extension of information, and the improvement in its quality and coverage, in the industrial and agricultural censuses, together with the availability from the census of population of information on employment earnings, which in 1911 were classified by occupation and industry. This suggests that the omnibus collection methodology may not perhaps have been as bankrupt as Coats and his fellow members of the departmental commission later judged it to be. On the other hand, the 1901 and

1911 results were achieved at markedly higher costs than their predecessors. In any case the methodology was doomed, simply because, as the report of the departmental commission was soon to emphasize, it was no longer sufficient to conduct industrial censuses at decennial intervals.

But in spite of the redeeming features of the 1901 and 1911 censuses, the methodological shortcomings of the censuses conducted by the Department of Agriculture appear to provide a far more profound explanation of their basic weaknesses than that relating to administrative discontinuity, which the institution of a permanent Census and Statistics Office in 1905 had sought, in part, to address. The latter view was put forward in an earlier official history,[17] perhaps on the authority of Coats's graphic argument: "A bad feature ... was that for four successive decades the census was compiled and indeed planned each time by a headquarters staff organized *de novo* from the ground up, and sunk without a trace just about the point that it was achieving competence – this for a job that requires both a unique administrative technique and as broad a background, statistical and general, as it is possible to secure."[18]

It is undeniable that, in the prolonged absence of continuous administrative arrangements, the status of the census function must have seemed very insecure. But the Canadian situation was never as bad as that described by Robert P. Porter, superintendent of the eleventh census of the United States, while testifying before a House of Representatives committee in March 1892 on the proposal to establish a permanent census bureau: "When I was appointed I had nothing but one clerk and a messenger, and a desk with some white paper on it. I sent over to the Patent Office Building to find out all I could get of the remnants of ten years ago, and we got some old books and schedules and such things as we could dig out ... I was not able to get more than three of the old men from this city ... I knew most of the old census people. Some of them were dead and some in private business. I succeeded in getting one from Colorado ... I was glad to get him ... With these men we started up the organization."[19]

For one thing, the institution, from 1885–86, of mid-decade censuses for Manitoba and what later became Saskatchewan and Alberta had the effect of smoothing somewhat the sharp cycle of peaks and troughs in decennial census activities. But more importantly, there was discernible continuity among the major personalities involved. Taché, in particular, had a continuous commitment to, and personal involvement in, census work up to the time of his retirement in 1888, and his successor, John Lowe, together with another departmental officer, J.G. Layton, had played important roles in the 1871, 1881, and 1886 censuses. A man who eventually became assistant Dominion statistician under Coats, E.H. St Denis, cut his teeth on census work in the 1870s and can be tracked with progressively increasing responsibilities in the records of every post-Confederation census up to that of 1911. By the time of the 1891 census, Lowe also had the assistance of George Johnson – the first person in the department to be designated as a full-time statistician – who had served in the 1881 census as officer for Nova Scotia. Johnson in turn overlapped with Archibald Blue, who came in as special census commissioner for the 1901 census.

As the responsible minister indicated at the time, the establishment of a permanent Census and Statistics Office in 1905 was aimed just as much at improving the effectiveness of the statistical function as a whole as at providing continuity in census taking. Coats was clearly of the view that the former objective could not be achieved by the 1905 arrangements. In his first annual report as Dominion statistician,[20] he emphasized the distinction between "a general statistical office charged with the taking of the Census," and the former Census and Statistics Office – "a census office *plus* specific independent duties." He went on to quote, with evident approval, John Cummings's concerns about the need for the US Bureau of the Census to demonstrate its value as a general statistical office: "The justification for permanent maintenance must ultimately be formed if at all in the work done by the office in its character as a permanent bureau ... The intercensal activities of the Bureau absolutely determine the character of the working force. If these activities are trivial, the Bureau itself will always be found incompetent to undertake the decennial census."[21]

In fact, the Census and Statistics Office's record of intercensal activities after 1905 was a creditable one, but it was soon to be submerged in the larger sweep of events. In assessing the post-Confederation statistical record of the Department of Agriculture, the pertinent question is whether the establishment of a separate Census and Statistics Office at, or soon after, Confederation would have resulted in substantive developments significantly different from those described in the preceding chapter. Would the detachment and security of a separate office with an adequate staff have made possible the development of a significant body of intercensal statistics, using methodologies for the collection of industrial and institutional information more appropriate than those applicable to censuses of population and agriculture? And could such an office have effectively exploited the possibilities for statistical collaboration with the provinces in those areas where the latter had exclusive or shared jurisdiction?

It seems doubtful. There was not yet, during the late nineteenth century in Canada, a sufficiently scientific and innovative statistical tradition,[22] and international precedents were scarce. The country with statistical needs and capabilities most closely resembling those of Canada was the United States, where a similar, if slightly more restrained, approach to census taking existed, and where, with the exception of agriculture, there was little intercensal statistical activity. Finally – and perhaps decisively, whatever the technical considerations – the disappointing pace of economic development during most of the thirty years following Confederation had not, as the introduction to this chapter suggests, encouraged a very positive view of the potential usefulness of statistics.

Thus, instead of judging the post-Confederation statistical record by the standards of later years, it should more realistically be seen as a necessary stage of evolution. The insights of the departmental commission of 1912 would not have been possible without forty years of experience, good and bad, to draw upon, and the arrangements proposed would have met with little genuine understanding and scant prospects of success in the immediate post-Confederation years. It is worth noting the concluding observation of Coats's 1946 critique, which appears to be more tolerant than his initial assessment: "The text ... may furnish yet one more example of how democracy so often meanders and stumbles (given an occasional push) to an objective, by the old method of trial and error."[23]

The Department of Trade and Commerce

The most important statistical products of the Dominion government during the latter part of the nineteenth century, other than those arising from the mandate of the Department of Agriculture, related to foreign trade. From the time of Confederation, the Department of Customs had generated primary statistics of imports and exports and published them, with little or no adornment, as the annual *Tables of the Trade and Navigation of the Dominion of Canada*. However, this situation changed following legislation in 1887 to create a Department of Trade and Commerce, as a consequence of what the prime minister, Sir John A. MacDonald, called "the rapid and largely increasing trade of Canada, both foreign and domestic."[24] Apparently for reasons of fiscal stringency, the act was not proclaimed until 1892, but the new department very soon began to compile what were later referred to as "trade statistics of an interpretive character."[25] The deputy minister, W.G. Parmelee, writing in the department's first annual report for the financial year ended 30 June 1893, explained the objective as follows: "It is now deemed advisable to show to the people of Canada in a comparative sense the commerce of the world and to point out new avenues through which increased trade may be brought to our shores or through which our increasing products may be carried to countries in quest thereof."[26]

The report showed a sophisticated appreciation of the difficulties of making valid comparisons between the imports and exports of any two countries, citing differences in valuation, the lack of a common statistical period, inconsistent bases for showing the countries of origin and destination, changes in commodity classification systems, and fluctuating exchange rates. In the second annual report, it was announced that quarterly reports had been initiated from September 1894, and within a few years some areas were being reported upon monthly. By the time of the 1905 report, it was possible to say that "times have changed and it now has come about that this department which only a dozen years ago started out in a very small way is called upon for and actually furnishes more commercial information than was given in combined annual reports published or up to that time attainable, notably as regards the tariffs and trade of foreign countries, trade openings, condensed comparative statistics with aggregate figures since confederation, etc., etc."[27]

The department also published special statistical reports from time to time, such as that prepared for a commercial conference in Sydney, Australia, in 1909. The effusive tone of this report[28] is reminiscent of the promotional piece written some twenty years earlier by George Johnson for the Department of Agriculture on the occasion of the Colonial and Indian Exhibition of 1886 in London.

The growth in Canada's trade described by the Sydney report was part of the worldwide burgeoning in international trade that was occurring as the new century proceeded. The concerns that this growth generated for standardized methods of statistical measurement and international comparison led to the founding of the Bureau International de la Statistique Commerciale, or the International Bureau of Commercial Statistics as it became known in English. It had its beginnings in an international conference called in 1910 by the Belgian government to draw up a common nomenclature of goods, with the objective of improving the international comparability of import and export statistics. The initiative came to fruition at the end of 1913, when the delegates of some thirty countries agreed to adopt a five-category nomenclature, on the basis of which returns would be made to a bureau in Brussels charged with the publication of an annual bulletin of international commercial statistics.[29] The bureau was to be managed by the Belgian government but financed by the contracting countries. Canada had declared itself as supporting the Brussels Convention in principle, and the question of its formal adhesion was under discussion during the early months of 1914. But there is no record of an Order in Council on the matter and, in any case, the outbreak of war prevented the convention from coming into force within the specified time limit.

LABOUR AND PRICE STATISTICS

At the turn of the century, a third major locus of statistical activity in the Dominion government emerged with the enactment of the Conciliation Act of 1900. This had as its primary purpose the establishment of machinery to promote the amicable settlement of what it called "trade disputes," and, with a view to providing statistical information for use in conciliation and arbitration proceedings, a Department of Labour was established to "collect, digest, and publish in suitable form statistical and other information relating to the conditions of labour ... [to] institute and conduct inquiries into important industrial questions upon which adequate information may not at present be available, and issue at least once in every month a publication to be known as the Labour Gazette, which shall contain information regarding conditions of the labour market and kindred subjects."[30]

In speaking of the proposed gazette in the House of Commons on 17 June 1900, the postmaster general, Hon. William Mulock, explained that it would "as regards labour, fill the same place as does the report of the Minister of Agriculture as regards agriculture, and the report of the Minister of Trade and

Commerce in the commercial world ... [it] will not be a medium for the expression of opinion, but for the registration of facts ... Canada is behind other countries in not having long since adopted a journal of this kind ... Great Britain established a gazette some years ago prior to the Conciliation Act, and that journal I think has been of very great importance in aiding the work of conciliation."[31]

Mulock took ministerial responsibility for the new department, and W.L. Mackenzie King,[32] at the tender age of twenty-five, was appointed its first deputy minister and editor of the *Labour Gazette*, with Henry A. Harper as associate editor. The gazette got off to a quick start, with the first issue, priced at three cents, appearing in September 1900. It soon became a mine of information on current industrial conditions across the country and the related employment situation, as well as the general conditions of employment, which covered such topics as labour legislation in various jurisdictions,[33] legal decisions, and proceedings under the Conciliation Act, along with statistics on wage rates, hours of labour, and the cost of living. In its early years, the gazette relied heavily upon a network of local correspondents for the collection of statistical information, but gradually a more rigorous approach was taken through the direct mailing to potential respondents of printed schedules.

The appointment of Robert Hamilton Coats, a twenty-seven-year-old Toronto journalist, to the fledgling Department of Labour early in 1902 came about under tragic circumstances. Harper, King's associate editor, drowned in December 1901 while attempting to rescue a lady who had fallen through the ice during a skating party on the Ottawa River.[34] Coats and King were known to each other,[35] but even so, Coats enlisted the good offices of his colleague at the Toronto *Globe*, Claude E. Bogan, in offering himself for the vacancy. Bogan wrote to King on 12 January 1902 to say that "Coats ... telephoned me last night to know if I would endorse his application ... I told him it would be a pleasure to remind you of his good qualities." He was himself considering a change of career at this time and had expressed an interest in the Ottawa position, albeit diffidently. He apparently had other possibilities in view and, in two further letters, continued to press on behalf of Coats, finally noting that "it will be an act of Providence for Coats whose health has been breaking down with work in the *Globe*."[36] King very quickly assured Coats that the job would be his, and Coats's letter of thanks on 22 January 1902 concluded with the assurance that "I shall bring into my new field all the enthusiasm and strength of purpose at my command."[37] His formal appointment as associate editor took effect from 30 January 1902.

Like his predecessor, Harper, Coats was soon effectively looking after most aspects of the gazette on behalf of a superior whose main preoccupation was conciliation work and the various special investigations with which the department was charged from time to time, and who thus spent much of his time away from Ottawa. However, Coats's interests soon converged on the area of employment conditions. On 1 September 1904 he wrote the first of a series of memoranda, addressed to King, on the need for a more systematic approach to the collection and publication of statistics of wages and the cost of living.[38]

The memorandum began by asserting that "to a labouring man the first question is the obtaining of employment; the second is the amount of remuneration he is to receive, and its relation to what he has to spend for subsistence." The gazette was, Coats said, dealing adequately with the first question, but as to the second, while investigations had been undertaken at different times both into wages and the cost of living, no effort had been made to make these statements appear at regular intervals, "or in accordance with a fixed and definite plan designed to be of the greatest benefit in future years." What was needed, Coats continued, was the establishment of a separate wages and cost of living statistics branch that could address itself exclusively to the organization of a system by which an annual enquiry might be undertaken and the results published separately in January or February each year as a supplement to the gazette. This would resolve the difficulty arising from the method of publishing such statistics in use at that time, which "is not only of insufficient scope and accuracy but, to a certain extent, dissipates interest in the subject as a whole owing to the smallness of the instalment which the limited space available permits."[39]

The necessity of maximizing public impact through the timely presentation of a critical mass of information was further stressed in a memorandum of 18 November 1904 in which Coats was reporting to King on the problems of dealing with material currently on hand on the subject of wages and hours. "It will be impossible to handle this matter in less than twelve or fifteen months, and, as five issues of the *Gazette* have already appeared since the circulars of inquiry were sent out, its value by the time it reaches the public will be greatly impaired."[40] Coats, like most English-speaking official statisticians at that time, had had no formal training in statistics,[41] but it was clear that he had done a great deal of homework since his appointment. The September memorandum had spoken of reducing the information from the wages and cost of living returns to "a system of index numbers so that comparisons might be made on a mathematical basis both as between wages and the cost of living in the several cities and provinces and also as to the relation between living expenses and the remuneration of labour at different points."

Neither of the 1904 memoranda appears to have elicited any response from King, and Coats returned to the topic with a further memorandum on 1 September 1905, which was essentially a restatement of his earlier proposals.[42] This was followed by a memorandum on 20 September urging that the annual report be supplemented with "a monthly article and table relating to current prices of selected staple commodities, including the more important necessaries of life designed to illustrate, by a series of index numbers or charts, important conditions and tendencies affecting the cost of living throughout Canada."[43] In this memorandum, Coats addressed for the first time the technical issue of "weighting" the various components of an aggregated index number so that their relative importance would be appropriately reflected. For this purpose, he suggested the construction of a budget for a family of five with an income of two dollars per day. An interesting handwritten addendum to this memorandum read: "*Alternative plan; on wholesale basis (Dun's)* Take complete list of commodities of consumption; secure frequent quotations; multiply prices of each commodity by average per capita consumption in the Dominion (if statistics are available) and add the totals. Result = index number."

This clearly suggested that Coats was aware of the practical difficulties he would encounter before long in collecting retail prices. The problem was essentially one of what the department could afford to spend. Retail prices needed to be carefully specified and collected *de novo* from a great many individual retail outlets, whereas wholesale prices were, comparatively speaking, easily and abundantly available by precisely defined varieties and grades from the business press.[44]

Coats continued writing memoranda on how to improve wages and cost of living statistics. One dated 8 February 1906 proposed a card index system to provide easy reference to the department's growing body of information on rates of wages and hours of labour. The first evidence of any reaction from King came in a memorandum of 6 September 1906, in which he informed Coats that "I have arranged with Dun's agency to supply us through their correspondents in the cities with a monthly statement of quotations of current retail commodities."[45] He also asked for a list of commodities that he could pass on to Dun's, and Coats politely reminded him that he had furnished such a list in his memorandum of 20 September 1905. A memorandum to King of 15 July 1907 provided further confirmation that King was at last paying attention to Coats's proposals. "In accordance with your recent instructions," wrote Coats, "I beg leave to offer the following suggestions as to the organization of a 'cost of living' branch in the Department and the method in which the work of collecting and presenting statistics on the subject might be carried out."[46] On this latter point, he commented on the desirability of a family expenditure survey as conducted in England, Germany, and the United States but acknowledged that it would not be practical at that time.

Just a few weeks earlier, Coats's emerging status as an expert on wages and the cost of living had been demonstrated for the first time outside the anonymity of the gazette. The files contain a brief, dated June 1907, that he had prepared privately on behalf of the Civil Service Association[47] for presentation to the Royal Commission of Enquiry into the Civil Service. Entitled "The Cost of Living, Ottawa, 1897-1907," the brief demonstrated that the average weekly expenditure on staple foods, lighting, and rentals for a family of five living in Ottawa with an income of $750 per year had gone up by 34.3 percent. This level of income, which had not increased in many years, was quite common in the lower grades of the "inside service," as the Ottawa establishment was called, and Coats's findings thus demonstrated clearly the hardship they were suffering. The brief also provided confirmation of the validity of growing public concerns about price increases generally, and it perhaps helped bring about King's apparently more sympathetic attitude towards Coats's repeated advocacy of a program of wages and cost of living statistics. Even so, King still did not take the plunge and a year later, on 6 August 1908, Coats wrote yet another memorandum, restating and elaborating all his earlier arguments.

Much of Coats's problem with King stemmed from the latter's increasingly high profile as architect and administrator of the new Industrial Disputes Investigation Act and *diplomate extraordinaire* on the questions of oriental immigration and the opium traffic. On 21 September 1908 King submitted his resignation as deputy minister, giving as his reason "a sense of public duty and a belief that the larger sphere of politics afforded ampler opportunities of public service."[48] Shortly afterwards he successfully ran for Parliament in the general election of October 1908. On 19 May 1909 royal assent was given to an act elevating the Department of Labour to the rank of a separate portfolio with its own minister, and on 2 June King was sworn in as minister of Labour.

The legislation attracted unfavourable comment from the opposition, which argued that there were too many in the cabinet already, that it was unwise to create a portfolio that did not address the needs and interests of all Canadians, and that, in this particular case, there would be so little for the minister to do that he should not be paid as much as ministers in the traditional portfolios.[49] One member, a Mr Henderson, drew attention to the departmental estimates for the coming year, which provided for a staff of nineteen. "To this list," he noted, "we are now adding $7,000 for a minister. With all this retinue of officials, there will be little left for a minister to do."[50]

There was no criticism of King's qualifications for the position, although another member, Mr Sproule, some weeks before the legislation had even been passed, inquired facetiously about the whereabouts of "the prospective Minister of Labour," who at the time was in Shanghai attending the sittings of the international committee dealing with the suppression of the opium trade. "The Minister [Rodolphe Lemieux] might tell us," Sproule asked, "whether he has been taken possession of by the Mikado or in what part of the habitable world he is resident at the present time, and, if ever, when he is likely to return."[51]

King was succeeded as deputy minister by F.A. Acland, who had served as secretary of the department for some time and would thus have had more direct and continuous exposure to Coats's thinking. But what really tipped the balance towards action was the fact that the cost of living had by this time become a vexing social and political issue. As the February 1910 issue of the *Labour Gazette* put it: "For some years past, and especially since the beginnings of the present century, one of the most important features of the general industrial and economic situation, as in several other countries, has been a continuous and pronounced advance in prices and the cost of living ... It is safe to say that no public question at the present moment equals in general interest, that of the abnormal cost of living."[52]

It was expedient, then, for King as minister to demonstrate his department's willingness and capability to respond with an enhanced program of statistics addressed to the understanding of the issue. Thus, elsewhere in the same issue of the gazette, it was announced that the department was adopting "a more comprehensive and systematic method of dealing with the subject," and that "for several months past arrangements have been in progress looking to the inauguration of a periodic statistical review of prices."[53] The new approach provided for the separate treatment of retail and wholesale prices, and its first outcome was a monthly table in the gazette, starting with data for January 1910, showing "the retail prices of thirty-four commodities which enter largely into the cost of living at the more important centres of population across Canada," with the promise that, at a later stage, "by the employment of averages, and the application of a carefully selected workingman's budget to the statistics, some interesting comparisons and generalizations will be rendered possible."[54]

The Study of Wholesale Prices

The February 1910 issue of the gazette also announced plans for a monthly summary of fluctuations in the wholesale prices of 225 commodities "which enter largely into the trade of the country and which may be considered as reflecting the more important phases of its industrial activity."[55] This new series was to be buttressed by a special benchmark study on the course of wholesale prices between 1890 and 1909. Because much of the current concern about the rising cost of living was centred upon the high prices of meats, advance information on this topic was released immediately. Although wholesale prices were, in principle, more accessible than retail prices, the compilation of data for twenty years was a formidable task. King wanted it done by the existing staff at no additional expense. But Coats was, in some instances, obliged to offer the local correspondents extra payment for digging out the historical data. Even so, John Appleton, the Winnipeg correspondent, complained that "I have hired two men and promised each of them $5.00 to look over the files of the *Free Press* and those of the *Commercial*, the most reliable record there is in existence as to prices prevailing as far back as you require them. But both of them failed me. It is a laborious work and men capable of doing it will not look at it at the price you offer."[56]

The work was nevertheless completed, and the results of the study,[57] published in June 1910, were hailed in the following month's gazette as "undoubtedly the most comprehensive statement on the subject of prices ever published in Canada."[58] Even more notably, the appendix[59] that accompanied the tabulations was without precedent in Canada as a work of statistical scholarship. The portion dealing with methodology demonstrated Coats's easy familiarity with the work of such authorities as Jevons, Edgeworth, Palgrave, Giffen, and the US Departments of Commerce and Labor. He dealt more extensively with weighting than with any other single topic and, after a careful review of the practices underlying the better-known British and United States indexes, summarized his conclusions as follows:

> It would seem strongly advisable, not only that a weighted index number should receive the preference, but that care should be taken in the choice of the particular method of weighting. The dictates of common sense and the abstract reasoning of the mathematician alike appear to support this view. Nevertheless, in proceeding to the actual problem, one is met on the threshold by the fact that, however strong in theory the argument in favour of a system of weighting appears, in practice many of the most important considerations urged for it tend to disappear. Not only has it been demonstrated by numerous experiments that differences between the various systems of weighting are slight; but the difference between any one of them and no system at all is little.[60]

Coats went on to argue that the use of a weighted mean was called for only in two contingencies: "when the general trend of prices is interrupted violently by circumstances of a special character, as in the United States during the civil war of 1861-1865, or in Europe during the Franco-Prussian war of 1870-1872; and when the number of commodities included in the survey of prices is limited."[61] Since neither of these considerations was thought applicable to the Canadian situation, Coats opted in the official index for a simple arithmetic average that assigned equal importance to each commodity.

Nevertheless, as corroboration of the unweighted index, he showed elsewhere in the study the results of an experimental index based upon an approach taken twenty years earlier by the British Association for the Advancement of Science, in which major commodity groupings were weighted according to relative expenditures on them.[62] Whether this influenced Coats's choice of an unweighted index is not clear. He later commented, however, that "in recent years the weighted number has been advancing more rapidly than the unweighted number as a result of the comparatively greater rise in the prices of farm products and foods," and he conceded that "the weighted number just described ... is probably on the whole a better index of tendencies in cost of living than the unweighted index number."[63]

This major initiative was appropriately followed by a reorganization of the department's now more extensive responsibilities. As the annual report for 1910-11 put it: "The work ... has been increasing steadily for some time past, until a point has been reached where further progress is possible only on an enlarged and thoroughly comprehensive basis. Especially is this true of the statistical work of the Department as applied to the very important subjects of wages and the cost of living."[64] Accordingly, a new Labour Statistics Branch[65] was created with Coats in charge. His persistence had finally been rewarded.

The wholesale prices report had been purely technical and its text made it quite clear that "no attempt has been made to deal with causes,"[66] although it did conclude with a general discussion of some of the factors contributing to price change. But it was in no sense a direct response to the continuing intense public interest in the cost of living, an interest that the introduction to the report characterized with a dramatic quotation from a current issue of *Bradstreet's Journal*: "'when the history of 1910 comes to be written, not the least memorable of its happenings to be chronicled will probably be the great agitation, partaking of the proportions of a national revolt, against the high prices of food.'"[67]

The Cost of Living Inquiry

Such a response did not come about until 1913, when a sharp decrease in employment, in conjunction with the continuing prevalence of high prices, finally provided the necessary impetus for the appointment at the end of that year of a board of inquiry to conduct "an investigation ... into the increase in the cost of living in Canada and into the causes which have occasioned or contributed to such result."[68] Coats's professional standing in this field made him a natural choice for membership on the board.

The board's report, completed in mid-1915,[69] looked an impressive effort, comprising more than two thousand pages in two volumes. The first of these two volumes was the report proper, signed by all the commissioners[70] except Coats. The second volume, described as Coats's supplementary report, was in effect an alternative report. It came about because, from the very beginning of the board's work, Coats was concerned about the unstructured approach being taken to the gathering of evidence and the lack of any framework within which to assess it. On 22 June 1914 at the board's final meeting for the taking of evidence, Coats suggested that a memorandum be prepared in his department outlining general economic tendencies in recent years, so as to provide a basis of understanding for the rise in prices. The board agreed, and Coats subsequently secured the consent of his minister, Thomas W. Crothers.

The board was to have met to discuss its report later in the summer but the outbreak of war intervened, and, as Coats reported later, "I did not see the Chairman [John McDougald] until the autumn when he was under the impression that consideration of the report would of necessity be indefinitely postponed."[71] Coats decided to continue with the memorandum anyway since it would be of value to the Department of Labour. But on 21 December McDougald advised Coats that the prime minister, Robert Borden, wanted the report as soon as possible and asked for the materials he had undertaken to prepare. Coats was unable to comply immediately but furnished much of the memorandum in instalments over the next few weeks, and when a meeting of the board was called for 22 February 1915 he was able to bring the balance, except for a summary of findings then in preparation. McDougald would not allow it to be considered, however, on the grounds that there was simply no time to take up the matter. He said he had instructions that the report should be signed that week and added that the meeting had been called to consider a draft report which he himself had prepared.

Not only was consideration of the departmental memorandum ruled out but there was apparently to be no serious discussion of the McDougald draft either. Coats wrote to McDougald after the meeting as follows: "I am unable from a hurried and only partial reading to discuss it in detail, but in general I would suggest that it be made to include a broad definition of the *economic* causes of the great price rise, which is perhaps two thirds of the whole cause ... I wish ... to renew very strongly my suggestion that you print the 'exhibit' of the Department of Labour in full as an Appendix to the Report ... The findings have the approval of the Minister and its publication will be to the credit of the Board and of the Government as it contains several quite new essays in statistical and economic research."[72]

Coats's fellow board members, J.U. Vincent and C.C. James, supported McDougald and signed his draft report, but when Coats received it on 26 February, he felt unable to sign and immediately wrote again to McDougald: "Please do not interpret my answer to Mr Lynton [secretary of the board] ... as a refusal to sign the draft report. It was simply to repeat that I cannot sign it till I have had an opportunity of going into it fully, and pending your reply to my letter of February 24 ... If, however, as Mr Lynton informs me, it is imperative that the report go to the PM on Monday, I would ask under the circumstances that the exhibit ... which embodies the point of view mentioned in my previous letter be regarded as my contribution to the work of the Board. I repeat, however, that I think it preferable that it should be discussed by the Board."[73]

In spite of this plea, the McDougald draft was forwarded to the prime minister on 1 March without further discussion, but there was attached to it an "Exhibit by the Department of Labour through R.H. Coats." This comprised some four hundred pages of essentially descriptive matter from the departmental exhibit,[74] leaving out the analytical material that Coats regarded as its *sine qua non*. The apparent concession did not placate Coats, who wrote to McDougald again on 4 March to "ask the PM through you, that my name be withdrawn in this connection. When I stated ... that I was agreeable to having the Departmental exhibit regarded as my contribution to the work of the Board, I did not refer to the exhibit in its present form, of which I strongly disapprove."[75]

Coats's objections up to that time had been mainly procedural, but as the disagreement with McDougald continued through the rest of the year, he focused more and more on the substantive inadequacies of the board's report as agreed to by the other members. Writing to Crothers in March, he argued that, while the report contained useful information on the production, distribution, and consumption of the major Canadian food products, it was not organized from "the proper point of view." "In fact," he went on, "the report does not seem to have any clearly defined plan at all ... some interesting and important data have been overlooked ... at the same time, the report would gain by condensation and the omission of certain matter that appears trivial, and by a further attempt to digest the evidence."[76] Again, writing to Arthur Meighen, the solicitor general, he urged that the chairman be induced to withdraw from the report the page devoted to recommendations. "The Order in Council appointing the Board did not ask for recommendations ... [those] in question do not grow out of the Report, but are simply lugged in by the scruff of the neck."[77]

As the preceding illustrates, various cabinet members were at one time or another drawn into the controversy, including the prime minister, and also Sir George Foster after Coats's appointment as Dominion statistician in June 1915. At one point, it seemed that there would have to be a majority and a minority report, making public the board's discord. Eventually, however, an awkward compromise was reached by which the McDougald text, augmented by the seven appendices referred to earlier and prefaced by the summary (Part III) from the Department of Labour exhibit, "The Rise in the Cost of Living in Canada and its Economic Causes," made up volume one of the board's report, published in February 1916. Coats's unabridged material, comprising some one thousand pages, was published as volume two and referred to as the "Supplementary Report."[78]

Coats's introductory exhibit to volume one offered the view that the advances in prices were the growing pains of an unprecedented era of economic and social change: "The great rise in prices that has taken place in Canada is ... found to centre largely in the new distribution problem which has been created by the lessening of expenditures on capital account ... almost an exact counterpart is to be found in the experience of the provinces during the 1850's while the original railway and canal systems of the country were under construction ... [and when] there was a real estate boom of enormous proportions and in rapid growth of the cities at the expense of the rural districts."[79]

The report proper paraphrased this explanation and also cited the increase of the gold supply as a factor in rising prices. A great deal more attention, however, was addressed to what might now be called early manifestations of marketing technology: "advertising designed to exploit the public rather than to make known the merits of commodities ... the increased use of package goods instead of food bought in bulk ... the greater cost of frequent delivery and of small packages, increased by the growing use of the telephone in ordering supplies." The expenditure of twelve million dollars a year on automobiles in Canada prompted the observation that "reasonable recreation and reasonable luxury may be necessary for modern progress, but the price has to be paid and the bill is found in our high cost of living."[80]

Volume two – Coats's supplementary report–was singularly devoid of observations of this sort and emphasized the general economic factors at work. It embodied all the material published as appendices to the majority report and to this extent it was, as noted earlier, duplicative. But this material, which made up the larger portion of Part I of volume two, "Facts," was required for the volume to stand as a self-contained report. The unique character of the volume stemmed from Part II, "Causes," a three-hundred-page review of monetary and general economic conditions including trade, capital, labour markets, production, and consumption, much of this information being set in a historical and international context. A third part of the report distilled the preceding analysis with a summary account of the economic causes of the rise in the cost of living. Like the background material provided in the wholesale prices report of 1910, the supplementary report, particularly Part II, was a formidable piece of statistical scholarship, monumental in its scope and erudition and truly remarkable for the speed with which it was put together.

The work attracted favourable attention from professional colleagues the world over. Coats received a complimentary letter from the venerable Alfred Marshall of Cambridge University, and Wesley Clair Mitchell, an ardent proponent of the need to base economic analysis on observation and measurement, wrote from Columbia University that "this investigation of yours seems to me precisely the kind of work which is most needed for bettering our understanding of current economic developments, and for guiding our economic policy wisely. It is sound in method; it supplements one branch of statistical inquiry by another; it is lucid in arrangement, and its inclusions are of great significance ... this piece of work is a real contribution to economic science, as well as a document of much practical interest to Canadians ... your inquiry is in several respects wider in scope than any other known to me."[81]

TOWARDS A NATIONAL STATISTICAL SYSTEM

Even before its involvement in the cost of living inquiry, it was clear that the Department of Labour had developed a significant statistical capability during the decade or so of its existence, and that there was a booming market for the kinds of statistics that the Conciliation Act required it to collect. At the same time, the climate for economic growth that prevailed during the early years of the century was extremely favourable to the Department of Trade and Commerce's mandate to "develop ... and maintain ... everything connected with our trade and commerce." That department, too, now had a highly competent statistical facility, particularly on the analytical side, but to work at its full potential it required a comprehensive body of statistics covering the production of primary and manufactured commodities and the trade in them, both domestic and foreign. However, major elements in the schema, notably those relating to internal trade, were lacking.

There was no evidence that the Department of Agriculture's Census and Statistics Office was interested in filling the gap. Instead, as noted earlier, it still regarded its mandate as the conduct of omnibus censuses and the provision of less-detailed but more frequent and timely information on the agricultural and industrial elements of those censuses. In the provinces too, there was a growing awareness of the need for statistical information relating to provincial conditions and development, and collection programs had gradually been established to meet the need. But the resultant products lacked mutual consistency as between provinces and frequently duplicated work being done at the Dominion level.

The time was clearly ripe for a new initiative in statistical leadership that would define the requirements of a comprehensive national system and harness existing capabilities, both Dominion and provincial, to work in close cooperation towards its achievement. The last few years of Laurier's long tenure as Liberal prime minister were probably fraught with too many major political problems for such an initiative to be possible. The occasion was provided, however, by the election of a new government late in 1911 and the appointment of a remarkable minister of Trade and Commerce, George Eulas Foster, who moved quickly and decisively on the statistical issue. And it does not need hindsight to see that Robert Hamilton Coats was sure to be a central figure in subsequent developments.

CHAPTER FOUR

1912–1918
The Years of Change

Introduction

The year 1912 was a watershed in the history of official statistics in Canada, not least because it brought onto the stage the new minister of Trade and Commerce, George Eulas Foster. The portfolio was a natural focus for all the imperatives towards statistical reform that had been emerging during the previous two decades. Foster's previous cabinet experience as minister of Finance between 1887 and 1896 gave him a ready-made understanding of the issues and – most crucially – he was to serve in Trade and Commerce continuously for almost ten years. Thus, his vision, commitment, and political authority were the driving forces behind the remarkable sequence of statistical developments during his time in office.

The sequence began with the transfer of the Census and Statistics Office from the Department of Agriculture to the Department of Trade and Commerce on 1 April 1912.[1] Just a few weeks later, on Foster's initiative, a departmental commission was appointed with a mandate to look critically at the existing hodge-podge of official statistics and to make recommendations for a more systematic body of statistics appropriate to the needs of the time. Almost concurrently, Foster was named as the Canadian representative on a newly established Dominions royal commission.[2] The commission's mandate was primarily addressed to trade issues, but as its inquiries proceeded, these were seen to have important statistical implications. Its work, interrupted by the outbreak of war, continued until 1918.

Simultaneously, the work of the departmental commission, appointed to examine domestic statistics, was proceeding. Following the acceptance by Foster of its findings, R.H. Coats, who had served on the commission, was appointed Dominion statistician. He spent the next three years putting together a plan for a central statistical office for Canada and translating it into legislative form for enactment by Parliament. While the discussions of, and planning for, imperial statistics had no direct impact on the development of the Canadian statistical system, the reverse was not true. Canadian thinking and experience influenced both the statistical conclusions of the Dominions royal commission and also their disposition in the years following the end of the war. Canada's role in the latter process will be dealt in a subsequent chapter. Before looking at the work of the departmental commission and how it was followed up, however, the activities of the Dominions royal commission will be briefly reviewed.

Towards Imperial Statistics

The Dominions royal commission had its origin in a resolution of the imperial conference of 1911, which had called for an investigation of and report upon "the natural resources of each part of the Empire represented at the Conference, the development attained and attainable, and the facilities for production, manufacturing and distribution; the trade of each part with the others and the outside world; the food and raw material requirements of each and the sources thereof available; to what extent, if any, the trade between each of the different parts has been affected by existing legislation in each, either beneficially or otherwise; and by what methods consistent with the existing fiscal policy of each part, the trade of each part with the others may be improved and extended."[3]

The 1911 conference that proposed the commission was the most recent in a series of what were originally called colonial conferences going back to 1887, which had been convened from time to time as pressures on the part of the self-governing colonies for full autonomy in the making of trade agreements with each other and with other countries had grown.[4] These issues were of particular importance to Canada, which, since the early 1890s, had been concerned to lessen dependence on its two major markets, the United States and the United Kingdom, to find new outlets for farm products, and to seek customers for the range of manufactured goods developed under the protection of the National Policy. The Department of Trade and Commerce had been created in 1892 to carry out these purposes. Foster, as minister of Finance, had participated in the colonial conference of 1894 held in Ottawa and presumably welcomed the opportunity now provided to document and analyze the complex patterns of interdependency in imperial economic development and trade. Equally, it would have been clear to him that the task would require an extension and improvement of statistics – particularly as to their comparability – among the countries of the empire.[5]

By late 1912 Foster was taking part in the preliminary work of the Dominions royal commission in London, and he travelled in New Zealand and Australia with the commission between February and June of 1913.[6] In January 1914 the commission issued its second interim report,[7] which, like the report of the Canadian departmental commission discussed below, was strongly influenced in respect of statistics by the centralist views of A.L. Bowley, a leading English academic authority on statistics who had given evidence in London. The

Australian experience was also cited in the report. In particular, the 1906 conference of state and Commonwealth statisticians in Melbourne had resulted in "marked progress in the coordination of Australian statistics" and it was suggested that there was obvious potential for "useful application in the wider sphere of Imperial Statistics."[8] The work of the Dominions commission continued during 1914 in South Africa (without Foster), again in London, and in Newfoundland. It was to have been completed with a program of sessions in major cities across Canada, but these were indefinitely suspended on the outbreak of war. In the summer of 1916 Foster was named by the British government as one of four British representatives at the Allied Economic Conference in Paris and shortly afterwards received the singular honour of appointment to the Imperial Privy Council. He had already been knighted in June 1914 and thus could now be styled as "the Right Honourable Sir George Foster." His visit to London also resulted in a decision on the part of the Colonial Office to revive the work of the Dominions royal commission, giving rise to the cross-Canada tour (5 September to 31 October) that had originally been scheduled for the summer of 1914.

Most of the statistical evidence[9] consisted of replies to preset questions. Some of these were technical in nature, relating, for example, to the desirability of uniformity in weights and measures, the definition of the statistical year, and procedures for the valuation and classification of imports and exports. The two most interesting, however, sought views on whether there should be a conference of empire statisticians after the war and whether a permanent imperial statistical bureau should be established. Coats, by then heading the Census and Statistics Office with the title of Dominion statistician, did not testify, but his colleagues, E.H. Godfrey and W.A. Warne, both expressed support for the propositions. In other testimony, Ernest McGaffey, secretary of the British Columbia Bureau of Provincial Information, and G.E. Marquis, director of the recently established Quebec Bureau of Statistics, commented on the fragmented and uncoordinated state of Canadian statistics and argued for full-time provincial statisticians who would meet with each other and their Dominion counterpart at least once a year.

With all the evidence now in hand, the end of 1916 found Foster back in London helping prepare the commission's final report[10] – a report that W.S. Wallace, Foster's official biographer, subsequently described as "of profound significance for inter-Imperial trade after the war."[11] Its main statistical findings were, by this time, entirely predictable:

> an almost universal consensus of opinion among the various statistical authorities whom we have examined that progress towards uniformity could be most effectively and rapidly attained by means of a Conference representing the Government departments in the different parts of the Empire which are now engaged in statistical work, and including officers of the various customs administrations ... At present

> none of the administrations in the Empire is specially charged with the work of collecting, collating and preparing statistics for the Empire as a whole ... The establishment of a central statistical office for the Empire has been advocated by several witnesses ... and we are of the opinion that the creation of some office of the kind is eminently desirable.[12]

As noted earlier, the royal commission's work had no direct effect on developments in Canada, which had acquired their own momentum. But its report conveyed a strong message that effective statistical coordination and standardization at the international level must necessarily rest on sound national foundations among the participating countries. The recommendations quoted above were formally approved by the Imperial War Conference of 1918 on the basis of a resolution that read as follows: "The Imperial War Conference having considered the correspondence as to the improvement of Imperial Statistics arising out of the recommendations of the Dominions Royal Commission, is in favour of the proposal to hold a Conference of Statisticians after the war, and that such conference consider the establishment of an Imperial Statistical Bureau under the supervision of an Inter-Imperial Committee."[13]

Arthur Meighen of Canada, in speaking to the resolution on 10 July 1918, was by then able to observe that it was "simply an extension of the principle into the Imperial sphere which we have already adopted in the Federal sphere in Canada." The proper men to bring it about and to give it form, he said, were the experts of the Dominions. "We have in our country what we regard as a real expert in statistical work; he is a man of the type whom we should like to see taking part in the work of the proposed Conference."[14] Thus the foundation was laid for the first British Empire Statistical Conference, held in London in 1920, at which Canada, through its representation by Coats and Godfrey, began the tradition of participation in intergovernmental statistical consultations that has continued to the present time.

While these initiatives at the international level were in train, the departmental commission referred to earlier completed its assessment of the domestic statistical system, and work was begun to implement its recommendations.

The Departmental Commission on Official Statistics

The commission was appointed on 30 May 1912 by Order in Council PC 1485, and its terms of reference required it "to inquire into the statistical work now being carried on in the various Departments, as to its scope, methods, reliability, whether and to what extent duplication occurs; and to report to the Minister of Trade and Commerce a comprehensive system of general statistics adequate to the necessities of the country and in keeping with the demands of the time." In the preamble to the Order in Council, it was noted that; "with the exception of the enumeration and the compilation of the decennial census returns, no comprehensive system at present exists for the collection and publication of the statistics of production and distribution of Canadian commodities within the country itself, a matter which appears to [the Minister] to be essential to the proper appreciation of our own resources and the proper direction of our industrial trade development."

The preamble also took note of the work being done by the provinces in collecting statistical information relating to provincial conditions and development, and the commission was required to report on how Dominion and provincial statistical activities might be better coordinated so as to avoid duplication of effort and to provide "a body of statistical information which would be of the utmost use to all."

The chairman of the commission was Richard Grigg, who had most recently served as head of the British Commercial Intelligence Service in Canada and Newfoundland, and who had been recruited by Foster to overhaul Canada's Trade Commissioner Service. Although nominally the second ranking officer in the Department of Trade and Commerce, he was in fact paid more than the deputy minister, F.C.T. O'Hara, and was firmly committed to statistical reform. The Ottawa statistical establishment was co-opted in the persons of E.H. Godfrey from the Census and Statistics Office, W.A. Warne of the Trade Statistics Branch of the Department of Trade and Commerce, R.H. Coats of the Department of Labour, and John R.K. Bristol of the Department of Customs. Other members were Adam Shortt of the Civil Service Commission and C.H. Payne of the Department of Trade and Commerce, who acted as secretary to the commission. The commission held twenty-seven meetings, and individual members were extensively involved in visiting and corresponding with Dominion and provincial departments, as well as with numerous public bodies and individuals with a stake in official statistics. Time constraints[15] ruled out the possibility of public hearings and the taking of extensive formal evidence.

When the commission reported on 30 November 1912, it substantially confirmed the views of the minister as to the fragmentary and poorly coordinated nature of official statistics in Canada and explained how the situation had come about:

> Though many of the statistical reports issued by various departments and branches are of undoubted excellence and value, there is apparent in the body of Canadian statistics, considered as a whole, a lack of coherence and common purpose. This is traceable to imperfect appreciation in the past of the fact that the statistics of the country, whether the product of one agency or several agencies, should constitute a single harmonious system, with all divisions in due correlation. Under the British North American Act, 1867, the Dominion is given specific authority to deal with "statistics," and while this must not be regarded as precluding statistical activity on the part of local governments it does apparently imply that statistics are a matter of national concern and may therefore properly come under the general coordinating

> authority of the Federal Government. No such view-point or function, however, has in the past been assumed by the Dominion. On the contrary each department or branch, charged directly or indirectly with statistical investigation, has concerned itself primarily with the immediate purpose only in view ... while this detachment has characterized the departments of the Dominion government, still more has it been evident as between the several provinces and the Dominion, and between province and province, notwithstanding that the national importance of many of the functions of the provincial governments under Confederation calls urgently for statistical uniformity and homogeneity. This general condition we would consider to be the fundamental defect which must be met and overcome in the existing situation.[16]

The commission went on to characterize the consequences of this state of affairs – duplication of activity, differences in quality and value of the resultant statistics, and a lack of attention to timeliness, among others. Perhaps the most telling was that "the scope of Canadian statistics has been restricted ... there has been no general comprehensive answer to the question, What statistics should a country such as Canada possess? ... It may be argued that the demand for statistics may be trusted to create the supply; but to wait for the occasion to arise is often to be too late, and such a policy precludes the growth of a statistical system along consistent and logical lines."[17]

These considerations provided the basis for the lead recommendation of the commission, namely, "that there be created a Central Statistical Office to organize, in co-operation with the several departments concerned, the strictly statistical work undertaken by the Dominion Government."[18] The commission's report also reflected the views of A.L. Bowley, referred to above, who had characterized the essential role of a central statistical office as a "central thinking office." His description of the possible functions of such an office in Great Britain was thought to be so applicable to the Canadian situation as to warrant its embodiment as an integral part of the report:

> Such an office must have cognizance of all the statistics of more than departmental importance which are published officially ... Misleading statistics must be suppressed, overlapping must be stopped, careful plans must be devised for filling in the gaps at present left and preparations made for investigation of matters likely to become of public importance. All Bills involving or affecting the collection of statistics should be considered by it ... Publications for the use of the public should in some cases be edited by it, with careful definitions, and with short analysis and criticism, stating accurately and intelligibly the purport and meaning of their contents; in other cases, where a department already exists for such publication, there should be co-operation with a view to carrying out the purposes already indicated.[19]

To enable the central office to carry out its coordinating role *vis-à-vis* the statistical activities of Dominion departments, the creation of an interdepartmental statistical committee was proposed. Similarly, provincial cooperation was to be achieved through a continuing interprovincial conference on statistics. In this connection, a distinction was drawn between those statistics collected by the Dominion, which may or may not be duplicated by the provinces and in which cooperation would produce better results, and those that the provinces alone collected, such as statistics of vital events, education, and municipal finance, but for which it would be desirable to have some central coordination to ensure consistency and comparability.[20]

The most important subject-matter reform proposed by the commission concerned the census. As related earlier, the basic demographic content of the census had become increasingly overlaid with supplementary – largely industrial – information because of the apparent ease of its collection, but in fact with serious effects on its quality. The commission emphasized that there was no question as to the need for the supplementary information; the issue was rather one of devising more effective collection arrangements. It was therefore recommended that the census be regarded "as limited for organizational purposes to the enumeration of the population and of certain property, such as lands and buildings, and [that there be] set apart definitely under a separate scheme those statistics which more specifically bear on industrial conditions."[21] In another major recommendation, the commission urged the desirability of a quinquennial census for the Dominion as a whole, "having regard to the increased importance of immigration and the internal movement of population," and pointing out that this would merely extend a principle already adopted for the three northwestern provinces.[22]

As for statistics of production, the heading under which the commission grouped agriculture, forestry, fisheries, mines and manufactures, the recommendation to dissociate these from the decennial census for collection purposes was reinforced by the consideration that, in any case, they needed to be collected more frequently: "decennial statistics of production no longer meet the requirements of a rapidly expanding country."[23]

In agriculture, and in forestry, fishing, and mines, both the Dominion and provincial governments were engaged in the production of annual and, in the case of agriculture, subannual statistics, but with varying scope and using different methodologies. Here, the recommendations were addressed to collaborative efforts that would render more effective the work already being done. In manufacturing there were no regular annual statistics, and it was proposed that this void be filled by an annual postal census, like that of 1905.

Statistics of trade received a great deal of attention.[24] In the matter of foreign trade, the apparent duplication of effort between the Customs department and the department of Trade and Commerce was not seen as a matter of serious concern. "With regard to the two series of reports which have resulted, the

Commission do not think that in this connection alone serious loss in the way of expenses of compilation and publication is incurred, as some repetition of matter would be difficult to avoid under any circumstances of organization."[25] But inconsistency was a different matter, and more careful coordination of the work of the two departments was urged. Recommendations were also made for the development of commodity classifications more suited to the needs of trade, and for work to alleviate the problems arising from incomplete information on the countries of origin and destination of imports and exports.

The commission dwelt at length on the difficulties standing in the way of "a complete and accurate statement of interprovincial trade," in view of the absence of any machinery like that of Customs to record the internal movement of both domestic and foreign goods. It suggested, however, that a start might be made by "selecting a list of the more important articles and obtaining statistics as to their movement from producers, transportation companies and such other authorities as might be able to furnish them."[26]

On the matter of wages it was reported that "no comprehensive periodical reports ... are as yet available, and the want of them is distinctly felt."[27] The suggestion was made that the Department of Labour might collaborate with departments engaged in collecting statistics of production and persuade them to gather information on wages by a slight extension of their schedules. In considering the parallel question of the cost of living, the commission took note of the useful work that had been begun by the Department of Labour in the collection of retail prices but stressed that this information needed to be complemented by studies of family consumption. Finally, in a section of the report addressed to publications, it was recommended that the scope of the *Canada Year Book* be altered and enlarged, and that the Census and Statistics Office and the Publications Branch of the Department of Agriculture collaborate to eliminate the duplication between their respective monthly agricultural publications.[28]

Action on the Recommendations

An early and specific response to the report of the departmental commission was the changes effected by the Census and Statistics Office in the *Canada Year Book*. The preface to the 1912 edition, signed by Archibald Blue on 16 July 1913, noted that "although prepared largely along the lines hitherto followed, the Canada Year Book for 1912 comprises a considerable number of changes and additions." New subjects covered were vital statistics, climate and meteorology, labour, provincial revenues and expenditures,[29] and public lands. In addition, descriptive material was provided with the tables. It was noted too that the volume had been edited by E.H. Godfrey who, as a result of his work with the departmental commission, now had a much higher profile within the office.[30] The preface to the 1913 edition, which was signed by Godfrey as editor, reported that "progress has been made in the direction of greater comprehensiveness with a view to increased usefulness of the work for purposes of research." To the special features of the 1912 edition had been added illustrated articles by "competent authors" on the history and physical characteristics of Canada.

The Census and Statistics Office also launched an initiative to eliminate the duplication of activity and inconsistency of results between Dominion and provincial efforts in the area of agricultural statistics. Several years later, this won high praise in Coats's first annual report as Dominion statistician.

However, the main responsibility for following up the recommendations of the departmental commission's report remained in the hands of Grigg, who felt that, as a first step, discussions should be held with the provinces. He was committed to a long trip to China and Japan in the spring and summer of 1913 in connection with his responsibilities for the Trade Commissioner Service and therefore decided to visit the western provinces on his way. Accordingly, Foster wrote on 6 February 1913 to the premiers of Manitoba, Saskatchewan, Alberta, and British Columbia, recalling his correspondence with them in the previous spring shortly after the formation of the commission and asking them to put Grigg in touch with the appropriate provincial authorities so that; "after ... an interchange of opinions with the different provincial authorities, the way may be open for the calling of a more formal conference in which representatives of the Dominion and provincial governments may be called and a system of gathering and publishing statistical information be devised which will be adequate to the requirements of the country and worthy of its position and importance."[31]

Although he no longer had any official standing in commission matters, Coats continued as a fertile source of advice and suggestions. He strongly supported Foster's initiative and, in a letter dated 14 February 1913, counselled Grigg that "you could accomplish good by approaching the provinces now in the way of asking their co-operation in the preliminary thinking out of the details ... it is of the utmost importance that the good will of all concerned should be secured from the outset in this matter, and your visit to them without, in the first instance, any cut and dried, hard and fast scheme to advance, ought to be regarded as a token of the spirit in which the Government here is moving."[32]

But although Grigg found widespread support for the report and willingness to cooperate in the furtherance of its objectives, the promises that written submissions on the provinces' "views and desires" would be forthcoming were, without exception, not fulfilled. The reasons for this, Grigg explained to Foster in a letter of 20 November 1913, were that "the Provincial Governments feel that they do not possess officers of statistical acquirements to enable them to formulate such a memo as they promised to provide, in addition to which their more capable men are so fully engaged with the work of their respective departments that they cannot give the necessary attention to the subject ... It appears absolutely necessary to place the provinces in a position to criticize a scheme already formulated rather than to ask them to provide such a scheme themselves."[33]

Thus, by the end of 1913 it had been concluded that the details of the work involved should first be mapped out, subject by subject, so that the Dominion and provincial government departments concerned could be approached on the basis of specific plans related to their particular interests.[34] This made it a matter of urgency that a competent officer be appointed to do the necessary planning and then get the discussions under way.

The Appointment of a Dominion Statistician

For more than a year no action was taken to appoint an officer who would do the planning for a centralized statistical system. Archibald Blue was at this time the doyen of official statistics but, at seventy-four, hardly a candidate for the job. In any event, he died in office in July 1914, and less than a year later, on 19 June 1915, Coats was appointed to the Department of Trade and Commerce as Dominion statistician and controller of the census. The title of Dominion statistician was not new, having earlier been held by George Johnson. It was not formally defined at this time but was probably meant to be indicative of the broader responsibilities it would encompass upon implementation of the departmental commission report.

Given Coats's high profile, arising from his work with the Board of Inquiry into the Cost of Living and with the departmental commission, it would have been surprising if he had not received the appointment. E.H. St Denis, whose experience in statistics went back to the time of Taché and who, as secretary of the Census and Statistics Office, had taken temporary charge after the death of Blue, had applied for the post and his candidacy was supported by his friend P.E. Blondin, the minister of National Revenue. But Foster was clearly looking for new blood. Even before the departmental commission had been set up, he and Grigg had made discreet inquiries about the possibility of recruiting in Britain "a first-rate man who could help to reorganize the statistics of Canada," and Grigg had also mentioned the name of G.H. Knibbs, whose work in centralizing the Australian statistical system some years earlier had been taken note of by the Dominions royal commission.[35] It is doubtful whether Knibbs was ever approached, and Coats may well have had the inside track all along.[36]

Coats's appointment met with wide and favourable comment. The *Ottawa Citizen* of 26 June 1915 published an editorial noting his impressive credentials and commending Foster for "waiting till he could find the right man to undertake the work. He has finally found him without having to go outside the Dominion Civil Service." Coats also received a gracious letter from Mackenzie King: "I write to congratulate you heartily, and to say that I hope this new position, in affording the splendid scope it does for great ability, will lead you in the course of time to further recognition of your services to the Dominion and to the world of statistics generally. It adds to the pleasure to know that it is to your own splendid work in the Department of Labour that this appointment is due."[37]

Coats very soon made known to Foster his preliminary thinking on how statistics might be reorganized. Foster replied in encouraging terms in a letter of 7 July 1915, summarizing the challenge ahead as threefold: "First what we as a Dept. can do *of ourselves* (a) in gathering new statistics, (b) in bettering our methods, and (c) preparing plans for comprehensive operation; secondly in determining what methods can be adopted for co-operation with other Dominion departments; and thirdly what methods are to be adopted for co-operation with Provinces, and coordination of all activities within the whole system."[38]

However, he went on to outline a more specific and urgent concern – the requirement for statistics of "the yearly production and broad lines of its disposal of the principal striking industries of Canada" – and asked Coats to consider whether immediate work could not begin on some of these industries. On 13 July Coats confirmed that these questions had in fact been one of his major preoccupations since taking office but noted the urgent requirement to initiate work on the quinquennial census of the Prairie provinces in mid-1916, a matter in which he had no discretion. As to production statistics: "there is clearly need for an intercensal estimate of a fairly comprehensive kind in manufacturing," which, he noted, a repeat of the 1905 postal census of manufactures would go a long way towards filling, at least for the time being. He further pointed out that, "on its completion, we would be in a good position to decide on what lines it would be possible to continue such a record annually." Coats concluded his reply by assuring Foster that "this work falls within the first category mentioned in your letter ... viz: work which we as a Department can do *of ourselves*."[39]

A second postal census of manufactures, covering the calendar year 1915, was authorized later that year, and implemented during 1916, the results being published early the following year. The results of the census were well enough received at the time but did not find favour with those who, half a century later, compiled the first edition of *Historical Statistics of Canada*.[40] Only establishments with outputs of $2,500 or more had been enumerated. Thus, the census was said to have had limitations in its coverage of manufacturing establishments and their operations, and the 1915 data were omitted from the historical time series for manufacturing.

More interesting from a current standpoint than the substance of the census is the uncompromising policy it followed with respect to nonresponse. This policy, which may have been the first attempt to enforce the mandatory reporting requirements of the 1905 legislation, contrasts sharply with the cautious approach taken in later years after response burden became a public issue. One whole page of the four-page schedule was used to itemize "Offences and Penalties under the Census and Statistics Act," and the operational procedure was to follow up the initial mailing with two further requests by registered mail, after which the names of delinquent establishments were placed in the hands of the Department of Justice for further follow-up under the direct threat of legal proceedings.

By the end of October 1916, 121 names had been so submitted out of a total of some 21,000 establishments for which statistics were eventually compiled. Later the list was whittled down to thirty-eight names and the decision had to be made whether to actually prosecute. In correspondence with the deputy minister, F.C.T. O'Hara, Coats acknowledged that "a good many ... are of little account and their omission will not be serious." But some were of "first importance" and "it would be inexpedient to issue statistics that did not include them."[41] The list was further narrowed down to seven names, of which four finally came to court.

This approach, which was sustained after the census was annualized, appears to have generated surprisingly little friction at first, although the situation was to change considerably within a few years. Respondents in the early years frequently pleaded the absence of knowledgeable employees on war service; less apologetically, a few pointed out that the Department of Justice would be better occupied in prosecuting war profiteers. Coats's replies were always tactful but firm, as exemplified in the following letter:

> You can readily understand that the prosecution of delinquents under the Industrial Census is not only distasteful to us, but is a measure attended with heavy expense and inconvenience, and to a certain extent demoralization of our work. We resort to it only when we have exhausted every attempt to receive the information, which the Government must have if it is to successfully direct the administration of the Country's affairs. We are at all times ready to offer every explanation and assistance to producers in filling out their returns, and in making estimates where exact statistics are not procurable. If, however, after having given you five notices (where only one is required by the law), two of which contained explanations to the above effect we have still no reply from you, we have no recourse but to institute proceedings and proceedings having once been instituted it is impossible to withdraw.[42]

As required by law, the first full year of Coats's tenure as Dominion statistician and controller of the census saw the finalization and implementation of arrangements for the 1916 quinquennial census of the Prairie provinces. St Denis served as chief census commissioner and E.S. Macphail, who was next in seniority and who went on to become chief of demography in the Dominion Bureau of Statistics, was responsible for preparation of the report. This census continued the practice, introduced in the 1911 census, of providing timely publication of what it called "the main facts" through four bulletins issued early in 1917, the report proper following in January 1918.[43]

Planning for the Centralization, Reorganization, and Enlargement of Canadian Statistics

On the broader issue of the plan for reorganization Coats was now working alone, following the sudden death of his collaborator, Grigg, in January 1916. But by the middle of that year he had completed a section-by-section review of the field of national statistics, which he documented in a series of fourteen memoranda. In August 1916 Coats sent Foster, for submission to cabinet, a summary paper entitled "A National System of Statistics for Canada – Centralization, Reorganization and Enlargement of Canadian Statistics."

On the question of centralization Coats took as his starting point the existing Census and Statistics Office, which, as he noted; "is by law assigned practically the entire range of statistics, coupled with the most comprehensive powers; it is the only Government office having the collection of statistics as its sole administrative function and having its organization defined by law ... its general statistical experience and equipment are more complete than those of other branches ... the creation of a central statistical office should proceed in the first instance by joining on to the office such other activities as properly fall within the scope of a national system of statistics, and reorganizing the whole as a new entity."[44]

This central office would be directly responsible for the publication of all those statistics representing information collected primarily for its economic significance, while other statistical branches at present engaged in such work would be reconstituted as branches within it. On this latter point, Coats had in mind the collection of annual and sometimes more frequent statistics of industrial production by departments such as Marine and Fisheries, Mines, and Interior, as well as the statistical activities of the Departments of Labour and of Railways and Canals. Indirect control was to be exercised in the case of statistics that were records of administrative processes. Here the prime target was the external trade statistics of the Department of Customs, where "the method of collection and compilation should be visé-ed and the statistics edited by the Central Statistics Office, under interdepartmental arrangement, so as to ensure their coordination with the general scheme."[45]

Coats outlined various potential operational advantages of a policy of centralization, such as a more efficient use of machines and clerical staff, and better cooperation from the public through the more judicious exercise of "inquisitorial powers," or the authority to conduct statistical surveys of institutions, businesses, and individuals. These powers, he urged; "cannot be conferred indiscriminately, but only where they are necessary to administration. The Census and Statistics Office being the only branch covering the general field of statistics as an act of administration, general inquisitorial power for its own sake is limited to that office. Under the system of decentralization, however, many inquiries are being made by Departments which have no legal powers to demand a response. This has an unfortunate tendency in two directions: (1), it may lessen the seriousness with which inquiries are begun, and, (2), it inculcates carelessness in the public to which they are addressed."[46]

As a final argument for centralization, he also stressed the benefits that would accrue to government from "the extended and related view ... of economic and social phenomena ... [which] it cannot have if its statistics are produced by diverse methods in a series of 'watertight compartments.'"[47] Coats was addressing the general principles of centralization and, characteristically, did not at this time outline proposals for the administrative status of the central office. Clearly, however, he took the view that the effective discharge of its centralizing responsibilities required it to be, and to be clearly perceived as, independent of the influence of any particular department. The failure to embody this principle in the enabling legislation for the central office two years later was to prove a serious handicap to its subsequent operation.

As regards the substantive work of the central statistics office, Coats saw it as being organized in nine divisions.[48] The first of these was to cover the census of population and agriculture, thus confirming the view of the departmental commission that the census should be divested of industrial production inquiries. However, while the commission had included agriculture under the heading of industrial production, Coats's view was that agriculture, "in view of its great relative importance in Canada," must always be linked with population, and that satisfactory results could be obtained from the "low-paid field investigators" employed for the census of population.[49]

The census of population also needed to be correlated with the fields of migration and vital statistics. With respect to the former, Coats noted that statistics of immigrant arrivals were available, but that special provision would have to be made for statistics of emigration. Past attempts to collect a decennial record of deaths in the census year had repeatedly failed, and because of the absence, incompleteness, or inconsistency of provincial information, it had not been possible to develop vital statistics on a current basis in collaboration with the provinces. Coats pinned his hopes on a fresh initiative with the provinces. The key elements were to be the adoption of a uniform scheme of legislation and administration by the provinces covering births, marriages, and deaths, and the undertaking on the part of the Dominion, first, to secure certain benchmark data through the census and, second, to provide for centralized collection and publication of the data.[50] This was to be the responsibility of a second proposed division.

Mention was made in an earlier chapter of the work begun in 1913 to develop an effective scheme of collaboration between the Dominion and the provincial departments of agriculture for a system of annual statistics, and this was seen as the core element in the mandate of a division dealing with agriculture statistics. With respect to industrial statistics, Coats had already addressed the recommendation of the departmental commission for an annual postal census of manufactures, but he proposed, more generally, that the entire field of industrial statistics be covered by a program of comprehensive inquiries every ten years, supported by simpler annual updates. To underscore the need for coordination of the existing statistics of forestry, fishing, and mining, he noted that no fewer than twenty-five different departments, Dominion and provincial, were involved.

In the matter of the division of responsibility for foreign trade statistics existing between the Customs department and the department of Trade and Commerce, Coats was much more critical than the departmental commission,[51]: "It has been said that because each of these series contains analyses which are necessary and which are not in the other this method of publication is justified. This is not the case. Not only is 30% of pure repetition involved in the dual series of reports, but the final result is to give the statistics, considered as a whole, an illogical and confusing arrangement."[52]

Coats therefore proposed that the foreign trade statistics branch of the Department of Trade and Commerce be transferred to the central statistics office under an arrangement whereby the Customs department would carry out the collection and first compilation of the data, while the central office would be responsible for analysis, interpretation, and publication of a single series of unified reports. This, he argued, "would bring the statistics of trade into a position where they could be influenced and directed by the Department having to do with the promotion of trade, at the same time serving the interests of the Department having to do with the collecting of customs." He also recommended parallel arrangements for the systematic accumulation and study of data on internal trade from sources such as the statistics of railway and canal traffic, the production census, the foreign trade statistics, the marketing statistics of the Grain Commission, Fisheries Branch, etc., and the statistics of wholesale prices. This latter work, he suggested, should "supplant in time by arrangement the similar work of the Department of Labour, in so far as the trade aspect is concerned, leaving the cost of living aspect of prices and wages as the subject proper of that department."[53]

The Railway Statistics Branch of the Department of Railways and Canals was at this time the other major repository of inquisitorial powers for the collection of general statistics and provided information on railways, tramways, express companies, canals, telegraphs, and telephones. Certain shipping statistics were also published by the Customs department and republished by the Department of Trade and Commerce in a relationship analogous to that existing between the two departments with respect to foreign trade. Coats proposed that the Railway Statistics Branch be constituted as the "transportation division" of the central office, and that it should continue to furnish much the same reports as before, augmented by the navigation returns of the Customs and Trade departments. The need for improved statistics of public finance was also emphasized. Here the most pressing requirement was to bring a system of municipal statistics into being in cooperation with the provinces, "and to extend the work over the whole field of public incomes and expenditures, adjusting the statistics to census investigations in the same field."[54] Coats further recommended an extension of the Census and Statistics Office's existing work on criminal convictions to cover all statistics relating to the administration of justice.

The final proposal was for the establishment of a branch to be responsible for "the editorial study of administrative statistics in departmental hands, and for the abstracting, condensing and rearranging of general statistics." The compilation of the *Canada Year Book* was to be central to this work, and it was visualized that the *Census and Statistics Monthly*, at that time exclusively a vehicle for agricultural statistics, would be transformed so as to present all the latest official statistics, "highly summarized and coordinated for the guidance of trade and industry, constituting a comprehensive barometer of economic change from month to month in every section of the field, and combining all into a definite analysis of the current trade as a whole."[55]

In conclusion, Coats outlined the steps necessary to set the plans in motion. These were, first, the adoption by the government of statistical centralization as a policy and the amendment of the Census and Statistics Act, principally for the purpose of enabling the central office to confer its inquisitorial powers, by arrangement, upon officials of other departments. Secondly, arrangements for a series of conferences between the central office and the various departments for the purpose of ratifying arrangements incidental to centralization should be put in hand. It was not clear from the memorandum which was to come first, the legislative changes or the consultation with departments, and this was before long to cause some faltering.

Progress towards a Central Office

An Order in Council (PC 3056) of 8 December 1916 identified the Census and Statistics Office as "the central agency best adapted and equipped to effect [its] purposes" and authorized it, on the minister's behalf, to "confer ... with the various Departments publishing other statistics than the purely departmental records of their activities with a view to the early arrangement and completion of the system referred to." Coats's recommendation that legislative amendments be made was not heeded; rather, the Order's reference to "the wide powers conferred upon [the office] by the Census and Statistics Act of 1905" suggested that it had all the authority necessary to work out collaborative arrangements with the other departments.[56]

Concurrently with the drafting of the memorandum to cabinet on which the

Order in Council was based, Coats also outlined what might immediately be done within the Department of Trade and Commerce itself, "irrespective of any action that may be taken on the wider basis."[57] There was nothing new in this statement; principally it reiterated Coats's well-known position on the desirability of conducting a comprehensive industrial census for the year 1917, urgently implementing those elements of his proposals with respect to foreign trade that were internal to the department, and making a start on the work planned in the area of internal trade. But it provoked the sensibilities of the deputy minister, O'Hara, who, while repeatedly stating his concurrence with Coats's thinking, clearly felt threatened: "It follows ... that the Statistical Office shall issue all the various publications relating to statistics. That would mean that the present Annual and Monthly Reports of the Department of Trade and Commerce would be abolished. If the grain and trade statistical staffs are transferred to the direct control of the Statistical Office, the comparatively small inside staff of the Department of Trade and Commerce would be greatly reduced and the statistical office largely increased."[58]

Even more disturbing, however, was O'Hara's perception that "Mr Coats apparently desires to create more than a Branch of a Department. He is aiming at a Department with a Minister at the head thereof ... [an] increase in the number of existing Departments would be a move in the wrong direction."[59] Coats's response on the matter of the publication of trade statistics was forthright. "The general function of a Central Statistical Office would be to do the purely statistical work of the Government, leaving the annual reports of Departments for the discussion of administrative activities and problems." On the matter of a separate department, he was more diplomatic: "The expression 'Minister of Statistics' used in my Memo of October 27th does not imply a portfolio of statistics. It implies, however, that the Minister of Trade and Commerce should be regarded as directing the general statistical policy of the Government."[60]

O'Hara was certainly correct in his suspicion that Coats wanted to transform the Census and Statistics Office into something more than a regular branch of the Department of Trade and Commerce, accountable to a nonprofessional deputy minister. However, this did not surface again as an issue until several years later. Coats very soon reported[61] that he and Warne of the Trade Statistics Branch had come to an agreement about the integration of the three series of foreign trade statistics, and Warne's Branch was accordingly transferred to the Census and Statistics Office in March 1917. But O'Hara's objections had some effect, for the small Grain Statistics Branch stayed for the time being under his direct control. It remained, then, to secure the agreement of the Customs department as to its role in the overall plan.

As he had done earlier in his career with the wholesale prices and cost of living reports, Coats also sought external comment on his plans. A letter dated 19 March 1917 from G.M. Murray of the Canadian Manufacturers' Association offered practical suggestions on a number of the subject-matter proposals and added that "words almost fail me to express the importance I attach to the execution of a scheme such as you have worked out."[62] Professor H. Michell of Queen's University was less effusive but spoke of his department's plans to start up "a kind of research bureau for economic data and statistics" in which "such an organization as you plan would be of the greatest assistance to us."[63]

Planning for another postal census of manufactures to cover the year 1917 began at this time. It subsequently became an annual undertaking and was the cornerstone of what was eventually to be the more broadly based annual census of industry. Work was also put in hand in the area of internal trade statistics, which received a good deal of momentum from the statistics the Census and Statistics Office was compiling on behalf of two new wartime agencies, the Canada Food Board and the Fuel Controller.

As Coats had pointed out earlier, these activities were in areas where the department could take the initiative by itself. Where the cooperation of other departments was required, progress was sometimes more difficult. In the matter of the industrial census, Coats's first progress report to Foster assured him that "we can ... count on adjusting matters to our complete satisfaction with the Water Powers Branch, the Forestry Branch and the Fisheries Branch. The arrangement with the Mines Branch is less advanced, but I feel that we are steadily working towards a good solution, the end of which will be to make our office the repository of the statistics of production for the Dominion."[64]

But he had to admit to a lack of progress with the Railways Branch and the Department of Customs–exactly the areas where he had promised the largest benefits from centralization. The former had cordially acknowledged a memorandum he had sent them, but up to that time there had been no opportunity for substantive discussion. The situation with Customs was more delicate. They had not responded to his request for a conference, and now, Coats said, "I hear indirectly that the Customs Branch is remodelling its statistics in accordance with the forms and general method of presentation which we laid down in our Memo as the basis for *joint* action." This left him hesitant about approaching them again: "Any refusal on their part ... might prejudice further consideration of the question."[65]

A New Statistics Act

As a result of the difficulties outlined above, Coats urged upon Foster that it would be preferable to proceed towards a central statistical bureau through legislation rather than by serial negotiations with the various departments, as had been the intent of the December 1916 Order in Council: "We would encounter much less difficulty ... if it was seen definitely that the scheme of centralization was a large one, embracing all the Departments and involving a general principle, than by taking up each Department separately, which induces the Department in question to look on the matter as directed against itself alone ... Moreover, an Act would bring the whole matter before the public and place statistical reorganization where it properly belongs, namely, as an important section of the Government's policy of preparedness for reconstruction."[66]

Foster did not object in principle, but he saw no possibility of doing anything during the current session of Parliament. Coats, again short-circuiting protocol, thereupon wrote to the solicitor general, advising him of his exchange with Foster and asking him to keep a weather eye open for an appropriate opportunity. He supported his case by reference to the government's current emphasis on cutting down staffs and economizing, pointing out that "in the single section of Trade Statistics, we could, by proper organization and use of machinery, do away with 75 clerks and save at least $100,000 a year ... Similarly, we are building up an absolutely distinct statistical office in the Railway Department, though transportation companies should be treated statistically in the same way as other concerns, and we could perhaps save thirty per cent on expense by amalgamation."[67]

Coats had in fact been working on a draft statistics act since early in 1917, and his 26 May letter to Foster had included a first attempt put together without legal advice. He later submitted a more polished draft act to Foster, supporting it with a memorandum similar to the one he had written eight months earlier, adding that "arrangements which are made under a general Order in Council are always more or less unstable and I foresee that, even where satisfactory relations have been established, there will be more or less constant difficulty in maintaining them, in the face of changes in the officers of Departments, as well as in Departmental policies."[68]

What carried the day, however, was the fact that Foster now saw no procedural obstacle, and so events moved quickly. Coats was authorized to contact Francis H. Gisborne, KC, parliamentary counsel, and he worked with him during March on the drafting of "An Act respecting the Dominion Bureau of Statistics."

It was introduced by Foster in the Commons on 4 April 1918 as Bill 32, on the basis of the following resolution: "Resolved, that it is expedient to provide for a Bureau under the Minister of Trade and Commerce to be called the Dominion Bureau of Statistics to collect, abstract, compile and publish statistical information relative to the commercial, industrial, social, economic and general activities and condition of the people, to collaborate with all other departments of the Government in the compilation and publication of statistical records of administration according to the regulations, and to take the Census of the Dominion."[69] The bill prompted very little discussion in the House[70] and passed quickly, receiving royal assent on 24 May 1918. Subsequently known as the Statistics Act, 1918 (8-9 Geo. V, cap. 43), a copy is shown here as appendix H.

The reference to "other departments," unlike the broader definition used in subsequent amendments to the act, covered Dominion departments only, and the key phrase with respect to the bureau's collaborative responsibility, occurring in section 3, was "according to the regulations," leaving the details to be worked out later. As well as specifying in sections 16, 17, 18, and 19 the requirement to take the census of population and agriculture, the act made explicit provision for a census of industry, statistics of trade and commerce, transportation returns, and criminal statistics,[71] thus setting the stage for the transfer to the bureau of the statistical units of a number of other departments. The part of the act dealing with general statistics, sections 34 and 35, was open-ended but made particular reference to work that would need to be carried out in conjunction with the provinces, such as vital statistics, agriculture, education, and public and private finance. The arrangements for this collaborative work (section 9) were a greatly strengthened version of those that had been written into the act of 1905, and that now effectively treated provincial departments and officers as agents of the bureau.

The most notable provisions of general application (section 15) related to secrecy. As the marginal notations of the draft bill had put them: "no individual return to be published or divulged," and "no report to reveal individual particulars." These were supported by a prescribed oath of office for persons employed under the act, and penalties for its breach. The 1905 act, by contrast, had dealt with secrecy inferentially, requiring each employee to "take and subscribe an oath binding him to the faithful and exact discharge of such duties and to the secrecy of statistics and information collected for the oath." The "wilful neglect of duty" was declared to be an indictable offence.

For the new bureau to be fully viable as an instrument of centralization, it needed the regulations, provided for under section 3, that would make explicit its coordinating responsibilities *vis-à-vis* the statistical work of other departments. On 13 June 1918 Coats submitted for Foster's consideration a draft letter to the Governor General in Council setting out two basic principles: first, that all purely statistical investigations be conducted by the bureau; and second, that statistics that were by-products of the administrative activities of any department be produced by arrangement between that department and the bureau "insofar as possible in conformity with the methods and organization established in the Bureau, the object of such arrangement being the prevention of overlapping, the increase of comparability, and the utilization of Departmental organizations in the best manner for statistical ends."[72]

The recommended procedure to implement the latter principle was that the Dominion statistician should confer with the officers of the various departments and prepare plans as to how their statistical work might best be carried out. Such plans, after approval by the Governor General in Council, would then constitute permanent arrangements. A parallel recommendation was that "to further promote efficiency and economy, all statistical compilations for the Government be carried out insofar as practicable by mechanical appliances, and that for this purpose use be made of the machines installed in the Bureau of Statistics."[73]

On this latter point, "A National System of Statistics for Canada" had emphasized the potential of machine methods for savings in both money and time, noting that "in the United States, the cost of compiling the monthly trade returns is stated to have been reduced from $200,000 to $75,000 by the use of machinery, and two weeks gained in the issue of the reports."[74] This had first come to Coats's attention through a story in the *New York Times* of 8 July 1915. Subsequently, he had corresponded extensively with officers of the Bureau of Foreign and Domestic Commerce in the Department of Commerce, and this in turn had resulted in a visit to New York in January 1917 to look at the mechanical tabulation installations in the Customs House and some leading insurance companies. In seeking approval for the trip, Coats had argued that "we have about $80,000 invested in machinery. Up to the present its use has been confined almost entirely to the population census. We should now contemplate, however, an extension of its application."[75]

Coats's expeditious preparation of the draft statistical regulations was of no avail, however, for they were misplaced in O'Hara's office and, in consequence, could not be brought to Foster's attention before he left Ottawa for an extended vacation.[76] Coats complained that "the mix-up is going to handicap us seriously in our negotiations with the Customs Department."[77] Arrangements had already been made for the latter to cease publication of its monthly report, and the main outstanding issue at that point, in the resolution of which the proposed regulations were expected to be helpful, was the future of the annual Customs report. It was not until 12 October 1918 that Coats's centralizing mandate became fully explicit through Order in Council PC 2503, based on the recommendations outlined above.

There was, however, one recommendation in Coats's submission of 13 June 1918 that did not get embodied in the Order in Council. This was the proposal for an advisory statistical commission, with the Dominion statistician as *ex officio* chairman and with some of the membership to be drawn from outside the government, "to take into consideration from time to time matters appertaining to the general statistical policy of the Government, and in particular to advise when so required upon specific points of method and procedure."[78] Foster had not been enthusiastic when the idea had been broached earlier, but Coats had urged that he keep it up his sleeve, as it were, during discussions in Council. The proposal, unsuccessful then, was one that Coats put forward several times in later years, with no more luck than in 1918.

Conclusion

With the Statistics Act and its attendant regulations in place and the former Census and Statistics Office transformed into an organization ostensibly serving all Canadians, the stage was set for Coats to begin implementation of his 1916 blueprint for a "national system of statistics." The most urgent priorities were to arrange for the orderly transfer to the new bureau of the statistics of customs, railways, mining, forestry, and so on, deriving from the administrative procedures of the responsible departments, and also to reach agreement with the nine provinces for collaborative action with respect to statistics in areas of joint jurisdiction, such as agriculture and civil registration.

Rapid progress was to be made in most of these areas, as well as in others where the bureau could act at its own discretion. And as a result of Foster's work with the Dominions royal commission, Coats and others of his staff were to be pitchforked into the international statistical community, establishing a tradition that has flourished ever since. But it was not all to be plain sailing. Throughout the rest of his career, which lasted until 1942, Coats was to feel that his efforts were handicapped by the failure to accord to the bureau separate departmental status, with himself as deputy head, responsible only to a minister of the Crown. The effects of this failure and the efforts Coats made to combat them are dealt with in the following chapters of this history.

CHAPTER FIVE

1918–1939
The Dominion Bureau of Statistics – Putting Its Programs in Place

NTRODUCTION

Che early postwar years were ones of high achievement for the fledgling)ominion Bureau of Statistics. Building on the nucleus inherited from the Census and Statistics Office, the organizational framework outlined in "A National System of Statistics for Canada" was put in place through transfers rom other departments and the creation of new branches. As the framework ook shape, existing programs were strengthened and elaborated, and new ones ındertaken. In 1923 Coats summarized this progress as follows:

1) The Census (decennial and quinquennial) has been reorganized.
2) A national scheme of vital statistics has been established.
3) The monthly and annual statistics of agriculture have been brought under joint operation of the Bureau and the nine Provincial Governments.
4) The statistics of fisheries, mines, forestry, dairying, central power and general manufactures have been unified and placed on an annual basis (Industrial Census).
5) The statistics of foreign trade and of transportation and communication have been completely remodelled.
6) A branch dealing with the more important aspects of internal trade, including interprovincial trade movements, the marketing of staple commodities ... and a complete system of prices statistics, has been established.
7) Criminal statistics have been reorganized and coordinated with the Census and other social statistics.
8) Substantial beginnings have been made in the treatment of public finance and of education.
9) Relations between the Bureau and the Department of Labour covering the entire range of labour statistics have been reduced to formal working arrangement and overlapping has been eliminated.

10) A library of the statistics of all countries has been established, and a central mechanical tabulating service available for all departments has been put in operation.[1]

Coats emphasized the coordinated nature of these developments and claimed "the consequent establishment of a comprehensive survey of the country as a single 'going concern.'"[2]

These achievements were the more remarkable in that the bureau was obliged to operate in an administrative climate that was frequently unhelpful as regards relations with both departmental management and the civil service bureaucracy in general. This chapter first sketches early organizational and administrative matters, including accommodation and the function of mechanical tabulation, before looking at how the bureau dealt with the more urgent program challenges such as vital statistics, the census of population, agricultural statistics, the industrial census, foreign trade statistics, and transportation statistics, where its credibility was crucially at stake. It then considers program developments in areas where the bureau was under less immediate pressure and had greater scope for discretionary action, such as education, prices, labour, public finance, and the establishment of the central "thinking office" to which Coats so frequently referred.

Early Organization and Staffing

The organizational nucleus of the new bureau was the Census and Statistics Office of the Department of Trade and Commerce, augmented early in 1917 by the internal transfer of Trade and Commerce's Trade Statistics Division. Thus, a number of the subject-matter branches proposed in Coats's 1916 memorandum, " A National System of Statistics for Canada," were already in place during the bureau's first year. Some of them like population (demography), agriculture, administration of justice, and external trade, were operations of long standing and, notwithstanding plans for their further elaboration, could be considered as "going concerns." Others of more recent formation, like the industrial census and internal trade, were in the developmental stages.

The bureau's second year of existence, 1919–20, saw the organization of two completely new branches – education and general statistics, and finance. During the same year, the Transportation Branch of the Department of Railways and Canals was transferred to the bureau, and the industrial census, hitherto covering manufactures, forestry, and fisheries, was extended by the creation of a Mining, Metallurgy and Chemicals Branch with resources transferred from the Division of Mineral Resources and Statistics of the Department of Mines.[3] The fisheries work also blossomed into a fully fledged Fisheries, Furs, Dairy Products and Manufactured Animal Products Branch. The subject-matter branches were supported by an Administration Branch, which included Coats's immediate office, personnel and finance, as well as other centralized functions such as mimeographing, the compilation of the *Canada Year Book*, and publications distribution. The bureau's organization, as it stood at the end of fiscal year 1919–20, is shown in appendix C. The "division" numbers shown are those of the headings of Coats's 1916 memorandum. By the mid-1930s, as the developments in this chapter will demonstrate, the bureau had matured considerably, and its organization at the time, correspondingly elaborated, is shown as appendix D.

Overall, the bureau's staff utilization, exclusive of temporary census staff, more than doubled during its first five years, from 123 person years in 1918–19 to 253 in 1923–24. The proportion accounted for by permanent positions was approximately two-thirds. Some operations, however, like the census of industry, were heavy users of part-year temporary staff.

Just as important as numbers was the calibre of the staff. Those who became Coats's principal lieutenants in the early years were mostly the seasoned veterans of the Census and Statistics Office, and many of them continued to serve until after his own retirement. The doyen of them all was E.H. St Denis, who had been associated with the census in the days of Taché and had served more recently as chief of criminal statistics. Before retiring in 1924, St Denis was appointed assistant Dominion statistician. W.A. Warne, Coats's fellow member of the departmental commission, had been one of the Department of Trade and Commerce's first statisticians after its establishment in the early 1890s and served as chief of the bureau's External Trade Branch until his retirement in 1936. E.S. Macphail, chief of demography and associated with the census since the turn of the century, also served out his working career in the same position.

Macphail's assistant and eventual successor was A.J. Pelletier, who was to serve until 1944. The Agricultural Statistics Branch was the province of E.H. Godfrey, who had come from the UK. in 1907 to set up the program of crop reporting statistics and had been another of Coats's colleagues on the departmental commission as well as editor of the *Canada Year Book* for a number of years. The first chief of the industrial census was J.C. Macpherson, who had cut his statistical teeth with the industrial schedules of the decennial census of 1901 and had then conducted the first postal census of manufactures for 1905, which was repeated in 1915 and became an annual in 1917. He too served until the early 1930s. Col J.R. Munro, another veteran from the 1890s, became the first chief of public finance and probably established a record for long service when he retired in 1944.

Less visible, but no less important in a small organization, were those in staff functions. Writing on the occasion of the bureau's fortieth anniversary, Coats referred affectionately to those he had met when he first came to the old Census and Statistics Office in 1915. He remembered very well Joseph Wilkins and E. Skead, who assembled the *Canada Year Book* each year. "Wilkins and

Skead had worked as a pair at the same desk for over a quarter of a century," wrote Coats. "They were the first members of the staff to make a business call on me (they had worn out the desk and wanted a new one)." And then there were Miss F.A. Brown, Miss Gertrude Kehoe, and S. Swettenham, the messenger, all of whom were located immediately outside Coats's office. "Miss Brown had been Mr Blue's secretary, coming with him from Toronto; Miss Kehoe was the clerk in charge of personnel records and general files. Naturally they could give the lowdown on both the work in progress and the staff engaged on it in short order."[4] All three went on to serve until the 1940s; Miss Brown was promoted to take charge of fisheries, furs, dairy factories, and manufactured animal products within the industrial census.

But there was also important new blood in those early years. During 1919–20, Coats brought S.A. Cudmore to the bureau to head up a new Education and General Statistic Branch, which also involved serving as editor of the *Canada Year Book*.[5] At that time, Cudmore was a professor of Economics at the University of Toronto, a position he had attained after a Horatio Alger-like progression. He had come to Canada from Ireland as a child and had been obliged to leave school early and work as a "printer's devil" in Brampton, Ontario. Before long, however, he won a Prince of Wales matriculation scholarship that took him to the University of Toronto where he graduated with honours in Classics and English. This in turn led to a Sir James Flavelle scholarship at Wadham College, Oxford. During the next twenty years, Cudmore played a progressively more important role in the senior management of the bureau and succeeded Coats as Dominion statistician in 1942.

Cudmore's assistant in the Education and General Statistics Branch was another academic, Murdoch MacLean, who came in at about the same time. MacLean was given the job of developing an education statistics program, and this work was soon split off as a separate branch. His most enduring contribution to the bureau, however, came after he was appointed chief of census analysis in the early 1930s and went on to generate a brilliant series of monographs based on 1931 census data, before his accidental death in 1940. The other outstanding recruit of the early 1920s was Herbert Marshall, who, like Cudmore, had been a faculty member at the University of Toronto.[6] Marshall's first appointment was in the Internal Trade Branch, of which he became the chief after only a few years. He served in the branch for most of his career before succeeding Cudmore as Dominion statistician.

The Bureau's Accommodation

Shortly after Coats was appointed Dominion statistician in 1915, the Census and Statistics Office had moved to the Woods Building at 30 Slater Street. In 1918 it moved a little further east to the Canadian Building at 22 Slater Street near the Rideau Canal. In the following year it pulled up stakes again to go to the Daly Building at Mackenzie and Rideau streets, where it spent the next three years. The Woods and Canadian buildings were demolished in the mid-1960s to make way for Confederation Park. The Daly Building, although unoccupied during its final years, survived until 1992 on the basis of its perceived architectural merit.[7]

In 1921 the need to provide space for the 1921 census staff and its mechanical equipment dictated yet another move, this time to the Queen Building[8] on Vittoria Street at Bank, a site that now houses the Confederation buildings. A bureau employee, Mary Falconer, who retired in 1955 after forty-four years of service and had thus experienced the entire sequence of moves, said of the Queen Building that it "would have to be seen and lived in to be believed. It was thrown together to house some hapless World War I department. It consisted of 2 or 3 houses which had previously been stately homes with gracious gardens surrounding them. Well, the houses were denuded of all claims to grandeur and ramshackle shed-like structures erected to join them together. It was called the rabbit warren."[9]

In 1928 the bureau moved to the old Edwards Mill on Green Island, where it remained for twenty-four years. Even during the early years when overcrowding was not particularly a problem, these hand-me-down quarters were universally regarded as inconvenient and uncomfortable. After 1939, however, the bureau's expansion rapidly made conditions intolerable.

Mechanical Tabulation

One of Coats's a major objectives during the bureau's early years was to have all the government's mechanical tabulation work carried out at the bureau's central facilities. These had demonstrated their worth in the processing of the 1911 and 1916 censuses and, by 1918, were being used on a regular basis in routine work like the industrial census and statistics of agriculture. In the summer of 1918 the bureau undertook the compilation of returns from a national registration exercise. At its peak, this work employed more than four hundred temporary clerks but was quickly wound down after the end of the war.

At about this time, the regulations under the Order in Council of 12 October 1918 had just been approved, and with unused machine capacity now available, its use among other departments was vigorously promoted. Thus, in May of 1919 Coats circularized all deputy ministers, drawing their attention to the Order in Council, outlining the services that the bureau could provide, and concluding with the offer that "if there are any features of the work of your Department that you think could be handled to your advantage as above ... the Bureau will be glad to send an officer to confer with you and explain the application of mechanical tabulation in greater detail."[10]

Reactions were mixed. Coats's intention was simply that, where there was a potential for the use of machine methods, the cards should be punched in the departments and then transferred to the bureau for sorting and tabulation. But this was frequently interpreted as a stratagem on the part of the bureau to "take over" departmental responsibilities. Nevertheless, several satisfactory arrangements were negotiated during 1919, notably one with the Department of Finance for the compilation of income tax statistics.[11]

Coats continued to keep in close touch with developments in Washington, where experience was demonstrating that volume processing could yield important savings. This, he argued, would only be possible in Canada if the growing volume of departmental work could be centralized. In addition to straightforward efficiency considerations, Coats further argued that close bureau involvement with departmental applications could yield statistical benefits that a department by itself would perhaps not perceive, and that the public interest would also be served if the various supplying companies were obliged to deal with a single department with expertise in the field.

These arguments brought about the passage on 20 May 1920 of a new Order in Council (PC 1092), requiring that; "where the use of mechanical tabulation in the work of any Department or Branch of the Government is considered to be in the interests of economy and efficiency, application for the necessary equipment be made to the Dominion Statistician, who, on receipt of such application, shall forthwith, in consultation with the Department, submit a report dealing with the machines to be employed, the arrangements for securing them, the form of punched cards and other essential features."

Protection against the arbitrary use by the bureau of its new authority was provided by the stipulation that, in the event of such a report not being satisfactory to the department, it was to be referred for adjustment to the chairman of the Purchasing Board. There is no evidence that the new Order in Council was any more effective than the old in bringing departments to heel. In correspondence with the minister, Sir George Foster, early in 1921, Coats reported without further elaboration on its "good results" but also lamented that two substantial departmental facilities had slipped through the net, having been installed before the new Order in Council came into force. He suggested that "this policy would be improved if the bureau were in a position not merely to wait for the different Departments to approach it, but to adopt the point of view of a business concern interested in making as wide a disposition of its services as possible ... it might be worth our while to appoint an officer for the express purpose of drumming up business for tabulating machinery."[12]

Nothing came of this suggestion. Apart from any other consideration, the bureau was by then fast becoming its own best customer. As new programs were put in place, they were almost always serviced by mechanical tabulating equipment, and the 1921 census was close. In August 1920 seventeen new positions had been authorized for the bureau, fourteen of which – mostly for office appliance operators – were required for the new Vital Statistics Branch that had commenced operations at the beginning of that year.

Vital Statistics

Much of the spadework for a national system of vital statistics had been completed by the time the new Statistics Act came into force. The subject was one of the first addressed by Coats in the detailed memoranda outlining the proposals for statistical reform that he had prepared following his appointment as Dominion statistician. What was needed, Coats had argued, was: "(1) the enactment of uniform legislation and the adoption of uniform methods of administration by the provinces and (2) an engagement on the part of the Dominion Government to secure the proper data in connection with the population census, and also to use its machinery as a centralizing and unifying agency in collating and publishing from a national viewpoint the results of the provincial systems."[13]

The second point acknowledged the necessity of providing, through the census, information on vital characteristics not otherwise obtainable, but elsewhere in the memorandum Coats made it clear that the long-standing attempts to collect so-called "mortuary statistics" should be discontinued. The memorandum included, as an appendix, a draft vital statistics bill proposing uniform legislative and administrative standards for discussion with the provinces, and a draft Order in Council outlining procedures for the submission of vital records to the Census and Statistics Office by provincial officials. The Order in Council also provided for a biennial conference on vital statistics in Ottawa at Dominion expense.

Following informal discussions with provincial officials, Coats was able to report to Foster in November 1917 that his proposed initiative had been cordially received, and that several provinces had provided valuable suggestions and criticism. He was now ready for the next phase, the Ottawa conference, which took place on 19 and 20 June 1918 and was attended not only by Dominion and provincial officials but also by representatives of the Actuarial Society of America, the Canadian Medical Association, and the Union of Canadian Municipalities. In addition, a number of academics[14] took part, as well as the chief of the Division of Vital Statistics of the US Bureau of the Census.

A few days after the conclusion of the conference, Coats reported privately to Foster on its outcome, professing himself to be generally satisfied. He was disappointed, however, that his model bill had run up against what he obviously considered were inconsequential objections and had been referred back to a committee. Again, the frugal terms on which he proposed to pay for transcripts of registration documents were not enthusiastically received; the provinces put forward "a very vigorous plan for a subsidy on the ground that we were proposing to reap the fruits of years of administrative activity on their part."[15] A follow-up meeting was not possible until December, but the model bill was then approved without further ado, after which work started on seriatim negotiations with the provinces. Early in April 1919 Coats was ready to go forward with a draft Order in Council and was able to report that several provinces had already amended, or were in the process of amending, their vital statistics legislation for conformity with the principles of the model bill and were prepared to administer the legislation so as to ensure a ninety percent standard of registration.[16]

Recalling the attempts of the provinces to have the Dominion contribute to their expenses, the memorandum emphasized that there was no question of subsidizing them. They had been persuaded that the scheme "is a strictly co-operative arrangement for carrying out a line of investigation which falls under both Dominion and Provincial jurisdiction on the principle that each should do the work pertaining to its jurisdiction."[17] This principle was made clear in the wording of Order in Council PC 693, which was approved on 22 April 1919 thus laying the basis for a system that has continued, unchanged in its essentials, to the present time. But much still remained to be done to make the new system operational – securing final agreement on the prescribed forms that the bureau was committed to furnishing, setting the rate of payment for the transcripts of vital returns,[18] and, most importantly, getting reporting under way so that the bureau could start compiling and publishing.

While the Order in Council was going through, legislation was before Parliament for the establishment of a Dominion Department of Health. In support of its primary purposes, provision was made for the collection and publication of information bearing on public health, and Coats was concerned about the possibility that vital statistics might be thought of as part of this responsibility. However, the president of the privy council, the Honourable N.W. Rowell, was persuaded to have the bill amended to make it clear that the new department would not duplicate the work of the bureau.

The new act[19] made provision for a Dominion Council of Health, and Coats was able to arrange for bureau representation at its meetings. He used them to keep a watching brief on statistical matters generally, and also as a convenient forum for maintaining contact with the vital statistics officials who attended. Probably for this latter reason, no further Dominion/provincial conference on vital statistics similar to the two of 1918 was held until October 1943.

The regular submission of vital statistics returns by all provinces except Quebec began in 1920, and after some initial problems with the timeliness of returns, Coats was eventually able to publish a monthly report. January 1923 saw the first comprehensive annual report, covering the year 1921. Beginning in January 1926, Quebec, having overcome the difficulties relating to its system of registration, was able to accede to the national scheme, and from that year forward the annual report was truly a national one.

These developments threw a progressively greater workload on the bureau, and particularly on E.S. Macphail who had overall responsibility for demography. As the demands of the 1921 census began to make themselves felt, Coats thought it advisable to seek approval for a senior full-time position in vital statistics. The first appointee, Dr E.H. Chapman came to the position early in 1921, but resigned after only a few months due to ill health. He was replaced in February 1922 by W.R. Tracey who, like most of the other senior staff recruited by Coats, stayed for the long haul.

The 1921 Census

The 1921 census – the sixth comprehensive decennial census since Confederation – was uniquely important in assessing the success of the statistical reforms of 1918. Census taking had been the best-known and dominant statistical activity of the previous seventy years, and the departmental commission report of 1912 had singled it out as a prime target for both substantive and methodological change. These considerations alone would have generated high expectations for a successful outcome of the 1921 census, but the years since 1912 had brought others to the fore.

Thus, in reporting on the census after its completion, Coats wrote: "Within the decade just passed, Canada has celebrated the jubilee of her birth as a Dominion, when an appraisement of her status in fundamentals is particularly timely and necessary ... since the last census there has occurred the most profound upheaval in our history – The Great War – which left scarcely a feature of the national life untouched ... creating new stresses and strains ... [and] stimulating ... the demand for social and economic statistics as never previously; (and) the present census falls at a time when ... the relation of world population to national resources is being considered as never before in the present generation."[20]

The departmental commission report had recommended removing the industrial component (including agriculture) from the decennial census, thus limiting its scope exclusively to demographic questions. In 1916, however, Coats had argued both the desirability and feasibility of conducting the censuses of population and agriculture as a joint operation, and this principle had been enshrined in the new Statistics Act. The act had done away with the mortality schedule and made provision for a separate census of industry, so that the 1921 census was an affair of only five schedules: (1) population; (2) agriculture; (3) animals, animal products, fruits, etc., not on farms; (4) census of manufacturing and trading establishments; and (5) supplemental schedule for the blind and for deaf-mutes. However, there were in fact more questions – 565 by comparison with the 522 that made up the 13 schedules of 1911.

The first heading, population, covered only thirty-five questions. They were, as Coats noted, "in general conformity with international usage and previous practice in Canada."[21] Questions on "insanity and idiocy" were dropped, and the topic of fertility was avoided due to doubts about its practicability. Another new feature was a record of the birthplaces of the father and mother of each individual, which, in conjunction with the questions on citizenship and racial origin, would permit the segregation of Canadians who had resided for three generations or longer in the country and thus meet an insistent public demand.[22]

It was also claimed that an attempt was being made for the first time to obtain a record of unemployment for the census year. This was not entirely correct; in 1891 wage earners had been asked whether they had worked during the week preceding the census. In neither instance, however, did publishable information ensue.

The census of agriculture accounted for most of the questions in 1921. Schedules two and three accounted for 521, four times more than in 1911, thus offsetting the savings effected by the elimination of industrial inquiries. Many new topics were surveyed and considerably more detail was gathered on topics traditionally covered by earlier censuses. Much of the new or extended information was required to benchmark the more sophisticated system of monthly and annual crop reporting and other statistics of agriculture that the bureau was gradually developing in conjunction with the Dominion and provincial Departments of Agriculture.

The purpose of the fourth schedule was to assist the now-annual census of industrial production by collecting the names and addresses of business establishments, and similarly to help plan for a new census inquiry covering the distribution and merchandising of goods as an element in the bureau's new program of internal trade statistics.[23] The fifth and final schedule sought a record of the sex, age, and address of blind and deaf-mute persons in order to compile statistics for use by educational and other institutions involved in their care.

The departmental commission report of 1912 had recommended a change from the *de jure* to the *de facto* system of enumeration, and that the date for taking the census, which had been 1 June in 1911, be changed back to 1 April as in previous censuses. But the Statistics Act had stipulated "a date in the month of June," and 1 June was selected for 1921. The primary consideration was probably that April would be an unsatisfactory month for the agricultural component of the census, since acreages for the current season would not by that time have been determined. Again, there was no departure from the *de jure* system, which, it was said, "better portrays the permanent condition of the population, and is therefore better suited for the apportionment of electoral areas, the determination of municipal status, and the study of such subjects as housing, occupations and social conditions generally."[24]

The cooperation of the public was sought in advance of the census by a pamphlet entitled *The Coming Census – How It Is Taken, Why It Is Taken*, while the moving-picture service of the Department of Trade and Commerce produced a film depicting various census processes. Fieldwork was in the hands of 241 commissioners and 11,425 enumerators, who were responsible for corresponding numbers of census districts and subdistricts. In accordance with the requirements of the Statistics Act, the former were structured to correspond as far as possible to federal electoral constituencies, and the latter to polling subdivisions. The secrecy provisions of the new Statistics Act were given their first major public airing in the 1921 census. The enumeration instructions[25] required that respondents be assured of the confidential treatment of the information they were providing, and all temporary census employees, whether in the field as commissioners and enumerators or in Ottawa as compilers and clerks, had to swear the oath of office specified in the act.

The fieldwork, covering mainly the training of commissioners and enumerators and the checking and follow-up of census schedules for discrepancies or omissions, was conducted without the permanent field organization that was created in later years. The work of verifying and revising returns in the field and then shipping them to Ottawa for tabulation did not go as expeditiously as had been hoped. In 1911 87.8 percent of the returns had been received by the end of July; in 1921, the figure was only 76.8 percent, although much of the delay was made up during August. The report for 1921 commented that "in no previous census was so great difficulty experienced in obtaining satisfactory personnel for the field work of the census, and this applied with only diminished force in the case of the clerical staff engaged at Ottawa, the causes in both cases being the activity of general employment, the high rates of current wages, and the unsettled conditions following the war. A similar experience was reported by the US Census Bureau."[26]

In Ottawa, the compilation of results was undertaken by a special staff that was brought on stream as needed, rising to a peak of 350 by the end of August 1921 and tapering off to 120 by the end of the year. As in 1911, extensive use was made of mechanical tabulation methods. Preliminary population counts were given out piecemeal as they were completed, and the preliminary count for the Dominion as a whole was published on 24 February 1922. As revisions were completed, the final results of the census of population were published through a series of printed bulletins, some twenty in all. These were followed by bulletins on particular characteristics over the next eighteen months. A similar two-stage procedure was followed for the census of agriculture results, the bulletin series being completed in August 1923.

The basic tabulations having thus been produced with commendable expedition, the bureau was then able to proceed to the work of textual analysis and interpretation. By April 1924, three definitive volumes of the 1921 census, two dealing with population and one with agriculture, had been published. The remaining two appeared much later.[27] A sixth volume, to be made up of special analytical studies, was planned but never appeared, though two such studies were separately published: *Illiteracy and School Attendance in Canada* (1926); and *Origin, Birthplace, Nationality and Language of the Canadian People* (1929). Thus, Coats's claim in the administrative report that "no previous census ... will have supplied the public of Canada with results of equal volume and wealth of analysis"[28] was well justified.

Agricultural Statistics

The two decades prior to World War I had witnessed the development of monthly and annual agricultural statistics in most provinces. However, these varied so much in scope, methodology, and reliability that, when Canada acceded to the International Institute of Agriculture in 1908 and undertook to furnish national crop reports, the Census and Statistics Office had no choice but to initiate its own parallel program. Thus, as Coats put it in 1920, "for a considerable portion of Canada, a dual series of agricultural reports and estimates ... came into existence (and not infrequently into conflict) – a source of embarrassment to the many who required trustworthy agricultural figures, and the cause of constant friction among officials."[29]

The action required to rectify this unsatisfactory situation was in fact substantially completed before the bureau formally came into existence. Discussions between the Dominion and provincial governments about how they might best work together in the collection of agricultural statistics had begun in 1913, and within five years a cooperative arrangement with all nine provinces was in place. The first requirement was to determine each spring the acreages sown to field crops and the numbers of each kind of livestock. Hitherto, correspondents had been asked to estimate in the aggregate the percentage increase or decrease in each district by comparison with the preceding year. It was now agreed that actual information should be collected directly from as many as possible of the 640,000 or so holdings of five acres or more. This was thought difficult to do through the mail or by conventional enumeration. Instead, the assistance of rural schoolteachers was sought.

Schedules in card format prepared by the bureau were shipped in bulk to the various provincial departments of agriculture, which, in collaboration with their departments of education, forwarded them to the rural schoolteachers who had previously been advised and coached by joint circular of the two departments. The cards were then distributed to the children, to whom "a statement of the objects of the inquiry is read, making the whole a school exercise and a lesson in public service as well as in agricultural education."[30] The reverse route was followed in shipping the completed cards back to Ottawa for machine tabulation.[31] At harvest time, Dominion and provincial agricultural correspondents collaborated in making estimates of average yield per acre by county or crop district that were then applied to the acreage information to determine total yields.

Building upon the arrangement for crops and livestock, it was possible after 1919 to start extending the scope of the system to other areas of agricultural or horticultural production such as fruits, vegetables, sugar beets, tobacco, flax for fibre, and maple syrup. For many of these, the data collected in 1921 by the census of agriculture provided the starting point for annual statistics. These were published as soon as they became available in the *Monthly Bulletin of*

Agricultural Statistics. In January 1924, in fulfillment of a commitment made in 1917 at the time of the original Dominion/provincial agreement, a follow-up conference was held to assess the working of the system as it then stood, and to adopt recommendations for its improvement as a result of experience gained.

Industrial Census

In his plans for industrial statistics, Coats had proposed in 1916 that a separate and comprehensive census be conducted once every ten years in a different year from that of the census of population and agriculture, and that its findings be kept up to date by an annual postal inquiry of more limited scope. The Statistics Act provided that "a census of the products of industry shall be taken for the year one thousand nine hundred and eighteen, and subsequently at such intervals as may be determined by the Minister" and spelled out the details of the information to be collected. The frequency of the census proper was thus left open by the act, and it would certainly have been possible to conduct annual updates under the bureau's authority for the collection of general statistics.

In fact, the areas of statistical collection in which the bureau had been working towards cooperative arrangements with the responsible Dominion and provincial departments – fisheries, mines, forestry, dairying, and electric power – were already on an annual basis. This in turn had dictated that the bureau's own postal census of manufactures, originally introduced in 1905 as an intercensal supplement to the omnibus decennial censuses and repeated on that basis in 1915, should also be annualized. This was the situation from 1917 onwards, and there was no question but that it was a full-blown census.

The arrangements by which the other components of the industrial census were put in place were well summarized in a book prepared for the 1935 Commonwealth statisticians' conference held in Ottawa:

> In, say, mining, dairying or forestry statistics, where each province previously acted independently and often by differing methods, with the corresponding Dominion Department blanketing the work in whole or in part (the statistics being limited almost invariably to production alone), the following typical arrangement is now in force: (1) a uniform method and technique has been arrived at in conference between the Bureau and the Dominion and Provincial Departments concerned; (2) the Bureau of Statistics prints and provides the standard forms and schedules as agreed upon; (3) the Provincial Government Departments in most cases undertake the collection and visaing of the data; (4) the Bureau of Statistics compiles the schedules according to an agreed plan; (5) the publication of the data is made on a Dominion-wide basis by the Bureau, the provinces being given their own data for use in any way desired; (6) the Dominion Departments use the Bureau as their statistical agency and obtain from its appropriate branches such statistical services as they require.[32]

In publishing the statistics, those of the primary or extractive industries were separated from those of secondary production whenever possible. But in the former case, the statistics of immediately related manufactures were included for convenience of reference. Thus, the fisheries report included the canneries, salteries, and other fish-preparing establishments, as well as the catch, and similarly, the mines report covered contingent metallurgical operations.

Industries were classified according to the chief article of production and prevalent trade practice. The problem of secondary production was accommodated by asking for such production to be reported separately and then, by cross-compilation, deriving industry totals covering both primary and secondary production. However, the lack of an unambiguous and consistently applied product classification was a potential Achilles' heel for the new industrial census. As Coats put it, "if a grouping system contains such headings as 'leather' and 'clothing' within the same category, accuracy becomes impossible, as an article like boots and shoes cannot be placed in the one without rendering the other defective."[33] And with different interpretations as between different branches, reliable comparisons could not be made between production statistics and those of imports, prices, wages, etc.

In order to develop workable guidelines, the bureau set up a committee in May 1918 under the chairmanship of Professor W.C. Clark of Queen's University to canvass the views of interested Dominion and provincial departments and consult with a counterpart committee in the United States. It was recommended that any product classification for statistical purposes should be a tripartite system, grouping items according to either "chief component material," "purpose," or "source of origin," and that the three principles should not be intermingled in any one scheme. It was further urged that the first of these be adopted and adhered to as far as possible and the other two used for the presentation of analyses and broad totals. Thus, "boots and shoes" would be shown in the detailed presentation under "leather" but would also be included in the general analytical totals of "clothing" and among manufactured products ultimately derived from "the farm." Coats warned that "the method cannot be applied with 100 per cent success" but felt that "it can effect a considerable increase in accuracy over previous practices, and that by adopting it as a standard still further improvements can be worked out in time."[34]

Dealing with Non-response

The policy of diligently pursuing and, if necessary, prosecuting delinquent respondents that had begun with the 1915 census of manufactures was continued after the war for the entire census of industry. The rationale was that "by dealing with a few cases ... and giving publicity to the same, we would probably get in the rest without further trouble. I understand that the effect of a few enforcements of the Act with regard to Income Tax has had the effect of bringing in a great number of returns."[35]

The burden of preparing the cases and assisting counsel in presenting them in court fell largely upon J.A. Schryburt, assistant chief for industrial statistics. According to a letter from counsel to the minister reporting on the disposition of forty-three cases heard in a single day in Toronto: "Mr Schryburt, not only by his obvious efficiency and thorough grasp of the matters in question, but also by his fair minded attitude, created a very favourable impression, not only with the Court but with the Press, which was subsequently evidenced by their reports of these prosecutions ... his attitude in the matter [also] avoided unnecessary animosity being engendered among those who were prosecuted."[36]

Just a few weeks later, ninety-four actions were launched in Montreal, and judgments obtained in fifty-six of them.[37] This hectic pace slowed down in subsequent years. There was no perceptible decline in the number of delinquencies to be followed up, but fewer and fewer of them were taken to court. In any case, Schryburt's results appeared impressive; after one 1923 trip covering the principal cities and towns of Ontario over twenty-nine working days, he reported that he had "cleaned up" almost four hundred delinquents.[38] Schryburt's fieldwork could not have been easy. He was constantly asked questions such as:

– Why did you not prosecute us for your reports of 1919–20–21? Why should we feel that this year's report is more important than previous ones?
– Does a Government that fails to enforce the Sales Tax, a revenue measure, expect to frighten us by printing a law on a statistical form?
– I made all my reports except the 1922 one. John Smith has made none for five years. Why come after me?
– Are you willing to wait for our report until you can return and assure me that I am the only remaining delinquent in this city?[39]

But he always had an answer: "In most cases ... I convinced them of the value of statistics and the necessity of complying." And he never faltered in his conviction that "the Industrial Census will greatly diminish in value and even have a chance of absolute failure unless rigorous methods are immediately applied to bring all delinquents to time."[40]

External Trade Statistics

When the bureau formally came into existence on 1 July 1918, the confusing and anomalous division of responsibility for statistics of foreign trade,[41] which Coats had criticized in "A National System of Statistics for Canada," was already being addressed. The first step had been the transfer of the Trade Statistics Branch of the Department of Trade and Commerce to the Census and Statistics

Office in March 1917, making possible coordination of the analytical work with respect to trade statistics that each had hitherto undertaken separately.

Attention then focused on the remaining duplication between the reorganized Census and Statistics Office and the Customs department. Here the objective was that the latter should take responsibility only for the collection and primary compilation of data, their analysis, interpretation, and publication being left to the former. But dealings with Customs were uphill work. In December 1918 Coats wrote as follows to the acting minister of Trade and Commerce: "about two years ago this Bureau submitted to the Customs Department a memorandum on the improvement of trade statistics ... [they] did not seem desirous of discussing it with us, and we accordingly, about a year later, suggested the appointment of an interdepartmental committee to deal with the matter. This was also declined ... We accordingly, in passing the Bureau of Statistics Act last session, provided specifically for the handling of trade statistics."[42]

The operational details of the principles embodied in the act were to be worked out later and confirmed by special Order in Council, as provided for under the regulations set out in PC 2503 of 12 October 1918. The monthly customs report had in fact been discontinued before the passage of the Statistics Act. From 1 April 1918 the bureau began to publish detailed monthly statements of the quantities and values of imports and exports, by origin and destination respectively, based on information furnished by the Customs department. As to the annual report of the latter under the Customs Act, it was announced by the bureau that it would be "primarily an administrative statement of revenues collected, all purely trade statistical analyses being relegated to the report on that subject by the Bureau."[43] This latter task was addressed without delay, eventually resulting in an annual compilation of some fifteen hundred pages.[44]

The bureau continued to strive for improvements in both the monthly and annual trade reports. Timeliness was the dominant consideration in the monthly, and an advance monthly trade summary was introduced. A notable innovation in the annual report for 1926–27 was the use of index numbers of import and export valuations to show fluctuations in the volume of trade.[45] Another development on the analytical side was the regular preparation of special compilations for Canadian exporters and others, based not only on Canadian data but also on those of other countries.

The bureau was thus making tangible progress with its own direct responsibilities under the Statistics Act regarding external trade statistics, but the necessary accommodations with the Customs department were achieved neither as speedily nor as completely as with the departments that had been producing railway, mining, forestry, and other statistics as administrative by-products. Here the interdepartmental agreements called for by the regulations of the Statistics Act had been promptly developed and Orders in Council approved for the transfer of statistical functions and the staffs that had hitherto been responsible for the work in the parent administrative departments.

But this did not occur in the case of external trade statistics. Five years elapsed before the Customs department pruned its annual report back to anything like "an administrative statement of revenues collected." The reports up to that for the year 1922–23 continued to include several hundred pages of tables showing imports and exports by country and commodity, duplicating information provided in the bureau's annual publication. From the Customs side there was no public indication of why the changes had taken so long, and the bureau simply announced that "the Annual Report of the Trade of Canada, 1924, was the only detailed report published by the Government of Canada for that year, the Customs Annual Report being discontinued."[46]

In the difficulties between the bureau and Customs, personal animosities may have played a part. In mid-1918 John McDougald, commissioner of Customs for many years, had been appointed deputy minister. Four years earlier, as chairman of the Board of Inquiry into the Cost of Living, he and Coats, his fellow board member, had done battle over the board's report. In any case, however, external trade statistics were arguably different from those of the other departments mentioned above. They appear to have been thought of by Customs not so much as by-products as an integral and inseparable part of its mandate to collect revenues. Statistical cooperation with the new centralized bureau was desirable but could not be allowed to prejudice the department's core function. An important case in point related to the bureau's missionary efforts to promote the use of mechanical tabulation methods and to act as servicewide coordinator of this function. The net failed to catch the Customs department, and Coats, writing a decade and a half later, noted that "various difficulties ... prevented action until the present year, when a partial application of mechanical tabulation has been made in the Customs Department – to be made comprehensive in due course."[47]

Coats then listed a number of headings of needed improvements in the methodology of compilation and further possibilities with respect to the analysis of foreign trade statistics in which the bureau's more active involvement would be helpful. He concluded with the recommendation that "the statistical branch of the Department of Customs should be transferred and operated as a branch of the Dominion Bureau of Statistics under a plan whereby it should serve both the administrative needs of the former and the rapidly developing demands of a purely statistical character."[48] These arguments finally prevailed and the transfer was authorized by Order in Council PC 425 on 1 March 1938.

Transportation Statistics

Systematic collection of railways statistics had begun soon after the enactment of the Railway Statistics Act of 1873, which required all railways to furnish annual statements of earnings and expenses, traffic and operating statistics, finance, etc.[49] These returns were first made to the Department of Public Works, and then, from 1879, to the newly established Department of Railways and Canals. Similar but less-detailed information had been collected since Confederation for canals, and in the course of time statistics of express, telegraph, and telephone companies were added. After the Board of Railway Commissioners was established as a regulatory authority in 1903, railway statistics were extended and elaborated, the procedures and reports of the US Interstate Commerce Commission serving as a model. The Department of Marine and Fisheries maintained a register of the numbers and tonnage of Canadian shipping, and the Customs department provided information on vessels arriving from and clearing for ports in foreign countries, the trade statistics providing an analysis of their cargoes, but there were no corresponding statistics for the coasting trade.

The departmental commission report of 1912 had looked at transportation statistics not just as the mirror of one of Canada's most important industries but also for their potential contribution to a comprehensive body of internal trade statistics. Going further, Coats's 1916 memorandum, "A National System of Statistics for Canada," urged that transportation statistics should also be coordinated with the industrial census so that processes such as the manufacture of rolling stock would not be covered twice by different agencies and different methods. In addition, it recommended that the Railway Statistics Branch of the Department of Railways and Canals be constituted as the "transportation division" of the proposed central statistics office. The Statistics Act of 1918 assigned the bureau responsibility for the statistics of transportation companies, defined as "any railway, telegraph, telephone and express company and any carrier by water," with the formal transfer of such responsibility from the departments hitherto concerned to be arranged in accordance with the provisions of PC 2503.

Thus, railway statistics were transferred under Order in Council PC 1754 of 29 August 1919; central electric power statistics under PC 2036 of 1 October 1919; and statistics of electric railways under PC 2026 of 6 October 1922. PC 617 of 20 March 1919 put in place similar arrangements for canal statistics. The returns on which statistics of shipping in and out of Canadian ports could be based were generated by the Customs department, and negotiations for the assumption by the bureau of formal responsibility for these statistics were not successful until many years later. In the meantime, however, the Customs department continued to produce an annual navigation report, but this provided no information on coastwise, or domestic, shipping. Both the bureau and the department tried unsuccessfully to persuade shippers to agree to the preparation of cargo statements on coastwise traffic.

Complaints were received in the minister's office, but F.C.T. O'Hara, the deputy minister, showed little sympathy for the bureau in responding to them. In an exchange of correspondence with O'Hara, Coats made reference to the desirability of an Order in Council under the authority of PC 2503, dealing with shipping statistics, that would undoubtedly have given him a stronger hand in facing the industry. Even though PC 2503 was the key regulation under the Statistics Act, O'Hara chose to reply that "I know nothing of PC 2503, or at least it is impossible to trace an Order in Council by the number without the year being stated."[50]

Railway statistics got off to an uncertain start. The Department of Railways and Canals appears to have been keeping an anxious eye on how the bureau was handling its new responsibility, and in November 1920 J.L. Payne of the Office of the Comptroller of Statistics wrote to O'Hara that "a sense of duty impels me to advise you that very serious mistakes are to be found in Railway Statistics for 1919 as prepared by the Dominion Bureau of Statistics ... If these mistakes are not corrected, and the report is sent out in its present shape, it will be worthless and a reproach to Government."[51]

Payne attributed the mistakes to the inexperience of G.S. Wrong, the responsible branch chief. They were corrected before publication, but the resultant delays earned the bureau a further reproof. Payne again wrote to O'Hara in March 1921: "I merely wish you to know personally that the delay in getting out Railway Statistics has reached the point of being a real scandal ... This Bureau of Statistics we were told would handle public reports with greater efficiency than had been shown under the old system. What has actually happened is quite the reverse. Your Department is in a fair way of being discredited."[52]

After this initial aberration, steady progress appears to have been made with railway statistics. In a 1931 memorandum, it was possible to report that "Canadian statistics of railways are quite comprehensive."[53] Similarly, the statistics of electric railways and express, telegraph, and telephone companies were said to be "adequate in their essential features."[54] But statistics of water transportation were less satisfactory. A census of Canadian registered vessels covering the year 1918 had been conducted and the quality and scope of canal statistics had been improved, but Coats had to concede that "no statistics of Canadian water carriers on the same general lines as those obtaining for railways and tramways exist at present, and the gap has serious consequences for the general body of economic statistics."[55]

A further hiatus developed as a consequence of the restrictive definition of transportation provided by the Statistics Act, which excluded road and air carriers. As early as 1922, Wrong drew Coats's attention to the problem and recommended that the Statistics Act be amended to require the submission of statistical returns by such carriers. He met with no success, and the Statistics Act was not amended for this purpose until 1948. The lack of authority in the Statistics Act was not in fact an obstacle to the generation of useful information on aviation statistics. During the 1920s the fledgling industry was under the supervision of the Department of National Defence, which administered the federal air regulations, and the reports of the Air Board under these regulations provided a great deal of statistical information that was regularly reproduced in the *Canada Year Book*. The bureau did not begin direct surveys of civil aviation during the interwar period, but by 1936 there was enough information to warrant the publication of an annual report.

Work had begun during the 1920s on compiling from provincial sources statistics of nonurban road mileage and motor vehicle registrations – the track and rolling stock by analogy with railway statistics – but no action was taken to measure the transportation of passengers and goods by road. This deficiency became much more glaring when the Royal Commission on Railways and Transportation was formed in 1931 to address "the serious and continuing deficit of the Canadian National Railway System and the diminished revenue of the Canadian Pacific Railway System."[56] This was thought to have been in part the consequence of competition from other modes of transportation, and the statistics that would have shed some direct light on the problem were simply not available. The commission recommended that operators of road passenger services and common and contract carriers of freight "should keep accounts on a prescribed system and render returns to appropriate authority on a common basis."[57] The bureau naturally saw itself as the appropriate authority.

The lack of road transport statistics was noted at the Dominion/provincial Conference of Premiers in 1933. The subject was also discussed at the Commonwealth statisticians' conference in 1935, and the report of the Royal Commission on Dominion-Provincial Relations in 1940 provided implicit support for comprehensive transportation statistics in its recommendation with respect to transportation that there should be "continuous expert planning which can extend to all interrelated branches of this peculiarly intricate problem."[58]

Wrong continued to write memoranda, and shortly after Coats's retirement he reminded Cudmore, then acting Dominion statistician, that "for nearly 20 years I have been attempting to have the Statistics Act amended to include motor vehicles and aircraft in the definition of 'transportation companies.'"[59] The Second World War made it possible to act under powers granted to the wartime Transit Controller, and the bureau undertook a census of motor carriers for 1941. There were some challenges to the legal authority for this undertaking, but the real problems turned out to be purely statistical. They never really disappeared, as the following comments, made some forty years later, indicate: "While road transport has had the most vigorous growth of all modes of transportation, the quality of its statistics has been variable to an extreme. The development of this mode has long been in the hands of a large number of entrepreneurs who have been able to start business with a limited initial capital and to grow without large appeals to the capital market. Problems of definition as well as maintaining records of 'births and deaths' of trucking undertakings have been a formidable constraint on the provision of consistent statistical series."[60]

NTERNAL TRADE STATISTICS

oats's 1916 proposals for a system of internal trade statistics envisaged three
nain activities. The first was the use of monthly traffic returns to measure and
nalyze interprovincial and interurban flows of goods in broad outline. The
econd was cooperation with the marketing branches of certain other
lepartments, making it possible to round out and further analyze the traffic
lata with information on the movements of specific commodities like grain,
ivestock, and fish. The third was the development of matching price statistics –
or producers' prices and wholesale prices in particular – to provide the necessary
ink between quantities and values.

Wartime needs had intensified interest in all kinds of statistics, particularly
hose of production and trade. One important example was the study put in
nand by Sir George Foster early in 1917 to explore the possibility of establishing
n internal trade commission, modelled on the Federal Trade Commission of
he United States, to address the improper trading practices that had mushroomed
nder wartime conditions. Coats was a member of the committee appointed to
arry out the study, and his influence is clearly detectable in its draft interim
eport: "The establishment of an adequate system of statistics of production
nd internal trade is fundamental to work of any kind by any agency along the
ines now suggested by the Minister ... In this connection the committee has
onsidered the two memoranda prepared by the Census and Statistics Office,
lealing respectively with the Industrial Census and Statistics of Internal Trade.
t begs leave to endorse these memoranda and bring them to the attention of the
Minister with the suggestion that they be acted upon at the earliest possible
noment."[61]

At the same time, Coats was exerting direct leverage on O'Hara: "In further
eference to our recent correspondence re internal trade problems, you once
emarked that a good deal of the chaos in existing arrangements for statistics
vas due to the inactivity of the Census Office, which had compelled other
Departments to step in. I feel that we are taking a very considerable risk of this
ind in further postponing action re internal trade. We cannot go on indefinitely
'warning off' other Departments. I have reason to fear that if we do not within
he next few months occupy this field in a capable way there will be a strong
novement to cover it elsewhere."[62]

The entry of the United States into the war in the spring of 1917 forced the
ssue by creating massive new demands for food and industrial materials, which
bliged both Canada and the United States to put in place machinery for the
ontinental management of supply and demand. Thus, in Canada, a Food
Controller, Fuel Controller, and Board of Grain Supervisors were quickly
ppointed. Their operations generated extensive statistical records, the
ompilation of which, for the first two, was carried out by the Census and
Statistics Office in a newly established Internal Trade Statistics Branch. The

importance attached to this new branch by Coats was demonstrated in his recruitment of Dr R.J. McFall of the University of Minnesota to serve as its chief.

The approach to the measurement of internal trade through traffic returns was directly carried out by the Transportation Branch, which by 1921 had developed a monthly railway freight traffic report. This showed *inter alia* the loadings and unloadings – by province, and for the fifteen largest urban centres – of some seventy classes of commodities, making it possible to identify net movements. Later, weekly statistics of carloadings were initiated. But there were no corresponding developments on the side of water transportation, either through the canal system or by coastwise shipping, during the whole of the interwar period.

However, the Internal Trade Statistics Branch made a great deal of progress in the early postwar years in developing marketing statistics in collaboration with other federal departments and bodies. These programs were given official blessing through specific Orders in Council under the blanket authority of PC 2503 of 12 October 1918. The first of these (PC 1246), dated 31 May 1920, related to statistics of livestock and animal products, while a parallel Order (PC 3362) dated 13 September 1921 covered grain statistics, where the principal source of current information on the inspection, weighting, forwarding, warehousing, and shipment of grain was the Board of Grain Commissioners.[6]

A third Order in Council (PC 1892) of 12 August 1920 became necessary following the passage in 1919 of the Combines and Fair Prices Act – the outcome of Foster's 1917 initiative. The act had set up a Board of Commerce and, although provision had been made for the returns required by the board to be submitted either to the board itself or to the Dominion statistician, the Order stipulated that "where any periodical statistical return is required by the Board, application for its establishment be made to the Dominion Bureau of Statistics, and the work carried out under the immediate direction of the Bureau, subject to such conditions as to scope of data to be collected, method of collection, compilation and disposition, etc., as may be prescribed by the Board, the work of this character at present being carried out in the Economics Division of the Board and the staff thereof to be transferred to the Bureau, and reorganized in coordination with the general work of the Bureau."

These arrangements were soon working smoothly and were supplemented by others, for which Orders in Council were not necessary, covering cold storage, milling, sugar, etc. Successive annual reports of the Dominion statistician regularly noted the extension and improvement of the statistics. In 1927 F.J. Horning, who had taken over the Internal Trade Statistics Branch in 1920 after the resignation of R.J. McFall, was appointed chief of the Agriculture Statistics Branch following the retirement of E.H. Godfrey. He brought with him the program of commodity statistics, which was subsequently elaborated to cover the movement of virtually all farm products into domestic and foreign markets. But by this time the Internal Trade Statistics Branch had already staked out what was eventually to become its major responsibility – the wholesale and retail phases of the marketing cycle, together with the provision of commercial services.

Coats's early success in developing a comprehensive body of production statistics pointed the way towards an analogous census that would measure distribution activities. Accordingly, in the 1921 census, a list of establishments engaged in wholesale and retail trading was collected by the enumerators on a special schedule to serve as the basis for a postal inquiry in 1924 covering the year 1923. Returns were obtained from 66,814, or some two-thirds of such establishments. Budgetary stringency ruled out the possibility of follow-up but many of the nonrespondents were thought to be small, so that the figures finally published for capital, sales, etc. probably represented much more than two-thirds of the Dominion totals. It was therefore possible to assert in the report of the census, which appeared in 1928, that "while the data is [sic] therefore incomplete, it is considered to be indicative of real conditions."[64]

The continuing increase during the 1920s in the relative importance of distribution and related activities led to a second and more determined effort to measure them in the context of the 1931 census. It was decided that the Canadian census should be made as comparable as possible to a proposed census of distribution in the United States, with the difference that the Canadian census would also cover service establishments.[65] Follow-up after the mailing of questionnaires was considerably more vigorous, and it was estimated, for instance, that hardly more than five percent of the number of retail stores were missed. A few years later, the 1935 Conference of Statisticians of the British Commonwealth, held in Ottawa, was informed that:

> The Internal Trade Statistics Branch counts among its main achievements the taking of a complete Census of Merchandising and Service Establishments ... Some 23 kinds or sizes of such establishments were differentiated in the schedules sent out. Reports were subsequently received from 125,003 retail traders, 13,140 wholesale traders and 42,223 retail service establishments. These were carefully analysed by commodities traded in, by amounts of sales and by types of operation, by percentages of credit business, etc., as well as by provinces and localities ... This census was one of the first of its kind in the world, and has provided legislators, traders, economists and students of marketing and marketing areas with very detailed and extensive information regarding Canadian distributive organization.[66]

Apart from its considerable intrinsic value, this census also laid the foundation for an annual survey of retail and wholesale trade.

The second major component of the work of the Internal Trade Statistics Branch, as it took shape after 1931, was price statistics. The first such statistics had been those prepared by Coats in the Department of Labour for his 1910 study *Wholesale Prices in Canada, 1890–1909*, which was subsequently kept up to date by an annual publication. The study was a response to concerns about the rapid rise in the cost of living during the first decade of the century, and wholesale prices were chosen as a proxy because there was an abundance of ready information in the trade and financial press, and elsewhere. At the same time a parallel initiative was launched in respect of retail prices proper, for which the department's correspondents furnished quotations to measure monthly changes in a synthetic workingman's budget. The First World War elevated the profile of this work, and a separate Cost of Living Branch was established to meet needs such as those of the Food Controller and, later, the Canada Food Board. After the bureau was established in 1918, the collection of prices was taken over by the Internal Trade Statistics Branch, which furnished monthly and annual reports to the Department of Labour for publication in the *Labour Gazette*.

This arrangement was disrupted for a while during 1919-20 when the responsibility for price collection was transferred to the new Board of Commerce, which undertook to carry out the work in conjunction with the collection of other information from the same respondents. The experiment was not a success. The timeliness of reporting suffered, while the low esteem in which the business community held the board resulted in a diminishing rate of response. Thus, in August 1920, on the authority of PC 1892, the work reverted to the bureau's Internal Trade Statistics Branch. This arrangement was confirmed by a new Order in Council (PC 2109) of 16 October 1922, under which responsibilities in the field of labour and price statistics were formally allocated between the Department of Labour and the bureau. For most of the 1920s the prices work was directly managed by Herbert Marshall. It benefited considerably from the programs of industrial and agricultural statistics, which yielded producers' prices, and also from the branch's newly developed marketing statistics, which provided a new source of wholesale prices. The direct collection of price quotations was steadily expanded during the 1920s and the reliance on secondary sources correspondingly lessened. This made it possible to elaborate and extend the wholesale and retail price statistics, and also to break ground in a number of new areas.

During this period, one responsibility of the branch that had certainly not been visualized in the original planning of internal trade statistics was the development of balance of payments statistics. Rough estimates of the invisible items of the balance of payments had been made in 1915 by Coats, and his work attracted considerable interest among academics, notably Jacob Viner, who eventually published a major study in this area.[67] During the early 1920s the momentum was kept up by other academics such as Frank A. Knox, K.W. Taylor, and Frank Southard. In 1926 the bureau decided to develop balance of payments statistics and the task was assigned to Marshall. Special attention was given at the start to foreign investments in Canada and Canadian investments abroad because of their basic importance to the balance of payments and their role in economic development. To support this work, the Internal Trade Statistics Branch put together a set of corporation records profiling branch, subsidiary, affiliated, and controlled plants. The body of information that was eventually built up made possible a 1936 study of Canadian/American investment under the joint authorship of Marshall, Southard, and Taylor.[68] In 1939 Marshall won the prestigious Gold Medal of the Professional Institute of the Civil Service of Canada for his pioneering work with the Canadian balance of payments during the interwar years.

Other Program Developments

In addition to the urgent program initiatives that Coats launched or completed during the bureau's early years, there were others that, while of a more discretionary character – at least where timing was concerned – were also important building blocks in the ultimate program structure. These are reviewed below.

Education Statistics

The problems with education statistics faced by the bureau in 1918 were similar to those concerning vital statistics. Both involved areas of provincial jurisdiction where, to the extent that statistics were already available, interprovincial comparisons were at best difficult and valid national summaries and analyses impossible. Coats's 1916 report recommended that "statistics of education, which are at present published by the provinces in a form incapable of coordination, should be reduced to harmony by conference with provincial Departments of Education," and that "ultimately we should develop a central branch for the collection and publication of education statistics, as in the United States."[69]

The *Canada Year Book* had provided a special article on education in its 1916–17 edition, summarizing the census statistics on illiteracy and education and providing a description of the salient features of the existing Canadian systems of education, together with a tabular presentation of the principal annual education statistics by province from the beginning of the century. But as the *First Annual Report of the Dominion Statistician, 1918–1919* pointed out, "the results tended primarily to emphasize the blanks and discrepancies that must prevail under existing conditions."[70]

One of the detailed memoranda underlying the 1916 report had sketched out a scheme of statistical reform involving the modification of certain provincial practices, the delimitation of Dominion and provincial inquiries, and cooperation between the bureau and provincial education departments in a nationwide system of educational statistics. These proposals were submitted to the provincial departments for discussion and agreement was reached on their feasibility, the key point being that standardization rather than uniformity should be the goal. In 1918, after similar discussion, the Dominion Education Association endorsed by resolution the bureau's contemplated plan of action.

The establishment of an Education Statistics Branch, at first under S.A. Cudmore in conjunction with the General Statistics Branch and later on its own under M.C. MacLean, made it possible to proceed with the implementation of the plan. The first step was the convening of a Dominion/provincial conference in October 1920, which gave its blessing to the plan. The provinces continued to be responsible for collecting statistics of enrolment, attendance, teachers, facilities, accommodation, expenditures, etc. for provincially controlled primary and secondary schools, while the bureau began the direct collection of statistics on private schools and postsecondary institutions. In 1921 an *Historical Statistical Survey of Education in Canada* was published.[71] It can hardly have had access to much material that had not been available to the earlier yearbook study, but it was hailed in the annual report for 1921–22 as entailing "very considerable research in a hitherto undeveloped statistical field" and representing "an attempt for the first time to deal comprehensively with Canadian education."[72]

Subsequently, current data were used in the *Annual Report on Education Statistics in Canada*,[73] first published in 1922, and the branch began to edge into peripheral areas of inquiry like the operations of public libraries and playground associations. Notably, it also began to analyze current educational statistics in conjunction with census data, producing studies such as that on illiteracy and school attendance in Canada. The education statistics program was substantially in place by the end of the 1920s, and MacLean was succeeded in 1935 by J.E. Robbins, who continued with distinction MacLean's analytical tradition. One particularly notable study, *The Dependency of Youth*, a 1931 census monograph, was extensively drawn upon later in wartime and postwar social planning.

Health Statistics

The Department of Agriculture's short-lived initiative in the collection of mortuary statistics during the 1880s had been thought to complement and enhance the statistics being developed by the provinces in the area of public health, particularly those of communicable diseases. The connection was again stressed in the departmental commission report of 1912, which quoted the Committee on Public Health of the Commission of Conservation, Canada, as follows: "Correct and accurate vital statistics are the basis of modern sanitation; they are the gauge whereby we judge the progress made against diseases of all kinds, and whereby we obtain information for further advancement."[74]

of these or any other standards by the provincial and municipal authorities, so that, although statistics pertaining to both areas were regularly published, they were neither comprehensive nor consistent, and the branch's analytical skills were taxed to the utmost to render them useful or even intelligible. Statistics generated at the Dominion level during this period related to public finance only incidentally. In 1924, on the instructions of the prime minister, a statistical investigation of the number of employees of the Dominion government and the expenditure on salaries covering the period 1912–24 was undertaken in the context of the government's continuing, and frequently embarrassing, problem during the 1920s with civil service classifications and salaries.[82] The work was subsequently regularized as a monthly survey on the basis of procedures agreed with the departments to secure uniformity of method.

The branch's work languished until 1933 when, as a result of the Depression, public finance was pushed high on the list of political priorities. In that year a Dominion/provincial conference under the chairmanship of the prime minister resolved that "the necessity for accurate and comparable statistics relating to public finance is apparent, and the Conference recommends that the Dominion Statistician should communicate with the treasurers and/or statisticians of the several provinces with a view of securing uniformly classified statistical information."[83]

In September 1933 a conference between the bureau, the provincial treasury departments, and the Dominion Department of Finance agreed upon a set of schedules as the basis for future compilations of provincial finance statistics, the first annual report under the new system being issued in 1935. The subsequent development of the bureau's program of public finance statistics was determined by the needs of the Royal Commission on Dominion-Provincial Relations, to which this history returns in chapter 7.

The Canada Year Book and Handbook

In his 1916 memorandum, Coats had promised that centralization would provide the "fundamental data" required by government through systematic coverage of the major headings of social and economic statistics. The establishment of the various subject-matter branches and the development of their programs as described in this chapter resulted in substantial progress towards this goal during the bureau's first decade. But, as the memorandum had argued, "these are by no means all the statistics that are called for. With increasing frequency practical problems arise which require a new angle of approach, and new combinations of data"; hence the need for a "national laboratory;" or "central thinking office," to observe and interpret current economic and social phenomena from a broader standpoint. With this in place, Coats optimistically predicted, "'Cost of Living' and 'Economic Commissions', etc. would either not be necessary or would find the primary data they require ready at hand."[84] Coats was strongly influenced in this thinking by the formation in 1916 of the Honorary Advisory Council for Scientific and Industrial Research (later the National Research Council) to provide parallel arrangements for the physical sciences in Canada. He saw the bureau as the natural locus for the economic and social service, and the General Statistics Branch, under the newly recruited Professor S.A. Cudmore, as the organizational vehicle, the *Canada Year Book* constituting the nucleus around which it would be developed. As the subsequent history of the branch demonstrated, however, it fell sadly short of Coats's expectations for economic and social research. It was always known primarily for its work with the yearbook and handbook.

Under Archibald Blue, the *Canada Year Book* had been transformed into a purely statistical abstract. Following criticisms by the departmental commission of its narrow orientation, E.H. Godfrey was assigned the task of beefing it up with textual material. Cudmore took over from Godfrey soon after coming to the bureau, and the 1918 edition was published as a jubilee volume, with articles on "The Story of Confederation," and "Fifty Years of Canadian Progress." Further scholarly articles were published as the 1920s progressed. At the same time, the gradual development of the bureau's primary programs was providing additional statistical content. Although these developments were well received, the yearbook was in fact shifting away from its earlier popular objectives and being transformed into an encyclopaedic work of reference. The time was thus ripe for a companion publication of similar coverage, but more succinctly written and attractively packaged.

As part of the observance of Canada's Diamond Jubilee in 1927, the bureau had been directed by the organizing committee to prepare a handbook that duly appeared as *Diamond Jubilee of the Confederation of Canada: Sixty Years of Canadian Progress, 1867–1927*.[85] It was pocket-sized with 168 pages and seventy illustrations and diagrams. More than 180,000 copies were distributed in both French and English at the expense of the organizing committee, schools and clergymen getting blanket coverage. In the foreword by the Honourable James Malcolm, minister of Trade and Commerce, the hope was expressed that "the book will be convenient and suggestive for public speakers, teachers, and others who may take a leading part in the celebration, as presenting in readily accessible form the more salient facts of our national progress." The favourable public reception of the 1927 handbook prompted the issuance three years later, under the title *Canada 1930*, of what was hoped would become an annual publication. Since the bureau now had to assume financial responsibility, the press run was conservatively estimated. Fears of failure were groundless; the publication was an instant success and has appeared continuously ever since. The handbook was frequently adapted to meet special needs or to commemorate special occasions. Thus, in 1932 a deluxe edition was presented to the delegates of the Imperial Economic Conference, and the Italian Chamber of Commerce of Canada paid for its translation into Italian for printing and circulation in

Italy and other Italian-speaking countries. It also found its way to some unusual places. When *Canada 1936* was ready for release, J.G. Parmelee, the deputy minister, wrote to Coats suggesting that copies be sent to the Cunard White Star Line, which was "soliciting ready reference books for the First and Tourist Class libraries, especially of the new super-liner [*RMS*] Queen Mary."[86]

The responsibility of the General Statistics Branch for the *Year Book* also made it the obvious channel for the provision of statistical information to other organizations for republication, and for dealing with inquiries from various sources. The Dominion statistician's annual reports during the 1920s made regular mention of these activities. From the early 1920s the bureau also served the public as well as its own staff through a library that was mainly stocked with Canadian and foreign statistical publications and works on statistical methodology. The first librarian was Miss G.S. Lewis, who served with distinction until her retirement in 1951.

The Publicity Section

Early in 1932 James Muir, a former newspaperman, was appointed to establish the bureau's Publicity Section – the nucleus of what eventually became a fully fledged information function. This was located in the Administration Branch, possibly because Coats wanted it under his immediate supervision. Muir's first assignment was to produce for distribution to the English- and French-language daily press a summary of notes and excerpts from reports currently being issued. This, the *DBS Daily Bulletin*, first appeared in February 1932 and was followed in October of the same year by a weekly edition, the *DBS Weekly Bulletin*. This latter was particularly targeted at weekly newspapers, thereby serving small-town and rural Canada. In 1933 the idea was adapted to the needs of radio. Material was supplied daily to the Radio Commission of Canada for a two-minute broadcast entitled "A Fact a Day about Canada." These broadcasts were reprinted each month in a bulletin that found a large following among teachers.

"Barometric" Statistics

In parallel with these developments in the yearbook and related activities, there had also been progress in what Coats had described in 1919 as the need for "a more frequent summing-up of at least the main movements of production, trade, finance, immigration and the like, providing the basis for an analysis of the interdependence of such activities and the throwing of dominant tendencies into relief."[87] The first step towards publishing such "barometric" statistics, as Coats called them, was the transfer to the bureau from the Department of Labour of responsibility for the monthly index of industrial employment late in 1922. Specifically authorized by Order in Council PC 2109, dated 16 October 1922,[88] this was part of a broader agreement for the realignment of statistical responsibilities between the two organizations under the terms of PC 2503. The index had been developed in 1918 in support of the department's efforts to minimize the unemployment that was expected to follow the cessation of hostilities. The Department of Labour was apparently contemplating discontinuance of the underlying survey in 1922, and this no doubt influenced the timing of PC 2109. Along with the transfer of responsibility went a transfer of staff, including Miss M.E.K. Roughsedge, who continued to be associated with the series until the late 1950s,[89] by which time it also covered earnings and hours.

A year or two later, the General Statistics Branch began publication of two other barometric series: bank debits to individual accounts (January 1924), a measure of the volume of bank business; and commercial failures in Canada (February 1925). The monthly wholesale trade index, now located in the Internal Trade Statistic Branch, was a barometric indicator too, as also was the Transportation Branch's weekly report on railway carloadings, begun in 1923. Thus, ample materials were now at hand for a first attempt at Coats's "more frequent summing-up," and in January 1926 the *Monthly Review of Canadian Business Statistics* was launched. Most of the credit for this new publication, that later became the *Canadian Statistical Review*, must go to Sydney B. Smith, who had worked in the census of industry before securing a transfer to the General Statistics Branch – largely on the strength of the private work he had done in the monitoring of business conditions, using the methodology of US and British publications in this area. The *Review*, which soon acquired a paid subscription list of 1,300,[90] was careful to warn its readers that "the Bureau makes no attempt at the interpretation of these figures, its object being solely to place the materials required for such interpretation readily at the disposal of the public."[91]

Statistics of National Wealth and Income

The bureau's first statistics of national wealth and income were published early in the 1920s by the General Statistics Branch, although in his first annual report Coats had envisaged them as being most appropriately developed in conjunction with those of public debt and taxation in the Finance Statistics Branch that was then being organized. This initiative had its roots in private work undertaken by Coats some years earlier in which he had used census and related statistics to estimate the value of investments in agriculture, manufactures, real estate, public infrastructure, etc., as well as the incomes of persons on salaries and wages and those operating on their own account. His paper,[92] although unofficial, was widely circulated, and in 1919 Coats was induced to write a more polished version, presenting estimates of national wealth and income for 1911 and 1918, variants of which were republished by the financial press in Canada and the US.

He was careful to dissociate the bureau from the estimates presented. Before long, however, the extended scope and improved quality of information from the 1921 census of population and agriculture and the annual census of industry provided a basis for more confident estimates that were legitimized by publication in the *Canada Year Book* of 1922–23. National income was approximated by taking the aggregate of the incomes assessed for income tax purposes, "making allowances for evasion and estimating the income of those whose incomes fall below its lower limits," but readers were still cautioned that "statistics of this character are suggestive and indicative rather than strictly accurate."[93]

In 1923 a new annual publication, the *Survey of Production in Canada*, suggested that a rough estimate of national income could be derived by taking the net values of production in the commodity-producing industries, adding an estimate for the service-producing industries based upon the assumption of equal productivity per person employed in the two sectors, and making allowance for depreciation, etc. Such an estimate was published in the 1925 issue, and, with some adjustment and revisions, this was the method used to estimate national income in Canada for the next ten years.

The bureau's first comprehensive study of national income was published in 1934. It was based on the information collected in 1931 by the censuses of population, agriculture, and distribution, as well as the annual census of industry. Three checks on the national income for 1930, as estimated by the earlier method, now became possible. The first consisted of a direct estimate, based mainly on the census of distribution, of the net value of production of the service industries, which was added to the net value of production of the commodity-producing industries. The second check was to take the wages and salaries data from the census of population and add to them an estimate of property income, arrived at by applying to the total of wages and salaries in Canada the ratio of property income to wages and salaries in the United States. The third check was to estimate the expenditures made with the national income, using figures of retail sales, construction, insurance, education, and other data. These checks were thought to corroborate the results obtained by the original method, which continued in use until 1937.[94]

Soon after, in the face of external evidence of the weakness of the production approach, which could not provide valid measures of the net output of the service sector in intercensal years, the method was abandoned in favour of an attempt to use statistics of incomes received by persons. Unhappily, this initiative had also foundered by 1941, and it was not until later in the war that a fresh start was made in the bureau on the basis of new thinking in Britain and the United States. These developments are described in later chapters.

CHAPTER SIX

1918–1939
The Bureau's Battle for Status

Coats's Reporting Relationship

Between 1922 and 1926 successive changes in various administrative procedures and reporting relationships between the bureau and the departmental hierarchy in Trade and Commerce brought about a serious deterioration in the bureau's status – already regarded by Coats as unsatisfactory–and consequently in its ability to carry out the mandate assigned to it. This state of affairs was not fully resolved for some four decades, but it exercised such a persistent and pernicious influence during the interwar years that it warrants special attention here.[1]

It had its origin with Coats's response in the spring of 1915 to Foster's suggestion that he should take over the Census and Statistics Office with a view to carrying out the recommendations of the recent departmental commission report. "I am prepared to take hold of it," he wrote, "and feel confident that with your support it could be developed into the equal of any similar service elsewhere." But he expressed reservations about Foster's views on the standing of the office:

> I understand you to suggest that it might be necessary in the first place to transfer me at my present rank (that of a chief clerk). This, I venture to think, would be to impose a handicap.
> ... what the situation demands from the outset is aggressive and constructive work, both inside and outside the Census ... it would militate against the kind of success desired if a reduction were made in the status which the office has always enjoyed in the past–especially in view of the new developments in contemplation. Of course, I understand and fully appreciate your remarks that the position should ultimately have the standing of a Deputy Minister and that you were not discussing details in your recent conversation.[2]

In speaking of the past status of the office, Coats had in mind the appointment of Archibald Blue in 1900 at a salary higher than that of the deputy minister.

His reference to "aggressive and constructive work" concerned what the proposed central agency would have to do to integrate the statistical activities of other departments into the overall schema and to exercise its own data collection functions effectively *vis-à-vis* the business community and the general public. This was a question not just of authority but, more basically, of the perception of integrity and objectivity that the agency must convey. This in turn depended upon its demonstrated independence from departmental, as opposed to ministerial, control. There is no record of any response from Foster to this letter. Coats did in fact receive an increase in salary within his classification at the time, namely Division IA,[3] and he was apparently content to leave it to Foster to take action at the appropriate time. But Coats subsequently made it perfectly clear that his acceptance of the position had been on the understanding that the necessary independence would be given expression through deputy ministerial status.

The proposed central agency would in significant measure consist of statistical units – fully fledged branches in the administrative sense–from various program departments. The inducement for yielding up such units would have to be an assurance that their work could be performed more efficiently and serve the department's interests more effectively when developed in full harmony with other bodies of statistics. This in turn required that the new host organization could provide supporting professional expertise and be seen externally as free from subordination to any departmental interest. Thus, it would have been retrograde for those statistical branches to become components of what was nothing more than a larger branch within another department. Statistical publications were a case in point. Most departments expressed themselves as willing to see their own imprimatur replaced by that of the central office, but not by that of the Department of Trade and Commerce.

Returning to this issue in later years, as he frequently did, Coats cited the views of the commission that had advised on the constitution of a central statistical office for the Irish Free State: "We would emphasize the importance of granting the Statistical Bureau in the first place as much formal autonomy as is possible. Its parent Department should not in all cases have the first claim to, or most influence on, its common service. We suggest that the Statistical Bureau with its numerous staff on specialized work should be disentangled in its administration from other Branches, and given special direct access to the permanent officials in all Departments who have power to make final decisions."[4] Coats also recalled on this occasion that, during the nineteenth century, when the deputy minister of Agriculture, who was also chief officer of the census, submitted formal reports on the decennial censuses, he did so not in the former capacity but in the latter.

When the Statistics Act was in its final drafting stages, it became apparent that it was not going to deal with the status of the Dominion statistician. On 9 March 1918 Coats wrote to Foster urging that "in the Act constituting a Dominion

Bureau of Statistics ... the Dominion Statistician, as head of the Bureau, be given the rank of a Deputy Minister by inserting the words 'who shall have the rank of a Deputy Minister' after the words 'Dominion Statistician' in Clause 4."[5] He again recalled the special treatment given to Blue, cited the precedent of the office of dominion archivist, which had been given deputy minister status without thereby creating a new department, and reminded the minister that within Trade and Commerce two officers under the deputy had the same rank as himself. Again, there is no record of Foster having replied, and Coats once more let the matter drop; for as he subsequently commented in his "Valedictory Report," the act of 1918 "was not considered final, certain features being left in abeyance until actual organization was effected."[6]

With the one crucial exception of deputy ministerial status, all the elements of autonomy for the new bureau were in fact in place in the Statistics Act. The mandate statement transformed the now augmented Census and Statistics Office from a statistical branch of the Department of Trade and Commerce into an agency at the service of all departments. And the name "bureau," which, Coats claimed, bore at the time a significance applicable only to autonomous or quasi-autonomous bodies, was deliberately chosen to emphasize its separate identity.[7] The Dominion statistician was required, under the direction of the minister, to "supervise and control" the bureau, and, as noted earlier, two related Orders in Council, PC 2503 of 12 October 1918 and PC 1092 of 20 May 1920, gave him unprecedented authority, both executive and advisory, *vis-à-vis* other departments in matters statistical. Similarly, section 9 of the act made him the minister's direct agent for statistical negotiations with the provinces. Finally, it soon became standard practice for the bureau to be acknowledged as having primary responsibility for the provision of statistical information in new or revised legislation, such as that setting up the Department of Health in 1919.

Coats therefore seemed justified in assuming that the powers required for his office could be taken for granted from the nature of the duties involved, and that the eventual ratification of his status through legislative amendment was simply a formality that could be addressed at any politically convenient time. In the meantime, he was able to supplement the act as it stood by various administrative arrangements, notably direct access to the Civil Service Commission on staff matters. This worked well enough at first. Indeed, in 1920, for the purposes of a servicewide reclassification, O'Hara, the deputy minister, was persuaded to put forward the following:

> While the Dominion Bureau of Statistics is a Branch of the Department of Trade and Commerce, its functions are so individualized, so large and complex, that it constitutes work of a great importance and in certain respects greater than some of the existing departments so-called. All negotiations with reference to statistical organization between the Bureau, and other Departments, and between the Bureau and Provincial Governments, and the drafting of recommendations to Council based

> thereon, are made by the Dominion Statistician, and the published reports of the Bureau have always been made direct. The primary responsibility for the Bureau is borne under the Statistics Act and Regulations by the Dominion Statistician. He initiates and controls expenditures, subject always to the approval of the Minister, advises in all matters pertaining to statistical policy, determines official organization and procedure, administers the staff, etc.[8]

But in 1921, when Coats felt the time was finally ripe to seek legislative endorsement of his *de facto* status, he had left it too late to capitalize on the friendship and influence of his original patron. Foster, after a parliamentary and ministerial career spanning almost forty years, resigned from the government and later accepted a Senate appointment.[9] However, the prime minister, Arthur Meighen, who had been helpful to Coats on several previous occasions, took up the baton and agreed to bring in new legislation establishing the statistical council that Coats had pressed for earlier and otherwise rounding out the act and confirming the status of the bureau. But before this could be done, the general election of 1921 intervened, the Conservative government was defeated, and a new Liberal minister of Trade and Commerce, the Honourable James Robb, was appointed on 29 December 1921. Robb decided, as Coats put it, "not to go forward on the line of development to which the Bureau had been working. By gradual process the powers conferred on the Dominion Statistician were weakened, so that in the course of time, though not by direct action, the Bureau was reduced in status in some respects to that of an ordinary Departmental Branch."[10]

Among other things, the department revoked the bureau's direct access to the Civil Service Commission, stating that the latter had complained about the difficulties of working with it through multiple channels, and in any case expressing its own dissatisfaction with the short-lived arrangement.[11] Thus, while the bureau had enjoyed complete freedom of action in hiring temporary staff for the 1921 census, subject only to the predetermined budgetary ceiling, it was obliged in 1926 to work through departmental channels. The bureau's memoranda in staff matters to the commission or the minister were generally passed along without recommendation, or in some cases with comments not previously communicated to the bureau, "the whole inviting the interpretation that the Department was unsympathetic."[12]

On a day-to-day basis, these changes in the ground rules tended to be minor irritants rather than major impediments. They wasted time in getting things done and provoked unnecessary misunderstandings. What appears to have bothered Coats most was the department's lack of understanding of, and unwillingness to deal with, the bureau's staff problems. One particularly exasperating instance occurred in 1929 when the government set up the Royal Commission on Technical and Professional Services, with Edward W. Beatty, president of the Canadian Pacific Railway, as chairman. As demonstrated later in this chapter, the bureau's classifications and salaries were a major dimension of the status issue, and Coats must have viewed the commission's mandate as a potential avenue of relief. However, the department ruled that the commission's circular inquiries could not be shown to the Dominion statistician, and that he could not make direct representations to the commission. This was ironic, if not absurd, since the bureau worked closely with the commission's staff from the outset, assisting in matters such as budgetary inquiries and studies of general salary movements. Coats asked O'Hara at one point: "Could I have a copy of the correspondence from and to the Commission dealing with the staff of this Bureau. In particular, what were the original requests received from the Commission and what representations were made in reply by the Department re the Bureau?"[13] O'Hara replied: "It is not practicable for us to pick out ... references to the Dominion Bureau of Statistics in our correspondence with the Beatty Commission ... the Beatty Commission correspondence was all confidential. We were especially asked to keep it private and confidential. You were furnished with all the information we were authorized to issue."[14]

Another major set-back in the bureau's status, consequent upon Robb's appointment as minister, was the addition of the imprimatur of the Department of Trade and Commerce to the bureau's publications, starting in 1923 or 1924. Exceptions were made in the case of the *Canada Year Book*, because of the important contributions of a number of other departments, and of the statistics of agricultural production, where representatives of the industry successfully dug in their heels. Some fifteen years later, the knife was twisted still further after the bureau started to issue the *D.B.S. Daily Bulletin,* J.G. Parmelee, O'Hara's successor as deputy minister, instructed Coats that "any release of figures from the Bureau of Statistics in future should mention the Department of Trade and Commerce."[15] Coats responded temperately and agreed to do as he was directed, although he pointed out why he thought the step was ill-advised. His reaction while reading Parmelee's letter was far from temperate, however; he wrote in the margin, "This is plain silly."

The Battle over Classifications and Salaries

The particular issue of classifications and salaries was a constant element in the broader question of the bureau's status during the interwar years. It was not, of course, an issue unique to the bureau; it affected the civil service as a whole and had a particularly severe impact on the professional and scientific classes. But the bureau would have fared better had it been able to argue its case as a department in its own right, or if the Department of Trade and Commerce had shown more understanding and sympathy for one of its major branches.

When the bureau was set up in 1918, status and salaries in the inside, or Ottawa, civil service were determined according to a classification system introduced a decade earlier when the Civil Service Commission had been created. Three divisions, each with two subdivisions, were provided for as follows:

> The First Division shall be divided into:
> Subdivision A, consisting of officers having the rank of deputy heads but not being deputy heads administering departments, assistant deputy ministers, and the principal technical and administrative and executive officers;
> Subdivision B, consisting of the lesser technical and administrative and executive officers, including the chief clerks now holding office and not eligible for subdivision A.
> The Second Division shall consist of certain other clerks, having technical, administrative, executive, or other duties which are of the same character as, but of less importance and responsibility than, those of the first division. This division shall be divided into subdivisions A and B.
> The Third Division shall consist of the other clerks in the Service whose duties are copying and routine work, under direct supervision, of less importance than that of the second division. This division shall be divided into subdivisions A and B.[16]

This system had replaced one in which civil servants at all levels of responsibility below deputy minister were classified as one of five grades of "Clerk." During most of Coats's time with the Department of Labour, for instance, his duties with the *Labour Gazette* had warranted the rank of "First Class Clerk."

Salary ranges were provided for in the 1908 classification, running from $500 to $800 per annum in Division IIIB up to $2,800 to $4,000 in Division IA. Deputy ministers had a fixed salary of $5,000 per annum. The rates remained unchanged until a cost of living bonus was introduced at the end of the First World War. During 1918-19, Coats and his senior lieutenants, Macphail and St Denis, were in Division IA, with salaries of $3,975, $3,100, and $3,300 respectively. Godfrey, Warne, Macpherson, and McFall, all branch chiefs, were in Division IB at salaries varying between $2,100 and $2,800.

Wartime expansion of the service as a whole had greatly strained and distorted the 1908 classification, and the Civil Service Commission brought in an American firm of personnel consultants, Arthur Young and Company, to develop a new system based on modern techniques of job analysis.[17] Because of the promise this approach held out for the recognition of professional categories, it was no doubt welcomed by Coats and others responsible for the direction of scientific work. When the new classification was published in mid-1919, it proposed no fewer than seventeen hundred special classes, including "Senior Statistician" and "Statistician," supported by "Head Statistical Clerk" and "Principal Statistical Clerk." The first two of these required university graduation. However, the system met with widespread opposition, first in Parliament and then among the civil servants themselves. A particularly sore point was the consultants' assumption, in the determination of salary schedules, that the cost of living would soon revert to pre-war levels. In fact prices continued to rise all through the 1920s. One of the by-products of this opposition was the formation of the Professional Institute of the Civil Service of Canada, for which Coats served for many years as advisor on salary questions. Appeal machinery was set up, and some dozen or so of the senior positions in the bureau, including that of Dominion statistician, were slated to be reviewed. In the meantime, they were given "special" rankings, meant to be purely interim. But the appeals were never heard and the bureau was left with a set of makeshift classifications.

Coats himself probably fared the worst with a maximum salary of $5,400, which he reached by 1922–23, thereafter receiving no increase for ten years. St Denis, the assistant Dominion statistician, was awarded a maximum of $4,080. This was a largely honorific position, given in recognition of his previous service as secretary of the Census and Statistics Office. After his retirement in 1924, it was not reactivated until early in the Second World War, when Coats named Cudmore as assistant Dominion statistician. Cudmore, appointed in 1919, rapidly acquired a standing in the bureau in the area of economic statistics equal to that of Macphail on the social side, and the two of them were Coats's senior lieutenants during the 1920s with maximum salaries of $4,620 each, which Macphail, with the most seniority, was the first to reach.

The mainstream chief positions were external trade, occupied by Warne, internal trade, occupied by Marshall, agriculture, occupied first by Godfrey and later by Horning, and transportation, occupied by Wrong. These had maximum salaries of $3,720. The four components of the census of industry were classified at a lower level even though the officers responsible for them were all designated as full "chiefs." However, distinctions were made between the four. Manufactures, occupied by Macpherson, and mining, metallurgical, and chemical industries, occupied by Cook, were designated as "special" and given maximum salaries of $3,420. Lewis, chief of forestry and allied industries, was designated as "Statistician," with a maximum of $3,240, but Miss Brown, chief of fisheries, furs, dairying, and animal products, was only a "Principal Statistical Clerk" with a maximum of $2,400, presumably because she lacked a university degree. The classification "Statistician" was also used for chiefs of the junior branches, finance, education and justice, as well as for assistant chiefs and other senior positions within the larger branches. Again, because of her lack of a university degree, Miss Roughsedge, who was responsible for employment statistics under Cudmore, was designated "Principal Statistical Clerk" with a maximum of $2,400.

The continuing inflation of prices during the 1920s gave rise to a crisis with respect to professional and technical salaries as statutory increases within the existing ranges were exhausted. In 1929 Coats estimated for the Beatty Commission that, between 1914 and 1929, the increase in retail prices had been approximately fifty percent, and that taking this into account, "60% of such professional and technical salaries ... as are comparable are as low as or lower than in 1914." New appointees had generally done better because their salaries had to be fixed in relation to outside competition. Old employees who had transferred to new work had also done better, but those who had remained in the same positions "have fared much the worst of any class."[18] As a victim of this latter kind, Coats could hardly have been pleased when O'Hara, along with the other deputy heads, received an increase of salary from $6,000 to $8,000 in 1924, and a further $2,000 before the end of the decade. In the matter of absolute salaries, there was little he could do personally, but he continued to press for adjustment of salary relativities within the bureau. In 1928–29, he secured agreement for the chiefs of manufacturing and mining to be classified on a par with those of agriculture, transportation, external trade, and internal trade. All were to become "Senior Statisticians" in the range of $3,240 to $3,940, as originally provided for in 1920. But implementation was held up pending the outcome of the Beatty Commission's investigations.

Among the material that the commission had to ponder was a comprehensive brief prepared by Coats reflecting his view of relativities within the bureau and seeking parity with other professional and technical employees of the government. With regard to his own position, he recommended that "in view of the nature of the duties, executive and advisory, attaching to the office under the Statistics Act, a maximum rate be fixed in relation to the salary range of the higher officers similar to that relatively obtaining in other countries where similar organizations exist."[19] The position of assistant Dominion statistician had been vacant since 1924 and was not to be filled for another twelve years, but Coats bracketed it with two others as meriting special classification. These were chief of census and demography, and editor of the *Canada Year Book* and chief of general statistics, occupied by Macphail and Cudmore respectively, who were assistant Dominion statisticians in all but name. The salary range proposed for these three positions was $4,500 to $5,400.

For the remaining professional and technical positions – some twenty-four – Coats recommended a three-level classification as follows: Senior Statistician ($3,700–$4,800); Statistician ($3,000–$3,700) and Junior Statistician ($2,100–$3,000).

The chiefs of the major branches – Agriculture, External Trade, Internal Trade, Transportation, Mining, and Manufacturing – were to be "Senior Statisticians." The nominations for "Statistician" and "Junior Statistician" were an extension and elaboration of the structure that had been put in place earlier in the decade and that acknowledged parity between the chiefs of the junior branches and the assistant chiefs and other senior personnel in the larger branches. There was one brave gesture, however. Coats never directly challenged the Arthur Young requirement of university graduation for a professional position, but he considered that by 1929 the Misses Brown and Roughsedge had gained sufficient experience and expertise to be "grandfathered" as professionals. Accordingly, their respective positions, chief of fisheries, furs, etc., and chief of employment statistics, were put forward for classification as "Junior Statisticians." As Coats wrote to one of the Beatty Commission consultants: "Both of these officers are first-class, and if they were leaving, I would insist on their positions being filled by graduates."[20]

The Beatty Commission reported in February 1930 and proposed replacement of the existing proliferation of classifications by a seven-grade scheme in two divisions as follows:

First Division		Second Division	
Grade I	$1,800 – 120 – $2,160	Grade IV	$3,420 – 120 – $3,900
Grade II	$2,280 – 120 – $2,760	Grade V	$4,020 – 120 – $4,620
Grade III	$2,880 – 120 – $3,360	Grade VI	$4,800 – 240 – $5,520
		Grade VII	$5,700 – 300 – $7,200

Within the first division, advancement and promotion were to be determined by the deputy head, but promotions to and within the second division had to involve the Civil Service Commission.[21] Provision was made for special ratings in exceptional circumstances.

The position of Dominion statistician was recommended for Grade VII, and Coats reacted strongly: "this office has been seriously degraded and should be given the rank of 'special rating.' Though the office at the present moment is relatively much more important than at any previous time in Canada, the present classification places it lower relatively than in any previous classification. For over forty years the position of chief officer of the Census alone carried a salary equivalent to that of a Deputy Minister, and the classification of 1922 placed it immediately thereunder. The present classification places several positions above it, and over 30 on a parity, though demonstrably lower in responsibilities and range of duties."[22]

The positions of Macphail and Cudmore, the two most senior chiefs, were allocated to Grade VI, but that of assistant Dominion statistician (vacant at the time), for which Coats had sought parity with the latter two, was downgraded a notch to Grade V, apparently on the assumption that its duties were purely administrative. The chiefs of the six major branches were ranked in Grade IV, with a footnote in each case to the effect that they be promoted to Grade V on merit, on the recommendation of the deputy head. Coats urged that this promotion be effected forthwith: "These six positions were the subject of special review by the Civil Service Commission last year, when their regrading as Senior Statistician (maximum $3,960) was recommended ... The classification ... not only disregards this finding, but awards a scale which is $60 lower than the maximum laid down in 1920 ... I recommend strongly that the above-mentioned positions be regarded as in Grade V, which merely retains them in the order of precedence that they have always occupied in the Bureau's organization, viz., next to the positions of Chief of the Census and Chief of General Statistics."[23]

To demonstrate the inadequacy of the commission's recommendations, he noted that the chief of the Agricultural Branch (Horning) had left the bureau for private employment at an increase of seventy percent in salary, while the chief of the Mining Branch (Cook) was about to take up a less-exacting post classified twenty-five percent higher. Coats also found it inconsistent that the chiefs of junior branches such as Education, Public Finance, Forestry and Vital Statistics should be classified in Grade III since elsewhere the commission had proposed that the second division should, in its own words, "include all heads of branches and divisions in the technical, scientific, and professional service, as well as many senior positions involving the positions of subordinates." He acknowledged that the original 1920 classification of "Statistician" (maximum $3,240) had been appropriate at the time, given the tentative nature of most of these positions, but argued that they had now long passed the developmental phase and acquired "new proportions and importance."

But Coats's arguments went unheeded. Canada was already in the grip of the Depression and the recommendations of the Beatty Commission were never acted upon. Before long, on the direct order of the prime minister, civil service salaries were cut by ten percent and frozen at that level until further notice. A little later, Order in Council PC 44/1362 of 14 June 1932 reduced departmental establishments by the expedient of abolishing all permanent positions unoccupied on 30 July 1932. The bureau suffered a reduction of twenty in what had been an establishment of 258 permanent positions. However, the effect was not catastrophic, since temporary positions were less affected by the new staff control regulations. The bureau had always had a continuing complement of temporary positions to cover fluctuations in its workload and was able to increase this from time to time as, for instance, when the coverage of the Old Age Pensions Act of 1927, under which it was obliged to provide proofs of age to certain applicants, was gradually extended to all nine provinces. More importantly, it was able to retain many temporary employees from the 1931 census.[24]

As a consequence, the bureau had no fewer than 171 temporary staff in May 1936, compared with thirty-seven immediately prior to the freeze on permanencies. Some of these were highly qualified people who undertook responsibilities far greater than warranted by their nominal classifications. In effect, the bureau was getting professional help for clerical salaries. The staff control regulations were rescinded by Order in Council PC 1/2035 of 16 July 1935, and a little later, annual salary increases were restored. Coats then initiated the process of securing permanent appointments and, in appropriate cases, promotions for the great majority of the temporaries. He also returned to the longstanding issue of a more rational professional salary scale. In a letter to the deputy minister, Parmelee, in September 1935, he complained about "the great disadvantage under which the Bureau operates in the absence of coherent provision in the Civil Service classification for the higher statistical positions, i.e. positions requiring technical qualifications ... There should be provided at the earliest possible moment a consistent progression for positions of this class in a series of six or eight classifications, ranging in salary from, say, $1,800 to $4,800."[25]

The process was cumbersome and bureaucratic, involving the preparation of detailed justifications, their scrutiny by the Organization Branch of the Civil Service Commission, which had a keen eye for what it considered to be unjustifiable claims,[26] and, in most cases, submission through cabinet for approval by Order in Council. And the Department of Trade and Commerce was itself capable of throwing up roadblocks. In respect of one of Coats's earlier submissions, which had already been approved by the Civil Service Commission but had somehow slipped by Parmelee, the latter reminded him that "all these recommendations of the Civil Service Commission ... are conditional upon approval being given to the continuation of the new functions." Referring to section 34 of the Statistics Act, which stated that the governor in Council could authorize the minister to have any special statistical investigation made that was deemed advisable, he noted that he could find "no authorization with respect to the new undertakings," and that "the Minister asked me under what authority the new work and the expansion of former functions was being undertaken."[27] Coats, never easily browbeaten with legalities, replied that "most of this work would fall *ad interim* under Section 33(g) of the Act, Section 34 referring to special investigations *ad hoc* not definitely specified as under Orders in Council in other sections of the Act."[28] With this, Parmelee appears to have let the matter drop.

The flood of submissions being put forward by departments under PC 1/2035 prompted some backtracking on the part of the Liberal government that had succeeded the Conservatives in October 1935. A new Order in Council, (PC 84/978) of 22 April 1936 noted that the cancellation of the staff control regulations "has resulted in permanent appointments being made without regard to maintenance of a margin of temporary employees to provide for fluctuations in volume of work, greater flexibility of staff and increased incentive to new appointees."[29] It therefore decreed that "the proportion of permanent employees to the existing basic fixed establishment (normal staff requirements) of any unit of the Public Service shall not at any time exceed 80%." This restriction gave rise to a running argument between Coats and the departmental administration as to what constituted the bureau's "basic fixed establishment," but it was relaxed by Order in Council PC 2259, dated 11 August 1939, subject to the stipulation that no permanent appointment could be made until after one year of employment. Then, of course, the war brought fresh restrictions on permanent appointments.

However, Coats was successful with most of the submissions he put forward for permanencies, reclassifications, etc. in the late 1930s. Notably, Order in Council PC 75/2423, dated 30 September 1937, provided a new five-tiered classification for statisticians that upgraded most of the chiefs. Senior chiefs like Herbert Marshall, G.S. Wrong, T.W. Grindlay, and M.C. MacLean became Statisticians 5 at $3,840, while the remainder were distributed between Grades III and IV. Unfortunately, his strong representations on behalf of Misses F.A. Brown and M.E.K. Roughsedge still did not convince the Civil Service Commission, and they remained as Principal Clerks.

For the most part, then, the injustices and anomalies that had plagued the bureau since the days of the first makeshift salary structure had been put to rights as far as the need for relativity with Coats's own salary would permit. This had recovered from a low point of $4,860 in 1932-33 to $7,000 in 1937–38, but it still lagged behind that of the deputy minister at $9,000.

Summing Up

The bureau remained administratively subservient to the Department of Trade and Commerce, but with the onset of war in 1939, this was less and less an active source of friction. Massive new responsibilities were thrust upon the bureau and, more importantly, a statistical clientele began to develop within the government for the first time. Coats's nemesis, Parmelee,[30] retired, and a more cooperative relationship developed with subsequent deputies. The status issue became more of an embarrassing anomaly than anything else. What Coats's patron, Foster, could have done with a stroke of the pen during the honeymoon period of 1916–20 did not come about for almost half a century. It did so, however, in the context of a genuine appreciation on the part of government of the role that a fully independent central statistical office could play in developing and implementing its policies and programs. This was lacking during most of the bureau's first two decades, despite the intermittent lip service paid to statistics.

How much more effective might the bureau have been if it had enjoyed administrative autonomy from the start? It could hardly have done better in developing its programs during the 1920s, and the outside world certainly did not perceive it as a flawed jewel. There were different challenges and new constraints during the difficult years of the 1930s, but again, formal recognition of the bureau's administrative autonomy would, by itself, have made little difference to the outcome. Coats was sometimes quite despondent about whether the bureau could carry on much longer with its administration in the hands of an unsympathetic nonprofessional. On balance, however, he seemed to accept the situation as a drag – sometimes almost intolerable – on the bureau's efficiency, rather than as a threat to its professional integrity. "The situation is absolutely ridiculous,"[31] he wrote in 1934. "Of course, we make it work, but only at the expense of continuous latent friction."

Coats frequently spoke of the adverse effects of the unresolved status issue on morale, particularly on the ability to attract and retain first-rate professional staff. But turnover was slight during his tenure, and it was his "old guard" who continued to furnish the bureau's senior leadership for a decade and more after his retirement. Ironically, the tensions between the bureau and the department may very well have been good for morale. Coats's courage and persistence were bywords in the bureau, and, in spite of his not having had the formal administrative autonomy he desired, he acted as much as possible as if he did. And in professional questions, there is no evidence of the hierarchy ever challenging his judgment. The real problem was a lack of recognition on the part of the potential user community in Ottawa. It is to this problem, and Coats's efforts to resolve it during the 1930s, that the next chapter turns.

CHAPTER SEVEN

The 1930s
The Bureau's Quest for Professional Recognition

ACHIEVEMENTS AND EXPECTATIONS AT THE BEGINNING OF THE DECADE

The bureau's struggle for separate administrative status during the interwar years, dominant though it may have seemed at times among Coats's preoccupations, was essentially subordinate to the parallel quest for professional recognition. Without such recognition, the achievement of administrative independence would have been a hollow victory. During Coats's tenure as Dominion statistician, neither was in fact realized, but the bureau's continuing subordination to the Department of Trade and Commerce probably did little to impede progress towards its professional coming of age. That was to be dependent upon completely different considerations, principally the development of a sophisticated user community.

This began to emerge during the 1930s as the Depression deepened and radical thinking such as that of the Regina Manifesto[1] was gradually absorbed into political orthodoxy. But the real breakthrough did not occur until the mid 1940s when postwar reconstruction needs provided the necessary stimulus. Thus, most of the credit for the role that the bureau eventually came to play in the formulation and operation of economic and social policy fell to Cudmore and Marshall. However, as this chapter describes, much of the necessary foundation had been put in place by Coats.

One of Coats's recurrent themes was the need for centrally directed arrangements for the conduct and coordination of economic and social research. He frequently noted with approval the steps taken by the government in 1916 to establish what eventually became the National Research Council with a mandate covering the physical sciences, but he never visualized a parallel body for economic and social research. Rather, he considered that the Statistics Act authorized – indeed required – the bureau to do all that was necessary. This was to come about as a natural consequence of the development of a comprehensive program of primary statistics, knitted together with common or consistent concepts, definitions, and methods of classification. Individually, they would shed light on specific problems; collectively, they would provide what Coats was fond of referring to as "an articulated conspectus"[2] of Canadian society, making possible more complex cross-sectional analyses and interpretations. The Bureau would thus be "a national laboratory for social and economic research,"[3] serving the policy needs of government, acting as the research arm of royal commissions, and so on.

A great deal of progress had been made during the first few years of the bureau's existence in the development of primary statistics. Collaborative arrangements were put in place with other Dominion departments and the provinces to bring under central direction a wide variety of hitherto fragmented, uncoordinated, and often duplicated statistical material. This gave rise to such achievements as a national system of vital statistics, a comprehensive annual census of industry, and current statistics of agriculture, internal trade, and transportation. In addition, the precedent of half a century was broken with the conduct of a decennial census that now focused solely on households and farms, resulting in a considerable improvement in the quality of the information collected. But other fields of statistics in the 1916 blueprint, such as finance, the administration of justice, education, and general statistics, fared less well at first.

In common with the rest of government, the bureau sustained staff cuts during the mid-1920s, but Coats was able to report that "the work has been maintained with only slight curtailments."[4] By 1930, however, the losses had been more than made up and a slightly better balance of resources achieved between the mainstream and newer programs. However, the bureau's achievements overall fell short of the high hopes held out by Coats a decade earlier when, on the basis of wartime experience, the value of statistics as a tool of public policy appeared to have been well demonstrated. The unique understanding and support he had enjoyed from Foster was never matched by subsequent ministers, and during the 1920s Coats was left to his own devices in professional matters.

At the beginning of the 1930s, neither the Department of Trade and Commerce nor other departments were "users" of statistics in the modern sense of the term. The bureau supplied them with material relevant to their programs, but the use of statistics in the aggregate for broad policy purposes was a later development. The business community was provided with a mass of detail on production and related matters and presumably found it useful. In academe, demographers had plenty of material to work with, but economists – in Canada at least – had not yet developed quantitative methods of research.

There was thus a vacuum of informed criticism and guidance, which Coats sought to fill, from time to time, with his recommendations for a statistical advisory council. No such body was put in place during Coats's time, but as the decade proceeded, the shallow lip service paid to the bureau during the

1920s gradually gave way to more thoughtful assessments of its ability to respond to successive economic and social challenges.

One such assessment was provided in 1939 by Professor D.C. MacGregor of the University of Toronto for a committee – largely academic but with bureau involvement – that was looking at ways of fostering social and economic research in Canada and improving its organization.[5] MacGregor at that time had recently served as a senior researcher with the Rowell-Sirois Commission and was thus well acquainted with the bureau and its programs. He thought that the bureau had started out promisingly but had soon faltered. He found favour with the philosophy and goals of the 1916 blueprint, subsequently reflected in the Statistics Act, and noted that "whatever defects may have later appeared, the general scheme and classification bear evidence of an informed academic outlook." The initial work of development and integration had, he said, been substantially completed by 1924. But that year had been a high-water mark. "Retrenchment had already begun; the census of construction had been dropped and the coverage in the census of manufactures had been narrowed practically to that prior to 1917. Henceforth, the work of the Bureau was to consist of routine interrupted , modified and extended at many points by a multitude of forces other than the guiding principles of the first six years."[6]

MacGregor attributed this state of affairs largely to the bureau's status as "the tail end of the Department of Trade and Commerce" under the thraldom of generally unsympathetic ministers and deputy ministers whose pliancy made it vulnerable to shortsighted demands from special private sector interests. Such pressures, he thought, had had a pernicious effect on the way the bureau worked: "New sources of material are added before old ones have been tested, audited, revised and written up in a proper and scientific manner. The system rarely gets beyond the stage of extensive inquiry, rough editing and 'general purpose' material. In the effort to serve everybody, no one is served well; long-term problems of major national importance are given less attention than the work of providing schoolboys and the daily press with statistics without tears."[7]

Again, despite the importance Coats attached to statistical centralization, MacGregor thought the principle had been applied only superficially. For example, "various branches of the census of production – especially those which were already well established prior to 1918 – went their separate ways in their use of schedules and terminology." The work of completing the internal integration of statistics "does not appear to have been specifically entrusted to any one division, unless to the General Statistics Branch, and seems to have been forgotten."[8]

These and other charges could probably not have been answered without overstepping the bounds of bureaucratic discretion, and there is no record of any rejoinder. Indeed, some, such as that relating to internal integration, would have been difficult to refute. Many years later, Herbert Marshall conceded that "during this period quantitative considerations had sometimes to be given priority over considerations of quality in order to get things started."[9] Even so, MacGregor's assessment failed to give credit for the many positive achievements since the alleged high-water mark of the mid-1920s. The "retrenchment" at that time had been no more than a transitory phenomenon, and, in bad times as well as good – generally in the face of apathy or suspicion on the part of his bureaucratic and political masters – Coats continued to make progress.

Repeatedly during the 1930s, he pressed upon successive ministers his views on what had to be done to complete the work set out in his 1916 blueprint. One such submission was the "Memorandum on the Dominion Bureau of Statistics – Lines of Future Development" of August 1931.[10] It called for a revision of the Statistics Act with a more forthright affirmation of the bureau's role as a locus of statistical and economic research, and with confirmation of its status as a professionally independent organization under an officer of deputy ministerial rank who would be assisted by an advisory board.

In addition, there was a listing of "the various steps necessary to complete the program of statistical reorganization of subject-matter as originally laid down but later suspended."[11] These included the development of interprovincial trade statistics following completion of the organization of trade and navigation statistics and those of water transportation; completion of the organization of the industrial census in cooperation with the appropriate provincial departments; enlargement of the statistics of public finance, notably those of the municipalities; improved analysis of the trade balance, particularly the capital movements into and out of Canada; and a rounding out of the statistics of national income and wealth, to be accomplished in part by the coordination of bureau records with those of the Income Tax Branch. It was also recognized that the bureau's coverage of the service sector should be extended to cover the areas of public institutions and merchandising and distribution. And the memorandum was alive to the needs that were emerging, as the Depression deepened, for statistics of social welfare, including unemployment and "public benevolence."

Some progress was made on this agenda during the 1930s. Notably, the statistics of external trade were finally taken over from the Customs department, although this did not lead to the synthesis of interprovincial trade that Coats wanted because of the inability to complete the statistics of water transportation and to develop statistics covering the growing medium of transportation by road. Again, through agreement with the provincial treasurers and the Department of Finance, annual reports of provincial finance were launched, a new start was made on construction statistics, and statistics of the balance of international payments had been brought to a high degree of sophistication by the time war broke out in 1939.

THE 1931 CENSUS

Without doubt, the bureau's greatest professional achievement during the 1930s was the 1931 census. MacGregor implicitly dismissed the decennial census as the ritual satisfaction of a legal obligation,[12] but in two important respects, that of 1931 went much further. First, by conducting censuses of merchandising and services and of institutions,[13] and subsequently putting current collection programs in place in these areas, the bureau narrowed appreciably what had hitherto been a major gap in its statistical coverage. Secondly, the analytical studies of the 1931 census findings not only provided valuable understandings of economic and social developments during the interwar years but also lent credibility to Coats's claim for recognition of the bureau's research capabilities.

Like its 1921 predecessor, the census of 1931 had a turbulent decade to look back upon. Postwar boom and collapse had been followed by several years of sustained economic growth, which had been sharply reversed by the crash of 1929. In spite of the long lead time needed to plan census content and the requirement for continuity with earlier censuses, some accommodation to the changed economic and social circumstances was possible. Questions were asked to gauge the extent and severity of unemployment and to analyze its causes. In this latter connection, a new system of classification for industries and occupations allowed these two characteristics of the gainfully employed to be cross-classified for the first time. Again, the census of agriculture was expanded and elaborated to measure such phenomena as vacant and abandoned farms.

The collection methodology for the 1931 census was virtually identical with that of 1921. The public was again informed, and its cooperation sought, through a publicity campaign that made use this time of the new medium of radio in addition to the press and motion pictures. As well as newspaper advertisements, there was a series of press releases explaining census questions such as those relating to the family, the definition of a farm, nationality, and the *de jure* principle.[14]

Fieldwork was completed more expeditiously than in 1921, and in spite of increases in the population base, the amount of information sought, and the rates paid to commissioners and enumerators, its overall cost was only sixteen percent greater than in 1921. A major factor in this appears to have been the bureau's ability, as a consequence of the depressed labour market, to hire more competent staff than in 1921. Compilation and tabulation were again carried out almost entirely by mechanical equipment, but productivity was greatly increased through the use of a new sorter-tabulator developed by Fernand Bélisle of the bureau's mechanical staff. Three of these machines were built, and the administrative report on the census noted that "in the two years in which they have been in use [they] produced materials over fifty times as compendious as would have been possible with the equipment of 1921, and at materially lessened labour cost."[15] Nathan Keyfitz and H.F. Greenway later described how this had been done. It came about as a result of Coats's asking why, once the census data were on cards that could be read by machine, the machine could not take off all the data at one scanning instead of reading a column at a time, as commercial scanners did. Thus: "Starting with the device invented by Hollerith ... Coats and A.J. Pelletier ... supported and encouraged a Canadian of extraordinary talent, Fernand Bélisle, in making more extensive circuits and building a machine containing some five hundred counters ... Its counters could be wired directly to all the possible positions of the card, or by means of branching and relays could secure two- or three-way tabulations, still in the single reading of the card."[16]

Following the release of preliminary counts and summary results as soon as they became available, the definitive findings were issued between 1933 and 1936 as volumes one to eleven of the official report of the 1931 census. Volume one, after providing the administrative report, was mainly a revision and extension of the compendium of historical statistics assembled by Taché in volume four of the census of 1871. It was designed, as Coats put it in the preface of the administrative report, "to supply a much-felt need for data of a comprehensive nature as a basis for the study of the Canadian population problems."[17] This remarkable piece of historical scholarship was the work of A.J. Pelletier, at that time assistant chief of the Census Branch.

Volumes twelve and thirteen of the report comprised the monographs analyzing and interpreting census findings under such headings as the Canadian family, fertility, housing, illiteracy, dependency, and unemployment. The program had been planned by M.C. MacLean, chief of social analysis, who was also involved in writing several of the monographs. Unfortunately, the first of these did not appear until 1937 while the rest took four more years, and their impact was probably blunted by the delays.[18] However, they won many plaudits as outstanding examples of statistical analysis, and the scope and quality of the program set a challenging standard for subsequent censuses. They were also the vehicle for a new policy of author credits and thus brought to public attention a younger generation of statistical luminaries, including John Robbins, Nathan Keyfitz, and Alan LeNeveu.

The 1931 census was the swansong of E.S. Macphail, chief of the Census Branch, who, some thirty years earlier, had been chief assistant to Archibald Blue. In addition to his many contributions in the census field, he had also been the prime mover in the introduction of mechanical tabulation equipment and had played the lead role in the development of a national system of vital statistics. On his retirement in 1934, he was succeeded by A.J. Pelletier, another veteran of the pre-war Census and Statistics Office. The compilation of the census of agriculture was the work of O.A. Lemieux, who followed Pelletier as chief of the Census Branch after the 1941 census. The census of merchandising and service establishments was the responsibility of Herbert Marshall, while the census of institutions was conducted by J.C. Brady.

As already noted, the latter two censuses were followed up by corresponding programs of annual collection. On the face of it, in the light of the budgetary and staffing restrictions introduced in 1931, it is surprising that these and other statistical developments during the early 1930s were possible. But an awareness of the potential usefulness of statistics to government was perhaps beginning to dawn, since Coats was able, with little apparent difficulty, to more than offset the reduction in his establishment of permanent positions by such devices as extending the terms of temporary census staff. Perhaps this latitude in staffing was a tacit recognition by the Civil Service Commission that any gesture towards the relief of unemployment, however small, was worthwhile. In this connection, Coats became involved in 1933 in the planning of a project to make unemployed men with scientific training available to the bureau and the National Research Council for research work. This was to be a new refinement of the program under the Relief Act, operated jointly by the Departments of National Defence and Labour, which had already put thousands of generally single and homeless unemployed to work on what were essentially "make work" projects. The men were to be housed and fed army-style in an unused section of the bureau's premises on Green Island and given twenty cents in pocket money for each day worked. Coats's minister, H.H. Stevens, put the proposal to cabinet, but there appears to have been little political enthusiasm for it, and although there was never an outright refusal, it gradually withered on the vine.[19]

In any case, statistical awareness developed in a number of ways. Domestically, a succession of royal commissions attempted to grapple with the problems brought on by the Depression. Canada was also involved in the efforts of the Commonwealth and the League of Nations to resolve them through international cooperation. The bureau's contribution to this work was solid and some of its highlights will be recounted here.

A Radical Initiative – The Speakman Resolution

One of the earliest pleas for social and economic research as the basis for understanding and responding to the deepening national and world crisis came not from the government or the official opposition but from the western minority parties. In April 1931 R. Gardiner of the United Farmers of Alberta (UFA) and member for Acadia suggested that an economic research council would be "a thousand times more valuable to the people of this country than any tariff commission that might be set up."[20] A few days later, a UFA colleague, A. Speakman, member for Red Deer, introduced the following resolution:

> Whereas; the problem of production has been largely solved, assisted greatly by the application of scientific methods and the results of organized technical research; and
>
> Whereas; the federal government has contributed to that end by the establishment

> of the National Council of Scientific Research, and by the financial assistance given to that body; and
> Whereas; the problem of distribution, with the kindred questions of purchasing power and the exchange values of agricultural and other commodities, together with their relation to the growing problem of unemployment, are still unresolved, and demand immediate attention with systematized investigation and scientific study; and
> Whereas; this can best be done at the instance of the state and by men of scientific training enabled to devote their entire time and attention to the study of this important subject;
> Therefore be it resolved; that, in the opinion of this House, the government should give immediate consideration to the establishment and maintenance of some organized body for this purpose, which body might be known as the National Council for Social and Economic Research.[21]

There ensued a lengthy but inconclusive debate in which the government took the position that the problems Speakman had cited were already being addressed by the various departments. There was no reference to any leadership, or even supporting, role that the bureau might play in such work. In the following February Speakman again introduced his resolution. The need for action was now almost desperate, he argued; "like some deadly paralysis, [the Depression] is penetrating further and further into the system."[22] The House was more sympathetic this time, although King, leader of the opposition, took the view that the work could be done by extending the mandate of the National Research Council, while Stevens, the minister of Trade and Commerce, repeated his earlier assertion that the questions touched upon were indeed under study by government. Nevertheless, it was promised that the government would give careful and sympathetic consideration to the resolution during the ensuing year.

Gardiner and Speakman were part of the coalition of radical interests that established the Cooperative Commonweatlh Federation in Calgary later in 1932. The party's manifesto, adopted in Regina in the following year, challenged what it considered to be the do-nothing policies of the Bennett government by calling, *inter alia*, for the establishment of a welfare state with universal pensions, health and welfare insurance, children's allowances, unemployment insurance, and workmen's compensation.

The Imperial Economic Conference, 1932

In the meantime, Coats was drawn into what was perhaps the biggest and most concentrated effort of *ad hoc* research into economic questions ever undertaken by any government in Canada, as it prepared to host the Imperial Economic Conference of July-August 1932. This was the first such conference to be held outside the United Kingdom, and it had been called to find ways of increasing intra-empire trade in the face of world depression. Under an overall organizing committee, five subcommittees were set up to prepare background material for the Canadian delegation, and Coats chaired the general economic committee. In just over three months, this body prepared forty monographs that, together with the related tasks of providing statistical support to other subcommittees, notably in the preparation of positions on tariffs, kept the bureau's staff toiling long and hard all spring.[23] As its own distinctive contribution to the conference, the bureau also prepared a special edition of the handbook, *Canada 1932*.

When the conference opened, there were forty-two delegates of ministerial or equivalent rank and many times that number of advisers. Canada had thirteen delegates under the prime minister, R.B. Bennett, supported by sixty-four departmental advisers, including a fifteen-man contingent from Trade and Commerce. The bureau was represented by Coats and Cudmore together with four branch chiefs covering off the agenda's principal subject-matter headings.[24]

Coats's Proposal for a Social and Economic Research Body

Coats regarded the Speakman resolution as simplistic, and made this clear in a critique and counterproposal that he sent to Stevens following the imperial conference.[25] In the House, Gardiner provided a convenient peg for the submission by urging the minister to report on progress by those departmental officials who had earlier been said to be addressing themselves to the country's economic problems.

The basic flaw in the Speakman resolution, Coats argued, was its failure to recognize the difference in method distinguishing research in the natural sciences from research in the social sciences. In the former, the chief method of research was said to be experimental, such as the work carried on in the laboratories and experimental stations of the Departments of Agriculture, Mines, Forestry, etc., coordination and "an omnibus point of view" being provided by the National Research Council. In the social sciences, two roles were distinguished. The first was that of deductive and theoretical reasoning, which, while important in government policy making, was in Coats's view primarily the responsibility of private scholarship – mainly the universities. The government's role lay in the opposite field, that of inductive research – i.e., research based on observing and recording the various activities and characteristics of human society, and applying to them scientific methods of analysis and interpretation.

This, of course, was the method of statistics that Coats formally defined as "the science which treats of the measurement and interpretation of social and economic phenomena both as a whole and in their separate dimensions."[26] Only the government could engage in statistical work, partly because of the heavy expense involved but mainly because it alone had the inquisitorial powers needed to compel the giving of information. Coats recalled for Stevens the evolution of Canada's central statistical system and its progress – admittedly incomplete and not on a final and satisfactory basis – towards the parallel goals of providing a comprehensive range of information on particular subjects, and of integrating it into a comprehensive overview of social and economic conditions in Canada.

Thus, the challenge before the government was not to duplicate or confuse this mandate by extending the responsibilities of the National Research Council, or by creating an analogous body to deal with social and economic research as Speakman had proposed, but to strengthen and make more effective the arrangements already in place. To this end, Coats proposed action along two main lines. Central to the first was "the completion of the system of statistical organization and administrative machinery and control connected therewith mapped out when the Bureau was established."[27] This was to be accomplished by reconstituting the bureau as a "Bureau of Statistics and Civil Research," with statutory confirmation of the powers assigned to it by Order in Council and Regulation during the formative period of 1918–22.

Over and above this system, and using and controlling it as a "working arm," Coats proposed the establishment of a "National Committee of Social and Economic Research," to be chaired by a member of cabinet and with representatives of important organized economic interests,[28] with the following responsibilities:

> a) To keep under continuous advisement the general need as regards social and economic research; to undertake special investigations from time to time as found necessary; and generally to direct, promote and coordinate social and economic research within Canada.
> b) To undertake on behalf of industrial associations, or individual industrial concerns, special studies based principally or in part upon official data, and to charge costs to such associations or concerns for same.
> c) To co-operate with organized economic interests in planning production, expansion of capital, equipment, or other policies.
> d) To suggest coordination of the activities of Government Departments in the social or economic sphere where deemed expedient.
> e) To exercise supervision and control of the organization of statistics as the basic data required in social and economic research, and to act as a Board of Reference in problems of interdepartmental and interprovincial scope arising in connection with such organization.
> f) To publish such reports and findings as may be considered in the public interest.[29]

Coats concluded with the assertion that his proposals "would solve for some time to come what had undoubtedly developed into one of the prime needs of government, that of keeping abreast of economic thinking and of being continuously equipped with the materials required in the formulation of its broader economic policies, and of having more definitely recognized machinery to that end." He also stressed the economy of his proposals and the stimulus they would afford to private economic research. Finally, indulging his penchant for wrapping up arguments with impressive quotations, he noted that they "would set up for Canada what was so emphatically advised by the post-war Royal Commission in Great Britain headed by Lord Haldane on the Machinery of Government, namely, a special Department for the 'organized acquisition of facts and information as preliminary to policy.'"[30]

Stevens replied that he had read the memorandum "with tremendous interest" and complimented Coats on its completeness and illuminating character. He promised to "follow this matter up further" and said that he would "likely call on you for a conference in the near future."[31] Bureau records provide no evidence of direct follow-up on Stevens's enthusiastic acknowledgment of the memorandum, but it may have influenced the legislation brought in early in 1935, providing for "an Honorary Advisory Council on social and economic questions which shall be known as the Economic Council of Canada."[32]

The Economic Council of Canada, 1935

The council, under ministerial chairmanship, was required to:

a) study, investigate, report and advise upon questions relating to the general trend of social or economic conditions or to any social or economic problem of Canada, and to authorize the investigations in that behalf as hereinafter provided;
b) to make recommendations to promote and coordinate social and economic research within Canada;
c) to make recommendations to coordinate the activities of a social or economic character of the several departments of the Government of Canada;
d) to make recommendations as to the organization of statistics as the basic data required for social and economic investigations;
e) to publish such reports and findings as may be considered to be in the public interest.[33]

The Dominion statistician was designated as secretary of the council and was required to undertake, under the Statistics Act, any special statistical investigation that it might require.[34]

In committee discussion of the bill, Sir George Perley, the acting prime minister, used arguments reminiscent of those of Speakman three and four years earlier but added a new one: " The setting up of this economic council will ... save time and labour for members of the government of the day and especially for the Prime Minister. ... it has been evident for many years that the ministers of the Crown have too much detailed work to attend to, and that the Prime Minister especially under our system has far more to do than any one man should have." He was lavish in his praise of the bureau, particularly as regards its achievements in coordination since 1918. "[it] has done first class work and must receive commendation from every person who had to do with it. This bureau supplies statistics which are absolutely trustworthy and available for every person." But it was now essential to go further "and work from a wider and all-embracing viewpoint."[35]

The legislation was remarkably faithful to the spirit of Coats's 1932 memorandum, and it must have seemed that the millennium had finally dawned. In June 1935 he wrote to Bennett that "I have been trying to see you re the [Economic Council of Canada], mainly to let you know that preparatory details are fully in train when you wish to take them up ... I have drawn up and submit to you herewith a suggested agenda for the first meeting of the Council, to which is appended a draft address by yourself as the opening item."[36]

The letter went on to suggest that the address, which comprised twenty pages of typescript, should be given wide distribution in the press. No such meeting was held, and in October 1935 the Bennett government fell. Early in the following year, a private member on the government side, J.F. Pouliot, introduced a bill to repeal the Economic Council of Canada Act, explaining colourfully, if obscurely, that its purpose was "to put the axe of parliamentary control to a dry branch of the dead tree of so-called social legislation."[37] He was more direct in second reading, identifying two specific reasons for the bill: "First, neither this government nor the previous government have attempted to form an economic council. Secondly, there was an item of $20,000 in the estimates last year to cover the expenses under this act, but in the estimates for the coming year there is not a cent provided for that purpose. I therefore conclude that the government has thought it very wise not to take advantage of this legislation."[38] The prime minister, Mackenzie King, left no doubt on this latter point: "I am quite satisfied with my own council; I do not think I need an economic council to tell the present government what is necessary in the way of legislation."[39]

It would be pleasant to supppose that the initiative for the Economic Council of Canada Act had resulted solely from the force and logic of Coats's arguments for a "National Committee of Social and Economic Research." But its provenance was purely political, going back to the earlier Speakman resolution. It had proved convenient to put it forward at the beginning of 1935 as part of Prime Minister Bennett's "New Deal" – a package of proposals designed to arrest the decline in the fortunes of the Conservative party. The package included social reforms in areas such as unemployment insurance, health insurance, old-age pensions, hours of work, and minimum wages. It is thought to have been largely the work of W.D. Herridge, Bennett's brother-in-law, who, as minister in Washington, had been greatly influenced by President Franklin D. Roosevelt's "New Deal." The package was not convincing enough to win the October 1935 general election for Bennett, and in January 1937 the Judicial Committee of the Privy Council in London declared most of the Canadian "New Deal" to be *ultra vires*.

WORKING WITH ROYAL COMMISSIONS

The perceived inability of the bureau to respond to the statistical needs of successive royal commissions during the 1930s was a central theme of MacGregor's 1939 critique: "There was no good information on motor transport for the Duff Commission; inadequate information on the financial results of merchandising for the Price Spreads Commission; no satisfactory comparisons of Canadian and foreign prices for the Tariff Board and the recent inquiries into agricultural implements and textiles; inadequate statistics of business activity and public finance for the use of the Bank of Canada; unsatisfactory records of unemployment and relief administration for the Employment Commission, almost no good tax and income statistics for budgetary purposes."[40] As a consequence of its lack of interest or neglect, he asserted, the government had "time and again been 'caught with its pants down.'"[41] In their particulars, these charges were substantially correct, but it was certainly not the case that the bureau did nothing to assist the work of the royal commissions. Indeed, for one of them – the MacMillan Commission of 1933 – it worked in parallel with MacGregor himself, and in that particular context he provided a more balanced, and generally sympathetic, assessment of the strengths and weaknesses of bureau material.[42]

Coats's approach was to use royal commissions as potential leverage for pressing the bureau's claims as the government's primary source of economic and social research. His tactics were, first, to render all possible assistance to the commissions' staffs and those preparing for the hearings, and to impress upon such clients that the bureau, by virtue of legal authority and acquired competence, could actually or potentially satisfy all their statistical needs. Secondly, he lobbied for the inclusion in their reports of recommendations to fill any program gaps that might have been revealed by their investigations, and for their support in having the bureau recognized as a national research capability in the social sciences.

The approach was well illustrated in the bureau's dealings with three major royal commissions, the first being the Royal Commission on Banking and Currency, appointed in July 1933 to examine the operation of the banking and monetary system in Canada.[43] Its establishment had been proposed in the 1933 budget, with the purpose not only of generally examining the operations of the banking and monetary system, partly in connection with the approaching decennial revision of the Bank Act, but also of considering the advisability of a central bank. At the time, Canada was almost unique among industrialized countries in not having one. The traditional view was that the banking system had always worked well enough without central guidance. However, their establishment in countries that did not already have them had been regularly urged in postwar international conferences, and at the World Monetary and Economic Conference of June 1933 Canada supported a resolution to this effect. W.C. (Clifford) Clark, the deputy minister of Finance, strongly supported the establishment of a central bank, and the prime minister, R.B. Bennett, was of the same view. Later, after a favourable report by the commission, when legislation for a central bank was proposed in the January 1934 speech from the throne, Bennett stated that; "when I realized for the first time that the Dominion of Canada could not carry on direct exchange operations with London for any substantial amounts except through Wall Street, I personally was of the opinion that this country should have a central bank."[44]

The choice of chairman for the commission was Lord Macmillan, who had chaired a committee on "finance and industry" a few years earlier in Britain where there was a long tradition of central banking. Since a majority of members were thought likely to recommend the establishment of a central bank, the commission proceeded with what one writer called "nearly breakneck speed"[45] to conduct hearings and then prepare its report, which was in the government's hands by the end of September. By a three-to-two margin, the commission recommended a central bank.

Coats, properly enough, took the commission at its face value. The report of Macmillan's British inquiry,[46] published in 1931, had included a chapter on "Proposals relating to Information and Statistics" that was critical of the position of British statistics at that time. It made a strong impression on Coats, who prepared an assessment of the extent to which the statistical information regarded as desirable in Britain was also available in Canada, and what improvements and amplifications should be made in Canadian statistics. His conclusion was that "the Canadian statistical system is more complete than the British in respect of financial and economic statistics," referring particularly to the scope, quality, and timeliness of the Canadian census of production, and the decisive advantage conferred by centralization, which "greatly facilitates comparisons between one statistical field and another and promotes comprehensive treatment of the general economic situation." He did, however, note a number of shortcomings with respect to Canadian banking statistics, such as the need for periodic information on the industrial distribution of bank loans, and recommended that these be "carefully considered within the next six months in view of the approaching decennial amendment of the Bank Act."[47] There is no evidence, however, that the Department of Finance heeded this advice.

With Macmillan as chairman of the Canadian royal commission, Coats seemed assured of a sympathetic ear. An elaborated and updated version of the 1932 memorandum was submitted to the commission under the same title.[48] It now included a more detailed review of the bureau's statistics of finance, and the program's perceived gaps and deficiencies. Particular attention was drawn to the lack of statistics of profits, and the need for more detailed and frequent estimates of national income.

The only other assessment of the adequacy of Canadian statistics for the guidance of monetary policy was provided by Professor MacGregor.[49] It was generally sympathetic towards the bureau, acknowledging that it had "done as much as is humanly possible with the resources and legal powers at its disposal." In particular, he characterized the annual census of industry as "the most detailed and frequent record of its kind in the world," but, like Coats, he was concerned that "very little has been done towards the analysis and interpretation of these records, in spite of their great value." Again, he was critical of the quality of public finance statistics, observing that not much improvement could be hoped for until the provinces and municipalities could be persuaded to follow uniform accounting practices. He also singled out, more pointedly than Coats had done, the inadequacy or absence of data, such as current measures of wages and salaries, that would have made possible valid estimates of national income. A subsequent bureau review of these criticisms concurred in most of them, particularly that relating to wage and salary payments, which it called "the most glaring defect of Canadian statistics."[50]

A.F.W. Plumptre, an assistant professor of political economy at the University of Toronto, served as assistant secretary of the commission and, together with Clark, coordinated its research program. The bureau prepared for their use a portfolio of statistical data and also spent a great deal of time trying to fill some complex special requests. These included statistics to illustrate the relationship between wheat exports and exchange depreciation in Canada and other wheat-producing countries, historical statistics of metallic currency in British North America, measures of "investment" as the term was used by Keynes in his *Treatise on Money*,[51] and measures of the historical effect of price changes on debt burdens. The pill was occasionally sweetened with flattery. One of Clark's requests concluded as follows: "I hesitate to bother your overworked organization with these matters, but I suppose that is the price you have to pay for being an expert."[52]

When the royal commission made its report, there were no recommendations, as Coats would have hoped, relating to economic and financial statistics. The only reference of any kind to statistics was the following: "We have received both from Mr Coats, the Dominion Statistician, and from a committee under the chairmanship of Professor Jackson, suggestions as to the improvement of the various statistical returns which the banks are required to make. This is a matter of detail and largely non-controversial, and in our view is more appropriate for consideration by the Department of Finance, preliminary to the inquiry before the Standing Committee on Banking and Commerce to which the revision of the Bank Act will doubtless be referred by Parliament."[53]

It was perhaps imprudent of Coats in his submission to the commission to have emphasized so strongly how many of the statistical desiderata identified in the British Macmillan report were already available in Canada. In any case, by January 1935 he had revised his earlier memorandum, which was now entitled "Canadian Statistics for the Guidance of Financial and Monetary Policy" and went more directly to the point of what still needed to be done. He recommended an annual census of financial institutions as well as more work on the balance of international payments and capital movements and claimed the bureau was ready with plans to work with the income tax authorities in developing statistics of profits from their corporate tax returns.

He sent the memorandum to J.A.C. Osborne, deputy governor of the newly established Bank of Canada, suggesting that "it may serve as a 'starter' for our discussion."[54] Coats probably intended this approach as the beginning of a close relationship between their two organizations that would enable the bureau to launch new statistical programs, while at the same time serving the bank's operational and research requirements. There is no evidence that any special relationship developed. The bank soon established its own research division, and subsequent dealings with the bureau took on a routine character – as, for example, when the bank started its monthly statistical summary and coordinated its contents with related bureau series so as to avoid duplication of effort.

A second major instance of the bureau's work with royal commissions was the inquiry that later became the Royal Commission on Price Spreads. In February 1934 the House of Commons appointed a select special committee "to inquire into and investigate the causes of the large spread between the prices received for commodities by the producer thereof and the price paid by the consumers therefor." After concluding its investigation, the committee was required to recommend "such measures as ... may be considered necessary to secure as far as possible, fair and just practices in the distribution and marketing systems of Canada, with fair and just returns to producers, employees, and employers, not inconsistent with the rights of consumers."[55]

The initiative for the committee came from H.H. Stevens, the minister of Trade and Commerce, and he was appointed its chairman. Stevens had entered Parliament after an undistinguished career in small business. An instinctive champion of the underdog, he quickly established himself as a crusader against what he saw as the abuses of the free enterprise system by large manufacturing and retailing interests.[56] The committee immediately plunged into a flurry of hearings and investigations, and by late June it was clear that it could not complete its work before the imminent adjournment of Parliament. Accordingly, Stevens persuaded the prime minister, R.B. Bennett, to turn the committee into a royal commission with a similar mandate. Somewhat unusually, Stevens was allowed to continue as chairman, but at Bennett's insistence, L.B. Pearson of External Affairs was appointed secretary.

The bureau was soon centrally involved in the work of the committee. Marshall and Cudmore were appointed to a consultative committee of civil servants, and Coats was named as one of three consultants on the analysis and study of the evidence to be presented. However, the even tenor of this work was disturbed late in July when the bureau became peripherally involved in a scandal provoked by Stevens.

From the start of the hearings, Stevens had dealt very harshly with the heads of large businesses appearing before the committee.[57] On 26 June he gave a report on the work of the committee to a group of forty Conservative members of Parliament, speaking of the "incomprehensible disregard for ethics which has characterized some of the leaders of industry and finance in this country" and personally attacking Sir James Flavelle for his alleged manipulation of the stock of the Robert Simpson Company. Prudence would have dictated that such a bombshell be kept confidential, but shortly afterwards Stevens gave orders for three thousand copies to be mimeographed by the bureau, one of which found its way to the press. As O. Mary Hill put it, "the storm that followed was shattering."[58] The front cover of the twelve-page pamphlet showed the following subtitles: "Deplorable conditions in some Businesses Revealed. Hon. H.H. Stevens declares he will never rest until remedies are found. Does not care what happens," and "Wages Cut when Fabulous Profits Made. Minister of Trade and Commerce issues warning of gravity of outrageous situation and danger to our constitutional structure."[59]

This was an obvious violation of the doctrine of cabinet solidarity and led to Stevens's resignation in late October. His defence of a "leak" at the time when the speech was being mimeographed was unconvincing; the three thousand copies, most of which the department managed to recall, had clearly been meant for mass distribution.[60] The bureau appears to have suffered no loss of public esteem through its innocent role in the scandal; fortunately, its name did not appear on the pamphlet. Neither was there any official censure. This was perhaps one occasion on which the bureau was thankful for its administrative subordination to the deputy minister of Trade and Commerce.

In the matter of statistical support, no other government inquiry had hitherto made such extensive demands on the bureau. Before the end of the inquiry's first month, it had furnished information to the secretary of the committee as well as to its individual members, and Coats had appeared at the hearings to outline potentially useful areas of research, and to indicate what statistics were available to pursue them. As the work of the committee progressed, the annual censuses of industry and the 1931 censuses of population, agriculture, and merchandising and service establishments were heavily drawn upon, as also were the bureau's current surveys of wholesale, retail, and farm prices.

A great many requests for assistance also came directly from Stevens, who was generally seeking material to support his personal views on the issues. One such request was that Coats should get hold of a recent report by the Russell Sage Foundation in the United States, which had purportedly demonstrated that "the independent merchant gave generous credit in the small towns and villages to the unemployed, whereas the great chain stores and department institutions sold on a cold-blooded cash basis, and thus did not carry their share of the burden at all."[61] Political biases of this sort were pointedly commented on by Vincent W. Bladen of the University of Toronto, who, at the invitation of Lester Pearson, had worked briefly for the commission. In a note on its report prepared for the *Economic Journal*, he wrote that "there is much that is useless and much that is inconclusive and incomplete. There is too much opinion, and the facts were obtained by questioning on the part of examiners who were anxious to substantiate opinions ... It is hardly too much to say that the inquiry had all the characteristics of a 'witch hunt.'"[62]

Coats would have been trying to keep the committee and the commission on the straight and narrow in their use of statistics. However, they wanted much information that could not be supplied. The bureau assisted by drawing samples for *ad hoc* surveys from its own respondent lists, but deliberately distanced itself from the actual collection.[63] Coats was concerned that "the Bureau of Statistics as such should not come into the inquisitorial end of the enquiry, and this I think is understood, though the newspaper reports don't make it altogether clear. All returns made to us by individual concerns are of course inviolate, and the only materials I am to be called upon to supply are from the broad statistical standpoint."[64]

The bureau's work was not just restricted to the compilation of statistics; it also drew very heavily on the specialist knowledge of chiefs in the various branches. For instance, Coats urged on Stevens the desirability of calling Herbert Marshall as a witness: "He could present to the Committee a résumé of the outstanding points brought out by our 1931-2 Census of Merchandising; ... describe the operations of trade associations in the United States, with which he has been keeping in touch for some time past; ... also give a résumé of the functions of the Federal Trade Commission in the United States; ... make a presentation ... of the economics of merchandising, i.e. the economic characteristics of the various types of merchandising operations from a theoretical standpoint."[65]

Marshall's memoranda during the following year indicate that he went considerably beyond this role of furnishing background information and offered a good many policy recommendations, including the desirability of a "Fair Trade Commission" with powers of investigation and punishment against the abuse of monopoly conditions.[66] Again, Grindlay of the Agriculture Branch wrote an analysis of the burden of falling price levels on the livestock industry, with, *inter alia*, the recommendation for a board of live stock commissioners that would be responsible for developing and administering "a workable national marketing policy."[67]

Coats was not backwards in exploiting his formal status as "consultant on the analysis and study of the evidence." In July 1934, following a meeting of the bureau's senior staff with Stevens, he wrote him urging that "the best way ... of 'getting down to brass tacks' is to begin here and now the writing of a draft report." There followed a detailed listing of the ground that might be covered under twelve chapter headings, an addendum to one of which, he suggested, might be "a note on the statistical organization required for keeping proper tab on current trends in industrial and internal trading operations."[68]

This latter point was later picked up again by Coats in a letter to Pearson: "I have had a word with the Minister as to including some reference to statistics in the report of your Commission and have since drawn up the attached draft."[69] But Pearson, although sympathetic, refused to be rushed: "I quite agree ... that their [sic] should be some definite reference to statistics ... and it seems to me that the draft which you have drawn up might well provide the basis for that reference. I am wondering, however, whether it might not be wiser to leave the exact form until the remedial suggestions in general take more definite shape."[70]

He went on to say that if, for instance, some board of commerce were set up with power to carry on specific investigations from time to time, then it could be pointed out that its work would be seriously handicapped without an adequate basis of statistical information. Such a board was subsequently recommended – a Dominion Trade and Industry Commission – and the report's statistical recommendations were folded into the more general one that the proposed commission have the authority to conduct general economic enquiries: "A Commission of the kind which we have outlined would, we think, be a most suitable organization to conduct investigations, not merely into unfair competitive practices, but also into trade and business conditions generally ... Much of the work that we have done could, indeed, have been submitted to a Federal Trade and Industry Commission, if one had been available."

In drawing attention to the materials available for such investigations, the report commented favourably upon the broad scope and detail of existing statistics of production and distribution, but noted that "they . ... have been lacking in interpretation and analysis from a general point of view. ... there has been little study of the broader tendencies and characteristics of industry and distribution in Canada."[71]

This was a direct transcription of material submitted to the commission by Coats, as also was the recommendation that special studies should be made from time to time of "such phenomena as the integration of industrial operations, the relationship of capitalization to real capital and of the latter to numbers of employees, the relationship of wages to salaries and of both to net production and prices, the relative productivity of capital and labour in large-scale and small-scale operations, power supply in relation to the utilization of labour, etc." It was further recommended that "the general statistical work of the Bureau should be considerably extended and ... the [Trade and Industry] Commission should exhaust the information available to the Bureau before proceeding to its investigations into specific situations or into problems of the general economic significance of various policies between which it must choose."[72] The report also endorsed Coats's longstanding advocacy of an advisory body for the bureau.

The only detailed statistical recommendations related to labour where, in more than any other area of statistics, it was claimed, "the Commission has had to spend much of its own time and money on the unearthing of facts which should have been readily available."[73] In addition, it was further proposed that the collection of all labour statistics be centralized in the bureau. A national investigation into cost of living budgets was also called for in order to clarify the problem of regional differences in wage rates.

The report's mainstream recommendations were addressed in July 1935 by legislation, which, as part of the "New Deal" package, established a Dominion Trade and Industry Commission whose commissioners were to be the members of the Tariff Board, and whose primary duties were the administration of the Combines Investigation Act and commodity standards.[74] The commission was also authorized, when so required by the governor in Council, to "study, investigate, report and advise upon questions relating to the general trend of social or economic conditions, or to any social or economic problems of Canada."[75] A similar responsibility had been given to the recently established Economic Council of Canada. In recognition of this, presumably, the commission was also required to cooperate, "when necessary," with the council. Since the bureau was named as the council's statistical arm and the Dominion statistician as its secretary, the commission provided new leverage for the furtherance of Coats's research aspirations.

Coats accordingly sought the assistance of the Honourable George H. Sedgewick, chairman of the Tariff Board, in dusting off a proposal that Stevens had approved two years earlier, concerning the reorganization and enlargement of the Industrial Census Branch. It had two elements, the first being the creation of a new organizational unit to carry forward on an annual basis the work begun by the census of merchandising and service establishments. Secondly, a senior analytical position was to be created in the branch, similar to that of chief of social analysis in the Census Branch. Its function was to ensure continuing coordination of the various sections of the industrial census, and to carry out cross-sectional studies of the kind urged in the report of the Royal Commission on Price Spreads. Some progress was being made under the first heading with temporary staff,[76] but the new analytical position[77] and its supporting staff had not been established due to staffing restrictions.

Accordingly, Coats wrote to Sedgewick enclosing a memorandum setting out the details of this proposal and concluding as follows: "this reorganization is a necessary preliminary step in the carrying out of any investigations of the character specified in Section 25 of the Trade and Industry Commission Act. It is suggested therefore that the Bureau be authorized to confer with the Civil Service Commission as to the number and classification of the staff above mentioned with a view to the placing of the reorganization on a permanent basis at as early a moment as possible."[78]

But these hopes were soon dashed. As noted earlier, the Economic Council of Canada was never activated by the Bennett government and was subsequently abolished by the King government. Again, the Dominion Trade and Industry Commission never got the chance to undertake research. Its primary functions came under immediate jurisdictional challenge, and, while the issues were before the courts, it was largely inactive. Following resolution of the jurisdictional issues, the King government introduced legislation repealing certain duties of the commission and reassigning others. In so doing, it effectively eliminated the socioeconomic research function as originally visualized.

The Rowell-Sirois Commission

The royal commission with the most far-reaching impact on the bureau's programs and aspirations was the Rowell-Sirois Commission of 1937-40 on Dominion/provincial relations. The impact was not immediate, nor was the bureau able to influence it directly, as it had sought to do in the case of earlier royal commissions. This time the scope and scale of the inquiry precluded any possibility that the bureau might stake out a monopoly position as a provider of advice and information and secure recognition of this role in the commission's report. The commission's mandate was to conduct "a re-examination of the economic and financial basis of Confederation and of the distribution of legislative powers in the light of the economic and social developments of the last seventy years."[79] This clearly called for a very broad research program, touching upon many matters beyond the bureau's area of competence.

Little time was lost in developing an extensive program of studies under the three broad headings of economics, constitutional matters, and public finance, and these were carried out by an array of talent such as had never before been assembled for any Canadian royal commission. The studies were directed by Alex Skelton, chief of the Research Department of the Bank of Canada, who was also the commission's secretary. He was assisted by John Deutsch, also of the Bank of Canada, and the commission's report named close to forty eminent academic and public- and private-sector figures who contributed to the research program.[80]

A draft outline of the proposed research listed as a prerequisite for the task assigned to the commission "a study of regional wealth and income, and something approaching a regional economic history of Canada, which will show the changes in the relative wealth of various regions."[81] Data available for such a study were said to be as follows: "The Dominion Bureau of Statistics, the Department of National Revenue, and the statistical bureaus of some of the provinces have a large amount of crude material on this subject, but it requires extensive adjustment and analysis. The Bank of Canada has been gathering together the available material, and has been making a study of the extent to which useful estimates can be prepared on a provincial basis."[82] Professor D.C. MacGregor of the University of Toronto was noted as being "probably the foremost authority in Canada on the technical aspects of national income compilations," and it was suggested that he be in charge of the work.[83]

The discussion of studies needed in the area of public finance made it clear that, here also, there was no ready-made body of well-coordinated data on which to draw: "The most comprehensive effort to date at putting Dominion and provincial public finance statistics on a comparable basis is contained in the Red Books prepared by the Bank of Canada for the National Finance Commission."[84] The outline went on to say that questionnaires would have to be prepared and sent to the provincial governments to verify and amplify this material for the commission's use. A basis would thus be provided for the bureau to maintain comparative public finance statistics on a uniform basis for the future.

Thus, in two of the most basic areas of the commission's research, there were no expectations that the bureau would be able to play a central role. Even so, a great deal of assistance was given on a piecemeal basis. Book One of the commission's report was an economic, social, and constitutional history of Canada since 1867, and it is here that the bureau's input was most apparent. The report mentioned both Coats and Marshall in a listing of departmental officials who had given special assistance,[85] but some requests were beyond the bureau's capability at that time. In response to a request for population projections by province, Coats wrote: "We think it unwise to issue any statement regarding the future population of Canada. We have made calculations which give a variety of results ... but the whole problem is so speculative that I frankly think the benefits to be gained are not very practical. Even of Canada's population as a whole I am skeptical with our present knowledge of the population growth. As to distributing this by provinces, this greatly increases the dangers."[86]

In the course of its public hearings, the commission took over ten thousand mimeographed pages of evidence, and 427 briefs were filed. On 10 August 1938, when the hearings were substantially completed, Skelton sent Coats a list of recommendations relating to the bureau that had been noted in the evidence and the briefs. These were only sixteen in number and far from earth shattering. The bureau itself had dusted off its familiar recommendation for a Dominion council of statistics,[87] with representatives from the Dominion departments concerned with statistics and from the provinces.

The bureau's brief had been put forward in the context of the requirement imposed upon the commission to inquire into overlapping or duplication in the work of Dominion and provincial departments. The bureau pointed out that the Statistics Act provided for Dominion/provincial cooperation on the statistics of the various subjects that section 92 of the British North America Act assigned to provincial jurisdiction. An extensive network of cooperative arrangements had been developed since 1918, and while, as Coats advised Parmelee in submitting the brief, "arrangements of this nature are, of course, under constant modification to meet changing conditions," he could nevertheless assert that "there is no duplication of work that is not essentially of a superficial character or unavoidable in the subjects that have been definitely brought under review."[88]

When the commission made its report it emphasized that, wide and comprehensive as its terms of reference had been, they had nevertheless been concerned with the one great problem of relations between the Dominion and the provinces. "The Commission accordingly directed its inquiry strictly to this main problem. Many representations made to the Commission were concerned with other matters and, therefore, fell outside the scope of the inquiry."[89]

Thus, statistical policies and programs got very little attention in Book Two of the commission's report, which, building on the extensive historical survey of Book One, outlined recommendations for reallocating the burdens of government between the Dominion and the provinces. There were two explicit references to the bureau. The first was in the chapter entitled "Avoidance of Overlapping and Duplication." Here the bureau's evidence was recapitulated, with the conclusion that "the danger of administrative waste in the collection of statistics is considerable, but our inquiries did not bring to light any serious cases of duplication."[90] The influence of the Coats brief was also evident in the commission's endorsement of the need for close and intricate cooperation between the bureau and the provinces. It did not, however, identify itself directly with Coats's recommendation for a statistical council but said merely that "it was represented to us that the coordination would be strengthened by the creation of a Statistical Council which would be required to meet at least once a year."[91]

The second reference to the bureau was in the recommendation that the quinquennial census of the three Prairie provinces be discontinued, because the original rationale for instituting it – relating to the disproportionately rapid growth in their populations – was no longer valid. The growing tendency in other countries to take more frequent censuses was noted, but, it was said, "we have made no investigation as to the desirability of more frequent censuses for Canada as a whole and can, therefore, express no opinion as to their desirability. The point we make here is that there is now no valid reason for treating the Prairie Provinces differently from the rest of Canada in the matter of the Census."[92]

As Skelton had predicted, the commission was obliged to compile, as best it could, its own statistics of public finance, and its report provided numerous examples of the difficulties encountered. In the chapter dealing with municipal finances, which the commission had identified as "an integral part of the whole provincial picture, and consequently, to that extent, of Dominion-provincial relations,"[93] it was stated that the greatest obstacle to the analysis of the problems encountered was "the dearth of statistics, and the lack of uniformity in those available."[94]

In connection with the mechanisms it was proposing for keeping Dominion/provincial financial arrangements under review, the commission noted its awareness of "the need for further economic and financial research along the lines which we have attempted to develop, for continuation and improvement of the economic and financial statistics which we have gathered, and for refinement and development of technique in measuring the relative financial positions of governments and making equitable inter-governmental adjustments in the future."[95]

These functions would require "a small, but highly competent, permanent research staff and secretariat," and this was visualized as becoming "a clearing house for economic, financial, and administrative information relevant to Dominion-provincial relations and public finance policy."[96] In this context, no higher-order role was proposed for the bureau, but nothing was to be taken away from it either. As to the indicated need for improved statistics, the new body's role was presumably to have been only advisory, with the bureau continuing to do the actual work.

In the matter of national income statistics, the commission, following Skelton's suggestion, compiled its own estimates covering the years 1926-36 under the direction of D.C. MacGregor, and these were published in 1939.[97] As the introduction pointed out, the estimates represented "a fresh approach to the problem." For the purposes of the commission, it was explained, "it was desirable to improve the accuracy of the estimates and to give a breakdown of the national income by provinces. In the efforts to secure this breakdown, many difficulties and complications arose that are not encountered when only national totals are estimated."[98]

The bureau's own estimates of national income for the period 1920-34, based largely upon the annual census of industry, had directly estimated the net value of production in the goods-producing industries, and added to this an indirect estimate for the service industries based upon the proportionality of the gainfully employed and the assumption of equivalent productivity in the two sectors. This was the so-called "income produced" method. In 1935 MacGregor had been commissioned by the Bank of Nova Scotia to refine these estimates, following earlier pioneer work conducted on his own behalf. He retained the bureau's income-produced approach but prepared direct estimates for the service industries, rather than inferring their income from that of the goods industries. He also eliminated some duplication from the bureau's estimates of the net value of production in the goods industries by going further in the deduction of related expenses from the gross measures.

The income-produced method was unsuitable for the breakdown of national income by province that the commission wanted. Hence a shift was made to an income-paid-out method. The new estimates also included "the first thorough-going attempt to measure the net income from agriculture and the first direct estimate of bond interest and dividends received by Canadian individuals."[99] However, the most radical departure of the Rowell-Sirois estimates lay in their treatment of the contribution of government to national income – in particular, their recognition that government services to individuals provided by borrowing must be added to the total of income paid out to individuals. The point will not be elaborated here,[100] but with the onset of war and the consequent expansion in the functions of government – largely funded through deficit financing – it was the root cause of prolonged disagreement between the bureau and the new breed of economists advising upon war finance. In the process, the bureau's credibility was seriously damaged.

At the time of their release, however, the new estimates raised no alarm signals in the bureau. Skelton sent a copy to Coats in February 1939, and in his response Coats frankly acknowledged that "the subject is so large and many-sided that we have never been able in the Bureau to pursue either method of approach in detail."[101]

When the commission presented its report in the spring of 1940, wartime problems dominated the political agenda in Ottawa. In any case, there was provincial opposition to many of its recommendations, and they were left in abeyance until war's end. But the commission had left a legacy that the bureau could not ignore in the attention that it had focused on important weaknesses in bureau programs.

The deficiencies in the bureau's public finance statistics did not stem from any lack of understanding of what needed to be done. In the 1930s it had tried hard to put in place the necessary arrangements for Dominion/provincial cooperation,[102] but with a staff of one statistician and two clerks, it was impossible to provide effective follow-up. However, with the support of the deputy minister of Finance and the Bank of Canada, an accountant-statistician, J.H. Lowther,[103] was appointed and additional clerical staff secured to carry on the Rowell-Sirois Commission's work on provincial financial statistics. A steady process of improvement was set in motion.[104] In the area where the most immediate action was possible, municipal statistics, two Dominion/provincial conferences were held in 1940 to finalize and ratify the arrangements for uniform reporting of municipal activities and finance. A similar Dominion/provincial conference held in 1943 laid the basis for the resumption of bureau responsibility for the compilation of provincial public finance statistics in accordance with the specifications of the Rowell-Sirois Commission.

It took much longer for the bureau to acknowledge the defects in its approach to the estimation of national income, and, unhappily, a great deal of futile effort was expended before work was put on a track acceptable to the Department of Finance and the Bank of Canada, whose management of fiscal and monetary policy now relied heavily on valid estimates of national income. This is a story that continues in subsequent chapters.

Relations with the Academic Community

The need for the universities to be involved in statistically based research was a recurring theme in Coats's writings during the 1920s and 1930s. He saw their role as being on what he called "the 'pure' side" – the verification of theory by statistics. A case in point that he frequently cited was Jacob Viner's study of the classical theory of international trade, "a book started on its way, I am happy to say, by some crude statistics of our own."[105] But work of this kind was all too scarce.

Government, on the other hand, was responsible for applied research. The provision of statistics to serve needs in both areas was also the responsibility of government, which alone had the resources to collect and compile them on a comprehensive scale, as well as the authority to compel the giving of information. As a consequence of centralizing this responsibility in a specialized branch of government, logic demanded that it should be at the forefront in interpreting statistics and applying them to particular problems. Coats saw two further elements in the complementarity between government and academe, the first being the contribution the latter could make by advising on the content and assessing the quality of official statistics, and the second its responsibility for statistical education.

These views reflected in large part his observation of practices in the United States. The robust system of official statistics in that country, although decentralized, had, through such bodies as the Census and Labor Statistics bureaus, inspired the content and methodology of many of Coats's series, but he had been less successful in emulating its capacity to provide timely and relevant analysis of current economic and social issues.

Again, the meagre scope and quality of statistically based research in Canadian universities hardly bore comparison with the situation in the United States. This was not merely a question of scale; it represented a distinct cultural lag. Coats had diligently cultivated United States academics since the time of his work on prices in the Department of Labour, but he found few kindred spirits at home. During his entire tenure as Dominion statistician, his academic contacts in Canada were mainly with Queen's University and the University of Toronto through such men as W.C. Clark, W.A. Mackintosh, Harold Innis, Gilbert Jackson, D.C. MacGregor, H. Michell, and V.W. Bladen.

The American Economic Association and the American Statistical Association had large and active memberships that sustained flourishing periodicals and furnished the statistical agencies with advice and criticism. In Canada, the corresponding learned society was the Canadian Political Science Association (CPSA), an umbrella organization for a variety of social science disciplines. Coats had been a founding member in 1912, but until the mid-1930s, when for the first time it launched a quarterly publication, the membership list had never exceeded five hundred. One feature of the United States scene that was entirely lacking in Canada was the existence of private foundations that were active in economic and social research.

When Coats was elected president of the CPSA in 1936 – the first statistician to hold that office – his presidential address dwelt heavily upon these contrasts. The association's trust in the state of official statistics was, he commented sardonically, "well-nigh perfect."[106] This was in strong contrast to the situation in the US and the UK, where "in and out of season the ... societies advise and find fault. There are five Standing Committees of the American Statistical Association on as many different branches of official statistics. More, there is a permanent Advisory Council to the United States Census Bureau, six of its members being nominees of the American Statistical and six of the American Economic Association, – and they are advisory indeed! In Great Britain, the Royal Statistical Society has often memorialized the government, and the latter has invariably expressed respect and edification."[107]

It was the same with regard to statistical education: "By actual count there are this year in the colleges and universities of the United States nearly 1,000 courses in some form of statistical method, and more than 1,000 other courses in which a statistical unit is included. A diligent search in the calendar of Canadian Universities reveals twenty-two such courses in twelve institutions. Six Canadian universities do not mention the word! ... All twelve offer an honours degree in economics, but only five demand that this include statistics! Of course, no Canadian chair in statistics exists, and there is no text-book based on Canadian data."[108]

Coats urged the universities to provide statistical training from the outset – not just as an afterthought – in every social science program and to require a working acquaintance with the form and content of Canada's official statistics. He also wanted to see a course for the general student, "the citizen user-to-be of statistics, for I do not think anyone will pass as educated in the world of tomorrow who has not rudimentary knowledge of the laws of mass phenomena."[109]

There is no evidence, however, that this persuasively written survey and critique made any direct impact even on its target audience, let alone on government.[110] In the fall of 1936 Coats put to Vincent Bladen of the University of Toronto, then secretary of the CPSA, the idea of holding discussions on the bureau's program at the association's 1937 meeting and suggested that "our executive might discuss in the first instance what fields of statistics are of special importance and in need of development at the present time."[111] Nothing further came of this initiative, but early in 1938 a bureau colleague, J.B. Rutherford, chief of agricultural statistics, wrote to Coats suggesting that "one of the reasons for the lack of development in research in the social sciences in Canada has been the failure of the workers in this field to make their voices heard ... we have no official body which might make representations to the Government on various matters of importance to people in the social sciences ... Why not organize through the Canadian Political Science Association a 'Canadian Social Science Research Council'?"[112]

Coats took up the matter with Harold Innis of the University of Toronto, a past president of the CPSA: "Has not the time arrived when we should have some sort of definite organization for social sciences research?" His interest in the matter was, he explained, "to see some systematic use made of the materials we have in the Bureau, which are now becoming of quite respectable dimensions and which are badly in need of far more interpretation than we can give them."[113]

Innis was successful in interesting colleagues in other learned societies, and a meeting was arranged in Ottawa for 22 May to discuss ways of improving the organization of social and economic research in Canada. The meeting was chaired by Professor R.G. Trotter of the Canadian Historical Association, and John E. Robbins, the bureau's chief of education statistics, acted as secretary. Interest was sufficiently strong for the group to constitute itself as a continuing committee.

One of its early initiatives was to bring Wesley C. Mitchell of Columbia University to Ottawa to discuss the relevance of United States experience to the Canadian problem. Mitchell's advice appears to have strongly influenced the constitution, formally adopted on 22 May 1940, which set up the Social Science Research Council. During the next two decades the council received no funding from the Government of Canada and thus operated on a very modest scale, relying on grants from US sources – mainly the Carnegie, Ford, and Rockefeller foundations. With the establishment of the Canada Council in 1957, government support for the social sciences finally became available.

Another initiative of the Trotter Committee was to conduct a survey to show what research was being done – and what gaps existed – in the various social sciences. Professor MacGregor volunteered a paper on what was being done with statistics in the universities; this, as noted earlier, was in fact part of a longer paper that also covered the bureau under three separate headings.[114]

As for the universities, MacGregor's comments confirmed and amplified Coats's earlier contention that, by comparison with work done in Great Britain and the United States, there was in Canada a pronounced lack of studies based primarily on statistical data. Even in works where their role was secondary, statistics were used neither as carefully nor as effectively as they might be. "University economists," he said, "frequently display a surprising lack of knowledge of important Canadian data." He attributed this mainly to the strong influence of deductive and literary or philosophic traditions in Canadian economics. Consequently, few attempts had yet been made to achieve emphasis and precision on the basis of intensive statistical work. "Standards of workmanship in dealing with evidence, which recommend themselves to scholars in other branches of science ... have not usually been considered of enough significance to justify the additional work which they involve."[115] The natural consequence of this lack of interest in quantitative methods was that the ability of the universities to provide appropriate methodological training had never developed beyond rudimentary introductory courses.

MacGregor's general comments on the bureau and its products were touched upon earlier in this chapter. In a further examination of the usefulness of bureau material for research purposes,[116] he listed a number of "important branches of inquiry [that] have been omitted from the bureau's surveys" – a listing that was virtually identical with those prepared by Coats from time to time. But "the principal limitations of the Bureau's work," he argued, "do not lie as much in the absence of figures as in faulty methods of collection, compilation and presentation of the reports."[117] These included deficiencies in survey schedules and ambiguities in the instructions for completing them, shortcomings in the classification systems and inconsistencies in their application, and inadequacies in the textual statements accompanying statistics.

MacGregor's severest criticisms, however, were directed towards the bureau's personnel, the outstanding characteristic of which he judged to be "the small number and uneven distribution of persons and departments who possess the necessary technical capacity and initiative. Not more than half of those in positions of authority can be regarded as technically competent."[118] He acknowledged that persons whose academic discipline had been in other fields had made important and perhaps indispensable contributions to the bureau's work. And when the bureau had been built up at the end of the war, the backward position of economics and statistics in the universities would have rendered futile too rigid an insistence on qualifications in these areas. But he was driven to conclude that such training was now an essential requirement for the production of good official statistics, noting that "the effect of introducing four or five competent young men into the Bureau in recent years has been little short of phenomenal."[119]

He observed that few officials of the bureau had travelled extensively, even in Canada. Thus, an essential stage in scientific investigation was lacking, namely, direct contact with the conditions being measured. This, he thought, was due to the absence of branch offices outside of Ottawa and the failure to conduct field surveys, along with the failure to exchange officials with the provinces. The majority of senior staff lacked the ability to keep in touch with developments in economics and statistical method, did not feel at home at professional gatherings of economists, and were unable to make contributions to professional journals. Hence, there was ample justification "for those who call the Bureau a mere counting house and who doubt its capacity to assume greater responsibilities for the conduct of economic research."[120]

Conclusion

The years after 1945 were to bring about drastic changes, both in governmental support for important new statistical programs and in the calibre of personnel that the universities were able to provide by then. In the meantime, the "old guard," which MacGregor had praised with faint damns, held the fort and indeed met the flood of wartime demands upon the bureau most creditably. The next external scrutiny of the Bureau occurred in the early 1960s in the context of the work of the Royal Commission on Government Organization (the Glassco Commission), which had a mandate to inquire, *inter alia*, into the provision of economic and statistical services. Its findings were a very positive endorsement of the bureau's achievements and its potential for further contributions to the understanding of the structure and functioning of Canadian society.[121]

CHAPTER EIGHT

1918–1939
The Bureau's Role in the Development of an International Statistical Community

INTRODUCTION

Before the First World War, Canada and the other self-governing Dominions had no separate status under international law, which regarded them as colonial extensions of the mother country. However, their insistence on a say in the direction of the war effort commensurate with their contributions to it led to the establishment of an Imperial War Cabinet and the holding of an Imperial War Conference in 1917, which acknowledged, largely at the initiative of Canada's Robert Borden, that the Dominions were "autonomous nations of an Imperial Commonwealth."[1]

Subsequently, they became separate signatories of the Treaty of Versailles and members in their own right of the new League of Nations and associated bodies such as the International Labour Organization. The imperial conference of 1926 took matters further by proclaiming the complete equality in status of Britain and the Dominions, and the autonomy of the latter was confirmed and augmented by the Statute of Westminster in 1932. Canada's international coming of age was fully mirrored in the active role that the Dominion Bureau of Statistics played during the interwar years in the shaping and operation of an international statistical system to support, first, the work of postwar rehabilitation and development, and later, recovery from the crippling effects of the Great Depression.

EARLY DISCUSSIONS ON INTERNATIONAL COOPERATION

The first of many steps to this end was taken under the authority of Article 24 of the Covenant of the League of Nations, requiring new international commissions and bureaus to be placed under its direction and affording similar status to existing international bodies if they so wished. Thus, in August 1919 the Economic and Finance Section of the league's provisional organization invited representatives of the International Institute of Agriculture and the International Statistical Institute (ISI), together with other leading statisticians, to discuss possible relations with these particular organizations and, more generally, how the league might assist in the development of international cooperation in statistics.

The work of the International Institute of Agriculture had apparently continued with little disruption during the war, but the Permanent Bureau of the International Statistical Institute had experienced difficulties in proceeding with a planned international yearbook. Late in 1916 it had begun publishing demographic statistics, while preliminary work had been done in other areas such as statistics of strikes and lockouts, "want of employment," wages and hours of labour, and the cost of living. It was clear, however, that these latter fell within the mandate of the newly established International Labour Organization (ILO), which was required to collect information on all matters affecting industrial life and labour.

The unofficial status of the league conference meant that it could only put forward "suggestions." The most basic of these was that, "in principle, there should be a separation of the main classes of statistics, and that these should be entrusted to several different bodies or institutions working in conjunction with the League."[2] In the case of agricultural statistics, the International Institute of Agriculture was suggested as the responsible body; in the case of labour statistics, the International Labour Office; and for the time being, in the case of demographic statistics, the Permanent Bureau of the International Statistical Institute. A final suggestion, relating to the need for a separate coordinating body, was that a central advisory council on statistics be instituted. Further discussion was obviously needed, and it was recommended that "a committee be appointed to consider the definite distribution of statistical work between the various bodies connected with, or proposed to be connected with, the League of Nations, and to make suggestions, if thought desirable, for the establishment of other bodies than those already referred to."[3]

During the next two years the basis was laid for the resolution of these issues, and Canada played an important role in the key events. In January 1920, as described later in this chapter, the first Conference of British Empire Statisticians was taking place, and the delegates were invited to meet with league officials to submit their views on the above suggestions. They themselves were strongly disposed towards the centralization of imperial statistics, and Coats, the Canadian delegate, was one of the most forceful advocates of this viewpoint. Not surprisingly, therefore, they argued in favour of centralization at the international level also and expressed the view that the league conference's key suggestion should have read that "in principle there be no separation of the different classes of statistics, and that so far as possible the collection of all international statistics should be entrusted to a single International Statistical Bureau."[4]

Shortly afterwards, when the secretary general of the league recommended adoption of the proposal to appoint an International Statistical Commission, he nominated Coats as a member. Subsequently twelve members were formally appointed, including Albert Delatour and Henri Wilhelm Methorst, vice president and secretary general respectively of the International Statistical Institute, representatives of the International Labour Office, the International Institute of Agriculture, and the International Bureau of Commercial Statistics,[5] as well as others who, like Coats, were heads of national statistical offices. One of these, Luigi Bodio of Italy, who was appointed president of the commission, was also president of the International Statistical Institute.

The commission took note of a further seven international bodies with statistical functions, in addition to those represented at the meeting. One of these was the International Institute of Commerce, headquartered in Brussels, which had been established in 1919 by the International Parliamentary Conference for the purpose of coordinating and publishing commercial statistics, as well as information on commercial legislation and treaties. Some of its statistical responsibilities appeared to duplicate those of the International Bureau of Commercial Statistics, even to the extent of using that body's nomenclature for imports and exports. This particular overlap was not directly remarked upon, but, in a more general comment, it was conceded that "these institutions have certain features in common," and that "the same information may be collected or published by several of them." But, while pointing out the need "to establish perfect co-ordination in this kind of work by some permanent agreement," it was also emphasized that "the independence and autonomy of each would be respected."[6]

The commission's resolutions were adopted in part unanimously and in part by majority only. Those of the first kind proposed that the league should institute a continuing international commission to advise on all technical statistical questions, to facilitate the utmost possible use of the work already carried out by international statistical organizations, and to assist these bodies by its advice to delimit their respective spheres. With one abstention, it was resolved that the commission "would in each case, wherever possible, apply to the international institutions or offices which are concerned with the production of the said statistics, the said institutions to retain their autonomy."[7] The major difficulty came with the following article of the report, which was voted against by Coats, A.W. Flux of the United Kingdom, Royal Meeker of the International Labour Office, and Camille Jacquart of the International Bureau of Commercial Statistics: "The International Commission of Statistics should be supplied with two copies of the statistics produced, one of which should be transmitted to the International Institute of Statistics, in order to enable that Institute to formulate suggestions from a scientific point of view, and with regard to the standardization of methods."[8]

Coats, Meeker, and Flux signed a minority report urging, as the best means of unifying and standardizing international statistics, the establishment within the league of a statistical section similar to its other technical branches. Their disagreement with the majority position was stated as follows: "Especially objectionable do we consider the explicit provision, in the plan submitted by the majority, for reference by the proposed Advisory Council to another and a private organization, namely the International Statistical Institute. Our chief objection, however, is to the putting forward of an Advisory Council as a body competent to perform the urgent and difficult task involved in the co-ordination and standardization of statistics. This task ... can only be carried out by a properly constituted permanent office."[9]

The commission report also contained personal statements by Coats, Meeker and Jacquart. Coats wrote that "the argument that the International Institute, as a scientific body, is superior to political influences, seems not to realize that any policy laid down for official statistics is still dependent for practical results upon acceptance by governments, and that it is impossible in the final analysis to remove official statistics from official discussion and control."[10] Meeker's criticism was more direct: "I do not think it is at all possible to put into effect the Resolution recommending that the International Statistical Institute be made a sort of statistical Czar, to which statistics must be referred for approval and from which criticisms and recommendations to the International Labour Office to the Economic Section and to Governments would emanate."[11]

Writing about this meeting forty years later, J.W. Nixon stressed that the three officers of the International Statistical Institute on the commission (Bodio Delatour, and Methorst) had acted without consulting the other officers or any members in putting forward their proposals. He explained their action as a gamble for the institute's survival: "At that time, 1920, the Institute was about moribund. It had held no session since 1913, and saw no immediate prospect of calling another ... There seemed no other way of saving the Institute as a scientific body than that of attaching itself to, or having it recognized by, the new international bodies set up by the victorious nations of the war."[12] However the commission's recommendation that the institute should become an independent technical and advisory body to the League of Nations on statistical questions was formally rejected by the General Assembly in September 1921 and no action was taken to set up a continuing international commission on statistics.

Within a short time, a more concrete and ultimately productive initiative was under way. Following a recommendation concerning the uniformity of compilation of economic statistics originating from a conference held in Genoa in 1922,[13] the league established a mixed committee, made up of representatives of its own Economic Committee and the institute, to develop proposals. During the next five years reports were prepared in the areas of international trade statistics of production, and index numbers of prices of economic conditions

These were submitted for review to the first three postwar sessions of the institute in 1923 (Brussels), 1925 (Rome), and 1927 (Cairo). Coats attended the Brussels session as an "invité", a courtesy status distinct from that of "membres titulaires," or full members, who were elected on the basis of scientific merit, and whose numbers could not exceed one hundred and fifty.[14] The record shows him to have made a modest intervention on the subject of statistics of fisheries. The bureau did not take part in the Rome session, but at the end of 1927 Coats attended the Cairo session, where he commented on Canadian practices with respect to statistics of stocks of grain.

The International Convention Relating to Economic Statistics

The resolutions of these three sessions on economic statistics went back to the Economic Committee of the league, which in turn forwarded them to member governments for their consideration. The response was favourable enough for the council of the league to approve, in 1927, a proposal for a conference of official statisticians in 1928. The deliberations of this conference, held in Geneva in November and December of 1928, gave rise to the International Convention Relating to Economic Statistics, to which Canada acceded in August 1930 and which became the foundation for virtually all the league's subsequent statistical work in this area. Article 2 of the convention asked the contracting parties to compile and publish statistics of external trade and shipping, occupations, agriculture, livestock, forestry and fisheries, mining and metallurgy, industry, as well as index numbers of prices.

Article 8 provided for the appointment of a Committee of Statistical Experts to "make any suggestions which may appear to it useful, for the purpose of improving or amplifying the principles and arrangements laid down in the Convention concerning the classes of statistics dealt with therein. It may also make suggestions in regard to other classes of statistics of a similar character in respect of which it appears desirable and practicable to secure international uniformity." The committee, which did not have a fixed membership,[15] met eight times between 1931 and 1939 and generated a wide variety of methodological studies, a number of which were published in the League of Nations series *Studies and Reports on Statistical Methods.*[16] Coats took part in the eighth session in 1939, which *inter alia* drafted recommendations on price and quantum indices of international trade.

The International Statistical Institute had, through its collaboration with the league, played a key role in these developments, but the establishment of the league's own Committee of Statistical Experts effectively terminated the "mixed committee" arrangement with the institute. An attempt at collaboration with the International Labour Organization through participation in similar mixed committees to review the recommendations of that body's regular conferences of labour statisticians was less successful and was eventually abandoned at the instance of the ILO.[17] Thus, after 1927 the agenda of the institute's now regular biennial sessions reverted to their traditional format. As suggested by Nixon, the collaborative role had been virtually forced upon the institute by its precarious situation after the war, and even though it had been in part successful, some members had, in his view,[18] considered it inconsistent with the institute's independence and autonomy.

The International Labour Office

The statistical function of the International Labour Office, the secretariat of the International Labour Organization, arose out of the latter's responsibility for "the collection and distribution of information on all subjects relating to the international adjustment of conditions of industrial life and labour," assigned to it by the Treaty of Versailles. Although a statistical branch as such was not immediately formed, the office was in touch with member governments at an early stage, requesting that they regularly furnish "all official publications, bulletins, gazettes, reviews, reports and year-books relating to questions of labour, industry, commerce and agriculture."[19] The bureau's first direct contact with the office came about in October 1920 when, at the request of his former colleague in the Department of Labour, F.A. Acland, who was now the deputy minister, Coats substituted for the minister of Labour, the Honourable Gideon D. Robertson, as Canadian representative at the fifth meeting of the ILO's governing body. This came about because he was also attending the league's International Statistical Commission in Paris later that month.

Coats's subsequent report indicates that the meeting touched upon statistics only incidentally and fleetingly, but it gave him the opportunity of meeting Albert Thomas, the director, and Royal Meeker, who was organizing the office's statistical work and with whom he was shortly to find common cause at the commission meeting in Paris.[20] In a courtesy letter to Thomas as he left Geneva, Coats regretted that he had not had a chance to speak to him on the organization of international statistics.[21] When Thomas replied in very cordial terms on 18 October, the commission meeting had taken place, and he had apparently received a gloomy report from Meeker. He had been pleased to hear that Coats had aligned himself with the minority position, along with Meeker, and went on to say that, pending some more comprehensive framework for statistical coordination, "le Bureau International du Travail n'a plus qu'à aborder les quelques statistiques qui sont directement de son ressort."[22]

This it did with considerable success during the next decade and a half. In the spring of 1923 the governing body approved a proposal for the first of what became regular conferences of the official labour statisticians of the states members of the International Labour Organization. "This proposal was prompted," wrote Thomas, "by the feeling that, if statistics could be drawn up in such a manner as to render them internationally comparable, the scientific study of labour problems from the international point of view could be facilitated."[23]

The agenda for the conference, which was scheduled for the end of October, covered the classification of industries and occupations for the purpose of labour statistics, statistics of wages and hours of labour, and statistics of industrial accidents, thus straddling the mandates of both the bureau and the Department of Labour. The minister of Labour recommended that Canada be represented by Coats, noting that he would be in Brussels at the beginning of the month for the fifteenth session of the International Statistical Institute, and in London immediately afterwards, serving as the prime minister's statistical adviser at the Imperial Economic Conference.

Coats spoke only to the agenda item dealing with classifications, emphasizing the desirability of coordinating the ILO work with that of other institutions working on similar or connected problems. The recently concluded ISI session, for instance, had considered the classification issue from the standpoint of international trade. On the matter of industrial classifications, he argued what was by now his well-known position in favour of separate classifications of industries based on single principles rather than a single classification based on mixed principles.[24] Coats made little headway with his colleagues, but the secretariat's draft resolution endorsing the mixed classification principle was nevertheless withdrawn.

Classification issues surfaced again at the second and third International Conferences of Labour Statisticians held in April 1925 and October 1926, neither of which was attended by Coats. All that came out of the first was "a provisional list of the most important industries,"[25] prepared by the secretariat, which it was agreed in the following year should be elaborated "so as to show in greater detail the contents of each industrial group in the different countries."[26] Thus the bureau continued to have the somewhat negative satisfaction of knowing that single principle classifications had not been ruled out. Before too long, however, the initiative with respect to a classification of industries passed to the League of Nations in accordance with the provisions of the 1928 Convention Relating to Economic Statistics. In 1938 the league's Committee of Statistical Experts, with which the International Labour Office continued to collaborate, recommended a uniform definition of the "gainfully occupied" and two lists of industries–a minimum list and a more detailed one–for purposes of classifying the gainfully occupied population in a uniform manner for international comparison. However, the development and approval of an international standard industrial classification of economic activities had to wait until 1948, and an international standard classification of occupations did not come until 1954.

The outstanding achievement of the International Labour Organization during this period was the adoption by the International Labour Conference in 1938 of Convention No. 63 Concerning Statistics of Wages and Hours of Work. The preparatory work towards this convention had been undertaken by a specially appointed Committee of Statistical Experts, which met in 1933, 1935, and 1937. The convention, once adopted, assumed a significance unlike that of the various recommendations of the International Conferences of Labour Statisticians. These latter were simply circulated to member governments for consideration when changes in their statistics were being contemplated. The provisions of the convention, however, had the binding force of an international treaty on ratifying countries, which were obliged to submit an annual report on the manner in which the provisions were carried out.

The International Institute of Agriculture

The circumstances of the founding of the International Institute of Agriculture, the earliest of the intergovernmental organizations, and its influence on Canadian agriculture statistics have already been recounted. The promising start that the institute had made in promoting the worldwide adoption of uniform methods of crop reporting was disrupted by the outbreak of war in 1914, and there were concerns in the immediate postwar period that its role might be absorbed into the broader economic and statistical mandate of the League of Nations. This did not occur, and the institute was confirmed, with an unchanged mandate, as one of the group of intergovernmental statistical organizations, each operating in its own specialized area under the loose coordination of the league.

As it had done before the war, the Department of Agriculture continued to represent the government of Canada in its dealings with the institute, thus formally excluding the bureau from direct contact with the institute. The department was not particularly happy with this situation and wrote to the institute, at least once on its own initiative and again in 1922 following a complaint by Coats, suggesting that the bureau should be represented at the periodic meetings of its general assembly. But nothing was done. Just one visit might have been enough to open up a channel of direct communication such as existed with the International Labour Office where, in a parallel situation, the liaison role was officially vested in the Department of Labour.

The story of the bureau's indirect involvement with the institute mostly derives from two draft memoranda of uncertain date and authorship, one prepared as a working paper for the 1935 Conference of Commonwealth Statisticians,[27] and the second apparently written in 1945 at the time when the functions of the institute were about to be absorbed by the new Food and Agriculture Organization (FAO) of the United Nations.[28] A general assembly of the institute in 1920 had laid down what the 1945 memorandum called "a rather broad and comprehensive program." Here perhaps were the seeds of the bureau's future discontent with the institute, which prompted the following assessment in the 1935 memorandum: "The usefulness of the Institute has been impaired by two lines of policy: (1) in the statistical field the Institute has tended to extend its work into sections which are under direction by other international agencies, thus to a certain degree creating confusion and overlapping; (2) it has embarked on various undertakings outside of statistics that have not commended themselves to many of the adhering countries, with a certain dissipation of effort as a final result."[29]

At the same time as the Department of Agriculture was urging the bureau's direct involvement in the work of the institute, it was also relaying complaints about the institute's failure in what the bureau regarded as its primary tasks, namely, to achieve uniformity of methodology among adhering countries in the reporting of crop conditions, and to provide such reports in a timely fashion – particularly for European countries, which were important markets for Canadian grain. When these and other markets were later thrown into disarray by economic crisis, the institute's methods of analysis and presentation were judged inadequate to contemporary needs. The kind of analytical work that might have been helpful in formulating remedial measures fell to the lot of bodies like the Imperial Economic Conference and the Empire Marketing Board, and when the institute was invited to take part in the International Wheat Conference in Regina in 1933, it did not send a delegation.

Even so, in Canada at least, the institute did not entirely forfeit the goodwill built up in its earlier years, and its initiative in formulating draft schedules for a world census of agriculture in 1930–31 received favourable notice. In 1936 proposals for a second world agricultural census were discussed at an institute conference in Rome. Canada did not attend but was asked to provide comments on the proposed questionnaire and methodology. Grindlay, the bureau's chief of agricultural statistics, provided the bureau's response and, while urging that Canada support this initiative, commented unfavourably on the institute's current publications, which were defective in content and coverage and, in any case, generally too late to be of any practical value.[30] He recommended that Lemieux should attend the December 1937 conference to finalize plans for 1940, but Coats chose not to be represented.

From the late 1920s to the early 1930s the United States withdrew its support from the institute and built up its own system of international agricultural intelligence through its network of agricultural attachés in foreign countries. Canada's agricultural statistics had long been modelled on those of the United States; hence it is not surprising that, during the interwar years, the principal external stimulus to bureau practices came through its continued and close association with the US Bureau of Agricultural Economics.

The 1935 memorandum noted that "the United States has recently returned to the support of the Institute after an absence of some years, and it was demonstrated at the last General Assembly of the Institute that considerable benefit may arise from the renewed enthusiasm which this may infuse."[31] This sentiment was echoed by the 1935 Commonwealth statisticians' conference, which "noted with satisfaction that, at the General Assembly in October 1934, it was agreed that the Institute should concentrate its attention mainly upon its

statistical and economic work."[32] But this attempted rejuvenation was too lat
and fell victim to the onset of war in 1939. Canada, for one, suspended th
transmittal to the institute of statistics on agricultural production and trade
which were now information of strategic value.

The 1945 memorandum had been prepared after receipt of a letter to th
secretary of state for External Affairs from the secretary general of the institute
expressing the hope that "changed international conditions will now allow th
Institute to develop steadily its possibilities for service, and to make a definit
contribution to the study of the problems of economic reconstruction."[33] Th
bureau advised the rejection of such a role: "In view of the history of th
Institute and the difficulties that have been encountered in the past, it is suggeste
that at the earliest date possible the [new] Food and Agriculture Organizatio
should absorb its activities. However, when the FAO does take over, experienc
with the services of the International Institute emphasizes strongly the necessit
that this Bureau have direct access to the statistical organization of FAO on al
technical matters rather than reporting through some other Department of th
Canadian Government."[34]

THE COMMONWEALTH STATISTICAL CONFERENCES OF 1920 AND 1935

In its report of March 1917, the Dominions royal commission had recommende
that a conference of statisticians from different parts of the empire be held a
soon as practicable after the end of the war to consider arrangements for
central bureau to coordinate imperial statistics. The Imperial War Conferenc
of July 1918 had formally approved the proposal, and in 1919 the Colonia
Office asked the Board of Trade to make the necessary arrangements. Thu
there was convened in London in January 1920 what its subsequent report[3
referred to as the "First Conference of Government Officers Engaged in Dealin
with Statistics in the British Empire." The home government was represente
by thirty-one delegates, India by three, the self-governing Dominions by fiv
(including Coats and Godfrey[36] for Canada), and the colonies and protectorate
by four delegates.

In addition to the question of the central bureau, which was the prime agend
item, the delegates, under the chairmanship of A.W. Flux of the Board of Trade,[3
also addressed themselves to the consideration of statistical requirements an
practice under a variety of subject-matter headings. The original notificatio
by the Colonial Office of its intention to call the conference had suggested
subject-matter agenda limited to the concerns of the Dominions roya
commission, namely, trade, production and migration statistics, with th
concession that vital statistics might also be discussed because of their connectio
with the latter. In fact, it was unanimously agreed from the start that ther
should be no restrictions of the conference's mandate, and for this reason it sa
from 20 January to 26 February.

Committees were set up for each area[38] and were able to draft working principles that were unanimously approved as desirable and feasible for application throughout the empire.[39] Special mention is made here only of the committee dealing with trade statistics, in which Coats outlined the tripartite classification system recently developed in Canada for the industrial census and explained its applicability to other kinds of statistics, including those of foreign trade. The delegates were sceptical. When Coats remarked–perhaps a little too virtuously – that "we feel about our grouping that it is right," H.V. Reade of the Department of Customs and Excise countered that "with all respect to Mr Coats, I do not think there can be any question of a particular classification being right or accurate." Other delegates challenged Coats on apparent anomalies in the illustrations he had offered, to which his response was that "when I say we are right, I mean that the principle is right. We may have, by exercise of wrong judgment, put something in the wrong place."[40]

In spite of this rough passage in committee, Coats's arguments made an impact on the conference's final resolution with respect to "Uniform Classifications of Imports and Exports," which read in part: "The Conference ... does not consider that any single scheme could usefully be recommended for adoption by all parts of the British Empire, but regards it as highly desirable that, in order to facilitate aggregations and comparisons of trade statistics throughout the Empire, several schemes of classification should be prepared, under which the more important commodities could be arranged with reference to the particular object in view. Alternative classifications might be based, for instance, on the origin of the commodities, on their component materials, or on their purpose or use."[41]

The conference's agenda was, however, dominated by the question of how to establish an imperial statistical bureau, as recommended by the Dominions royal commission report of 1917. But the issue was now less straightforward than it had seemed three years earlier. The newly established League of Nations was concerning itself with coordination of statistics at the international level, and its recent London conference on this subject had acknowledged the potential role of the International Statistical Institute and specialized organizations such as the International Institute of Agriculture and the International Labour Organization.

Again, within the narrower imperial context, an Imperial Mineral Resources Bureau with explicit statistical responsibilities had been established by the Imperial War Conference, and a draft charter for a proposed Imperial Agricultural Bureau had been circulated to the delegates. As one of them put it: "One becomes afraid of our world statistical wheel having too many hubs."[42] It was recognized, however, that no system of international coordination could be devised that was entirely free of overlap, that an imperial statistical bureau could facilitate imperial participation in work organized under broader auspices, and that within the empire itself, common sense could avoid unnecessary overlapping between the imperial statistical bureau and bodies like the Imperial Mineral Resources Bureau.

But the contrast between the decentralized UK system and the centralized systems of the self-governing Dominions was a more basic problem. It was Coats who finally made an issue of this:

> I feel very strongly that we have got to make statistical centralization the cornerstone of our policy on Imperial statistical work ... It would be an impertinence on the part of a delegate from Canada ... to criticize the method of statistical work in any section of the Empire, but I do feel that, when we have set up a Central Statistical Bureau, one of the chief difficulties in the path of good work will be the fact that, in the largest section of the Empire, namely, the United Kingdom, there is no system of centralization. That is going to add materially ... to the difficulties of a Central Bureau ... if we are not going to lay down Imperial centralization ... there will be reluctance in my part of the Empire to come into this scheme.[43]

G.H. Knibbs of Australia was even blunter: "Unless this country shows that it can organize the statistics of the United Kingdom of a complete character like the statistics of the self-governing Dominions, the more doubtful it is that any organization we are going to suggest will do any better."[44]

The conference's final resolutions glossed over this difficulty, but it eventually proved to be fatal. The establishment of a "Central Bureau of Statistics for the British Empire" was proposed, its general function being "to obtain, co-ordinate, analyze and publish statistical information relating to the whole of the British Empire." The bureau was to be established by Royal Charter, its control vested in a council consisting of the prime minister of the United Kingdom and members nominated by the several governments in due proportion. The council in turn was to be assisted by an advisory committee representative of economic, commercial, and industrial interests. The director of the bureau, who would be responsible to the council, was to be "both an expert statistician and a man of approved administrative and official experience and ability," holding rank equivalent to that of a permanent secretary in the UK Civil Service. Following upon approval of the scheme by the several governments, the charter was to be drafted by their representatives.[45]

Some six months later, acting on the advice of Coats, the Privy Council of Canada approved the conference's proposals in principle and nominated the Honourable Sir George E. Perley, high commissioner for Canada in London, to represent Canada in the drafting of the charter.[46] South Africa also assented, but New Zealand, while approving the other recommendations of the conference, expressed its inability to support the establishment of an imperial statistical bureau. The decision of the Australian government was that such a bureau should be established *at the appropriate time*, but not before the United Kingdom had followed the lead of the self-governing Dominions by itself putting in place arrangements to bring together systematically the statistical products of the various departments. It was drily noted that "unless such an organization were first created, a large part of the work of the proposed Empire Bureau of Statistics would necessarily consist of formulating the statistical conspectus of the United Kingdom itself, a labour with which the Empire Bureau ought not to be charged."[47]

The United Kingdom's position was evident from the official response to an earlier petition by the Royal Statistical Society. This had stressed "the urgent need for a reorganization of the present system of official statistics,"[48] not only for domestic purposes but also in the broader context of imperial needs. The following reasons were cited for the inadequacy of official statistics: "(i) Absence of any general supervision of national statistics as a whole. (ii) Lack of co-operation between the different departments ... (iii) The fact that compulsory powers are too few and too seldom applied. (iv) Defective supervision of the collection of statistics in some cases, and the employment, especially for census purposes, of persons ill-paid and insufficiently educated and therefore uninterested in the collection. (v) Antiquated and anomalous legislation, such as that which prescribes different financial years for various annual returns. (vi) Inadequate financial provision for the collection of essential statistics."[49] The society requested an inquiry into the whole organization of official statistics, and the matter was referred by cabinet to a committee that, in May 1921, reported that "no case existed for such an enquiry, but recommended that a permanent consultative committee of official statisticians be constituted as the best means of obtaining greater co-ordination between Departments and effecting other improvements from time to time."[50]

The issue was placed on the agenda of the Imperial Economic Conference of 1923, and the secretariat's briefing memorandum, taking note of the New Zealand and Australian positions, ruled out any possibility of the original recommendation being acceptable to the various governments concerned.[51] It was suggested, however, that, pending the establishment of a definitive imperial organization, the Board of Trade should continue to prepare imperial statistics, but that an imperial advisory committee should be established "to supervise the work from an Imperial point of view."[52] In advising the Canadian delegation to the conference, Coats commented that little useful work could be done by the UK Board of Trade in the absence of a detailed and properly integrated scheme based on the recommendations of the British Empire Statistical Conference of 1920: "This is a work of considerable magnitude for experienced and expert statisticians in the first instance rather than for a purely advisory committee."[53]

In the end, all that could be salvaged from the 1920 recommendation for an imperial statistical bureau was a resolution instructing the UK Board of Trade to draw up a detailed scheme of empire trade statistics to be submitted to the various governments for their consideration. Little progress was made apparently, and the imperial conference of 1926 accordingly approved a recommendation that the existing statistical abstract for the British Overseas Dominions and Protectorates, prepared by the UK Board of Trade, should be modified and expanded in consultation with the interested governments, after which it might be desirable to hold a second meeting of empire statisticians to review the progress made and consider how to proceed further.[54] The imperial conference of 1930 reaffirmed approval of this suggestion, and it was agreed that Canada should act as host in September 1932.

At this same conference, however, Prime Minister Bennett of Canada persuaded the delegates to reconvene in Ottawa in 1931 to discuss ways of increasing intra-empire trade in the face of worldwide depression. Many pressing problems, including Britain's going off the gold standard, forced a postponement of what came to be called the Imperial Economic Conference, but it was finally scheduled for July 1932.[55] This in turn caused the United Kingdom to suggest, in February of that year, that the statistical conference be deferred for a year, principally on the grounds that this would enable the statistical needs identified by the economic conference to be assessed.[56]

The latter again endorsed the proposal for a statistical conference but also recommended the appointment of a committee to consider the means of facilitating economic consultation and cooperation between the members of the commonwealth, and, pending its meeting and report, no action was taken with regard to a statistical conference. After meeting in 1933, the committee held up the 1920 statistical conference as an outstanding example of the kind of cooperation it regarded as desirable. It noted that a second conference was to have been held in 1932 and urged that it be proceeded with at the earliest possible date.

Thus it was that on 13 September 1935 Prime Minister Bennett welcomed sixteen delegates, along with an observer from the Imperial Economic Committee, to the Conference of British Commonwealth Statisticians in Ottawa. This was considerably fewer than the numbers attending the 1920 conference in London, most of whom had been representatives of UK home departments. Of course, a great many bureau staff and officials of other departments assisted in the work of the Ottawa conference but could not be listed as delegates. Coats was unanimously elected chairman and Herbert Marshall served as secretary.

The fifteen years since the 1920 conference had seen an almost complete change in personnel,[57] and the conference report noted that; "of the delegates at the present Conference, only one – Dr Coats, the Chairman–attended the preceding meeting. Personal contacts between those responsible for the statistics of their respective countries have thus been lost, and the delegates to the present Conference have much appreciated the opportunity afforded to them of establishing such contacts ... It is the opinion of the delegates that the interval between successive statistical Conferences should be less extended than has been the case in the past."[58]

There was no predominant item on the agenda, as there had been in 1920 when the issue of an imperial statistical bureau had been paramount. There was, however, a discussion of the progress achieved in the modification and expansion of the UK Board of Trade's statistical abstract, as recommended by the imperial conferences of 1923 and 1926. The conference noted "the changes and improvements made during recent years ... which have resulted in the publication of statistical material of much value, both as regards the comparability of Empire Statistics and ... the direction of trade of each country,"[59] and made its own recommendations for further enhancing the usefulness of the abstract.

The agenda also called for "the examination, from an Imperial standpoint, of international obligations regarding statistics."[60] This had particular reference to those arising out of the League of Nations International Convention Relating to Economic Statistics of 1928 and the work of its Committee of Experts, as well as that of bodies such as the International Labour Office and the International Institute of Agriculture, there being obvious merit in the large block of English-speaking countries represented at the conference coordinating their own statistics as far as possible in accordance with international standards.

Thus, the resolutions in areas such as fisheries, mining, industrial production, statistical classifications, valuation of imports and exports, balance of international payments, and wholesale prices were studded with references to the reporting formats of the economic statistics convention and the recommendations of the Committee of Experts. Similarly, those in the broad field of "labour" – employment and unemployment, wages and hours of labour, and retail prices and the cost of living – reflected the recommendations of successive International Conferences of Labour Statisticians.

Novel items on the agenda reflected general economic and social developments since 1920 – road transport and traffic accidents, radio broadcasting, and the growing importance of "invisible" items, such as tourism, in the balance of payments. The discussion in all areas reflected a powerful awareness of the pernicious effects of worldwide economic depression. Censuses of population were not on the agenda as such, but–largely on Coats's personal initiative, it seems–there was a discussion on census tabulating machinery, which involved dragging the delegates away from their meeting rooms in the Centre Block to the primitive surroundings of the Edwards Mill on Sussex Drive where all the machines were located.

As the foregoing suggests, the major thrust of the conference was towards economic statistics. It was cryptically noted in the report that "reference was also made to the definition of the term 'Social Statistics', but no delimitation of the subjects which should be included under this general heading was found desirable."[61] The delegates were well pleased with the outcome of the conference: "The difficulties facing the Conference were fully realized when it was convened, but it was hoped that a substantial advance would be made beyond the stage that was possible when the previous statistical Conference was held in 1920. These hopes have been more than fulfilled. It is very gratifying to record that, after discussion, unanimity prevailed in the Conference with regard to the objectives of the resolutions proposed."[62]

In spite of the conference's expressed view on the desirability of more frequent meetings, no proposals were mooted for another, and it was not until November 1951 that the third Conference of British Commonwealth Statisticians was convened in Canberra.

A Venture into Technical Assistance

By the mid-1930s the bureau's international reputation was well established through its contributions to the statistical work of the League of Nations and the International Labour Organization, its participation in the International Statistical Institute, and – most notably, as far as the United Kingdom was concerned – through Coats's forceful performance at the first Conference of Empire Statisticians in 1920. It was probably the recollection of his enthusiastic advocacy of the virtues of statistical centralization that prompted the British government to inquire, early in 1935, whether the government of Canada would be prepared to allow a suitable officer to be seconded from the Dominion Bureau of Statistics for a three-year period as head of a proposed bureau of statistics in Palestine.

In conveying this request in a letter of April 1935, Sir Francis Floud, high commissioner in Canada for the United Kingdom, wrote to O.D. Skelton, under secretary of state for External Affairs, that "the Government Statistician ... should be a man of energy and initiative, and ... should have had considerable practical experience in the collection, compilation and analysis of public statistics as carried out in a government department ... an officer employed on the staff of the Canadian Bureau of Statistics would have had the training and experience necessary for such work."[63]

Coats was advised of this interest through the deputy minister of Trade and Commerce, James G. Parmelee, and put forward the name of S.A. Cudmore. However, on 28 May Parmelee wrote back that; "as this was a matter of Government policy, it was taken up with the Minister who, in turn, took it up with the Prime Minister. The Minister is in receipt of a note from the Prime Minister today in which he states that our Minister realizes, of course, that Mr. Cudmore is not a statistician, but an economist, and that it would be a mistake to put ourselves in a position which might result in our nominee not being what was wanted by the Palestine people."[64]

Coats's reply of 31 May politely but firmly challenged this assessment, pointing out that the Palestinian legislation was based "almost *verbatim* on ours," and that the government of Palestine was "desirous of creating thereunder an organization and body of statistics *mutatis mutandis* similar to ours in

Canada." Thus, he argued, they had correctly assessed the requirement for "an officer experienced in our methods" who could deal with the problems of administrative principle and set-up and the planning and implementation of statistical programs appropriate to Palestinian needs. Cudmore, as "the ranking Chief Officer of the Bureau," was amply qualified by experience and ability to meet such a challenge.[65] This vigorous defence persuaded the prime minister to reverse his position, and on 15 August Parmelee wrote to advise Coats that the appointment would be offered to Cudmore.[66]

Cudmore deferred his departure for Palestine in order to take part in the Ottawa conference during the latter part of September and arrived in Jerusalem in early November. His subsequent letters to Coats and other colleagues provide a fascinating commentary on the challenges he faced. These were basically the consequence of a longstanding and generalized lack of appreciation of the usefulness of statistics on the part of the Colonial Office but were greatly compounded in the case of Palestine by the country's heightening political tensions. The most obvious difficulty was the scant resources he was expected to work with. As he ruefully wrote to Coats: "It is a great nuisance ... to have the Government spending all its money for police and soldiers, and telling us that we must keep our estimates down and cut wherever possible." He reported that, to his embarrassment, two special policemen assigned to guard the Statistical Office presented arms whenever he went in or out. "They cost the Government as much as a couple of clerks who would do some work."[67]

Nevertheless, Cudmore was able to effect palpable progress. He improved the timeliness and detail of trade statistics – partly through the installation of Hollerith equipment – and instituted a monthly survey of employment and payrolls. He was diligent in pursuing other government departments whose operations gave rise to the raw material of statistics and was thus able to establish systems of judicial, vital, and banking statistics. The statistics of wholesale and retail prices were put in good order and an annual statistical yearbook and a monthly bulletin of statistics established as the basic elements of a growing repertoire of statistical publications. Perhaps the most radical departure from the traditional Colonial Office view of statistics was the emphasis Cudmore placed on getting statistics into the hands of people who could make good use of them.

In another letter to Coats, Cudmore reported on a conversation with a senior colleague who, just back from leave in England, had told him that "the Colonial Office was very much pleased with our work in Palestine, saying that they were getting better statistics from here than from any other territory under their administration." His reaction had been characteristically modest: "Realizing how elementary our work as yet is, I can only say 'God help the others.'" But he expressed the hope that "if my work here opens the eyes of the Colonial Office to the importance of establishing similar offices, as far as possible, throughout the 2,000,000 square miles or so of territories all over the world, with their 60,000,000 people, which constitute the Colonial Empire, I shall have made a real contribution to British colonial administration."[68]

As the time approached, in early 1938, for Cudmore's return to Canada, there were concerns about finding a suitable replacement for him. In Cudmore's view, no one in the office was as yet experienced enough to take over, and what had seemed to be the possibility of getting someone from Australia with a background like Cudmore's fell through. There was even talk of another Canadian, but Coats said firmly that "we have done our duty by the Palestine Government ... and we could not (again) send anyone without crippling ourselves considerably."[69] Finally, a Mr G.E. Wood of New Zealand was appointed but too late for any overlap with Cudmore's tenure.

On 3 August 1938 Cudmore left Palestine to resume his duties in Ottawa after a vacation in Europe. The curtain was drawn on this first venture into technical assistance with a letter dated 7 October 1938 from the office of the high commissioner for the United Kingdom in Canada to the under secretary of state for External Affairs:

> The High Commissioner for Palestine, in a despatch addressed to the Secretary of State for the Colonies on the departure of Mr Cudmore, has expressed the wish to place on record his sincere appreciation of the notable advance in the statistical records of Palestine which has been achieved as the result of this officer's experience and ability ...
>
> His Majesty's Government in Canada should be informed of the high appreciation with which the Government of Palestine viewed Mr Cudmore's services; of their recognition of the distinction which Mr Cudmore's temporary membership of the service in Palestine had conferred upon that service, and of their gratitude to the Canadian Government for having placed his services at the disposal of Palestine at so critical a period of the history of the country.[70]

Conclusion

It will be clear from the foregoing that during the two interwar decades, Canada had become a prime mover within the international statistical community, largely on the basis of Coats's technical skills and leadership abilities. With the outbreak of war in 1939 international contacts ceased, with the exception of continuing bilateral relations with the statistical agencies of the United States and, to some extent, with those of the United Kingdom. After the war, Herbert Marshall proved himself a worthy successor to Coats in contributing to the revival of existing intergovermental organizations and the establishment of new ones. In particular, his chairmanship of the new United Nations Statistical Commission provided valuable guidance to that body during its formative years. Again, as one of the few Commonwealth statisticians who had participated in the 1935

Ottawa conference, he became a key figure in reviving that forum in 1951 and ensuring regular meetings thereafter.

The provision of technical assistance in statistics to what were then called underdeveloped countries became a widespread practice in the late 1940s, and, with Cudmore's successful pre-war mission to Palestine still in mind, many would-be recipients looked first to the bureau for help.

CHAPTER NINE

1939–1942
The Closing Years of the Coats Era

INTRODUCTION

Coats's service of more than a quarter century as Dominion statistician began and ended while Canada was at war. After his appointment in mid-1915, the Census and Statistics Office conducted the 1916 census of the Prairie provinces, annualized the census of manufactures, undertook some work for wartime agencies such as the Canada Food Board and the Fuel Controller, and, towards the end of the war, participated in a national registration exercise. But given the office's small size and rudimentary development, its potential for assisting the wartime bureaucracy was limited.[1] In any case, it is doubtful how well equipped the latter was to make effective use of statistical information. During the Second World War the situation was much different, and almost from the beginning the talents and resources of the bureau were mobilized to serve the needs of Canada's war economy.

One notable contribution by the bureau was the conduct of the 1941 census, which *inter alia*, provided information needed for manpower planning and utilization and for the development of a postwar housing policy. Less successful were the bureau's efforts to provide national income statistics capable of meeting the needs of the new breed of economists in the Bank of Canada and the Department of Finance who were advising on the financing of the war effort and the overall management of the economy. Conceptual defects in the bureau's approach resulted in the production of national income statistics temporarily falling, by default, to the Bank of Canada. It was not until later in the war, during Cudmore's tenure as Dominion statistician, that the bureau was finally able to reclaim the initiative in this important area of statistical development. This chapter then looks briefly at Coats's so-called "Valedictory Report," written at the time of his retirement, which provided a review of past achievements, as well as proposals for legislative and administrative changes and for the further development of the statistical program.

The Bureau Goes to War

The outbreak of war ushered in an unprecedented expansion in the functions and machinery of government with the object of mobilizing resources for an all-out war effort. The government's role became far more pervasive and systematic than it had been a quarter of a century earlier, when its record had been marred by procurement scandals, profiteering, and inflation. From an early date it was realized not only that Canada's own fighting forces would have to be raised and supplied but also that food, raw materials, and armaments would have to be furnished to Britain and elsewhere. As the war progressed and victory eventually seemed assured, concerns shifted towards postwar reconstruction. All these activities generated enormous informational requirements, but the government now had a mature statistical system to call upon. The basic programs set out by Coats in 1916 were more or less in place, and the bureau was well able to respond quickly to new needs.

Although special budgetary allotments and staffing authorizations were provided, it was not easy for the bureau to assume additional work. It was mostly clerical and often intermittent in nature, with successive cycles of hiring and laying off of casual staff. From mid-1941 on, males of military age were no longer eligible for appointment to the public service, and the bureau was, of course, competing for staff with other departments of government. No permanent appointments could be made, but whenever possible the better casuals were absorbed into the continuing staff, which increased from under six hundred in 1939 to approximately nine hundred by 1945.

The bureau's ability to recruit new senior staff was similarly constrained, and a considerable burden fell upon the "old guard." They were already a disproportionately older group because of the staffing freezes and low turnover of the 1930s, and many of them were persuaded – as was Coats – to accept extensions of service beyond the normal retirement age.

The Major Wartime Committees

In its task of planning and implementing the economic and financial policies and related organizational changes required to put Canada's economy on a war footing, and later of restoring that economy to a peacetime basis as quickly and smoothly as possible, the cabinet had at its service a number of interlocking committees, notably the Advisory Committees on Economic Policy, Demobilization and Rehabilitation, and Reconstruction. Their mandates overlapped, as did their membership, which was largely drawn from the ranks of deputy ministers. This was thought to be a positive factor in avoiding duplication of effort among the various departments and in ensuring effective coordination. There was also, under the direction of External Affairs, the

Canadian Section of the Joint Economic Committees, an arrangement for cooperation between the governments of Canada, the US, and the UK.

The Dominion statistician was formally named only to the Advisory Committee on Demobilization and Rehabilitation, but in practice Coats worked with and for all of them. Particular initiatives undertaken by the bureau in connection with manpower mobilization, nutritional standards, and the work of the Wartime Prices and Trade Board, for instance, generally had their origin with one or another of the advisory committees.

Work for the Wartime Prices and Trade Board

One of the first of the new agencies of government, this was set up by Order in Council PC 2516 under the War Measures Act on 3 September 1939 "to provide safeguards under war conditions against any undue enhancement in the prices of food, fuel and other necessaries of life, and to ensure an adequate supply and equitable distribution of such commodities." More bluntly, its mandate was to supply the subsistence needs of the civilian population with minimum disruption to the demands of the war machine. From April 1940, when the "phony war" came to an end, these latter were made the responsibility of a new Department of Munitions and Supply, formed to expedite the procurement of war supplies and to facilitate, where needed, the creation of new industrial capacity. The department operated in part through a system of controllers in various industrial sectors, who together constituted a Wartime Industries Control Board. This maintained direct liaison with the Wartime Prices and Trade Board to ensure coordination of their frequently overlapping activities. Both boards made heavy demands upon the bureau's resources. The work of the various branches of the census of industry was particularly relevant for the former, and many new monthly reports showing the production, shipments, and stocks of metals, minerals, etc. were instituted.

But the needs of the Wartime Prices and Trade Board were perhaps the most exacting and continuous. Indeed, it virtually conscripted the Internal Trade Statistics Branch into its service. Within days of its formation, Herbert Marshall, chief of the branch, was seconded to it by Order in Council PC 2632 of 11 September 1939 "for service during such period as the board may require." The Board, like most of the other new agencies, recruited its senior staff from the top echelons of business and the universities, so that the bureau's managers were dealing with people who were fully their professional equals.[2]

The bureau's biggest single job for the board resulted from the decision to license all retail, wholesale, and manufacturing establishments in Canada. Operationally, this involved using business census records and other sources to develop a mailing list on addressograph plates, coded by kind of business. A machine room was then set up to handle the board's regular mailings – as many as two million pieces per month – to the 350,000 licensed establishments. This involved the erection of a new building (No. 7 Temporary) adjacent to the Edwards Mill premises. Once the work was organized on a routine basis, it was taken over by the board, although a nucleus of bureau staff remained for liaison purposes. The licensing records were regularly updated and were thus a valuable check on the completeness of the mailing list for the 1941 census of merchandising and service establishments. This was of the same general scope as that of 1931, but the tabulation program was extensively revamped and expedited to accommodate the processing needs of the board and other wartime users.

While the slack in the economy was being taken up during the first two years of war, inflation was not considered to be a problem.[3] The board's efforts were mainly addressed to organizing the supply of specific commodities and preventing the occurrence of avoidable shortages. Thus, the Internal Trade Statistics Branch was called upon to initiate the collection, at short notice, of statistics of stocks, consumption, and prices of coal, and of hide, skins, and leather. As 1941 progressed, however, the cost of living index began to rise sharply, and an overall price ceiling, to be administered by the board, was imposed on 1 December of that year.[4]

The bureau was well prepared for this development. In 1938 it had conducted its first family expenditure survey, and this provided the weights for a new national cost of living index, which it introduced in the summer of 1940. Later, eight city index numbers were compiled to measure regional differences in living-cost movements. The new index superseded not only the bureau's own previous index, which dated from 1926, but also that of the Department of Labour, originally developed by Coats and published monthly in the *Labour Gazette* for more than a quarter of a century.

When the government first introduced a limited program of wage stabilization measures in December 1940, the new index was designated by Order in Council as the basis for determining authorized cost of living bonuses. To coincide with the introduction of price ceilings in 1941, the wage stabilization measures were generalized for all employees. This intensified official interest prompted the bureau to send personnel all across Canada to check on a regular basis the representativeness and accuracy of the prices reported through the mail by retail outlets.[5] However, the user criticisms that developed as the war progressed were more in the nature of conceptual challenges, such as the alleged failure of the index to reflect concealed price increases and the effect of tax changes, as well as changes in the patterns of consumption.

Mobilizing Canada's Manpower

Satisfying the enormous needs for manpower, both civil and military, was basic to the war effort, and when a Department of National War Services was established in July 1940 under the newly enacted National Resources

Mobilization Act, its first major initiative was to undertake a national registration of Canadian manpower. The bureau had had experience with a similar undertaking in the final months of the First World War, and was again called upon to compile the results. In a very short time, the Census Branch developed a register of almost eight million persons over the age of sixteen years, classified by age, marital status, education, and occupational experience. The first use of the register was for the selection of single men of specified age groups to be called up for military service in Canada. Occupational compilations were also made to assist in satisfying the demands of the war industries for skilled labour. Subsequently, arrangements were put in place to keep the records up to date.[6]

Government intervention in the operation of the labour market made new demands on the bureau's monthly employment statistics, which had hitherto served wholly as barometric indicators. Now they were also required to support decision making on such issues as the location of wartime industries, the transfer of labour to areas of special stringency, and the curtailment of nonessential production. It was reported at the time that "the transformation of the data to permit their use in ... these functions (resulting wholly from the War and differing greatly in purpose and kind from that for which they were originally collected) has constituted a heavy drain upon the energy and resourcefulness needed to carry on what even in peacetime is generally recognized as an unusually difficult statistical job."[7]

The administration of the wage stabilization programs required not only timely and valid cost of living information but also statistics of earnings. Thus, early in 1941 the monthly survey of employment became a survey of employment and payrolls. This was again reported to have "*considerably more than doubled the regular work of the Branch*, necessitating the use of complicated questionnaires, the building up of a completely new technique to handle the returns, the quadrupling of the statistical calculations required, and the solution of many difficult problems to ensure the comparability of the statistics compiled upon the new basis with those previously prepared."[8]

In 1944 man-hours were added to the data collected by the survey, making it possible to calculate weekly and hourly per capita earnings, payroll index numbers, and averages of hours worked. Miss M.E.K. Roughsedge, who had worked in this general area for more than twenty years, supervised the new developments.

Another responsibility assumed by the bureau in the area of labour statistics that did not arise out of wartime needs but that nevertheless assisted the government greatly in managing the labour market was the statistical analysis of the operations of the new Unemployment Insurance Commission, which began working on 1 July 1941. The work was assigned to the Social Analysis Branch, which had already carried out studies of the supply of labour and its utilization.[9] One of the first tasks was to gather information on the age, sex, industry, occupation, and place of work of each person covered by the act. This provided an important body of baseline information, which was referred to as the "corpus" of the Unemployment Insurance Act.

Early in 1942 a more rigorous approach to the problems of labour supply was thought necessary, and a director of national selective service was appointed under the minister of Labour. An inventory of employable persons was required as a basis for his work, and in this connection, the records and personnel of the National Registration Division of the Department of National War Services were transferred to the Department of Labour. These records had ostensibly been kept up to date since 1940, but it was decided that a fresh approach should be taken by enlisting the good offices of the Unemployment Insurance Commission.

The commission's operating procedures required a recall and reissuance of insurance books each year, together with a reregistration of employers and their insured workers. Accordingly, the April 1942 reregistration extended[10] and elaborated the original "corpus" so as to yield the additional information needed for a new manpower inventory. The *Canada Year Book* for 1943-44 reported that "these manpower records have been compiled by the Bureau of Statistics: they cover more than three million persons and such information as age, conjugal status, occupation, additional skills, industry and other pertinent data that will enable each to be placed in a position where he can contribute most to the national effort."[11] This, then, was yet another of the massive one-time jobs taken on by the bureau, involving a special staff of six hundred at its peak.

Agriculture and Nutrition

The war changed Canada's food situation from one of apparent abundance to one of absolute scarcity, and almost all sectors of agriculture gradually came under government control or regulation. With one of the bureau's oldest and best-established programs, the Agricultural Statistics Branch was generally well equipped to respond to the statistical demands of the various regulatory bodies.[12] Even so, new statistics had to be developed for products like coarse grains and oil seeds where output was being rapidly expanded, and the detail and frequency of others like farm income, farm labour, and operating expenses had to be increased.

As the war progressed, sophisticated procedures were developed to determine targets for agricultural production,[13] and the branch provided statistical support for this work. This led, in 1943, to participation in a study of comparative nutrition levels in the United States, the United Kingdom, and Canada to address the questions of whether and how, in the face of the priority needs of the war effort and emerging supply problems, the nutritional requirements of the civilian populations in these countries could be adequately met.

The bureau's participation in the international exercise of 1943 came about after Cudmore attended a meeting of US and UK experts in Washington, where he argued that any useful study would have to include Canada. On his return to Ottawa he quickly convinced External Affairs as well. In a letter explaining how he thought available data on the quantities of food purchased or consumed might be converted into nutritional measures, he suggested that "we shall have to reconsider our whole agricultural situation and our agricultural statistics from the nutritional point of view, and it will be advantageous that as many as possible of our agricultural experts, our nutritional experts and our statisticians should be given the opportunity of readjusting their minds to this new and most important development."[14]

In the event, nutritional conversions did not become a permanent feature of the bureau's work as Cudmore had urged. However, a one-time exercise was conducted for each of the war years to date, with 1935-39 as a base. These data served as Canada's contribution to the international study and were also published separately by the bureau.

War Finance and Foreign Exchange Control

The recommendation of the Rowell-Sirois Commission for more comprehensive and consistent statistics of public finance was a reflection of peacetime needs, but its rationale was greatly strengthened by those of the war effort and the reconstruction that would follow. As noted earlier, the commission had been obliged to develop by itself most of the statistical material on which its substantive recommendations were based.

As the war progressed, the statistical needs of those responsible for war taxation, debt management, and so on tended to be met by piecemeal updating of the Rowell-Sirois data. By agreement with the user community, the bureau's Public Finance Branch concentrated on the task of developing a sound statistical foundation for Dominion/provincial cooperation in postwar reconstruction by bringing its statistics of public finance for all three levels of government into line with the recommendations of the commission. A notable milestone in this work was the Dominion/provincial Conference on Provincial Financial Statistics of October 1943.

In the area of national income, the bureau was again unable to respond to user demands. It had ceased publication of annual estimates with those of 1934 and, at the outbreak of war, was engaged in the preparation of new historical estimates on the basis of what it represented as a substantially improved methodology. When these appeared in 1941, however, they did not make the desired impression on the user community, which continued to rely, as in the case of public finance statistics, on extrapolations of material prepared for the Rowell-Sirois Commission. Only later in the war was the bureau able to make a fresh start in the area, in effect discarding the 1941 study and using an approach consistent with that of its counterparts in the US and the UK.[15]

However, in another dimension of war finance the bureau was able to be of much greater service, and the operation of wartime controls made possible a considerable improvement in the related statistics. In the immediate pre-war years, the Internal Trade Statistics Branch had made steady progress in developing new data sources for the balance of international payments, thus reducing the dependence of this statistic on estimates. In 1939 a special report was published, *The Canadian Balance of International Payments – A Study of Methods and Results*,[16] which described the improvements in methodology and provided a great deal of new statistical information.

Thus, when the Foreign Exchange Control Board was established at the outbreak of war, the bureau's facilities and expertise in this area were soon called upon to assist in monitoring trends in the balance of payments, capital movements, etc. C.D. Blyth, the officer in charge, was seconded to the board along with other staff to assist in drawing up the forms and schedules for its administrative controls, and subsequently to ensure that effective statistical use was made of the information they generated. The cooperation of other interested departments was secured by the formation of an interdepartmental committee, and this gave rise to two important developments.

First, the basis of valuation for both exports and imports was changed to reflect the actual monetary value of transactions. Second, there was a considerable improvement in the coverage and quality of tourism statistics. The work of compilation, hitherto carried on at customs ports, was transferred to the bureau, where a new section was set up to handle it. Methods of securing samples of tourist expenditures were also improved. By the end of the war, the comprehensive synthesis of primary statistical series represented by the balance of payments had definitively established the first subsystem of the macroeconomic framework that eventually became the System of National Accounts.

The Bureau's Publications

As the government's major publisher, the bureau encountered special difficulties. At an early stage in the war, prohibitions were placed on the public distribution of information relating to the production, export, and import of strategic materials. This was with the bureau's willing concurrence; indeed, the initiative came from the bureau itself. Censorship was the responsibility of a directorate within the Department of National Defence, and in a memorandum of 17 September 1939, the director, Colonel Maurice Pope, reported on a conversation with Coats as follows: "When a few days ago the weekly report on grain supplies was about to be issued, it had occurred to him that it might not now be in the public interest to publish anything ... [this was] but one of a great number with respect to which it would now possibly be in the public interest to observe a certain measure of reticence."[17] Subsequently, a Censorship Advisory Committee on Statistical Publications was formed, and it had held nine meetings by mid-1944. Its work was not always prohibitory; as the war progressed, a number of the earlier restrictions were relaxed.

The most serious threat to the bureau's publications emerged in August 1942 when a Directorate of Government Office Economies Control was established under the minister of War Services.[18] It was given overriding power to examine and approve or reject all requisitions for office supplies, furniture and equipment, and printing. As far as the first two of these targets was concerned, the bureau dutifully toed the line: "Under the existing conditions, drastic economy should be observed in the purchase of supplies for government offices, and all waste should be eliminated ... The Order in Council [PC 4428] deserves the support of all patriotic citizens and has been wholeheartedly carried out in the Bureau."[19] A typical example of the directorate in action was the memorandum of 2 October 1942 from the director, Colonel John Thompson, to "all Departments, Commissions and Boards," stipulating that "in future, no erasers will be issued unless one is turned in for each eraser indented for."[20]

But printing was a different matter. The Statistics Act required the bureau to publish and it saw this obligation as having been enhanced rather than diminished by wartime conditions. Hitherto, the only constraint on its freedom to publish had been the budgetary powers of the Treasury Board. Now the prospect of interference by what it called "an external authority that is not fully acquainted with the obligations of the Bureau to the Government of Canada and to the general public"[21] was seen as a serious threat. Rota-printed and mimeographic reports that were prepared by the bureau itself were not affected; what were at risk were the formal print publications that had to be requisitioned from the King's Printer.

By trimming the list of such publications and shortening their print runs, the bureau, on its own initiative, had reduced the related printing costs to half the 1939–40 level by the time its budgetary plans for 1943-44 were finalized. This was perhaps less of a sacrifice than the bureau might have cared to admit since, as the war progressed, it made proportionally greater use of its own reproduction facilities to minimize delays in the provision of reports to its governmental clientele. It correctly judged, however, that little credit would be given for its own attempts to economize, and it took the line that, like the War Information Bureau, it should have been exempted right from the start from the provisions of PC 4428 as regards printing.

Early in November 1942, Cudmore, now the Dominion statistician, decided that, rather than submitting each individual publication to Thompson as it was compiled, it would be better to obtain his views on the entire publication program for the balance of the fiscal year. Accordingly, a list of twenty-four publications was submitted in the expectation that this would be the prelude to a serious assessment of individual merits and relative priorities. Within days, however, the entire list was returned with the dismissive comment that "the following are not to be printed during the War."[22]

An appeal mechanism was available in the form of an Advisory Committee on Government Office Economies Control, chaired by the auditor general, Watson Sellar, but the bureau was not notably successful with the cases it put forward. In 1941–42, the year before PC 4428 came into force, fifty print publications (mostly annuals) had been issued. In 1942-43, the figure fell to thirty-seven, and in 1943–44 to nineteen. The *Canada Year Book* for 1943 was a casualty but a combined 1943–44 edition was approved, so that continuity did not suffer.

The bureau's outstanding success was in saving the Canada handbook. When it became known early in March 1943 that Thompson's decision to cancel it for the duration of the war had been overturned by Finance minister J.L. Ilsley, the *Ottawa Journal* of 4 March 1943 reported the story with headlines such as: "'Crazy Waste' Stymies Economy Director," "Thompson Charges Work is Hampered," and "'Evasions, Subterfuge and Trickery' Are Being Used." Cudmore wrote to the minister the next day to set the record straight. After an explanation of Thompson's summary action in cancelling the handbook ("no reasons were given, nor were we invited to present our case"), he recounted everything that had been done for the appeal process to provide information on costs and sales of the handbook, its users, and uses and concluded that "under these circumstances, since the information must have been available to Colonel Thompson, it is most difficult to understand how such distortion of the actual facts could have found their way into print."[23]

The handbook had been the bureau's best-selling publication before the war, with 26,000 copies of the English edition and 4,000 copies of the French edition printed in 1938. Its popularity increased greatly after 1939 because of its value as a morale booster on the home front – largely through school distribution – and as a propaganda tool abroad. These new demands reached their peak just as Colonel Thompson's veto was imposed, but even though this was successfully appealed there were still difficulties in printing sufficient copies to meet them. The Royal Air Force had been provided with a special edition of *Canada 1942* for distribution in England to trainees about to come to Canada under the British Commonwealth Air Training Plan, and it put in a further order for 5,000 copies of *Canada 1943*. The War Information Board also asked for 7,000 copies of the latter for use by its Washington office. And because of the stepped-up interest in trade with Latin America, special Spanish and Portuguese editions were requested by the Trade Commissioner Service.

These and other problems were generally resolved by pressures from the client departments. As a parting shot with regard to the handbook, Thompson's office persuaded the Treasury Board to insist on an austerity version of *Canada 1944*, but in February 1944 Cudmore successfully argued with the minister, Hon. J.A. MacKinnon, for a restoration of the higher standard for *Canada 1945*.

Questionnaire Nuisance

An earlier instance of attempted interference with the bureau's work had occurred in September 1940, when Hon. J.L. Ilsley, minister of Finance, wrote to Coats asking him to prepare "a report showing the various information returns now required by city, provincial and Dominion authorities across Canada, and the possibility, through combination of these reports, of eliminating the cost of compliance and saving time to those who must comply with these requirements."[24] Coats's response a few days later, based upon an extensive memorandum from Cudmore, firmly fended off what would have been a monumental task: "A detailed report on this subject would be a very considerable undertaking ... In view of the governmental pressures of work on the thinking staff of this Bureau, at a time when the National Registration is in hand, the decennial census in the offing, and various branches of the Bureau are under pressure for special compilations relative to Canada's war effort, I doubt whether it is feasible to prepare a detailed report at the present time. The fact, however, is that we are all the time at work on this problem."[25]

The message was driven home by a typical Coats lecture. The great expansion of statistics in the previous quarter century had resulted from the wider functions undertaken by governments. After the passage of the War Measures Act, statistical needs could not possibly be reduced. The best way to collect information with the minimum of inconvenience to individuals and businesses was through the operation of a system of statistical centralization that would reduce overlapping and unnecessary questionnaires. And so on. There is no record of Ilsley having returned for a second dose of this treatment.

The 1941 Census

In spite of the many, frequently onerous, responsibilities assumed by the bureau in response to wartime pressures, the 1941 census was still its biggest undertaking during those years and probably its most important contribution to the war effort. In the early months of the war, however, there had been some concern that the government might consider cancelling the census on the grounds of wartime economy. A contingency memorandum prepared for Coats's possible use with the minister[26] outlined the consequences of not proceeding with the census and pointed out that, in the gravest months of the First World War, there had been no thought of cancelling the 1916 census of the Prairie provinces. Finally, it warned that, while the government could legitimately cancel the census under its wartime powers, the action would constitute a threat to the stability of Confederation.

These concerns appear to have been without foundation. Only minor savings would have resulted from cancellation[27] and could not have outweighed the benefits of being able to assess the social and economic effects of the most severe depression in Canadian history and of two years of mobilization for war. In the event, the census was planned and carried out much as it had been a decade earlier. The most visible indication of wartime exigencies was that the beginning of enumeration was put off for nine days in order to avoid a public conflict with the launching of the first Victory Loan.

The main determinant of the content of the 1941 census was the need for comparability with those of 1931 and 1921. Even so, there were some important changes. Hardly any of these were direct responses to the needs of the wartime departments and agencies, which were more interested in the speedy tabulation of standard information than the provision of new information. However, the justification for some changes was reinforced by wartime circumstances. Thus, the new residence questions had originally been designed to measure the internal migration that had taken place during the 1930s as large numbers of people moved from one end of the country to the other.[28] These shifts of population continued unabated during the war.

It was clear that a postwar housing policy would be needed to deal with the major population shifts of the 1930s. Accordingly, the "Description of Home" questions on the population schedule were supplemented by a census of housing, which sought more extensive information on the nature of the dwelling, its facilities, tenure, rents, values, mortgages, etc. For comparative purposes, it was directly modelled on that taken by the United States a year earlier. The schedule, which was addressed to every tenth household, was the first use of sampling by the census.[29]

The other major innovation in 1941 was the inclusion of questions on fertility – a topic considered to be too sensitive for the 1921 and 1931 censuses. Two reasons were cited for the inquiry:

a) The Vital Statistics now published annually have covered the nine provinces only since 1926. It was felt that it would be most desirable to secure some information on fertility rates over a longer period.
b) While the birth registration procedure requires the filling out of a detailed form, it cannot secure all of the information available on the census schedule. By incorporating the special inquiries on fertility with the general Population Schedule it was possible to relate fertility to earnings, schooling and other significant characteristics of the family.[30]

The census was launched with a vigorous publicity campaign that stressed the theme of patriotic responsibility: "Accuracy and despatch in your replies will promote good administration in your country, now under stress of war and facing crucial post-war reconstruction."[31] The assurances of confidentiality covered immunity not only from the traditional bogies of tax collectors and courts of law but also from the military authorities. When it came to the collection of results, the deferment of the date of the census delayed matters, and there were difficulties in recruiting and retaining qualified enumerators. When the returns arrived in Ottawa, the application of the *de jure* residence principle was more difficult than in previous censuses. The records of an unusually large number of civilians, temporarily absent from home at the date of the census, had to be transferred to their usual place of residence. Again, the names and census information of approximately 70,000 persons on active service at the census date and not enumerated in the normal fashion had to be obtained from the Defence department and added to the schedules. These were largely workload problems, but they were aggravated by the lower quality of wartime staff.

However, improvements in the bureau's machine facilities made possible the output of a wider range of census information than in any previous census, and with greater expedition. These facilities were still in the inventive hands of Thornton and Bélisle. The census administrative report, after recalling their contribution to earlier censuses, noted their most recent achievement as "the adaptation ... of the 1931 electrically operated equipment to compressed air. This change eliminated many of the difficulties which had been encountered through the use of heavy current in the electric machine."[32]

Wartime urgency made it imperative to circumvent the delays involved in the composition and printing of entire final volumes. This was achieved through an extended program of some 280 individual bulletins – more than for any census in the past. Organized under the broad headings of population, agriculture, housing, and merchandising and service establishments, they were available to users free of charge and most had been issued before the war's end. Meanwhile, the 1943–44 and 1945 editions of the *Canada Year Book* provided summaries of the various sections of the census. During the closing months of the war, two of the eleven planned volumes of the final report appeared, and the rest followed during the next two years. A planned twelfth volume was to comprise "a series of special studies and monographs based upon the interpretation of the preceding volumes of the census report as well as of previous censuses."[33] Unfortunately it was not possible to proceed with the scheme as originally planned, but one important monograph, *The Changing Size of the Family in Canada* by Dr Enid Charles, was eventually published in 1948.

The administrative report properly gave credit to the key individuals who, working under far from ideal conditions, had made the 1941 census an unqualified success. But there was a poignancy about some of the acknowledgments, marking as they did the departure of the bureau's "old guard." First and foremost among these was Coats himself, whose vision and leadership had laid the foundation of modern census taking in Canada, and who had retired in 1942. He was followed as Dominion statistician by Cudmore, who thus assumed responsibility for tabulating and publishing the results of the census. But Cudmore died suddenly in October 1945, and the administrative report, formally submitted on 21 November 1945, had to be signed by his successor, Herbert Marshall.

A.J. Pelletier, who had worked with Coats's predecessor, Archibald Blue, and who followed E.S. Macphail as chief of the Census Branch, had retired in October 1944. His long career had concluded with a two-year secondment to the Government of Jamaica, during which he supervised the taking of the Jamaican census in January 1943. The planning of the 1941 census owed much to M.C. MacLean, one of Coats's early recruits to the bureau and chief of the Social Analysis Branch since the mid-1930s. MacLean, however, had died accidentally in 1940 and his work on the 1941 census was ably carried forward by A.L. Neal, his successor as chief of the branch. Associated with Neal were Nathan Keyfitz, who later established himself as an international authority on demography, and Enid Charles, who had been brought to the bureau in 1942 to analyze the information gathered on fertility.[34]

Honours for Wartime Services

After the war, personal contributions to the war effort by bureau staff were recognized in a public service honours list.[35] At that time Canadian honours were still part of the British system, and while Canadians were no longer allowed to accept titles, lesser awards were open to them. Herbert Marshall was appointed Officer of the Order of the British Empire, while C.D. Blyth, H.F. Greenway, O.A. Lemieux, and M.E.K. Roughsedge were made Members of the Order. Marshall and Blyth had toiled mightily for the Wartime Prices and Trade Board and the Foreign Exchange Control Board respectively; the others had contributed in their own subject-matter areas. While the honours were ostensibly personal, their levels nevertheless appear to have reflected the relative standing of the bureau in the governmental pecking order. For instance, among the colleagues who had worked with Marshall and Blyth on the two boards but who enjoyed a more prestigious departmental or academic pedigree, there were several appointments as Commander of the Order of the British Empire, and at least one as Commander of the grander Order of St Michael and St George.

National Income Estimates

The bureau's work on estimates of national income made no contribution to the statistical needs of the war economy, largely because of its persistent adherence to methods that did not command the confidence of potential users in the Bank of Canada and the Department of Finance. The work had been mostly in abeyance since 1937 or so, but beginning in 1939 there was a major revision and updating of its interwar estimates in which, following the lead of MacGregor's work for the Rowell-Sirois Commission, it switched from a methodology based on income produced to one based on income received.

Cudmore set up a Committee on National Income Statistics and persuaded three xternal representatives to serve on it – J.J. Deutsch of the Bank of Canada, R.B. Bryce of Finance, and Professor MacGregor. Sydney B. Smith, the bureau fficer responsible for national income, prepared a memorandum on the scope of the enquiry and the methods of approach for consideration at the committee's irst meeting.

In transmitting the Smith memorandum to the committee members, Cudmore oted that:

> there are in different countries various avenues of approach to the measurement of the national income, the methods employed depending mainly upon the quantity and the quality of the available statistics. Thus in the United Kingdom and Germany, chief reliance is placed upon the amount of income coming under the cognizance of the income tax authorities ...
>
> In the United States, on the other hand, the availability of excellent statistics of production and of the distribution of incomes resulting from production has led to the use of other methods of approach. Thus, studies of national income and its distribution are now published annually by the Department of Commerce (income produced and paid out) and by the National Bureau of Economic Research (aggregate income payments and accruals) ...
>
> For Canada, where the statistics available are roughly comparable with those of the United States, it has seemed desirable, after making an exhaustive study of the methods used in various countries ... to follow, as far as possible, United States methods, as exemplified in the publications of the National Bureau of Economic Research and the Department of Commerce.[36]

Cudmore went on to describe Simon Kuznets as the outstanding North American worker in this field and referred glowingly to his *National Income and Capital Formation, 1919-1935*, published in 1937. This study, which became the dominant influence on the bureau's work during the next two years, incorporated the simpler view of the contribution of government to national income that the Rowell-Sirois study had endeavoured to transcend. Essentially, it equated the value of government services with the taxes raised for their financing. Ironically, later work by Kuznets indicates that he modified his position to take account of the changing role and fiscal practices of government in consequence of New Deal economic and social policies.

The subsequent meeting of the Committee on National Income Statistics held on 14 November 1939 did not challenge the approach proposed by Cudmore. One reason may have been that Deutsch, the lead hand in the Rowell-Sirois study and thereafter the severest critic of the bureau's work, was not present. The minutes quoted Smith as referring quite explicitly to "the differences between the forthcoming report of the Rowell Commission dealing with National Income and the Bureau study," but even so, it was resolved that "the Committee after study generally approves the memorandum on National Income – its scope of enquiry and methods of approach – as prepared by Sydney B. Smith."[37]

The committee next met some seven months later, on 27 June 1940. Again Deutsch was unable to attend. Like those of the first meeting, the minutes[38] mostly reported technical discussions on data sources and possible procedures including the suggestion that additional questions might be asked in the 1941 census to secure information on incomes by income groups and small geographic areas. Alternatively, it was suggested that the regular income tax records and those of the new national defence tax be explored as cheaper and more frequent sources of the same information. However, it was also recorded that Smith provided a summary and analysis of the general results of the bureau's study covering the years 1919 to 1938. No material had been distributed in advance and the only reaction it produced was a resolution that work notes for the study should be prepared for confidential circulation among members.

Early in 1941 Smith had completed part one of *National Income of Canada, 1919–1938*[39] and sent it to committee members in anticipation of a meeting. Apparently he received only two written responses, the first of which was from his colleague, Neal, who began: "The purpose of this report is stated to be as follows: 'The object of the present report is to provide one clearly defined and clearly labelled estimate of national income for common use.' It seems to me unfortunate that one had to read through 124 pages of text, tables and graphs ... most of which deal with various relationships and analysis of national income rather than the construction of the estimate itself, before reaching this statement of objectives."[40]

He found the analysis, when not merely superficial, to be questionable or sometimes completely erroneous. The main thrust of his criticism, however was that the report provided little or no explanation of how the estimates had been constructed. For example, Smith had written at one point that "owing to lack of sufficient data, totals were made up to a certain extent by estimating and interpretation should be qualified accordingly."[41] Neal commented that "if we knew the basis of estimation, we would know how to qualify the interpretation. When this information is lacking, the warning to qualify is of little value." He concluded with the following observation: "It is stated on page 128 that one of the merits of the Sirois Commission Report was the thorough explanation of the method. It is regrettable that the example was not followed in the present report."[42]

On 28 April Deutsch sent Cudmore a copy of the comments he had prepared. Like Neal, he criticized the format of the report, its failure to describe source materials and methods, and apparent errors in specific estimates. His main target, however, was what he called "faulty concepts of income and inaccuracies of method," focusing particularly on the bureau's treatment of income produced by governments. It had been obtained, he said, from "the sum of government payments for interest (net), salaries, wages, pensions, relief, military pay and allowances, public welfare services, plus increase in productive assets less new government borrowings." His assessment was that "this hodge-podge is both meaningless and misleading. The net effect of these calculations is to say that income produced by governments is equal to the total amount of taxes collected less government purchases. The inconsistencies which result from this assumption are obvious. If the government chose to pay for the war wholly out of taxes, the government contribution to the national income would rise precisely by the amount of the war expenditures. If, on the other hand, all the required funds were borrowed, war expenditures would have no effect on the national income, regardless of the amount of such expenditures."[43]

Deutsch concluded with some proposals for the future. Knowledge of the magnitude and fluctuations of the national income, and of its composition and distribution, was important at any time but absolutely indispensable in times of war. Consequently, "the preparation of reliable estimates of the national income should be the most important item in the statistical investigations undertaken by the government." But the outlook was bleak: "The estimates of national income which have just been completed by the Bureau of Statistics are unsatisfactory and cannot be corrected without a major operation; one which would constitute virtually a new start. The study prepared for the Royal Commission on Dominion-Provincial Relations is now almost ancient history. It can no longer be extended from one year to another on the basis of piece-meal projections."[44] Therefore, in Deutsch's view, it was urgent that the estimation of national income be put on a sound and permanent footing as soon as possible.

A first essential was to get someone to take charge of the work with "a thorough background in economic theory and ... a wide knowledge of *Canadian* economic organization and economic conditions."[45] Even so, it was important that the work should still be carried on in the bureau, which already had, or could collect, the necessary statistics. The practical work should proceed with the minimum of duplication and wastage of money. In this connection, he thought it vital that information acquired by the income tax authorities be made available so as to determine the distribution of income by sizes, and to estimate such magnitudes as property income received by individuals, incomes received in the service industries, total income by province, and monthly estimates of changes in the national income.

Predictably, the meeting of the Committee on National Income Statistics that took place on 16 June did not go well. Nothing had been done to follow up the suggestion of the previous meeting regarding the use of income tax records, and Smith continued to defend the Kuznets methodology despite criticisms of its inability to accommodate the new reality of massive deficit financing.

The discussion of alternative methodologies prompted the following suggestion from MacGregor: "The Dominion Bureau of Statistics should not attempt to publish a national income figure at all but rather publish the concepts which should be rearranged to produce various estimates for various purposes, and regard that as its main contribution. It may be necessary to become arbitrary. The Bureau might in addition give some account of the various ways in which the basic material may be employed and the purpose to which this may be directed, and I doubt whether it can go very much further. It is not like a population figure."[46]

This elicited no response at the meeting, but it was reminiscent of MacGregor's earlier scepticism about the bureau's ability to engage in research and analytical work.

Smith's obvious rigidities did not help him at this meeting, but it is difficult not to sympathize with his discomfort. The external members of the committee had known for almost two years how, for better or worse, he intended to proceed, so that whether able to attend earlier meetings or not, they could presumably have found some way to intervene constructively at an earlier stage and avoid a confrontation. The resolution that followed, however, was somewhat muted: "The Committee feels that the methods used in estimating income produced by governments could be improved, and should be clarified in the report for publication."[47] More bluntly, it was resolved that the report's distribution of income by provinces was not acceptable.

Shortly after the meeting, Cudmore sent Coats the following assessment of its outcome: "The Committee had little to say in criticism of our estimate of national income produced, except in connection with our estimate of national income produced by governments. Their criticism in this field was practically confined to the assertion that our method of estimating such income would not work well in wartime."[48] He suggested that a modified version of Smith's report could be published – one embodying some of the procedural explanations recommended by the committee and excluding for the time being the provincial breakdowns. Coats at this time was six months away from retirement, and Cudmore, in not explaining the gravity of the issue, may simply have been reluctant to alarm him about matters that could not be resolved during his remaining tenure.

In any case, Coats perhaps did not have a profound understanding of the subject. R.G. Bangs, Smith's assistant, told Bryce that the unsatisfactory nature of the national income report could be attributed to Coats, who had told Smith to give it a more or less popular and general character and not to provide too much information on how he got his figures. Bryce said he got the impression from Bangs that "Coats has not taken too much interest in the national income work and, in fact, did not understand very much about it."[49] Cudmore, on the other hand, probably understood the problem well enough, but, as he later wrote to L.D. Wilgress, the deputy minister of Trade and Commerce, "the guiding thought behind my attitude in the question is my strong reluctance to allow a great deal of good work which has been done in the past to go into the discard because of its rather inadequate presentation."[50]

In the months following the June 1941 meeting, Bangs worked diligently at following up its recommendations. In May 1942 Bryce wrote to him that, "in general, I think this material that you have sent me is a very great improvement over the report which Mr Smith prepared last year."[51] Cudmore was also monitoring his progress and had written three months earlier that "when [new totals] are prepared, I think the presentation then may well stand as the definitive presentation of the national income for the interwar period from 1919 to 1938." But, he said, "that statement ... does not mean that further changes and improvements will not be possible with the further development of our statistical system."[52] Meanwhile, the Bank of Canada continued to prepare independent estimates of the national income based largely on the Rowell-Sirois methodology and monitored the developments that were taking place in Great Britain and the United States under the influence of Keynesian thinking.

Deutsch and Bryce had also provided Clark, the deputy minister of Finance, with their own assessment of the situation at the bureau,[53] repeating Bryce's earlier suggestion that a special branch, headed by a person of superior qualifications, be set up in the bureau to take charge of the work on national income. Bryce came back to the issue a few months later, putting the national income issue in a broader context. Echoing MacGregor's earlier criticisms, he advised Clark that:

> the state of the national income statistics is really symptomatic of a more fundamental weakness in our statistical and economic information. Broadly speaking, our statistical system is based on Dr Coats' work in the 1920s, when the main purposes were to inform businessmen and the public what was happening in particular fields, to provide certain standard statistics of population, agriculture and business–not very much interrelated or integrated. This was somewhat modified and patched up in the 1930s with some new figures added, but not fundamentally altered.
>
> I think the time has come, or is rapidly approaching, when the whole system should be reviewed and overhauled to fit it for the far different world of the 1940s – both war and aftermath.[54]

Graham Towers was making similar representations on behalf of the Bank of Canada, and in April he met with Clark and Wilgress as well as Cudmore, Bryce, Deutsch, and other departmental representatives, including Fraser Elliott of the Income Tax Division.[55] Bryce furnished Clark with a briefing note before the meeting[56] and also wrote up its proceedings.[57] The Kuznets methodology, in spite of the criticisms, was not rejected outright. It was thought that the issue should be resolved by the experts who would be responsible for reorienting the work. The most urgent task was to secure the necessary basic information regardless of what methodology might be adopted. In this connection, there was an apparent breakthrough in the matter of access to income tax data. Elliott expressed himself as "glad to co-operate fully in providing all the information that could be usefully obtained from the income tax material."[58]

A new and more broadly based interdepartmental committee was proposed to oversee the bureau's continuing work on national income. Cudmore acquiesced in this but was more hesitant on the matter of setting up a special unit in the bureau for national income. He was apparently overridden, for, shortly after, Wilgress began the search for a candidate to head up the national income work. However, during a period stretching well into 1943, one effort after another came to naught. At different times, Deutsch, C.D. Blyth (at that time seconded from the bureau to work with the Foreign Exchange Control Board), and Walter Duffett were in the running, but each was found to be indispensable in his current assignment. When a breakthrough finally occurred early in 1944 under circumstances to be described in the next chapter, it was the relatively junior George Luxton of the Bank of Canada who was appointed chief of the bureau's newly established Central Research and Development Staff. He was given responsibility for a complete reorganization of the work on national income statistics in accordance with the new Anglo-American concepts he had been working with at the bank under Deutsch's guidance.

In the meantime, the bureau continued to prepare and publish national income estimates. Although the estimates were modified following the June 1941 meeting, Smith remained faithful to the Kuznets methodology, with no acknowledgment of the new approach being applied by Luxton to Canadian data. The 1943–44 edition of the *Canada Year Book* provided a definition of national income identical with that of the 1941 report.[59] The 1945 edition offered the same definition but noted that "methods and concepts of national income estimation are under extensive revision at the present time. This work is in the hands of the Bureau's new Central Planning and Development Staff."[60] In the 1946 edition, none of Smith's estimates were provided and all references to the Kuznets methodology had disappeared. Instead, there was a description of the new national accounting approach and its component elements of gross national product and expenditure at market prices, net national income at factor cost, and income payments to individuals.[61]

Coats Steps Down as Dominion Statistician

In July 1939 Coats had reached the age of sixty-five. During almost a quarter century as Dominion statistician, he had conceived and planned a central statistical system for Canada, established it organizationally, and developed its programs. The bureau's impact on public and private affairs had made him a household name in his own country, and he was regarded internationally as a leader in his profession. He had received doctorates of law from McGill in 1934, the University of Toronto in 1937, and Dalhousie University in 1938 and had served as president of the Canadian Political Science Association in 1936[62]–the first statistician to do so–and as the first Canadian president of the American Statistical Association in 1938.[63]

He would normally have been required to retire at this time but, with war clouds on the horizon, he was persuaded to accept a year's extension and, after that, another. Finally, in mid-1941, after leading the bureau through two difficult years that culminated in the successful launching of the 1941 census, he insisted that there must be no further delay in replacing him. As he put it in his retirement speech, "I don't believe in hanging on to a job by the eyebrows."[64]

It was finally agreed that he should serve for another six months, and he therefore retired from active duty on 25 January 1942 after more than twenty-six years as Dominion statistician, five days short of the fortieth anniversary of his appointment to the Department of Labour under Mackenzie King. In recognition of this impressive record of public service, he was designated Dominion statistician emeritus, to take effect after six months retirement leave. S.A. Cudmore was simultaneously appointed acting Dominion statistician. He had been Coats's principal lieutenant for many years and, as assistant Dominion statistician since 1939, was virtually the heir apparent, even though, at sixty-three, he was himself close to retirement age. When his appointment as Dominion statistician occurred in the following April, Herbert Marshall, the next ranking bureau officer, was named as assistant Dominion statistician.

Coats's retirement party was a family affair, exemplifying the camaraderie that he had developed with all levels of his staff during their long association.[65] On their behalf Cudmore presented Coats with a thirteen volume set of the *Oxford English Dictionary* and, befitting his classical education, made a speech replete with literary references. Coats, although himself a classicist, chose to reply in a lighter vein. The dictionary was, he said, a clear hint from his colleagues that, now that he was going out into the world, he should learn to spell before it was too late. Speculating about his future plans, he said the idea of military service had occurred to him: "Having quarrelled and scratched and bit and gouged with Treasury Boards and Civil Service Commissions and so on, I should be good for the very front firing line."[66] A number of the old hands also paid him their tribute, including the dean of them all, Colonel J.R. Munro, chief of the Public Finance Branch, who had made his debut in statistics as secretary to George Johnson in the 1890s and, in earlier service as a page boy in the House of Commons, had heard the announcement of the death of Sir John A. MacDonald.

The Valedictory

Coats left behind not only a mature organization with a formidable record of achievement but also a blueprint for further changes in its structure and programs. In mid-1941, he had urged that "there should be a review of the present position of the Bureau in view of the heavy demands on it which the war has already made and which the post-war period will accentuate. I have a report in process which I will be glad to leave as a 'last will and testament.'"[67] This was what came to be known as Coats's "Valedictory Report," a 111-page typescript with copious appendices. It was divided into two parts, the first dealing with constitutional and administrative machinery, and the second addressing the various statistical programs.[68]

Dominating the former heading was the issue of the bureau's status, which had bedevilled Coats ever since he had lost the understanding and support of Sir George Foster twenty years earlier. As an immediate measure lying within the minister's powers, he proposed a regulation under section 7 of the Statistics Act to give the Dominion statistician powers of staff administration consistent with the bureau's professional independence. This was to be followed as soon as possible by an amendment to the act conferring upon the Dominion statistician "the rights and privileges of a deputy head of a department, so far as regards matters relating to or arising out of the administration of this Act," or, alternatively, designating him as "the officer of the Government in all matters arising out of the administration of this Act."[69]

A point that Coats had not previously made in relation to the bureau's status was the requirement for appropriate accommodation. He noted that the Edwards Mill was ultimately to be demolished as part of the Ottawa Improvement Plan and urged that the bureau's special needs be made part of the general building program; "to house the Bureau in an ordinary departmental 'block' is an unsuitable arrangement." He cited a report made some years earlier by the International Statistical Institute, setting out the specifications for the type of building required for a central statistical office. These featured "a central 'main' section for administrative and central services with a series of radiating wings that can be extended as the work expands."[70]

A second general concern was the inadequacy of the machinery for consultation with the provinces. As described earlier, the procedure developed for coordinating the statistics derived as by-products of their administrative activities had involved the drafting of proposals by the bureau and their discussion with each province in turn, followed by Dominion/provincial conferences to iron out difficulties and formalize the arrangements agreed upon. This had made possible early successes in the areas of vital and education statistics and had also been used, in the 1930s, to begin the work of coordinating statistics of provincial and municipal finance. Arrangements had also been developed with provincial departments of agriculture, fisheries, mining, etc. and their Dominion counterparts for the cooperative production of a broad range of economic statistics. These had generally been ratified by Order in Council under the provisions of PC 2503 of 12 October 1918.

But little had been done to keep these agreements up to date. "In every year or oftener," Coats wrote, "one or more of the several fields embraced require full-dress review, as new statistics or modifications in existing statistics become necessary. At present such discussions may be arranged *ad hoc*, but in practice they tend to be intermittent and infrequent." Coats therefore proposed that the Statistics Act be amended to require that a conference of Dominion and provincial officials be held at least once a year to review on a rotating basis the arrangements in the various subject-matter branches involving Dominion and provincial cooperation, and to advise on any new arrangements that might seem necessary. This, he argued, "would systematize what now tends to be sporadic."[71] The proposal was clearly addressed to the need for rectifying the statistical deficiencies that had become evident when the Rowell-Sirois Commission began its work in 1937. Coats also observed that the centralization of responsibility for statistics within each province would contribute to more effective Dominion/provincial cooperation in statistics,[72] and suggested that the bureau should put in place regional branches.

Coats underscored these points by proposing a broadening of the bureau's mandate statement. The overall coordination of the statistical system was at that time addressed in the Statistics Act through an injunction to "collaborate with all other departments of the Government in the compilation and publication of statistical records of administration." His new draft act, set out in appendix 1 of the "Valedictory Report," added to this a requirement "generally to organize a co-ordinated scheme of social and economic statistics and intelligence pertaining to the whole of Canada and to each of the several Provinces thereof."[73]

The third cross-cutting issue dealt with in Coats's "Valedictory Report" was the bureau's role in economic and social research. A quarter century earlier, in "A National System of Statistics for Canada," he had sketched out a role for the bureau as "a national 'laboratory' for the observation and interpretation of current economic trends." Since that time, two branches had been developed for the analysis and interpretation of statistics, namely, the Social Analysis Branch, which dealt mainly with census data, and the Industrial Research Branch, which drew upon production, trade, and general economic statistics. These branches had certainly not had the public impact that Coats might have wished for them.

As described earlier, there had been a number of efforts during the 1930s– largely ineffective – to extend this kind of work and to give it a higher public profile. Coats now proposed the following addition to the Statistics Act: "There shall be an Institute of Statistical Research, of which the Dominion Statistician shall be Director, and for the administration of which the Minister may appoint an honorary advisory committee whose duties shall be ... to keep under advisement the relations of the Bureau to social and economic research; to recommend special statistical investigations to be undertaken from time to time; and generally to advise as to the organization of statistics as basic data for research purposes."[74]

This proposal revived Coats's well-worn recommendation for an advisory committee, but rather than addressing the general aspects of the bureau's management, it now focused exclusively on professional questions–much as the terms of reference of the defunct Economic Council of Canada had done. The membership of the committee was to be drawn in part from existing research bodies, including the government's Advisory Committee on Economic Policy, and the president and secretary of the National Research Council and the Social Science Research Council respectively.

In summarizing this first part of the "Valedictory Report," Coats wrote that "the main need is for final clarification of the place of our national statistical system in the general scheme of government, i.e., as the central statistical agency for the several Dominion Departments and for the government as a whole; as the gauge and measurement of provincial activities; and as representing the inductive approach in the study of national problems of a social and economic character. A good deal of basic organization has already been provided, but it requires to be completed and placed in a position that enables it to be fully recognized and developed. This its present administrative status and machinery does not realize."[75]

The major part of the "Valedictory Report," however, was a review of the history and achievements of the bureau's various statistical programs and an identification of what further work was needed, either to complete the blueprint of a quarter of a century earlier, or to refine and extend it in response to newer needs. This material was essentially an updating of a similar review prepared for the 1935 Commonwealth Statisticians Conference.[76]

The Years of Retirement

Coats enjoyed eighteen years of retirement before his death in February 1960 in his eighty-sixth year at his home in Rockcliffe Park. His first wife, Marie-Josephine Halboister, had died in 1938, and in 1942 he married his former secretary, Maida Skelly, who survived him. He remained active professionally for several years. One of his first postretirement tasks was to complete a study, *The American-born in Canada*, originally begun by M.C. Maclean before his accidental death in 1940. It was published under their two names in 1943.[77] Always at ease with the academic community, he served during 1942-43 as special lecturer in the Department of Political Economy at the University of Toronto and was visiting professor of Statistics there from 1943 to 1946. His article, "Beginnings in Canadian Statistics,"[78] was written as a lecture for the university's graduating class in economics in 1946. During this period he also served as president of Section Two of the Royal Society of Canada[79] and as treasurer of the Inter-American Statistical Institute from 1942 to 1947. He worked for the new Food and Agriculture Organization for a short while until 1947, when heart trouble forced him to give it up.

Coats kept in constant touch with his former colleagues. On the occasion of his eighty-third birthday some fifteen years after his retirement, a number of them sent him a bottle of Scotch, and he wrote a witty letter of thanks recalling early associations.[80] Only a few weeks before his death he wrote to his friend of long standing, Nathan Keyfitz, quoting George Bernard Shaw's aphorism that "every man over forty is a scoundrel," and asking what then of people like himself who were over eighty.[81]

In 1961 Nathan Keyfitz and Harold Greenway published "a first attempt to sum up his effort and achievement." They described his special contribution to official statistics in Canada as follows: "Coats did more than produce data and encourage the use of good techniques on their interpretation; he stressed again and again a different and no less important condition of statistics to the community: the impartiality and disinterestedness of the statistician, his independence of people's wishes and interests, even those of his own employer ... partly as a result of Coats' work, both the trustworthiness of statistics and technical standards have advanced, through an increasing professionalization of the field, [and] the increasing and wholesome tendency of statisticians to look to their fellow statisticians rather than to their employers for approval and criticism of their methods."[82] The article provided a bibliography of twenty-nine books and articles written over a period of more than forty years on a range of topics by no means restricted to statistics, illustrating vividly Coats's formidable powers of scholarship.

Because of his unique pioneering role, Coats defies comparison with any of his successors. The only comparable career was that of his contemporary and friend G.H. Knibbs, Australia's first Commonwealth Statistician, who had played a similar role in developing a centralized system of statistics for his country.[83] But in addition to the Coats of monumental achievements, there was also Coats the man. As Keyfitz remarked in the obituary that he wrote for the Royal Society of Canada: "These achievements, great as they are, and solidly as they are commemorated in the present Bureau of Statistics, are only a part of what those who know and worked with Robert Coats think of when his name is mentioned. Far brighter in their memories of him are his salty wit, his vast knowledge, his perception of movements in Canadian and world society, his fine judgment of men and events. No one was quicker to encourage colleagues and employees or more skilled in bringing out what was best in them; no one was more impatient with the friend or opponent who had not troubled to get his facts straight."[84]

CHAPTER TEN

1942–1945
Cudmore's Tenure as Dominion Statistician

Introduction

Sedley Anthony Cudmore had served as Dominion statistician for not quite four years when he died suddenly in October 1945. Nevertheless, he was a key transitional figure in the bureau's history. On assuming office in January 1942, Cudmore's immediate challenge was to continue serving the wartime bureaucracy, taking on additional temporary responsibilities and strengthening regular programs in certain areas. The appetite of the war machine for statistics was such that other departments and agencies, notably the Department of Munitions and Supply and the Wartime Prices and Trade Board, had also begun to collect and analyze statistics. This was a cause of concern in the bureau,[1] but even if it had not itself been hard pressed, it would have been rash to have argued the principle of statistical centralization at such a time.

As Cudmore's term progressed and the outcome of the war seemed more certain, the emphasis in economic management shifted towards postwar planning. In September 1943 the Advisory Committee on Reconstruction recommended that the reconstruction policies of government should seek, among other aims, to provide full employment, satisfy as rapidly as possible the pent-up demands for consumer goods, and put in place a social security system with particular emphasis on the educational and health needs of children.[2] This prescription was subsequently endorsed in the 1945 White Paper on employment and income.[3]

The bureau was not well placed to respond to these challenges, which, as it later conceded, required "statistics of the very highest quality."[4] Its organization and programs were still those of Coats's 1916 blueprint. This had sought to centralize and coordinate Canadian statistics under a single comprehensive scheme within which duplication would be eradicated, gaps filled, and uniformity of quality attained. During the interwar years these objectives were continually pursued, with the results that have been outlined in previous chapters. But as the bureau's critics were increasingly saying, and as it had itself cautiously admitted from time to time, most of the effort went into extensions and far too little into improvements of quality. In the many specific areas of wartime management and planning that required detailed data, the bureau had generally been able to satisfy the Ottawa establishment from its existing corpus of statistics or could respond quickly when a new need was identified. But for the economy as a whole, including fiscal and monetary policy where new tools of planning and management were being fashioned, the bureau's failure to develop valid estimates of national income was an embarassment for which the improvisations of the Bank of Canada could only partially compensate.

The challenge was thus a formidable one. This chapter looks at three main areas in which Cudmore harnessed the bureau's talents to prepare itself for what Bryce had called "the far different world of the 1940s."[5] These were the reorientation of the national income work along modern lines, the development of a systematic approach to statistical classifications, and the institution of a sampling capability.

THE DEVELOPMENT OF THE NATIONAL ACCOUNTS

In the first area, the bureau was initially at a tactical disadvantage owing to its perceived unresponsiveness between 1941 and 1943. Even so, its critics had never suggested that the bureau's mandate be overridden or bypassed and a fresh start made elsewhere. It was always presumed that the bureau could be revitalized–primarily through the proposed national income unit, which would serve as a fulcrum for raising its programs in their entirety to a satisfactory level of performance.

At the time of Cudmore's appointment, the deputy minister of Trade and Commerce was searching for someone to take charge of the national income work. But little consideration was being given to the organizational arrangements under which this person would work and to what exactly his responsibilities would be. It was Cudmore himself who took the decisive step. Late in 1943 he concluded that a definite plan should be developed in conjunction with other interested departments and endorsed by cabinet. He chose to work through the Advisory Committee on Economic Policy. A parallel body to the Advisory Committee on Reconstruction, this had originally been set up in 1939 to advise on questions relating to the war effort, and at the beginning of 1943 its responsibilities had been extended to cover postwar planning.[6]

On February 15 1944 Cudmore wrote to the Honourable James A. MacKinnon, minister of Trade and Commerce, outlining the statistical preparations that needed to be put in hand to deal with postwar problems.[7] These included making a fresh start on national income statistics and continuing the statistical work begun by the new war units. To accomplish these and other necessary improvements, certain organizational changes had to be made, among them the creation of what Cudmore now called "a planning and development staff," perhaps to disarm those who might argue that he was not going to the root of the bureau's problems. Within this new staff, there was to be a facility for using sampling techniques more extensively and systematically than in the past, in such connections as monitoring the labour force and measuring consumer income and expenditure and housing conditions. Finally, a standing interdepartmental committee on statistics was proposed.

A supplementary note by Herbert Marshall dated 15 March 1944 indicated that these recommendations had been put before the Advisory Committee on Economic Policy, with the purposes of the statistical committee elaborated as follows:

> The existence of such a Committee would serve several important purposes. The Bureau is frequently asked to inaugurate a new statistical series, or it may wish to commence one of its own accord. Different views may prevail as to the essentiality of the series. Before undertaking the new work, the subject could be threshed out in the Statistics Committee. The approval of a properly constituted Committee would strengthen the case for collection of the statistics. On the other hand, its disapproval would discourage the commencement of unnecessary statistics. Such a Committee would be of assistance in resolving differences of opinion between the Bureau and the departments concerning the methods of collection, presentation or interpretation of statistics compiled in the Bureau. It would suggest improvements in or extensions of the Bureau's output, and question the importance of series now collected.[8]

An Interdepartmental Standing Committee on Statistics was set up almost immediately with Cudmore as chairman and Herbert Marshall as secretary, together with J.F. Booth from Agriculture, R.B. Bryce from Finance, A. Peebles from Labour, and Oliver Master, the deputy minister of Trade and Commerce. Again, there was prompt action in establishing what was designated as the Central Research and Development Staff, and in appointing George Luxton as its chief in the spring of 1944.

Luxton had joined the Bank of Canada's research department in mid-1940 after postgraduate work on fiscal policy and statistics at Harvard. After cutting his teeth on updates of the Rowell-Sirois estimates of national income, he was soon experimenting with broader concepts of income, output, and expenditure, drawing on the work of Milton Gilbert of the United States Department of Commerce, and of J.E. Meade and J.R.N. Stone of the United Kingdom, who were attempting to flesh out with statistics the accounting identities underlying the Keynesian model of income determination. Following the formal entry into the war of the United States, an elaborate mechanism was developed for the coordinated direction of the war effort and for postwar reconstruction.

Luxton had recognized very early on that this required comparability between the national income estimates of the three Allies.

The point was dramatically underscored at the Post-War Economic Talks in London in the fall of 1942. During a session on statistics of national income, output, and expenditure, J.M. Keynes, Stone[9] and Meade spoke about the methods and purposes of the recent British White Paper on sources of war finance. Keynes expressed the view that "it would be of great value if similar estimates, framed so far as possible on a comparable basis, could be prepared by other Empire [sic] governments."[10]

Luxton now began the task of completely reorganizing the bureau's national income statistics. Events moved quickly in the few months before his tragic death in January 1945 at the age of thirty. Goldberg's review article of 1949 summarized the key developments as follows:

> First, a memorandum analyzing and comparing the concepts used in the United States, the United Kingdom and Canada was prepared. Discussions between representatives of the three countries were held in Washington, in September 1944, and a large measure of clarification and agreement was reached. Secondly, an interdepartmental committee was formed which examined in great detail the decisions reached in Washington from the point of view of their practical application. Finally, a committee on methods and sources was formed in the Bureau, which carefully examined relevant statistical series, their sources and methods of compilation, in all government departments. Those which contained the possibility of double-counting were scrutinized with special care and, where necessary, adjustments were made. At the same time attempts were made to fill the important gaps as quickly as possible; new questionnaires were designed, others were revised.[11]

The memorandum referred to[12] also recommended methods that should be adopted for Canada in the numerous cases where variations existed. Its introduction acknowledged the assistance given to Luxton by M.C. Urquhart (Department of Finance), Miss A.L. Chapman and W.E. Duffett (Bank of Canada), and S.B. Smith, R.G. Bangs, D.H. Jones, and G.L. Burton (Dominion Bureau of Statistics).

When Luxton went to Washington in September to negotiate with Richard Stone of the United Kingdom and various United States experts such as Milton Gilbert and George Jaszi, he was the sole representative of Canada but had no difficulty holding his own. Edward Denison of the US Department of Commerce subsequently reported that the discussions had led to substantial agreement on most of the principal questions, and that "uniformity of definition among the three major countries should greatly simplify the problems of the users of national income statistics."[13] The meeting was a double milestone for Canada. First, it directly demonstrated the ability of Canadian statisticians to participate on equal terms in what was to become a continuing process of international collaboration in the development of national accounts. Second, through subsequent endorsement of its conclusions by the interdepartmental committee referred to by Goldberg,[14] it laid the foundation for future Canadian work in this area.

Luxton's death shortly afterwards was an incalculable loss. In only three and a half years he had made a disproportionate contribution in several areas bearing upon the management of the Canadian war economy, but the writer of his obituary, Alex Skelton of the Bank of Canada, correctly stressed that "of outstanding importance ... and nearest to his heart was his work in the national income field. He was early seized with the concept of national income as the keystone of the whole statistical arch, and with the new vistas of economic research and practical planning which competent national income analysis opens out."[15]

Luxton's contribution was to have shifted the bureau from a unilateral approach to the estimation of national output, based on the measurement of incomes received, to a double entry approach by which parallel and theoretically equivalent measures were derived, first, of the gross national product, or net incomes accruing to the various factors of production, plus indirect taxes and capital consumption, and second, of gross national expenditure, representing the disposition of that product through various forms of expenditure, changes in inventories, and the balance of trade.

Luxton was succeeded almost immediately by Claude M. Isbister, a colleague from pre-war days whom Luxton had recommended as his successor during his terminal illness. At the time Isbister was completing a PhD in Economics at Harvard University and was thus well qualified to hold his own with the best academic talent the bureau's client departments could muster. In acknowledgement of the growing importance of the national accounts, Luxton had been appointed as senior economic statistician shortly before his death. Isbister was similarly designated as senior economist and, maintaining the momentum developed by Luxton, ensured that work on the conceptual side proceeded in parallel with the construction of tentative estimates. These latter were keenly awaited not only by the Bank of Canada and the Department of Finance but also by the newly established Department of Reconstruction, which had been given responsibility for planning and managing the Dominion/provincial conference on reconstruction of 1945. In order to assist with the assessment of Dominion proposals relating to public investment policy, social security, and financial arrangements, the bureau provided preliminary income and expenditure accounts for the years 1938-44.

Even at this early stage, the work on the national accounts was demonstrating its capacity for identifying gaps and inconsistencies in the body of primary statistics.[16] Almost immediately, for instance, it brought to light the requirement for statistics of manufacturing inventories, shipments, and orders, and of corporate profits. As the measures were subsequently extended and elaborated into what became known as the System of National Accounts, they made possible the "articulated conspectus" so frequently referred to by Coats. "A true national statistic," he had written in 1929, "is not a mere aggregation of the statistics of different activities, but also involves a purview of the totality of phenomena".[17] On another occasion, he argued that "the purpose is simply to see the structure whole and as a unison, so that when an essential is missing we shall know continuously (a) that it is missing; (b) why it is missing; and (c) just how and where to make it good".[18]

Statistical Classifications

A second important and enduring contribution by Cudmore to modern Canadian statistics was the impetus he gave to the further development of classification systems. Once begun, this work continued into the Herbert Marshall era and beyond, but for the sake of continuity its main outlines are reviewed in this chapter.

The importance of classifications as frameworks for integrating statistics from different sources had been recognized by Coats from the outset, and one of his earliest initiatives had been to develop what became known as the tripartite classification system.[19] His view was that the classification of a group of commodities and, by derivation, that of a related industry could only be based on one of three possible principles: chief component material, purpose or use, or origin. However, since no single one of them could accommodate all possible analytical interests, there had to be three parallel classifications for alternative use in different analytical contexts. In practice, chief component material became the most widely used principle. Applied in industrial classifications, it could only accommodate goods-producing industries, and when, in the 1930s, the bureau began to measure the economic characteristics of service industries, they had to be classified by kinds of institution – banks, garages, retail stores, etc. Coats was a persistent advocate of the tripartite system in international forums,[20] but the thinking at this level tended to favour a mixture of principles within the same classification.

Whatever the merits of the tripartite approach, the bureau's main problem between the wars in this area was the lack of any arrangement for keeping the system up to date and enforcing its application. With the increasing variety and sophistication of Canadian industrial processes – particularly after the outbreak of war – it became progressively more difficult to apply the principle of chief component material, and the comparability of industrial statistics was severely inhibited because of variations between the classifications underlying them.

The situation at the beginning of 1944 was summarized as follows:

> There appears to be an immediate need for a study of occupational and industrial classifications ... even in the Bureau classifications are not uniform. It is understood that in the various branches of the Industrial Census, there are some variations, each Chief being to some extent a law unto himself. The classification used by Employment Statistics is one which has been taken over from the Department of Labour and is a very old one. It also appears that Mr McKellar in Unemployment Statistics and Mr Cohen in the Industrial Census do not agree in the classifying of the activities of certain firms ... Mr Cohen treats the output of the Massey-Harris Company as an output of agricultural implements, although at the present time their output consists mainly of implements of war. Mr McKellar, on the other hand, treats the output on the basis of what it actually is.[21]

The memorandum went on to cite further consequences of the *laissez-faire* approach to classifications, including the use by the Department of Labour, in connection with National Selective Service, of a US Dictionary of Occupations that was far too detailed for Canadian conditions. It concluded with a plea for a senior interdepartmental committee to determine what should be done, and a continuing working committee to monitor the work.

Cudmore responded by setting up an Interdepartmental Working Committee on the Classification of Industry with McKellar as its chairman. A parallel committee on occupational classifications was set up at the same time under A.H. LeNeveu of the Census Branch but was disbanded after a year or so in the face of what were thought to be insuperable difficulties.[22] However, it did not take long to develop a new industrial classification that, in the case of manufacturing, augmented the criterion of "chief component material" with that of "purpose" to accommodate more complex industrial processes. It received its baptism of fire in the 1946 census of the Prairie provinces but was not published until 1948 because of the need to ensure its convertibility to the international classification then being developed by the United Nations. McKellar also played a lead role in this work,[23] which picked up from where the League of Nations Committee of Statistical Experts had left off immediately before the war. It resulted in the adoption by the United Nations Statistical Commission, during its third session in April 1948, of an International Standard Industrial Classification (ISIC)of all Economic Activities.

In the case of commodity classifications, the international work came first. Almost immediately after the publication of the ISIC, the statistical commission initiated the development of an international standard commodity classification, and McKellar, whose international credentials were by now fully established, was once more seconded by Marshall to assist in the work.[24] This was completed in 1950.

In the same year Marshall established a committee – again chaired by McKellar – to develop a standard commodity classification. A first draft was ready in 1951 but it took several more years to complete the work in all its ramifications. The criterion chosen for the allocation of commodities was the *state of fabrication*[25] and this gave rise to three principal categories: "crude materials," "processed materials," and "end products." Perhaps the most difficult problem in the development of the classification was its adaptation to the needs of external trade statistics. These had traditionally been based on the nomenclature of the customs tariff and thus could not readily be reconciled with those of production, internal trade, wholesale prices, etc. It was therefore necessary to develop separate export and import commodity classifications. These provided considerably less detail than the standard commodity classification, but were fully reconcilable to it.

The bureau's first rigorous classification of occupations, developed for the 1931 census of population,[26] was used again in 1941 with some revision. But it did not satisfy the more exacting wartime demands, such as those of National Selective Service, and Cudmore tried to put in hand the development of a multipurpose system. As noted above, this work had to be laid aside and was not in fact resumed for some twenty years until the bureau, in collaboration with the then Department of Manpower and Immigration, developed the Canadian Classification and Dictionary of Occupations.

However, the momentum of international work on statistical classifications did not slacken during the first postwar decade. The subject of the classification of occupations was placed on the agenda of the Seventh International Conference of Labour Statisticians in 1949, and a classification of nine major groups was approved at this time. The system then had to be developed in more detail, and McKellar, at the invitation of the International Labour Office, was seconded for a year to Geneva, where he was involved in the work that led to the final adoption in 1958 of the International Standard Classification of Occupations.

Incredibly, during a decade of continuous involvement in classification work both in Canada and on the international scene, McKellar remained chief of unemployment insurance statistics. Finally, the value of a full-time continuing capability in classifications was recognized, and he was appointed consultant on classifications under the wing of the assistant Dominion statistician – Statistical Integration. The small staff that was built up made possible the regular and systematic updating of the main classification systems.

The Beginnings of Sampling Work

The development of a sampling capability in the bureau arose from the need for regular and timely information on the characteristics of the population and labour force to monitor the effects of the policies and programs of postwar reconversion and reconstruction. Hitherto such characteristics could only be measured through the periodic censuses. Because of the lengthy processing time involved, the measures were mostly of historical interest when published, and considerations of cost and feasibility, as well as the requirement for continuity between successive censuses, tended to restrict flexibility in the choice of content.

The situation with regard to current measures of labour force activity had improved through wartime elaborations of the longstanding survey of employment in industrial establishments and the availability of completely new data on employment and unemployment arising from the operation of the Unemployment Insurance Act. As a purely wartime expedient, the register of National Selective Service showed the current occupational or nonoccupational status of every civilian sixteen years of age and over. But this was due to be discontinued at the end of December 1945. Keyfitz and Robinson, in their account of the beginnings of sampling work in the bureau, summarized the situation as follows: "There were no data on the size and chief characteristics of the labour force as a whole ... The agricultural labour force was completely omitted, as was employment in small establishments and occupations which were outside the coverage of the Unemployment Insurance Act. In respect to population, no current data on interprovincial migration or on families were to be had. It was also clear that data on specialized aspects, such as the rehabilitation of veterans, housing accommodation, sickness, etc., would be required from time to time."[27]

The decision was made to obtain the required data through a sample survey. Although scientific sampling had an academic pedigree dating back to the nineteenth century, it was not until the late 1930s that it had come into use in the collection of official statistics. The first major application relating to current statistics was the national monthly sample survey of households initiated by the Works Progress Administration of the United States in 1940 and taken over by the Bureau of the Census two years later. This had required the development of new methodology to deal with the problem of a universe of unprecedented size and uneven geographic distribution. The Canadian survey adopted a similar questionnaire and the Canadian methodologists, Nathan Keyfitz and Douglas Dale, drew heavily upon the advice of their US counterparts, William Hurwitz and Morris Hansen. This initiated a process of scientific cooperation between the two agencies that has continued to the present time.

The Canadian Labour Force Survey, as it was called, was directed by R. Warren James, who had come to the bureau from the Wartime Prices and Trade Board. The impending demise of National Selective Service made it necessary to conduct the initial enumeration in time for there to be an overlap of the two independent sets of data. It was therefore an urgent matter to put in place a field organization, and in mid-1945 regional offices were established in Halifax, Montreal, Toronto, Winnipeg, and Vancouver to cover the five natural geographic and economic regions of the country, exclusive of the territories. Difficulties in recruiting supervisory staff and in procuring satisfactory accommodation delayed the recruitment and training of field staff, and when enumeration finally started at the end of November, procedures frequently had to be improvised.[28]

Experience in the United States had demonstrated that a sampling ratio of one-tenth of one percent provided satisfactory results. To attain the same sample yield and accuracy with a population one-tenth as large, the Canadian ratio had to be one percent, covering about 25,000 households. The first results accorded well with statistics derived from the National Selective Service records, and the survey was subsequently conducted quarterly until November 1952. By this time, however, the volatility of the labour market was such that major federal government users persuaded the bureau to change to a monthly frequency. This was clear evidence of the perceived usefulness of the survey statistics as against alternative indicators of the employment situation.[29]

Organizational Changes

The establishment of the Central Research and Development Staff early in 1944 was the first in a series of organizational changes that completely transformed the bureau during the next four or five years and provided the model that served it for two decades. Early in Cudmore's tenure, he and Herbert Marshall sought to clarify the latter's duties as assistant Dominion statistician. Marshall had been appointed to this position not so much from administrative necessity but rather to formalize his standing as favourite son and heir apparent. Cudmore did, however, ask Marshall to submit a memorandum outlining what he thought the duties of the position should be. He replied that "the first duty should be to relieve you of details which interfere with your handling of larger problems ... there are many administrative tasks which you might wish to delegate."[30] He was referring to such functions as personnel, printing, supplies, publicity, and publications distribution, which Coats had kept in his own hands and which, with their growth in scale and complexity, were not getting the attention they deserved.

He did not, however, want his position to be wholly administrative. Surmising that his present work as a branch chief would eventually be taken over by others, he hoped that "some special inquiries of a general nature might be entrusted to me from time-to-time. Perhaps you might also wish me to make special studies of the existing statistical output as a basis to assist you in deciding policy with regard to expansion, contraction, modification, co-ordination, and so forth." With uncharacteristic humility, he asked to be allowed to "do work as would train me in a general way to carry on in your place should you be absent."[31]

While these matters were being pondered, arrangements were made for the continuance of the former statistical responsibilities of both Marshall and Cudmore. Marshall's longstanding (and by now misleadingly titled) fiefdom, Internal Trade Statistics, was broken into three separate branches: Prices, Merchandising, and International Payments. Similarly, Cudmore's General

Statistics Branch was dismantled to yield the Employment and Payrolls, Business Statistics, and Canada Year Book Branches.

When Cudmore had first invited Marshall's views on what he might do as assistant Dominion statistician, both would have conceded the necessity, sooner or later, for a Central Research and Development Staff, with the primary function of rehabilitating the bureau's work on national income. But neither perhaps would have foreseen the enormous weight of external expectations it would carry. These latter were probably the determining factor in convincing Cudmore that he needed two lieutenants – one to handle the slate of administrative responsibilities to which Marshall had referred, and a second to oversee the new research and development staff and to ensure that it got all necessary support from the branches responsible for primary statistics. In mid-1945 this proposition was put to senior Trade and Commerce management and the Civil Service Commission in the context of a more general proposal for reorienting the bureau and was approved by them in principle.[32] But for Cudmore's sudden death in October of that year, it would have been implemented with Herbert Marshall as the obvious choice on the subject-matter side.

Conclusion

During his three years and nine months of office, Cudmore laid the foundation for transforming a collection of pre-war programs of uncertain quality under an archaic system of management into a bureau recognizable by modern statisticians as being in direct continuity with their own outlook and practices. When he died suddenly on 17 October 1945 in his sixty-seventh year, he was attending the first conference of the newly formed Food and Agriculture Organization in Quebec City. His death was announced by Lester B. Pearson, conference chairman, while a longstanding Ottawa colleague, Dr G.S.H. Barton, deputy minister of Agriculture and head of the Canadian delegation, issued a statement of regret, emphasizing Cudmore's devotion to duty in the face of failing health.

Cudmore had been recruited from the University of Toronto in 1919 with glittering academic credentials and was arguably the bureau's leading scholar during the interwar years, Coats not excepted. Unlike colleagues who made their marks in specific subject-matter areas, Cudmore was a generalist whose books, articles in and editorship of the *Canada Year Book*, and contributions to a variety of learned journals demonstrate the breadth of his interests and the insights he brought to every topic he touched upon. A reticent man, it could not have been easy for him to flourish in Coats's shadow. Nevertheless, he was accorded peer recognition as a fellow of the Royal Society of Canada, as one of three Canadian members of the International Statistical Institute at the time of his death, and as a charter member of the Inter-American Statistical Institute. He was also a past secretary and vice-president of the Canadian Political Science

Association. A few months before his death, his Alma Mater, the University of Toronto, had conferred upon him the honorary degree of Doctor of Laws.

Many eloquent obituaries were written about him, but the one Cudmore himself might best have appreciated was that of his former Jerusalem colleague, Mr E. Mills, for the *Palestine Post* of 3 December 1945:

> It is sad that his penetrative mind, his knowledge and his wisdom are no longer at the service of mankind; but his work was always creative, and his influence is now spread through Canada, Palestine, the West Indies and the West Coast of Africa.[33]
> The public statistics of Canada are held to be an example to all countries.
> He came to Palestine in 1936 and returned to Canada in 1939. In that period, he established our Office of Statistics which is a model for the whole dependent Empire.
> He and Mrs Cudmore were devoted to Palestine, and his letters to me since he left ... reveal that the three years they spent in this country were among the happiest of their lives.

CHAPTER ELEVEN

1945–1956
The Marshall Years I: Preparing to Meet the Challenges of the Postwar Decade

Introduction

Herbert Marshall's term as Dominion statistician, which began on 18 October 1945, coincided with a decade of almost unprecedented social and economic change. Fuelled by a liberal immigration policy and accelerating birth rates, the population grew by thirty-one percent between 1946 and 1956. The industrial structure, greatly enlarged to meet wartime needs, made a smooth transition to the satisfaction of pent-up civilian demand. Gross national expenditures in constant dollars, led by a threefold increase in gross fixed capital formation, increased by sixty-eight percent, or at an annual rate of 5.4 percent. The corresponding increase in the civilian labour force was barely twenty percent, but unemployment rates were lower perhaps than ever before in peacetime and certainly than in any subsequent period. The annual rate averaged 3.2 percent between 1946 and 1956 and never exceeded 4.6 percent.

Major building blocks in a national system of social security were also put in place during this period. Already in 1940 the British North America Act had been amended to permit the introduction of a nationwide program of unemployment insurance, funded through employer and employee contributions. This became fully operational in 1942, although total payments to beneficiaries were very small while the war continued. In 1944 federal legislation was passed to introduce family allowances for each child up to sixteen years of age, funded from general revenues, and in 1948 federal grants were provided under Orders in Council to support the development of provincial health services. In 1952 old age security was introduced – a program of universal pensions initially paid by the federal government to all qualified residents seventy years of age and over. At the same time, provincial old age assistance for persons sixty-five to sixty-nine was put in place on a cost-sharing basis with the federal government, followed two years later by a program of allowances for totally disabled adults of working age, again on a cost-sharing basis. A final step during this period was the introduction in 1956 of a provincially administered cost-shared program of unemployment assistance. Thus, the prosperous but caring postwar society, visualized by the wartime White Paper on employment and income, was becoming a reality.

To plan and implement these remarkable developments, new administrative mechanisms had to be created, notably the Department of Reconstruction and Supply, set up in January 1946 from the former Departments of Reconstruction and of Munitions and Supply. Some elements of its far-reaching mandate and powers, such as those relating to the liquidation of the war program, were transitory, while others were addressed to longer-term industrial and economic development needs. The Economic Research Branch, for instance, was essentially an economic intelligence unit, designed to appraise and keep under observation the state of the Canadian economy. Again, the Research and Development Branch provided a technical information service to make available to industry the results of government and other research. It also sought to encourage research work not undertaken by any existing government department or agency and conducted overall assessments of research activities in government, industry, and the universities.

As the department was eventually wound down, these continuing functions were taken over by regular departments and agencies. The Research and Development Branch went to the National Research Council. The Economic Research Branch was combined with the Industrial Development Division of the Department of Trade and Commerce to form an Economic Research and Development Branch. This was able to capitalize on the department's foreign trade intelligence work to provide a continuing review of both domestic and external developments affecting the country's economic welfare.

Another new agency was the Central Mortgage and Housing Corporation, formed in 1946 as a successor to Wartime Housing Limited and responsible for all aspects of government housing policy. The principal locus for the development of social security programs was the Department of National Health and Welfare, successor to the former Department of Pensions and National Health. In effect it was two departments in one, with a deputy minister on both the health and welfare sides.

These and other program departments, such as Labour, Agriculture, and Transport, which now had at their disposal analytical skills of a kind and calibre previously associated only with the Department of Finance and the Bank of Canada, confronted Marshall and his colleagues with a user clientele of unparalleled sophistication. To oversee and coordinate relations with users, Marshall set up an Interdepartmental Advisory Committee on Economic Statistics.[1] In a 1949 progress report to the minister, C.D. Howe, Marshall wrote: "On this I have Mr Skelton and Dr Isbister, Mr Beattie from the Bank of Canada, Mr Mitchell Sharp from the Department of Finance and some of my best men in the Bureau ... This committee will ensure, I think, that the best use is being made of our resources in the Bureau and will keep us posted on the needs for economic statistics in all departments of the Government."[2]

This letter indicates the calibre of the staffs the bureau was dealing with in the client departments, and it was fortunate that, by the late 1940s, many of the senior staff D.H. MacGregor had criticized a decade earlier had retired, with their places being filled by a new generation of young professionals versed in Keynesian economics.

The government's original blueprint for postwar reconstruction was designed as a joint Dominion/provincial undertaking. A major objective of the 1945 Dominion/provincial conference on reconstruction was to put in place financial arrangements for carrying out shared projects.[3] However, the inability of the conference delegates to agree on such arrangements left in abeyance the government's proposals for a comprehensive social security scheme and a coordinated program of public investment. The 1946 Dominion budget subsequently provided a basis on which individual provinces could enter into tax agreements with the Dominion government until such time as a general tax agreement could be concluded. Hence, as discussed later, there emerged among the provinces a user market for general economic statistics, the locus of interest being the Treasury or parallel departments with the responsibility of advising premiers in the general context of Dominion/provincial relations.

The Marshall years began with a major organizational restructuring aimed mainly at strengthening the bureau's administrative capability and providing appropriate recognition and leverage for the key task of making up lost time in the development of internationally comparable statistics of national income. The work of compiling and analyzing these statistics and of broadening and elaborating their underlying primary statistics was accomplished with only a modest overall increase in staff. But Marshall was not able to convince his minister that the bureau had a mandate to analyze the statistics that it collected and compiled. Nor was he successful in arguing the case for an enhanced status for the office of Dominion statistician, an issue that remained unresolved until it was decisively addressed by the Glassco Commission in the early 1960s.

In 1948 Marshall brought in a new Statistics Act that, *inter alia*, legitimized the practice of sampling and strengthened the bureau's coordinating mandate *vis-à-vis* the statistical activities of other departments of government, both federal and provincial. Marshall's term of office was in fact an era of unprecedented federal/provincial cooperation in statistics, paralleling the political cooperation through which new social programs were being put into place.

Marshall recognized what would now be called the infrastructure requirements for an effective statistical program and, towards the end of his term, set in motion the process that irrevocably launched the bureau into the computer age. He was also determined that a revitalized bureau should have appropriate accommodation. Since the late 1920s it had been housed in the old Edwards Mill on Green Island, where working conditions had gradually deteriorated to the point that employee productivity was severely prejudiced. The move to new quarters in Tunney's Pasture was accomplished in 1952.

Organizational Changes

Immediately after his appointment, Marshall took steps to finalize the establishment and staffing of the senior positions Cudmore had decided upon before his death. An internal announcement at the end of 1945 explained that "it has become impossible for the Dominion Statistician and an assistant to handle the mass of administrative work necessary in the Bureau of today and at the same time give proper attention to the numerous problems of statistical integration which arise. To meet this situation, the position of Assistant Dominion Statistician has been discontinued and replaced by two positions, viz. Chief Administrative Officer and Chief Economist."[4]

J.T. Marshall – no relation to Herbert – was appointed chief administrative officer and assumed responsibility for personnel, repairs and maintenance, supplies, printing, mechanical equipment, and accounting. A specialist in vital statistics, he had come to the bureau from British Columbia to take charge of this work, but he had a talent for administration and was well thought of by the departmental secretary, Finlay Sim. He continued for over three years as acting director of vital statistics,[5] which now embraced institution statistics and criminal statistics, and was also given the formal responsibility of acting for the Dominion statistician in his absence. The more crucial appointment, however, was that of chief economist, with responsibility for the Central Research and Development Staff. The requirement here was for an appointee who could sustain the newly restored confidence among key Ottawa users in the bureau's handling of national income statistics.[6] The mantle fell upon Dr C.M. Isbister, who had come to the bureau to fill the vacancy caused by the death of Luxton and had proved to be a great success.

These appointments of late 1945 appear to have been an interim compromise to secure quick action from the Civil Service Commission, for within weeks of their announcement a further submission was put to the commission,[7] seeking the designation of J.T. Marshall as assistant Dominion statistician–Administration, and of Dr Isbister as assistant Dominion statistician–Research. The requirement for positions at this level was stressed in the strongest terms, as were the unique qualifications of the candidates. Of Isbister it was declared that there was no one else, inside or outside the bureau, who could do the job.[8] "Although he hasn't been with us very long, he has greatly impressed officials of the Bank of Canada, the Department of Finance, and the Dominion-Provincial Committee on Reconstruction, and has put Canada on the map in International Conferences in National Income and related economic series."[9] Giving him the recommended status, it was said, would not only facilitate his work in the bureau but would also assist him in his extensive liaison work with other departments, and at international gatherings. And finally: "If we do not give him proper standing, we shall lose him. Since coming here he has had offers of professorships in Universities."[10] Action on the appointments was not immediately forthcoming, but Marshall's annual report for 1947–48 records them as having been made during that fiscal year.

Another notable senior appointment at this time was that of Nathan Keyfitz as mathematical advisor, reporting within the Central Research and Development Staff directly to Isbister. Keyfitz, a demographer, had come to the bureau in the late 1930s with impressive academic qualifications and had made his reputation with work on the 1931 Census Monograph program. He had emerged to considerable prominence with his contribution to the quarterly labour force survey launched in 1945. In seeking his reclassification as a statistician grade six, Marshall stressed the impossibility of holding him in the bureau at his present salary and warned that:

> It would be a staggering blow to the Bureau if we lost Keyfitz. He has a most ingenious and original mind which, combined with his advanced knowledge of mathematics, has been of outstanding assistance in the analysis of very complex statistical problems. He is held in very high esteem in Washington by the mathematical experts in their sampling and other statistical fields requiring the application of higher mathematics. He is the mathematical expert on whom we rely for the formulation of our sampling patterns. Our new sampling organization must have a man of his calibre as mathematical advisor. In the field of Social Analysis his work is indispensable. In short, if we were to lose Keyfitz we would have to employ another mathematical statistician. None could be obtained with his wide knowledge of Canadian statistics.[11]

Keyfitz was eventually lured away to academe where he made a glittering second career. In the meantime he continued in the role described by Marshall, establishing himself as the unchallenged father of scientific methodology in the bureau's survey work.

The higher visibility given to the positions of Isbister and J.T. Marshall was part of a more general reorganization in which some twenty subject-matter branches, the chiefs of which all reported directly to the Dominion statistician, were regrouped into twelve divisions, headed by directors. A primary objective was the better coordination of certain areas of related statistics. Concomitantly, it reduced the Dominion statistician's span of control, and with a classification system that now had nine grades instead of five[12] it was possible to reward some loyal old hands, while opening up new prospects of advancement for those further down the ladder.

The Prices Branch was combined with the Employment and Payrolls Branch to form a Labour and Prices Division[13] under H.F. Greenway. This division also took over the compilation of unemployment insurance statistics, hitherto a responsibility of the Social Analysis and Economic Research Branch. The International Payments Branch was combined with the External Trade Branch to form the International Trade Division, with C.D. Blyth and L.A. Kane working in parallel as chiefs of international trade statistics for the balance of payments and exports and imports respectively.[14] The Business Statistics Branch, still under S.B. Smith, went to join National Income, the Sampling Organization, and Housing Statistics as part of the Central Research and Development Division under Isbister.

Of vital importance to the estimates of national income were the production-type statistics generated by the census of industry and the census of merchandising and services. The January 1946 memorandum on bureau reorganization commented that "there are glaring gaps in our data. We lack adequate information on inventories which constitute an indispensable barometer for those concerned with a policy of high employment. More current statistics are required on important commodities. Our index of physical volume of production needs to be improved greatly. In short, a thorough reorganization job has to be done in the Industrial Census field."[15]

Accordingly, the branches responsible for the census of industry, the Merchandising Branch, and the Construction Statistics Branch, were combined under W.H. Losee into a new Census of Industry and Merchandising Division, which also took on the job of conducting an annual survey of forecast repairs and capital expenditures.

Elsewhere, organizational changes were less radical. As noted above, J.T. Marshall's Vital Statistics Branch absorbed the branches responsible for institutional and criminal statistics. The new grouping, at first called the Social Welfare Statistics Division, became the Health and Welfare Division after a couple of years. The Social Analysis Branch, which had shed its responsibility for unemployment insurance statistics and classifications research, became part of the Census Division. The branches responsible for statistics of education, public finance, transportation, and public utilities, remained organizationally unchanged. Two elements of the former group of administrative services – those responsible for press and publicity, and publications distribution – were held back from J.T. Marshall's sphere of operations and set up as a separate Information Services Division. Later, in September 1948, a centralized Mechanical Tabulation Division was established under C. Scott, consolidating the tabulating sections that had formerly operated independently in the International Trade Division, the Health and Welfare Division, and the Labour and Prices Division. At this time, and indeed for many years into the future, the Census Division retained its own mechanical tabulation facilities.

In the spring of 1951 a new division, General Assignments, was created by the transfer to the bureau from the Economic Research and Development Branch, Department of Trade and Commerce, of statistical facilities that had been developed as a basis for the forecasting of new investment. These were amalgamated with the Capital Expenditures Section of the Industry and Merchandising Division, whose Construction Section was transferred two years later to the General Assignments Division, along with responsibility for the quarterly corporation profits survey, which had hitherto been conducted by the Research and Development Division. The new division was strongly committed to the research needs of Trade and Commerce, but it was soon able to contribute to the improvement and extension of the bureau's primary statistics, its array of economic indicators, and the national accounts. It was first headed by Morgan Mahoney, who had transferred from Trade and Commerce, and then by H.L. Allen, formerly the bureau's personnel officer.[16]

In 1949 the bureau lost the services of Isbister as assistant Dominion statistician – Research. Two years earlier he had been loaned for a time to the Department of Reconstruction and Supply, and in 1948 he had been seconded to the Economic Research Branch of the Department of Trade and Commerce. Finally, in the following year, he was appointed acting director of the Commercial Relations Division of Trade and Commerce,[17] and the Central Research and Development Division was subsequently divided into two parts. The work of the Sampling Organization and the management of the regional offices became the responsibility of a new Special Surveys Division. The remaining components of the Central Research and Development Division, responsible for the work on national income and business statistics, then made up a division with the shorter title of Research and Development.

The gap left by Isbister was not filled immediately. For a short time, A.S. Abell served as director of the Research and Development Division, but following his move to the Department of Finance he was succeeded by Simon Goldberg, who had just returned from doctoral studies at Harvard. Then in April 1954 Goldberg was appointed to the newly created position of assistant Dominion statistician – Integration and was in turn succeeded as director of the Research and Development Division by F.H. Leacy. Goldberg's new position was similar to that held earlier by Isbister but was now vested with functional authority over the whole range of primary statistics. This authority was subsequently used by Goldberg to great effect in developing Coats's "articulated conspectus."

The organization resulting from all these changes, which is depicted in the chart of appendix E, served the bureau with only marginal amendments until well into the regime of Marshall's successor, Walter Duffett.

Establishment and Staffing

The program achievements that ensued under the organizational structure just described, and that are highlighted in the next chapter, were accomplished with surprisingly small increases in staff. Marshall foresaw the need for an expanded and upgraded staff, but at a very early stage he was thrown on the defensive. In

April 1947 he had prepared a lengthy memorandum on the bureau's staff situation for M.W. Mackenzie, the deputy minister of Trade and Commerce. It began and continued on an urgent note: "In order to enable the Bureau to ... turn out the quality of statistics necessary to meet the *absolutely key needs* of departments and the general public, some further expansion of professional staff is needed."[18]

It focused on national income statistics, labour and price statistics, and international trade statistics. The unit responsible for the first of these had been weakened by outright staff losses and the assignment of senior people to meet other pressing needs. At the same time, it was being called upon to undertake new responsibilities, including the preparation, for the purposes of Dominion/provincial tax agreements, of a second estimate of gross national product incorporating changes in methods and new data, over and above the primary estimate based on the methodology and data sources already agreed upon.

Of labour and price statistics, Marshall said that "it is in this field that we are the weakest."[19] Here the bureau was under continuing criticism from the Canadian Labour Congress across virtually the entire range of its activities. While Marshall rejected many of their proposals as impractical or inappropriate, he argued strongly to Mackenzie for revamping the cost of living index to reflect postwar expenditure patterns, and for a program of productivity measurement. In the area of international trade, a new research section had been established under Douglas Fullerton, formerly with the National Income Unit, and it had identified the need for work on nomenclature and classification in trade statistics, and on problems of origin and destination.

In all, Marshall was looking for twelve professional and nine support positions. Shortly after delivering this memorandum, however, he wrote again to Mackenzie in some agitation: "When I went to see you last Friday, I had no idea you were under criticism because of the expansion of the Bureau. It was certainly an inappropriate time to present my memo on staff needs. It was meant, however, to indicate the staff development over a period which would eventually ... make the Bureau of Statistics an organization of which you would be proud. I should like to withdraw that memorandum and replace it by one with much more moderate requests which might tide us over for the time being."[20]

The criticism referred to went back to the House of Commons discussion the previous August of the bureau's 1946–47 estimates – a sum of $2,090,670. J.M. Macdonnell, MP for Muskoka, Ontario, had commented on the "large increase here of nearly half a million dollars. We all believe in statistics and I have a high opinion of the head of the Bureau; nevertheless it can run riot if there is no check. Who assumes responsibility for the size of the institution? It can be developed without limit unless there is someone keeping check on it. I do not know what it was the year before last, but it has increased twenty-five percent this year."[21]

The official answer was that "a very large portion of that amount is required for services which the bureau has been asked to provide for the Department of

Health and Welfare in connection with various activities."[22] These latter were said to include the validation of family allowance claims and the provision of vital statistics.[23] It is difficult to believe that Marshall had been unaware of the opposition's criticism. More probably, he had perhaps not believed that Trade and Commerce would take it seriously and could not now admit it.

In any case, the episode prompted Marshall to include in his annual report for that year a lengthy explanation of the factors that had contributed to the increase in the bureau's staff since 1939.[24] The continuing staff, i.e., permanent and temporary staff other than those on fixed-term census appointments, had increased from six hundred in 1939 to approximately twelve hundred on 31 March 1948. He cited the new and improved series compiled to satisfy wartime needs, the demand for which had increased rather than diminished in the postwar period; the expansion of work resulting from the extension of social security legislation; the new initiatives in national income statistics and sampling; demands arising from the development of research functions in other departments; and the need to satisfy the reporting requirements of international agencies, to mention some of the more salient factors.

In the responsible divisions, the staff increases had been quite dramatic. The Labour and Prices Division had increased its clerical staff by 113 as a consequence of its responsibility, assumed in mid-war, for unemployment insurance statistics, and for the field staff put in place to improve the quality of the cost of living index. The National Income and Sampling Organization units, which had not existed in 1939, now required the services of ninety clerks. The Health and Welfare Division required a hundred more to handle the new responsibilities cited in the estimates debate. The International Trade Division was now responsible for tourism records, and this had necessitated twenty more clerks. And to provide appropriate support to these various activities, the Administration Division now had fifty more staff than in 1939.

Subsequent annual reports provided details of hiring and separations, permanent appointments, reclassifications, the ebb and flow of temporary census staff, etc. The continuing staff had increased to about fourteen hundred by the end of the 1950–51 fiscal year, but the annual report for that year noted that "in line with the Government's plan for economy, the establishment of the Bureau was reduced by 75 positions on 31 March, 1951."[25] For the next three years, the staff level stagnated at slightly more than thirteen hundred. By the time of Marshall's retirement, however, at the end of the 1955–56 fiscal year, it had recovered to 1,411. Even so, there had only been an eighteen percent increase in eight years.

The composition of the staff as between permanent and temporaries shifted significantly during Marshall's tenure. In 1948 there were only 304 permanents, amounting to about a quarter of the continuing staff. The annual reports provided no details on permanent appointments after the 1952–53 fiscal year, but up to 31 March 1953 close to four hundred permanent appointments had been made, so that by 31 March 1956, when the continuing staff numbered 1,411, at least half were probably permanents. An appreciable number of professional and supporting technical officer positions were reclassified to higher levels during the period, and there were two revisions in the salary scales. Both these factors were helpful in enabling the bureau to upgrade the calibre of its professional staff.

In putting forward candidates for promotion under the new extended range of professional classifications, those belonging to the Central Staff were referred to as economists in keeping with the designation of Isbister's position. The most eminent of these was Agatha Chapman, who had come with Luxton on secondment from the Bank of Canada and continued to serve as Isbister's principal assistant during his early days at the bureau. Her continuing services were deemed essential for the further development of national income statistics, and she was recommended accordingly for appointment as an Economist Grade 7 ($4,200–$4,800). It was explained that:

> The economist has won an increasingly important place in the fields of government and business ... in the past the Bureau has been somewhat lacking in economic statistics, and particularly in their analysis from broader economic points of view. One of the principal reasons for the creation of a Central Staff was to remedy that situation ... The Central Staff will not be another statistics collecting branch of the Bureau, its work will be to integrate and analyze existing statistics and to develop new economic sources. When the latter are organized, they will be handed over to appropriate branches to carry on. The Central Staff will, therefore, be advisory, interpretive, analytical. Its members are economists first, statisticians second.[26]

This kind of mandate, it was said, could attract high-calibre graduates in economics, many of whom would not want to be statisticians as such. Furthermore, "it should lessen the growth of economic research units in other departments. When the Bureau's central staff is functioning fully, the need for such would diminish where they must be based on statistical data."[27] The first argument was certainly borne out then and later, when many highly qualified young economists came to the Central Staff. Some, like C.L. Barber, Gideon Rosenbluth, and J.A. Sawyer, eventually went on to make their names in the academic world. Others, like A.S. Rubinoff, F.H. Leacy, R.B. Crozier, and D.H. Fullerton left for senior positions in other departments of government where their bureau experience stood them in valuable stead. And some, like V.R. Berlinguette, H.J. Adler, and Jenny Podoluk, stayed the course, rising to the senior levels of bureau management. The most illustrious member of this latter group was Simon Goldberg, who had joined the Central Staff at its inception while still in air force uniform. As noted earlier, he was eventually appointed assistant Dominion statistician – Integration after taking leave of absence to complete a Harvard PhD. He held this position with great distinction until 1972 when he left for the United Nations to become director of its Statistical Office.

The second argument was almost certainly wishful thinking on the part of the bureau. Trade and Commerce did not, during Marshall's time at least, accept the argument that the bureau had a mandate to analyze the statistics it collected and compiled. In the parliamentary discussion of Trade and Commerce's 1955-56 estimates, the minister, Hon. C.D. Howe, was asked about the duties of economists both in the bureau and in Trade and Commerce. Howe at first replied that "there are no economists in the bureau of statistics; they are statisticians." He further explained that "their work is that of collecting information and making it available to anyone desiring it. The purpose of the staff in the Department of Trade and Commerce is to make an analysis of that information and to issue forecasts based upon information gathered by the bureau of statistics and through economic surveys." When pressed further, Howe conceded that "the bureau has people with economic training, but they are employed as statisticians." He emphasized firmly that "the bureau of statistics is not encouraged to do forecasting or to do other than present facts as disclosed to them by figures they collect."[28]

The Status of the Dominion Statistician

Howe's characterization of the bureau as the statistical arm of the Department of Trade and Commerce and his other unflattering references to its perceived mandate were typical illustrations of the status issue that had bedevilled Coats for a quarter of a century. "We are," lamented Marshall in 1951, "a cinderella of the service or, to use another simile, 'the hewers of wood and drawers of water' for others."[29] The issue of the status of the Dominion statistician was one that Coats had bequeathed to his successors through his 1942 "Valedictory Report." Cudmore had understandably taken no action in the matter, but the prospects for some resolution during Marshall's time must certainly have looked better, given the fact that the bureau's work in such areas as the national accounts and the conduct of sample surveys had made allies of many of its former critics.

As noted earlier, some much-needed salary raises for the bureau's professionals had been granted at war's end. In July 1948 Marshall wrote to the deputy minister, expressing his appreciation of this development but went on to say that "it would be only justice and certainly ... a great satisfaction to myself if the generally approved salary scale could be capped by one for the Dominion statistician."[30] The letter purported to show that, while salaries at the director level had gone up by about forty percent since 1939, the Dominion statistician's salary had increased by only seven percent. This latter calculation was based on a comparison of Marshall's current salary of $8,000 and Coats's retiring salary of $7,500. The letter also noted that the Dominion archivist and the superintendent of insurance were currently being paid $10,000 per annum.

There is no record of any direct response to Marshall's suggestion, and in December he returned to the matter: "I am by no means alone in holding the view that the position of Dominion Statistician should carry a higher salary. Is [the delay in action] ... because the Bureau is viewed as a branch of Trade and Commerce in the same sense as others? If that is the obstacle which prevents justice being done, is there not a remedy? Could the Dominion Statistician not be given the rank of deputy-head?"[31]

Again the question went unanswered, this time for more than two years, although Marshall's salary did increase to $9,000 in 1949–50, and to $10,000 in 1951–52. But the issue was never really just one of money. Writing once again to the deputy minister in February 1951, Marshall suggested that section 5.4 of the Statistics Act implied a status for the Dominion statistician equivalent to that of a deputy head. He went on to elaborate how such a status would facilitate the work of the bureau: "It would make co-operation and the co-ordination of statistical work with other departments easier since approval must often be through deputies ... the fact that the Bureau is a branch of a department not infrequently prevents Bureau persons from securing as good salaries as people in other departments with no greater responsibility."[32]

In pressing his point for deputy status, Marshall surprisingly stopped short of what would have been the most logical suggestion, i.e., the establishment of the bureau as a separate department or agency: "If the Dominion Statistician cannot have the status of deputy unless there is a separate department of statistics, then, of course, there is no more to be said. There is certainly no need for a separate department of statistics, and it would be absurd to suggest it. Is there no possibility of having the Dominion Statistician remain the Dominion Statistician but be ranked as equivalent to a deputy or associate deputy in the Department of Trade and Commerce? We are quite happy in the Department. My idea is that if such status were given, the Bureau would continue to work through the Deputy Minister of Trade and Commerce and the Minister."[33]

It may well have been the case that Mackenzie, would have preferred to be rid of the bureau rather than to have the Dominion statistician elevated within the department to near parity with himself. However, in his reply of 16 March 1951, he told Marshall that "the only way this could be accomplished would be by an amendment to the statute and ... I do not think the Government would be prepared to introduce an amendment to the Act solely for this purpose." He professed himself anxious to further "the better standing and morale of the Bureau, but ... more important than the technical question of status is the relationship between the Dominion Statistician and his staff vis-à-vis the Treasury Board and the Civil Service Commission on the one hand, and the salary level of the Dominion Statistician on the other."[34] There was in fact some loosening of the administrative apron strings during the remainder of the Marshall tenure, and his salary was further increased to $12,000 in 1953-54. But there matters stood for some years more. As a later chapter will describe, it was the scrutiny of the bureau by the Glassco Commission in the early 1960s that made possible the bureau's eventual emancipation as a separate department of government.

A New Statistics Act

The bureau's strengthened commitment to the user community during the postwar years was given practical and symbolic expression through the new Statistics Act of 1948. Virtually unchanged since 1918, the act had long been in need of revision. Introducing the second reading of Bill 326 respecting the Dominion Bureau of Statistics, G.J. McIlraith, parliamentary assistant to the minister of Trade and Commerce, complimented the bureau elaborately on its work since 1918 but went on to stress [the] "enormous increase in the number and complexity of the economic and social problems with which governments, business and private individuals have had to deal, and the greatly increased amount of statistical information [that] has been required in order to deal with these problems."[35]

The Statistics Act as it then stood was, he continued, an inadequate instrument for meeting the need: "First, it does not mention specifically many of the economic and social fields on which statistical information is now being obtained."[36] In consequence, the bureau had to rely on the voluntary cooperation of respondents in these areas. A notorious example was the bureau's difficulties in collecting statistics of road and air transport because of the narrow definition of the term "carrier."[37] "Again," noted McIlraith, "[the act] does not contain statutory authority for new collection techniques, such as the technique known as sampling."[38] This deficiency left the bureau open to complaints of discrimination among respondents and was a threat to the viability of the relatively new quarterly labour force survey.[39]

These matters were satisfactorily resolved in the new act, which also provided the bureau with a broader and bolder statement of mandate. It was now required, by section 3 (d), "generally to organize a scheme of co-ordinated social and economic statistics pertaining to the whole of Canada and to each of the provinces thereof." The Dominion statistician, in addition to being responsible for the administration of the Act, and for controlling the operations and staff of the bureau, was also required by section 4 (1)(a) and (b) "to advise on all matters pertaining to statistical policy and to confer with the several departments of government to that end; [and] to organize and maintain a scheme of co-operation in the collection, classification and publication of statistics as between the several departments of government."[40]

These were admirable objectives, but as Marshall's successor noted fourteen years later in a submission to the Glassco Commission,[41] there was no reciprocal obligation on anyone to collaborate with him. The following section demonstrates, however, that self-interest was sometimes a powerful motive for provincial departments.

New Dimensions of Dominion/Provincial Collaboration

The stronger mandate for the bureau was in fact, if not in intent, complementary to the new mode of Dominion/provincial cooperation for the planning and financing of social and other programs that had begun to emerge with the Dominion/provincial conference on reconstruction of 1945. Statistical collaboration with other departments of government, both Dominion and provincial, had been a central feature of the first Statistics Act and Coats had achieved some striking successes, for instance in the area of vital statistics. In other areas, however, like public finance, the imperative for success had been less compelling and little was achieved.

All this was changed by the Rowell-Sirois Commission and subsequent wartime and postwar developments that gave the Dominion and provincial governments common cause across a broad range of programs. As a consequence, an era of extended and continuous Dominion/provincial statistical collaboration began, and the work of several divisions in the bureau came to be significantly determined by the requirements of the policies and programs worked out in the political arena by the two levels of government. In particular cases, as well as working with the responsible Dominion and provincial departments, the bureau also sought to involve relevant professional and industry groups, thus ensuring the broadest possible inputs into the determination of new statistical programs.

A notable example of this new way of working was provided by the Public Finance Division. Its agenda had been set, first, by its commitment to carry forward the work initiated by the Rowell-Sirois Commission towards developing comprehensive and comparably classified statistics of public finance for the three levels of government, and second, by its service role in support of the 1945 Dominion/provincial conference on reconstruction and the subsequent follow-up conferences.[42] Between 1945 and 1953, for example, four Dominion/provincial conferences on financial statistics were held. These involved not only provincial and bureau officials but also representatives of the Department of Finance and the Bank of Canada. Continuing committees were set up to serve as interconference secretariats. As the division made progress towards its basic objectives, it was increasingly in a position to contribute to other areas of bureau work, such as obtaining and analyzing data on provincial finances for the quarterly estimates of national income, as well as data related to current and intended capital investment for use by the new General Assignments Division.

In the area of vital statistics, Coats's early work in developing model legislation and securing its adoption by the provinces had provided the basis for a national system that worked well for many years. Following the two

Dominion/provincial conferences on vital statistics of 1918, a quarter century elapsed before a third was held in 1943. By that time, new problems had surfaced. More comprehensive, timely, and efficiently produced vital statistics were needed, both by the provinces and the Dominion – in the latter case not the least as a basis for administering new and emerging social security programs, where such information could determine eligibility.

To address these needs, Dominion/provincial conferences on vital statistics were held in October 1943 and September 1944 respectively, and agreement was reached to draft a new model vital statistics act with a view to its adoption by all the provinces, and to develop national indexes of births, marriages, and deaths. To monitor the progress of this and other work, a Vital Statistics Council was set up and held the first of what became regular annual meetings in May 1945.

Vital statistics were only one of the responsibilities of the Health and Welfare Division, which also included judicial statistics and statistics of institutions and public health. With respect to institutions, the division again worked primarily in partnership with provincial authorities. In this connection, Dominion/provincial conferences on hospital statistics were held in February 1949 and May 1951 to develop and approve new reporting requirements, classification standards, etc. Similarly, a Dominion/provincial conference on criminal statistics was held in May 1949.

In the area of public health, the division worked in collaboration with the Department of National Health and Welfare, which had very quickly built up a strong research capability. An important joint undertaking by the two departments was the Canadian Sickness Survey of the early 1950s. The findings of this survey, which covered the extent of ill health and the patterns of health care as well as family expenditures on health services, attracted a great deal of attention at the time and underpinned much of the later research on the need for and costs of a national public health care system.

The conference method was particularly well suited to advising and assisting the Agriculture Division in its responsibility for planning and carrying out current surveys of crops and livestock, and also the Census of Agriculture Section of the Census Division. Provincial departments of agriculture advised from time to time on census content, and the census findings provided periodic benchmarks for the semiannual crop and livestock surveys. In the administration of these latter, the provincial departments played a particularly active role, selecting crop correspondents jointly with the bureau, for instance, and frequently tabulating survey results.

The great number of special interests involved in agriculture and the complex nature of their interrelationships required an unusually elaborate system of conference and committee arrangements. There were, during Marshall's tenure as Dominion statistician, five Dominion/provincial conferences on agricultural statistics, and between conferences continuity in their work was ensured by a

Continuing Committee. In addition, at the Dominion level, there was an Interdepartmental Committee on Agriculture Statistics with no fewer than six subcommittees, in the work of which national associations such as the National Dairy Council and the Canadian Federation of Agriculture took part from time to time.

In January 1953 the first of a new kind of Dominion/provincial conference was held, relating to economic statistics. It differed from those described above in that responsibility for the topics discussed was dispersed among a number of bureau subject-matter divisions, and that, correspondingly, there was no obvious locus of responsibility within the organizational structures of the various provinces. Historically, interest in the generality of economic statistics as a basis for articulating and implementing broad matters of policy probably developed at different times in different provinces. Certainly, however, the requirement to respond to the massively detailed information demands of the Rowell-Sirois Commission during the late 1930s would have precipitated such an interest if it did not exist before.

After 1939 the centralized management of the war economy muted this interest, but with the advent of peace the provinces began to play a vigorous role in the process of reconstruction. Thus, they had an equal stake with the Dominion government in developing a body of statistics that would serve their respective obligations for promoting inflation-free growth and high and stable levels of employment and income. The bureau had always tried to accommodate provincial statistical needs, but there were many kinds of local data that could not be provided from national programs; hence small statistical units had developed in some provincial departments. In some of the larger provinces, the evident success of centralization at the Dominion level had led to the centralization of local statistical work in separate provincial bureaux.[43]

The idea of a Dominion/provincial conference dealing with economic statistics appears to have been first mooted by R.M. Putnam, director of the Bureau of Statistics of Alberta. Writing to Herbert Marshall in September 1947, he remarked that "there have been some conferences between the statisticians of provincial departments and the Dominion departments on such subjects as agriculture, public health, vital statistics and finance (public accounts etc.), but I do not think there has yet been a conference where all the persons who act in the capacity of provincial statisticians have met."[44]

During the next eighteen months there was discussion and correspondence on the idea of such a conference. On 11 July 1949 Marshall wrote to the heads of all provincial statistical offices asking for their views on three questions: "(1) How could a Dominion-provincial conference on Economic Statistics benefit your work in [province]? (2) In the event of holding such a conference, should it deal with other subjects than economic statistics? (3) What is the most outstanding problem that you would like to have discussed at the Conference?"[45]

Some, like H.J. Chater of Ontario, were not enthusiastic at first. When it became clear, however, that Marshall was determined to hold a conference anyway, none of the provincial representatives chose to be left out. The conference eventually took place from 26 to 28 January 1953 with Marshall in the chair and was opened by the minister of Trade and Commerce, the Honourable C.D. Howe. On the basis of the prior consultation that had taken place, the agenda addressed the establishment of arrangements to avoid duplication of effort in the collection of economic statistics and the securing of a maximum degree of cooperation through available resources in terms of the sometimes divergent needs of Dominion and provincial authorities as well as both the permissive and restrictive provisions of the Statistics Act. It was planned to acquaint the provinces with the development of current bureau thinking regarding the industrial census on such issues as lessening the response burden on industry, increasing the usefulness of the data, and decreasing the time lag in publication. Also included on the agenda was a discussion of the relationship of industrial statistics to the national accounts.

Among the resolutions of the conference was one approving the use of the sales (or shipments) concept in place of gross value of production as a basis for reporting to the industrial census. Another recommended regular conferences on economic statistics, and yet another the formation of a continuing committee to review existing questionnaires and to prepare for subsequent conferences. In April 1955, during the second of what became a continuing conference series, the emerging issue of regional statistics was a featured item on the agenda.

The Dawning of the Computer Age

During the Marshall years, the technology in use for the more sophisticated operations of the bureau's Mechanical Tabulation Division was based on punched cards and updated from time to time as the principal supplier, International Business Machines,[46] developed faster or more versatile models of its card punchers, verifiers, sorters, collators, tabulators, etc. The main elements of the division's organization were a key punch unit that served all client divisions,[47] a number of tabulating units geared to the special requirement of particular clients, and an auxiliary machine unit that supported the tabulating units through services provided with various specialized items of equipment that they did not normally use. There was also a calculating unit equipped with calculating and adding machines and pegboards that performed simpler kinds of compilations directly from the completed statistical returns. At the end of March 1949, the division had 202 employees working with 173 units of tabulating equipment and twenty-seven adding machines or comptometers.[48]

The division advised on the planning and implementation of tabulation requirements for the 1951 and 1956 censuses, but these were unambiguously the responsibility of the Census Division itself, which had the experience, and was provided with the resources, to deal with the enormous volume of work generated at the processing peaks, both in Ottawa and at the regional offices. The Mechanical Tabulation Division did, however, undertake special tasks for the Census Division from time to time, such as the production of an alphabetic index of all persons enumerated in the 1921 census to assist claimants of federal old age security benefits.

In the mid-1950s Scott was appointed chief administrative officer and was succeeded by his deputy, W.I. Moore. Later in the decade the appointments of Moore and A.B. McMorran, director of the Special Surveys Division, were switched, and McMorran continued to serve as director of Mechanical Tabulation (and its later incarnations) until his retirement in the 1970s.

In Marshall's last annual report, which covered 1955-56, it was noted that "much study is being given to the question of adding an electronic computing machine to the Bureau's mechanical equipment."[49] For almost a decade, the bureau had been able to monitor the experience of the US Bureau of the Census, which had used UNIVAC in the processing of the 1950 census and was, by the mid-1950s, tabulating its current business survey, current population survey, annual survey of manufactures, and foreign trade statistics with this equipment. These developments did not take place uneventfully. There were continuing concerns about whether the right system had been chosen, and problems had occurred that might have arisen whatever the choice of system. A bureau officer, R. Ziola, who had visited the Bureau of the Census early in 1956, referred to them in a subsequent report to Marshall: "Subject-matter people ... are not entirely convinced that the UNIVAC system has given them the results which might be expected from a computer system. Undoubtedly UNIVAC has given a great deal of trouble–much of it probably not the fault of UNIVAC at all. Factors such as poor programming, inadequate analysis of the job, inexperienced operating staffs, maintenance problems, and even friction between the three operating groups, i.e., the subject matter staffs, the Central Operations Group, and the Central Electronics Unit are reflected in the performance of the UNIVAC system."[50] At this time, alternative equipment configurations for the processing of the 1960 census were under active study by the Bureau of the Census.

Considerations of the kind outlined by Ziola may well have been influential in persuading Marshall that no further time should be lost in addressing the issue of computerization in the bureau. In any case, he soon launched the bureau on a course of change that it is still pursuing four decades later, and that has completely transformed the nature of statistical operations. "The time has arrived," he announced in a memorandum, "for the Bureau to embark on a systematic program of preparedness for the installation of an electronic computer."[51] In this connection, the memorandum reported that a committee had been appointed "to study the statistical series of the various divisions from the point of view of their suitability for processing by electronic computers and the benefits to be derived."[52]

In the same memorandum Marshall appointed a second committee, with representation from the Research and Development Division, in the persons of Goldberg and Rubinoff, as well as Moore and Ziola. They were required to "explore the needs of users of Bureau data in the various government departments which can be satisfied better, or exclusively, by electronic processing." In particular, it was noted, "the mass deseasonalization of economic series and seasonal adjustment appears to be well adapted to electronic machines."[53] This second committee very promptly reported that, after discussions with the Departments of Labour and Trade and Commerce, as well as the Bank of Canada, it recommended that three hundred of its monthly postwar economic series be seasonally adjusted by computer. It had called for alternative cost tenders and found that the work could be done most cheaply with the UNIVAC program of the US Bureau of the Census at a cost of five dollars per series.[54]

The Marshall memorandum was effective as a rallying cry to bureau personnel, but it was misleading in permitting the inference that the acquisition of a computer for the bureau could be a unilateral decision. Even at the time it was written, the bureau was involved willy-nilly in the work of what was called the Government Committee to Study Developments in Electronic Computing Machines and Their Application, which would presumably have expected some say in departmental decisions.

This committee was later transformed into an Interdepartmental Committee on Electronic Computers with a mandate to assess particular departmental needs in a servicewide context and to assign priorities in the use of facilities, once installed, from a similar standpoint. Thus, the planning and decision making that resulted in the installation in the bureau of an IBM 705 – later supplemented by an IBM 1401 – was, ostensibly at least, influenced by the potential needs of other government departments as well as those of the bureau itself. These latter were, of course, dominated by the processing requirements of the 1961 census.

The Bureau's New Building

A major initiative of the Marshall regime, one that he rightly saw as crucial to future employee morale and productivity, was the bureau's move in 1952 to a brand-new building in Tunney's Pasture[55] in the west end of Ottawa. The move was symbolic of the bureau's coming of age. More than thirty years of public service in both peace and war had firmly established the bureau's reputation as the nation's gatherer and publisher of statistical information, and after so many years of performing this function in makeshift quarters, it finally had a worthy home. As noted earlier, the bureau had been housed in the old Edwards Mill on Green Island since 1928. Although providing some compensating benefits by its agreeable location near the Ottawa River, the building could never overcome the limitations of its original purpose. The steady increases in staff after 1939 resulted in scandalous overcrowding,[56] which was only partially relieved by the erection of temporary buildings.

When conditions were at their worst, a journalist who had come to interview Cudmore in 1943 wrote:

> The seamiest rabbit warren among the government properties houses the Bureau. It manages in some way to function in a mouldering brick excrescence that straggles over a fine site above Rideau Falls on the high bank of the Ottawa River, looking more like a defunct brewery than a Government Department.
>
> Through what looks like a barn door entrance and a series of horse stalls, up a back staircase and down a narrow corridor where you trip over gals bending over files, you find Professor Cudmore in an unprepossessing office of which the only distinction is its magnificent view over the river.[57]

The new building was formally opened on 26 September 1952. Under a headline that proclaimed, "Sunlight Plus Space the Keynotes of Vast New 'Factory of Statistics,'" Marshall was quoted as saying: "For the Bureau of Statistics staff the feeling is gone that they were working in an old shed or maybe a former stable. Vanished are the elbow-to-elbow sweatshop conditions."[58] Planning of the building had begun in the late 1940s and its location in Tunney's Pasture was dictated by the Capital Improvement Plan, one element of which was the decentralization of government buildings. From the beginning, bureau management worked with the architects to ensure that the building's design and amenities would accommodate the special needs of statistical work. It was described after completion as "a three-storey building, except in the centre part where it is five floors high ... [with] four pairs of wings." Much was made of the large number of windows, which were said to be "of particular importance for the close work necessary in the production of statistics."[59]

For a time in mid-1950, when the cold war seemed likely to escalate, there was talk of putting a stop to construction. Marshall wrote to the deputy minister to stress that, if war should come, the bureau would again have much additional work to do and extra space would be required; hence construction should be rushed, not stopped.[60] Construction went on, but by early 1952 there was concern that the building and its conference facilities would not be ready in time for the bureau to act as host to two consecutive international conferences scheduled for October of that year. All turned out well, however, and the formal opening took place shortly before the arrival of the first batch of delegates.

The bureau's press release on the opening date of the building boasted: "It is amazing what variety and aesthetic appeal has been introduced with little or no extra cost" and claimed that "the building is basically equipped for complete air conditioning, only requiring the addition of refrigeration units to the present system."[61] However, the bureau's repeated emphasis that the new building was, in effect, "a statistical factory"[62] did not stand it in good stead in the continuing guerrilla warfare over the status of the Dominion statistician and the classification of his professional staff.

Euphoria over the new building soon faded and there were frequent complaints about draughts, the lack of heat in winter, and the excessive heat in summer. Sometimes these found their way to the floor of the House of Commons. In discussion of the bureau's 1955–56 estimates, for instance, a Mr Nicholson, who had evidently not read the press release of 26 September 1952, thought it "a great pity that, when such an expensive building was being constructed, provision was not made to have it air conditioned."[63] The minister, C.D. Howe, replied that "as far as I know ... the members of the House of Commons are the only servants of the people in Ottawa who are entitled to air conditioning. It is a rule of the government that there is no air conditioning in Ottawa."[64]

The new building also provided ammunition for the periodic attacks on the government over the erosion of the term "Dominion." For example, John Diefenbaker, leader of the opposition, remarked that "I saw an example of it in the dominion bureau of statistics building in this city, that magnificent structure, the proper description of which, according to the statute, is the dominion bureau of statistics. But, on the two pillars in front of the building, the word 'Dominion,' which is the official title under the statute, had not been added. It simply says 'Bureau of Statistics Building.'"[65]

No explanation was offered at the time, but when the topic came up again later, the minister, C.D. Howe, rashly speculated that it might have been "an economy move on the part of the Department of Public Works." This prompted the following response from Diefenbaker: "I have heard all kinds of explanations for the removal of the word 'dominion,' but I think in this case the Minister of Trade and Commerce has achieved the ultimate in the matter. Cost is the reason why the word 'dominion' does not appear on the plaques in front of the bureau of statistics building. I commend the Minister for the novelty of his explanation."[66]

As far as its functional properties were concerned, the new building housed the bureau satisfactorily for at least a decade, but the expansion that took place in the 1960s[67] again necessitated resort to the use of temporary accommodation.[68] By the end of that decade plans were being developed for a major addition to the bureau's accommodation – the twenty-six-storey R.H. Coats Building, immediately to the south on Holland Avenue of what then became known as the "Main Building."

CHAPTER TWELVE

1945–1956
The Marshall Years II:
Program and Related Developments

INTRODUCTION

The salient program development of the Marshall years was the construction of what later became known as the System of National Accounts. Some parallel developments in areas such as income size distributions and population projections are also addressed in this chapter.

The decennial census of 1951 embodied significant developments, both substantive and methodological, in Canadian census taking and marked a sharp departure from the more gently evolutionary tradition of the Coats era. Marshall was further responsible for the first mid-decade census of the whole of Canada, conducted in 1956 and subsequently repeated every ten years. In addition, the bureau was involved during the Marshall years in the work of two royal commissions, the 1948 Curtis Commission on prices, and the much further reaching Gordon Commission of 1955–57 on Canada's economic prospects.

The late 1940s also initiated what became an extended process of rationalizing and streamlining its publication program, for which considerable resource savings were claimed. At the same time, arrangements made with the Queen's Printer confirmed the bureau's longstanding *de facto* practice of primary responsibility for the distribution of its own publications.

Although the domestic agenda was always paramount among Marshall's priorities, he was, like Cudmore and Coats before him, a committed internationalist. Thus, as the pre-war intergovernmental statistical organizations began to resume their activities, and as others emerged to meet new needs, Marshall reasserted the bureau's role as a leader in the development of international statistical standards and in the provision of technical assistance to statistical offices in many parts of the developing world.

DEVELOPMENTS IN THE NATIONAL ACCOUNTS

As noted in an earlier chapter, there was considerable pressure on the new Central Research and Development Staff to prepare estimates of national income and expenditure for use by the planned Dominion/provincial conference on reconstruction. The work proceeded during the spring and summer of 1945 under the direction of Luxton's successor, Claude Isbister, with what was referred to as "the Sub-Committee on National Income under the Interdepartmental Committee on Financial Arrangements of the Dominion-Provincial Conference on Reconstruction" looking anxiously over his shoulder. This subcommittee, chaired by Herbert Marshall with Isbister as secretary, also included Agatha Chapman, J.R. Beattie and Walter Duffett of the Bank of Canada, O.J. Firestone and M.C. Urquhart of the Department of Reconstruction, R.B. Bryce of the Department of Finance, and Simon Goldberg, A.S. Abell, and C.D. Blyth from the bureau.

In the fall of 1945 there appeared, ostensibly on a limited-release basis, a publication entitled *National Accounts, Income and Expenditure 1938–1944*, subtitled "Reference Book for Dominion-Provincial Conference on Reconstruction." In addition to the three bureau officers on the subcommittee, acknowledgments were given to Clarence Barber, Miss K. Muttitt, Miss E. Ferguson, D.H. Jones, S.B. Smith, and R.G. Bangs. Copies of the study reached the press, and in the *Financial Post* of 1 December 1945, J.W. Edmonds hailed it as a new and more relevant measure of "the net production of Canada," which could now be compared with corresponding measures for the UK and the US.

In April 1946 an updated and revised set of estimates was compiled for general release as *National Accounts, Income and Expenditure, 1938–1945*.[1] In addition to descriptions of concepts and methods of estimation, the publication provided provincial data on salaries, wages, and supplementary labour income, as well as the income of individual enterprises.

In September 1947, under the terms of the Dominion/provincial taxation agreements that had by then emerged, the Dominion statistician formally provided estimates of gross national product per capita and provincial population ratios to serve as the basis for calculating Dominion payments to the provinces. This became an annual affair and constituted a milestone in the recognition of the bureau second only to the role of the census in determining parliamentary representation.

Marshall's annual report for the year ended 31 March 1949 reported "a marked advance ... in the presentation of the National Accounts. A system of balancing accounts was published for the years 1938-1947, in which it is possible to trace the flow of income and expenditure from one account to another. At the same time each account summarizes an important group of economic transactions. The two Budget 'white papers' prepared during the year drew largely from this material. A historical series of national income, gross national product and expenditure, and personal income and expenditure was prepared for the years 1926–1937."[2]

Subsequently, the industrial distribution of national income and the provincial distribution of personal income were completed and published. Work also began on the deflation of the components of gross national expenditure. Two years later, the results were embodied in a milestone publication consolidating all the work of the previous five years: *National Accounts, Income and Expenditure, 1926–1950*. The annual report for 1951–52 noted that "one member of the Division began a statistical study of inter-industry commodity relationships."[3] The reference was to J.A. Sawyer, whose work, based on W.W. Leontief's pioneering study of input-output relationships in the pre-war US economy, gave rise to the publication in 1956 of *Inter-Industry Flow of Goods and Services, Canada, 1949*. The preface stated that "The primary reason for constructing this set of inter-industry accounts was to bring together, in an integrated framework, industrial and other economic statistics collected by the Dominion Bureau of Statistics in order to draw attention to possible inconsistencies in classification and to possible gaps or errors in the data ... The table may be regarded as an extension of the National Accounts in that it provides the industrial detail which underlies the Accounts. This detail may be used to further the analysis of determinants of the national income."[4]

Quarterly estimates of gross national product and expenditure and personal income and expenditure, in current and constant dollars and on a seasonally adjusted basis, began to be published later in 1953. These data, which went back to 1947, provided a powerful new statistical tool for studying current economic trends. A regular monthly index of industrial production was also developed and progress made towards extending its scope to provide real output measures for the economy as a whole, thus making possible an independent check on the validity of the income and expenditure accounts. A final noteworthy initiative during the Marshall years was the launching of a pilot study aimed at extending the existing framework of the national accounts to include purely financial transactions.

None of these extensions and elaborations would have been possible without the parallel development of the underlying primary statistics. Particular mention may be made of monthly inventory statistics, first collected, along with shipments and orders data, for the manufacturing industries and later extended to include wholesale and retail trade; monthly estimates of consumer expenditures; and a quarterly survey of corporation profits.[5] Improved estimates of savings were also developed, and gaps in the area of incomes were filled by surveys of professional earnings.

Other Research and Development Work

Elsewhere within the mandate of Research and Development, income size distributions for nonfarm families were published for 1951 and 1954 on the basis of data collected in conjunction with the periodic labour force surveys. An early attempt at income distribution by L.M. Read had been published as an appendix to the national accounts release for 1938–45. Covering the year 1942, it was based on 1941 census data and income tax statistics for 1941 and 1942. These latter were, of course, far from being representative of the population as a whole. Some income data were collected in the 1948 survey of income and expenditure, but the primary emphasis was on expenditures. It was subsequently decided that separate and continuing surveys of household incomes and household expenditures should be initiated. Responsibility for the income surveys was given to the Research and Development Division, while the Labour and Prices Division undertook the conduct of the family expenditure surveys.

In conjunction with the second labour force survey in February 1946, the Sampling Organization conducted the first of what became a regular succession of supplementary surveys, frequently sponsored by other departments for use in their own program planning. This first survey was addressed to the multiple occupancy of dwellings and conditions of overcrowding. Soon after, a survey was undertaken to obtain information about the re-establishment of veterans in civil life. August 1947 saw the beginning of what became the present annual survey of household facilities and equipment, and in the following year the first postwar family expenditure survey was conducted as a basis for updating what was by then an outmoded cost of living index. This was a difficult assignment for the regional offices, given the length of time required and difficulty for respondents in completing the recall-type questionnaire, and the sensitive nature of the questions relating to income, savings, debts, etc.

On 1 January 1949, as noted in the preceding chapter, the sampling unit was given separate and enhanced status as the Special Surveys Division. At this time, the new division absorbed the field representatives of what had become the Labour and Prices Division. These had been appointed during the war to ensure the maintenance of high standards of price collection. The newly strengthened regional office capability now began to take on responsibility for the follow-up of nonrespondents to the mail surveys of other divisions such as Industry and Merchandising and the Employment Section of the Labour and Prices Division. A regional office was also opened in St John's, Newfoundland, to accommodate the inclusion of that province in the labour force survey. In September 1952 the bureau was directed to increase the frequency of its labour force surveys from quarterly to monthly, and to accelerate the processing so that results would be available within four and a half weeks from the start of enumeration. As a consequence of the former requirement, new regional offices were opened in Edmonton and in Ottawa-Hull.

Population Projections

Soon after the end of the war, the bureau made its first population projections. As late as 1938, in connection with a request from the Rowell-Sirois Commission, Coats had expressed the view that "we think it unwise to issue any statement regarding the future population of Canada."[6] In 1946, however, the bureau published *The Future Population of Canada,*[7] Bulletin F-4 in the 1941 census monograph series. Its introduction made it quite clear that there were no longer any concerns on the bureau's part about the validity or propriety of such an undertaking: "The value of population projections lies, not in their prophetic qualities, for it cannot be too strongly emphasized that no attempt is made to predict what the total population of a community will be at some future date, but in their examination of what consequences must ensue if no unforeseen agencies intervene to affect drastically past trends."[8] The methodology was very simple. It extrapolated past trends to 1971 on the basis of different assumptions as to mortality and fertility. No account was taken of the possible effects of migration.

But the bureau's assurances did not satisfy the Department of Trade and Commerce. On 6 March 1946 the deputy minister, M.W. Mackenzie, wrote to the assistant deputy minister, Oliver Master, commenting on discussions stemming from the release of Bulletin F-4: "The Minister is concerned, and I think rightly, as to the propriety of ... engaging in this field of crystal gazing. I was under the impression that the Bureau restricted its releases to factual material, from which others are quite at liberty to draw predictions or conclusions."[9]

Marshall wrote a long memorandum defending the practice, stressing that "in many countries population trends are giving great concern to statesmen, economists, sociologists" and noting that the projections "were prepared initially because information was required by the Dominion-Provincial Committee on Reconstruction to assist them in their deliberations on old age pensions and on provincial subsidies." He argued that "the contents of our bulletins are purely statistical. Naturally it suggests nothing as to policy concerning population ... There have been many estimates of Canada's future population, many based on wishful thinking. It seems desirable that there should be an official estimate based on carefully stated unbiased assumptions."[10]

These arguments were apparently acceptable. Towards the end of the Marshall regime, Keyfitz's office compiled a "Memorandum on the Projection of Population Statistics, 1954," with an even stronger cautionary statement: "Despite ... improved procedures, the fact remains that there are no methods at present available to forecast with reasonable accuracy the forces ... determining population magnitudes and movements." It went on to say that, "for this reason, and because this calculation has not the same factual basis as other Bureau publications, this memorandum, like its predecessor, will not be given general distribution. It will be available only on request and for their own use to those interested in the subject."[11] This was probably a reasonable precaution against the possibility of further official complaints, but the circulation of bulletin F-4 had certainly not been restricted. In any case, the bureau continued to maintain a low profile on this topic, and it was not until the early 1970s that it began to issue "official" population projections.[12]

The 1951 and 1956 Censuses

The 1951 census provided a unique opportunity to shed light on the social and economic developments of what had been a decade of considerable turbulence. Marshall later called it "one of the most significant in the country's history. Coming at the mid-point of the century, it provided a means of measuring Canada's development during the first half of this century. Following a decade of great international upheavals, viz. World War II and the immediate post-war adjustment period, it reflected the widespread economic and social changes which have occurred during this period. With the union of Newfoundland and Canada in 1951, it represented Canada's first census since becoming a nation of ten provinces."[13]

From an administrative perspective, the many methodological innovations that characterized the 1951 operation are of considerable interest. The 1951 procedures were comprehensively described in the administrative report,[14] but a few salient points can be touched upon here. Planning began early in 1947 under the direction of a Census Executive Committee chaired by the Dominion statistician and made up of the senior subject-matter and functional experts who were to be involved at various stages. Primary responsibility rested with Dr O.A. Lemieux, who had followed A.J. Pelletier in 1945 as director of the Census Division.

The lead time was longer than ever before, since it now had to accommodate the preparation, conduct, and evaluation of a test census that explored the possibility of decentralizing to the bureau's regional offices the conduct of enumeration and the initial processing of questionnaires by "mark-sense" technology. This latter involved the recording of respondent information by means of special markings in designated positions on the enumeration document from which punch cards could be generated by a document punch without the intermediate step of manual punching.[15] Subsequent processing of the cards was carried out on what was called an "electronic statistical machine," or high-speed tabulator. The technology was not new, but it had not so far been used in a major statistical undertaking. The willingness of the commercial tabulating industry to work with the bureau in the statistical application of mark-sense technology effectively drew the curtain on the Bureau's long tradition of building its own machines.[16]

Mark-sensing, which was used only for the population and housing questionnaires, greatly reduced processing time and costs. The administrative report later estimated that "to produce a million punched cards completely edited and ready for tabulation, as achieved on 17 document punch machines during the week of peak processing in 1951, would have taken at least 650 key punch operators. Even then document punch machines operated at not more than 70% of their effective capacity."[17]

Reflecting postwar interest in the size, composition, characteristics, and activity of the labour force, which had been the subject of a regular current sample survey since 1945, ten of the twenty-five enumerative questions on the basic population questionnaire requested similar benchmark information from all persons fourteen years of age and over. Accordingly, for full consonance with the current measures, it was necessary to abandon the "gainfully employed" concept reflecting a person's usual activity that had been used in previous censuses in favour of a definition that determined employment status on the basis of current labour force activity.

The changes that had taken place during the 1940s in the industrial structure and its occupational composition set a premium on the accurate coding of labour force data. Thus, extensive changes were made in the classification manuals, including revisions of the major occupational and industry groups and a considerable extension of the detailed component classes. The larger industrial and commercial firms were also asked to supply each employee with a description of his or her job, to be furnished to the census enumerator, and the questionnaire required that the firm name be supplied, as well as the nature of the business. Finally, a key to the coding of firm names was provided as an aid for the coding staff.

In 1941 every tenth dwelling had been asked a set of questions designed to provide a comprehensive picture of housing conditions in Canada. In 1951 the adequacy of the housing stock was an even more important issue of social policy than it had been a decade earlier, and the sample was enlarged to include every fifth dwelling so that housing results could be published for smaller areas. However, the experience of 1941 had shown that certain questions, such as those relating to house values, property taxes, mortgage payments, and interest rates, gave results of doubtful accuracy when asked in a general census, and it was decided that such information could be better collected through a postcensal supplementary sample survey. In this inquiry, conducted in June 1952 with an expanded version of the quarterly area sample then being used to measure the current labour force, the housing questions were bracketed with a parallel group from the census of agriculture on such items as mortgage indebtedness and the costs of operating power farm equipment, which had presented similar difficulties in 1941.

The census of agriculture itself was greatly scaled down from that of 1941, which, under the pressures of wartime needs, had asked 941 questions. Including a number of questions that were to be enumerated on a twenty percent sample basis, the total for 1951 was 337. The threshold acreage and value of production for the definition of a holding as a "farm" were increased, and this was estimated to have accounted for about one-half of the decline in the count of farms in Canada, excluding Newfoundland, from 733,000 in 1941 to 620,000 in 1951.

The fishery, as the fishing industry was called, was surveyed in a decennial census for the first time since 1911 – a decision no doubt stemming from the entry of Newfoundland into Confederation. Although the fishery, like agriculture, was largely a household industry, the census test had shown that the general house-to-house census enumeration should not include the detailed fishery questionnaire dealing with such questions as the quantity, kinds, and value of catch, numbers and types of boats, gear, and equipment, etc. Instead, a simple form was used in specified fishing areas of Canada at the time of the general enumeration to elicit the names and addresses of commercial fishermen and to collect some basic information on the number of days spent fishing and the resultant income. Area samples were then drawn up for a special follow-up survey to enumerate a more extensive and complex body of information.

Procedures for what was now called the census of distribution were similar to those of the 1931 and 1941 censuses of merchandising and service establishments, with the field enumerators for population, housing, and agriculture collecting information for the provision of an office mailing list of all business firms coming within the scope of the census. The subsequent mail survey, covering the calendar year 1951, took place in January 1952.

The processing and tabulation program for the 1951 Census was planned on the basis of the statistical tables that were to appear in published form. This was to avoid any tabulations that did not have a definite place in the scheme of publication or analysis. The matter of special tabulations was deferred to the postcensal period when the possibilities of using sampling methods could be applied to particular tabulation requirements as they arose.

Another departure from earlier census practices was the plan adopted for the publication of the 1951 census reports and bound volumes. Hitherto, tables had been prepared on subjects of general interest and printed in the form of offset reports. They had then been prepared a second time in a different format for linotype printing in the census volumes. The bureau's switch to the use of varityping and offset printing, described later in this chapter, eliminated the need for this kind of duplication, and the film negatives of the photocopies of the tables used for the individual census reports were simply recompiled for the printing of the census volumes. The number of individual reports produced in 1951 (ninety-seven) was little more than a quarter of the figure for 1941 (353), and approximately seventy-five percent of their tabular content went directly into the volumes.

The careful planning and improved technology that underlay every phase of the 1951 census resulted in a more expeditious publication of census volumes than had been the case with the three preceding censuses. The administrative report noted that, of the nine planned subject-related volumes, six had appeared in less than three years after the census date, and the rest were expected to be published by March 1954. But the 1951 census did not attempt a series of research monographs like those that had adorned the 1931 census, and that would probably have been repeated after the 1941 census but for the war. Instead a general review was published as volume 10 of the series. This dealt chapter by chapter with the various subject-matter fields covered by the 1951 census under such headings as "The Growth of the Canadian Population," "Rural and Urban Distribution," "Families in Canada," etc.

A final important innovation of the 1951 census was the use of comparative checks to determine the order of size of the discrepancies to which all enumerative censuses are subject, regardless of how carefully they are conducted. The comparable and independent estimates used for the checks were provided by the June 1951 labour force survey. The documents of the two surveys were matched and compared to show the degree of divergence in answers to the same question by a matched group of respondents and also to provide an indication of the amount of underenumeration. Subsequently, in the census metropolitan areas of Montreal and Toronto, samples of the matched documents in which major differences occurred were re-enumerated to determine the reasons for differences, which questions were misunderstood and warranted more instruction and clarification, and the relative effectiveness of the two sets of enumerators.[18]

Prior to 1956, mid-decade, or quinquennial, censuses had only been conducted for the provinces of Manitoba, Saskatchewan, and Alberta. Covering population and agriculture, they had originated at the time of admission of the latter two provinces to Confederation and were an acknowledgment of what was then a rate of economic development higher than in the rest of Canada. In 1956, however, this requirement was incorporated into, and superseded by, a nationwide census of modified design. After the event, the administrative report noted that "the decision ... was influenced by the extremely large increases and shifts in population shown by intercensal estimates since 1951, and by the rapid changes occurring in the agriculture economy of the country."[19]

The report then addressed the perceived statistical implications of these changes: "Such rapid developments in population and agriculture indicated the need for bench marks at the five-year period in order to provide a more accurate basis for annual estimates. Further, one of the chief values of the 1956 census, both for population and agriculture, is that it provided information for small areas ... which cannot be obtained from inter-censal estimates."[20]

In the mid-1930s Cudmore had similarly argued for a Canadawide census in 1936 in order to update such information as that on unemployment. "Economic change," he had argued, "proceeds at least twice as rapidly as it did even a generation ago."[21] As the bureau developed its campaign for cabinet approval of a 1956 census, these arguments were supplemented by assurances about the probable costs. In the past, unacceptably high cost had been the great obstacle to more frequent national censuses. Now, however, it was said that "new methods and equipment had reduced this cost. Further developments of the economical methods used in the 1951 Census and additional new methods will enable the Bureau to take a Canada-wide census of population and agriculture for not much more than it would cost to take the prairie census as in the past."[22]

The census was described as a "simplified" count, meaning that there would only be five basic questions in the population count and some seventy in the agricultural enumeration. This reduction in agricultural questions would, it was suggested, "in a large measure set the pattern which would be followed in all succeeding censuses, thus reducing their cost."[23] The savings could then be used to conduct sample inquiries in intercensal years. But the proposition was not an easy sell. There were in fact some Ottawa users of statistics who took the view that the quinquennial census of the Prairie provinces could be discontinued without much harm to the public interest. Mitchell Sharp, associate deputy minister of Trade and Commerce, acknowledged that he had been one of them when he wrote to R.B. Bryce, now clerk of the Privy Council, enclosing for him a copy of the bureau's arguments. However, he added, "after looking into the matter a little more closely ... I find that the accuracy of our agricultural estimates in the Prairie Provinces depend to a considerable extent upon a Quinquennial Census of acreage and livestock numbers. That being so, I think there is a pretty good case for converting the Quinquennial Census into a country-wide count of population and country-wide survey of agriculture."[24]

Bryce responded to Marshall almost immediately: "By and large, I think the idea of extending and simplifying the Quinquennial Census is a good one."[25] But K.W. Taylor, deputy minister of Finance, to whom the same material had been sent, took longer to reply and was clearly not convinced. Referring to consultations with his senior colleagues, he wrote to Sharp that "I find we have somewhat divided views. Most of us favour dropping the quinquennial census entirely. Personally, I am a bit undecided and part of my indecision rests on a lack of cost data." Referring to the rough estimates quoted earlier, he thought that "there has to be a strong positive case to justify a $4 to $5 million expenditure." He further observed that "professional statisticians appear divided on the real value of a quinquennial bench mark. As a comparative layman, I would have thought it very valuable as a basis for good sampling. But I understand some experts do not think so. I would not attach much weight to the 'market analysis' or 'provincial grants' arguments"[26]

Nevertheless, the bureau's plan for a nationwide census in 1956 was approved by cabinet on 26 October 1955 (PC 1955–1609). There had been some discussion of the appropriate legal authority, but it was concluded that the provisions relating to "general statistics" in section 32 of the Statistics Act made it possible to extend the explicit provision of section 17 for a quinquennial census of the Prairie provinces to Canada as a whole. Planning had begun late in 1953 under the same kind of executive committee structure as that used for the 1951 census.

A test census was conducted in March 1954 to evaluate the feasibility of mark-sensing for the census of agriculture and to see whether the clerical coding of households and families that, in 1951, had necessitated one or more codes being placed on 14 million documents could be eliminated. In both cases, the outcomes were positive.

The abbreviated content of the 1956 census greatly simplified its collection, processing, and publication. Enumeration and the primary checking of questionnaries for acceptability were, as in 1951, directed by the regional offices, but because of the reduced requirements for machine processing, this work was carried out at head office. Again, table planning was much easier since there were eventually only about 1,500 pages of tables where there had been 8,000 in 1951. Population characteristics, for example, could be tabulated directly from the summary punched cards. Final results were issued in several series of offset printed reports, which were prepared in such a way that their tables could be collected in loose-leaf binders, or bound in volume form.

The labour force survey again provided the basis for a population quality check, using the May 1956 data. For the first time, such a quality check was also undertaken for the census of agriculture. This involved a re-enumeration of all farms in an area sample survey conducted during the months of July and August 1956. The 1956 census enjoyed the distinction of being the first to use television in its publicity program. Provision was also made for the approximately 4,500 municipalities to register disagreement with the preliminary counts of population, so that revisions, if appropriate, could be made before the issuance of final figures. One hundred and thirty-five municipalities, or three percent of the total, took advantage of this provision. Following investigation, changes were made in the preliminary totals for fifty-two municipalities, those for forty-seven being increased by 22,837, and those for five being decreased by 5,256.

Working with Two Royal Commissions

The apparent success of the macroeconomic management and social engineering practised by Ottawa's new breed of technocrats during and after the war did not, as might have been expected, deal a mortal blow to the royal commission industry. Already, at war's end, a royal commission on coal was at work, and by 1948 the transportation industry – a hardy perennial for this particular mode of analysis – was again under the microscope. The Marshall years witnessed several others – not all economic – culminating in the launching in June 1955 of what may have been the most ambitious in Canadian history, the Royal Commission on Canada's Economic Prospects. Before looking at the impact of this commission on the bureau, I shall examine the work of what became known as the Curtis Commission.

On 10 February 1948, a resolution of the House of Commons appointed a select committee to examine the causes of the recent rise in the cost of living. Consumer prices had been remarkably stable during the war, in part due to the successful imposition of a price ceiling late in 1941. During six years of war, the bureau's cost of living index had risen by less than twenty percent, with more than half of the increase occurring in the first two years. But the index had gone up by more than nine percent between 1946 and 1947 and was gathering momentum, so that a fourteen percent increase was registered in the following year. Later in 1948 the committee turned its work over to a royal commission, chaired by Professor C.A. Curtis of Queen's University, whose members were required "to continue, after familiarizing themselves with the work initiated by the Special Committee ... the inquiry into and concerning price structures, factors leading to price and cost increases and increased profit margins in Canada, paying particular regard to essential commodities and services in common daily use."[27]

The bureau provided much of the statistical underpinning for the commission's findings, but with its role in the Ottawa polity now more firmly established, it no longer needed to use the commission's work as a vehicle for promoting its image as it had done in similar situations during the 1930s. The findings, tabled on 8 April 1949, were complex and varied, but it was judged that "in the main, the post-war price rise in Canada was a consequence of the War, of rising prices abroad, of large export demands financed to some degree by the Canadian Government, and of the capital boom." Selective price ceilings had been reimposed in 1947 and 1948, but the commission took the view that "general price control should not be relied upon as an important instrument for stabilizing prices in peacetime ... (it) is no substitute for action designed to bring overall demand into line with overall supply."[28]

The commission also made a number of recommendations relating to price statistics. The cost of living index in use when its inquiries were being conducted was based on a budgetary survey conducted among families of urban wage earners in 1938. Not surprisingly, therefore, the need was felt "for the development of a continuing program of sample surveys such as are now carried out at infrequent intervals. Thus, when the articles in the base budget change in importance, or if new articles should be included, adjustments can be made to present a more accurate index number."[29] Dissatisfaction was also expressed with the methodology used for measuring changes in shelter costs and the failure to calculate explicit changes in the cost of children's clothing. In other areas of statistics, the commission endorsed the recommendation of the House Committee that the bureau "publish periodically an analysis of the way in which the consumer's dollar is divided among the various productive and distributive processes having to do with the price of basic commodities."[30] It also called for a "broadening and refining" of statistics of consumer credit, for quarterly information on corporate profits, and for a statistical study of productivity, which it considered to be an important factor in the explanation of price changes.

The bureau appears to have made no direct acknowledgment of, or response to, these recommendations. It was in fact working on a revision of the cost of living index when the House Committee was formed, and a new family expenditure survey was conducted in 1948-49. The results provided the item content and weights for a new index published in 1952[31] with a base period of 1949 and linked to its predecessor to provide a continuous record of retail price change. This satisfied two specific recommendations of the royal commission, first by providing a separate and direct measurement of changes in the price of home ownership[32] and second, by the inclusion of children's clothing among the items regularly priced for the clothing group. The change in the index's title from cost of living index to consumer price index was an attempt to avoid the inference that the index was a measure of all changes in living costs rather than those resulting from changes in the cost of purchasing a base-period "basket of goods."[33]

The bureau began to publish statistics of the quarterly profits of industrial corporations in 1954 and statistics of consumer credit followed in 1957. In 1949 an interdepartmental committee on productivity analysis began to review the conceptual and measurement problems that were involved, but it was not until the late 1950s that work actually began in the bureau on the development of productivity measures at both the aggregate and industry levels. The commission's recommendation for periodic analyses of the consumer's dollar into the fractions accounted for by the successive processes of production and distribution went unanswered by the bureau, no doubt as a consequence of reservations not only about the technical feasibility of such calculations but also about their credibility with different groups of users.

On 17 June 1955 a royal commission was appointed to look into the long-term prospects of the Canadian economy. Some weeks earlier in his budget speech,[34] the minister of Finance, Hon. Walter Harris, had acknowledged some faltering of economic growth in the fall of 1953, but he expressed himself satisfied, then and since, that the basic strength of the economy was not in question. Nevertheless, he believed the time had come to spend a little time, thought, and money on carefully documenting the reality underlying the widespread euphoria about Canada's great opportunities and shining prospects.

Walter L. Gordon, who was appointed chairman of the Royal Commission on Canada's Economic Prospects, was in fact its true father. He had long been uncomfortable with what he regarded as the continentalist economic policies of the St Laurent government, and his memoirs subsequently related his concerns about "the complacency with which Canadians were witnessing the sellout of our resources and business enterprises to Americans and other enterprising foreigners."[35] He had been invited to join the cabinet in 1954 but had not been offered a specific portfolio and hence refused.

Rather, he thought that an article questioning various aspects of the government's policies and advocating the creation of a royal commission to examine the issues involved might prod the government into action. He submitted a draft to K.W. Taylor, the deputy minister of Finance, and asked whether it would embarrass the department. Taylor replied that he supported the proposal for a royal commission, and that Gordon could expect to hear soon from the minister, Harris. Gordon recalled Harris asking him "if I would mind very much if the government took over my idea. He said that he would like to put forward the proposal for a royal commission in his forthcoming budget speech, but this would mean I would have to forego the original plan of publishing the article."[36] Gordon agreed with alacrity, and Harris subsequently came to him with a request from the prime minister that he serve as the commission's chairman. It was a bold initiative on Harris's part and reflected the relative growth of his influence in cabinet *vis-à-vis* that of C.D. Howe, who opposed the inquiry from the beginning.

The commission's mandate was as follows:

> To inquire into and report upon the long-term prospects of the Canadian economy, i.e., upon the probable economic development of Canada, and the problems to which such development appears likely to give rise, and, without limiting the generality of the foregoing, to study and report upon:
>
> a) developments in the supply of new materials and energy sources;
> b) the growth to be expected in the population of Canada and the changes in its distribution;
> c) prospects for growth and change in domestic and external markets for Canada's production;
> d) trends in productivity and standards of living; and
> e) prospective requirements for industrial and social capital.[37]

The scope of this mandate was thus comparable to that of the Rowell-Sirois Commission eighteen years earlier. Before publishing its final report in November 1957, fifty days of hearings were held across Canada, and 750 witnesses spoke to 260 of the 330 submissions received. The commission's own research staff published thirty-three supporting studies. Many of the submissions made use of bureau data, which were more comprehensive and reliable than they had been at the time of Rowell-Sirois. And, in addition to providing the research staff with "off the shelf" series, the bureau also collaborated with them in developing new compilations and analyses. Notable among these was a set of financial transactions accounts for the years 1946–54.[38] This work, which linked changes in the stocks of financial claims within the various sectors of the economy to the production of goods and services, provided the conceptual basis for the development and eventual publication of financial flow accounts, representing a further step in the articulation of the System of National Accounts.[39]

The commission's generous acknowledgment of the bureau's cooperation, which singled out in particular Herbert Marshall and Simon Goldberg, was a compelling testimony to the ease with which the postwar generation of the bureau's professional staff was able to work with the cream of the economic establishment in both government and academe. This stock of goodwill paid dividends a few years later when, for the first time, the role of the bureau within the federal government and its relations with users generally was critically examined by the Glassco Commission.

Publications and Their Distribution

The annual report of the Dominion statistician for the year ended 31 March 1950 noted that "for the past three or four years the Bureau of Statistics had had, as a prominent part of its program, the streamlining of its operations. The demand for statistics from the general public, from government departments and agencies and from international organizations has increased to such an extent that special efforts have had to be made to increase the efficiency of operation, and at the same time to keep staff and general costs to an essential minimum."[40]

Some of this "streamlining" was conceived and implemented by the subject-matter divisions. Thus, one of the initiatives commented on was the adoption by the industrial census of so-called "short forms" for use by the 10,000 or so small firms that accounted for only about five percent of the gross value of product reported to the census.[41] However, it was on J.T. Marshall's Administration Division, with its mandate "to study and apply the principles of up-to-date organization and methods to ensure the use of the most efficient equipment, improve work flows, [and] eliminate superfluous operations",[42] that the heaviest responsibility for results rested. Probably the most enduring and far reaching of his initiatives was the establishment on 1 September 1948 of the Advisory Board of Publications, charged with keeping the bureau's publishing program under constant review with a view to the elimination of unnecessary publications, ensuring that each publication retained or newly proposed met a demonstrable and fully justified need, effecting improvements in layout and the structure of tables and related text, and promoting uniform editorial and production standards across the bureau.

The task was a formidable one. The bureau's publications had developed between the two wars not as an organized program but as a collection of individual divisional initiatives. Wartime censorship and resource shortages had cut them back considerably, but growth resumed after 1945. The annual report of the Dominion statistician for the year ended 31 March 1948 reported the output of the Printing Section as 28,900,000 impressions[43] – an increase of sixty-four percent over the previous year. Most of this increase would have derived from publications rather than questionnaires and forms. The actual number of publications during that year was 2,470 (including separate issues of subannual publications). The publications were produced by at least three technologies: mimeograph, multigraph, and rotaprint, the latter being mainly a letterpress operation.

In the technical aspects of printing, some rationalization had come about before the formation of the advisory board. A shift was taking place from printing by letterpress to the cheaper offset process, using varitype machines for composition. The annual report for 1949–50 noted that savings of $55,000 were made by printing the four volumes of the 1946 census of the Prairie provinces in this way, and it was further claimed that $200,000 could be saved by the use of offset technology in printing the 1951 decennial census volumes. Again, the bureau had been thinking for some time that even greater savings could be made by turning over its Printing Section to the Department of Public Printing and Stationery. The agreement to this effect, completed during 1949–50, provided for the continuing location of the section on bureau premises and for bureau work always to be given priority.

Succeeding annual reports dealt extensively with the work and successes of the advisory board. One early initiative was the development of a manual, *Rules and Principles for the Guidance of Officers of the Dominion Bureau of Statistics in the Preparation of Copy for Reports*. This document embodied a directive that Herbert Marshall had issued late in 1946 outlawing the use of academic honours by authors and others mentioned by name in bureau publications. This had prompted an anonymous wit to write: "Democracy comes to the Bureau with a bang – Degrees and honours can go to hang – American influence we must embrace – The old school tie is in disgrace – The trappings of learning will be put to bed - Sufficient the honour a Branch to head."[44]

The annual report for 1948–49 provided an illustration of the progress being made in the item-by-item scrutiny of existing publications.[45] In summary, eighty-three reports out of a total of some 450 were eliminated. These initial successes were, no doubt, the easier ones since progress in subsequent years was less spectacular. However, a major saving came about by eliminating the reprinting by letterpress, for purposes of permanent record, of periodical publications made by the offset process. Offset reports were henceforth printed once only, by varitype, in such a form as to permit their being bound into annual volumes, thus avoiding double editing, proof reading, and printing costs. The cumulative effects of the board's work were summarized in the 1951–52 annual report, which noted that fifty-six reports had been entirely eliminated and 120 transferred to the "Reference Paper" or "Memorandum" classes.[46] These eliminations and transfers, together with reductions in the size of publications and the elimination of free lists, had brought about a saving of over 5,000,000 pages annually.

While the bureau had, on its own initiative, turned over its printing operations to the Department of Public Printing and Stationery at the beginning of the 1950s, it continued to adhere to its longstanding view that it could do a better job of distributing its own publications than the department. The latter was exclusively responsible for distributing the publications of other departments, but with the exception of a few publications – notably the Canada Year Book and Handbook, which it distributed jointly with the bureau – the great majority of bureau reports were distributed directly by the bureau's own Publications Distribution Unit.

This was a legacy from Coats who, since the bureau's inception, had insisted that publishing was its *raison d'être*, and that the right to publish, unhampered by external constraints, was guaranteed by the Statistics Act. In any case, he argued, the bureau understood its clientele and could look after their needs better than any general-purpose publishing organization. During the 1930s at least two attempts had been made – allegedly in the name of administrative efficiency – to put the bureau on the same basis as other departments, but Coats had successfully fended them off.[47] In 1956 the issue resurfaced when John Deutsch, secretary of the Treasury Board, wrote to Herbert Marshall reminding him of the authorization by cabinet two years earlier of a joint Treasury Board/Public Printing and Stationery Committee that was to discuss with departments "(a) the extent to which the mailing lists of departments might be curtailed, and (b) the desirability of transferring such lists and the printing arrangements to the Queen's Printer for mailing out such publications when adequate facilities become available in the new building."[48]

The recommendation that emerged for the bureau from this process was that it "continue to handle automatic distribution, i.e., distribution pursuant to subscription lists, as an agent of the Queen's Printer. All other sales to be effected at the Printing Bureau."[49]

The response to this latter proposition echoed the arguments of the 1930s: "There is a constant pressure on the Bureau from the users of the statistics ... for the earliest possible release of data ... I do not think there can be any doubt that the Bureau, being kept constantly aware of this situation, would have a greater interest in supplying the need than would be possible where the interest would necessarily have to be divided among many departments servicing divergent needs. This I believe to be true regardless of how conscientious the other agency may be.[50]

Again, the bureau carried the day but in what appears to have been a remarkably cooperative climate, judging from the mutual congratulations that were subsequently exchanged. The key points in the formal agreement signed by the Queen's Printer and the Dominion statistician read as follows:

1 Dominion Bureau of Statistics to continue to handle automatic distribution of their publications offered to the public on a subscription basis.

2 Subscriptions to publications and individual copies of publications for over-the-counter sales to be available to the Dominion Bureau of Statistics acting as agent of the Department of Public Printing and Stationery.
3 Surplus copies of the publications referred to in 1. and 2. above to be transferred to the Department of Public Printing and Stationery to meet current public demand or stored for future sales.[51]

The agreement also set the financial basis on which the two bodies were to operate for the next quarter century. The bureau was to pay all printing costs, half of the selling price being recoverable from Public Printing and Stationery; monies received by the bureau from the sales of publications were to be deposited in the Consolidated Revenue Fund.

International Cooperation

In 1945 the United Nations was established as the successor body to the League of Nations, and, in association with it, a number of relatively autonomous functional organizations were revived or came into being. Within the United Nations proper, a Statistical Commission was established in June 1946 for the purpose of carrying forward the statistical work begun by the League of Nations before the war. A subsidiary body of the Economic and Social Council, it was charged with:

a) promoting the development of national statistics and improving their comparability;
b) the co-ordination of the statistical work of Specialized Agencies;
c) the development of the central statistical services of the Secretariat;
d) advising the organs of the United Nations on general questions relating to the collection, interpretation and dissemination of statistical information;
e) promoting the improvement of statistics and statistical methods generally.[52]

Canada, represented by Herbert Marshall, took part in the first nine sessions, missing only the fifth in 1950, when it was not a member.[53] Marshall's international standing was reflected in his election as chairman of the first three sessions.

From the start, Canada was actively involved in the commission's work on national income. One of the earliest projects, in which C.M. Isbister and Agatha Chapman took part, was to review and complete, in the light of wartime developments in the area, a study of the measurement of national income and the construction of social accounts that the league's Committee of Statistical Experts had begun before the war.[54] Again, N.L. McKellar, working with his U.S. counterpart, V.S. Kolesnikoff, quickly earned recognition as an international authority on statistical classifications. And the bureau's successful application of modern sampling methods enabled it to contribute to the work of the Sub-Commission on Statistical Sampling, established in May 1946 to consider how far sampling methods might be used in meeting the increased postwar need for statistics.

While the Statistical Commission was charged with the general task of improving statistics and making them more comparable at the world level, the statistical problems it encountered were not identical from region to region, and the means of solving them also differed. Within the framework of world standards, there needed to be provision for regional adaptation and for the separate discussion of specifically regional problems. Accordingly, the Economic and Social Council made arrangements to facilitate and encourage consultation among representatives of national statistical agencies in the different regions of the world. The Economic Commission for Europe (ECE) convened meetings of European statisticians in 1949, 1951, and 1953, and the participants agreed to meet thereafter as a continuing body, to be known as the Conference of European Statisticians. Canada was not at that time a member of the ECE and did not become one until 1973, but from the mid-1960s the bureau participated informally in the work of the conference.

Another of the Economic and Social Commission's subsidiary bodies was the Population Commission. With responsibility for studies and advice on population changes, migratory movements, and the interrelationships of economic and social conditions and population trends, its orientation was primarily statistical. Canada was a member from 1947 to 1950 and from 1954 to 1957, and J.T. Marshall was delegate during both terms, being appointed chairman at the eighth session in 1954. Priority tasks addressed by the commission included the improvement of statistics of migration and the preparation of guidelines for the 1950 round of population censuses so as to render more comparable the various national findings.

Before the war, the two major intergovernmental organizations collaborating with the league in international statistical work had been the International Labour Organization and the International Institute of Agriculture. The former, which had spent the war years in Montreal, returned to Geneva and quickly resumed its pre-war range of statistical activities. In August 1947 the sixth International Conference of Labour Statisticians was held – the first meeting since the war – followed by others in 1949, 1954, and 1957. The sixth conference adopted a resolution concerning cost of living statistics, superseding that of the second conference of 1925, and the work that it began on statistics of the labour force, employment, and unemployment was extended and elaborated in a resolution adopted in 1954 by the eighth conference The most outstanding achievement of the conferences, to which McKellar made a key contribution, was the adoption in 1957 by the ninth conference of an International Standard Classification of Occupations, embodying major, minor, and unit groups. During this first postwar decade, bureau officers served twice on the ILO's prestigious Committee of

Statistical Experts,[55] a group convened from time to time to advise the governing body on criteria for determining the member states of chief industrial importance – a status that entitled them to automatic membership of the governing body.

The International Institute of Agriculture had not been thought equal to the postwar challenges of rehabilitating world food production and the channels for its distribution. It was thus replaced in October 1945 by a new Food and Agriculture Organization, the long-term objectives of which embraced not only the market-related roles of the IIA, but also the work begun by the League of Nations during the 1930s on problems of nutrition and their relation to health. The bureau's Agriculture Division was involved in the organization's statistical work right from the beginning, and its director attended no fewer than five meetings in 1946 alone. This officer, J.B. Rutherford, was appointed to the organization's staff in the following year. One of the organization's earliest statistical projects was for a world census of agriculture to be held in 1950, and the director of the Census Division played a major role in its planning.

Another new specialized agency with links to the pre-war responsibilities of the League of Nations was the World Health Organization(WHO), established in July 1946 with a mandate to promote the attainment by all peoples of "the highest possible level of health." The bureau had worked with the league's Health Section since the early 1920s, and the association had been particularly helpful in developing its own program of public health statistics. Prior to 1939 the bureau had participated in two decennial revisions of the international list of diseases, injuries, and causes of death.[56] Such revisions had, for more than forty years, been carried out under French government auspices, but after the war they became the responsibility of WHO. The bureau was involved from the start in preparations for what became the sixth decennial revision of the list, which was adopted in Paris in 1948, and hosted one of the preparatory conferences in Ottawa in February 1947.

Yet another example of a new specialized agency with roots in a pre-war function of the League of Nations was the United Nations Educational, Scientific and Cultural Organization (UNESCO), established in November 1945 with a mandate to contribute to peace by promoting cooperation within the fields of education, science, and culture. This was a successor organization to the league's International Institute of Intellectual Co-operation, set up in 1925. John E. Robbins, director of the bureau's Education Branch, had worked with the institute in the 1930s, and this was probably instrumental in his appointment as a Canadian delegate to the founding conference of UNESCO in London in November 1945. He was subsequently a member of an expert group to advise on the collection of international data on education and served as a delegate to the second annual general conference of UNESCO in Mexico City, and a third conference in Beirut.

Among the numerous other specialized agencies of the United Nations, mention may be made of the International Monetary Fund (IMF), which was established at the Bretton Woods Monetary and Financial Conference in July 1944 for the purpose of stabilizing international monetary exchange rates, and which began operations in 1947. The chief of the then International Payments Division, C.D. Blyth, worked extensively with IMF officials in the drafting of uniform principles for the construction of international accounts.

The International Statistical Institute had virtually ceased operations with the onset of war in 1939. Its first postwar meeting took place in Washington in September 1947, in conjunction with a World Statistical Congress sponsored by the United Nations and the meetings of other related bodies, including the newly formed International Association for Research in Income and Wealth.[57] The reactivation of the institute was largely the work of Stuart A. Rice,[58] who was also responsible for transforming its constitution – unchanged since 1887 – in recognition of the United Nations' role as the primary locus of international statistical cooperation. Its new aims dropped the 1887 references to "inviting the attention of governments to the various problems capable of solution by statistical observation" and "stimulating the interests of governments ... in the study of social phenomena"[59] and defined the institute as "an autonomous society devoted to the development and improvement of statistical methods and their application throughout the world."[60]

The postwar years saw a steady expansion in the institute's membership, which went from 171 to 307 in the first postwar decade. Following the 1947 session in Washington, the pattern of biennial meetings was resumed. Starting with the twenty-eighth session in Rome in 1953, at which Herbert Marshall and J.W. Hopkins of the National Research Council were the official delegates for Canada, the bureau never subsequently failed to send at least one representative. By the time of Marshall's retirement, O.A. Lemieux, J.T. Marshall, Nathan Keyfitz, and Simon Goldberg had been elected members, and Herbert Marshall served as vice-president from 1953 to 1960.[61]

At the 1955 session in Rio de Janeiro, Marshall broached the idea of Canada playing host to the institute for its 1959 session and, once home, initiated the lengthy process of securing approval. Sessions outside Europe were expensive to host because the practice had been adopted of host countries subsidizing the costs of air travel. With the support of the National Research Council's Advisory Panel on Science Policy and the blessing of the minister, Gordon Churchill, Marshall put forward a cabinet submission shortly before setting off for the thirtieth session in Stockholm in July 1957. Anxious to make the announcement while in Stockholm, he cabled back to find out whether cabinet had given its approval, but alas it had not and did not, and Japan stepped into the breach to host the thirty-second session – delayed a year until 1960. Canada's honour was finally redeemed when the thirty-fourth session took place in Ottawa in 1963.

When links with Europe were broken by the outbreak of war in 1939, the desirability of close political and economic ties between the United States and the rest of the hemisphere indicated a corresponding need for closer statistical cooperation. Stuart Rice had been chairman of the Arrangements Committee for the proposed 1939 meeting of the ISI in Washington and had planned to give it an inter-American emphasis. When the meeting was cancelled, Rice persuaded the US Department of State to embody its program into that of the Eighth American Scientific Congress, held in May 1940. At the same time, a new continuing organization for statistical collaboration, the Inter-American Statistical Institute (IASI), was formed, with Rice's group serving as a Temporary Organizing Committee. When political relations among the Americas were formalized by the establishment of the Organization of American States (OAS)in 1948, IASI became the statistical arm of the inter-American system. IASI created both individual and institutional memberships, the latter being mostly those of adhering countries of the OAS, the principal source of funding. As a nonmember of the OAS until recently, Canada was allowed to pay a grant directly to IASI.

IASI's first major initiative was the 1950 Census of the Americas (COTA), planned and supervised by an "all nations" committee of persons with direct responsibility for the conduct of the various national censuses. O.A. Lemieux and Nathan Keyfitz contributed significantly to this work, earning for Canada the reputation of a friendly source of expertise with no political axe to grind. COTA's success inspired the establishment in 1950 of the Committee for the Improvement of National Statistics (COINS), with the object of applying similar methods to statistical work in general.

COINS first met in Washington in 1951, and in the following year Canada played host to the Inter-American Statistical Conference, which featured the second session of COINS.[62] A third such conference was held in Brazil in 1955, and thereafter conferences were held at more or less biennial intervals, with COINS focusing on intergovernmental matters, and the meetings of IASI proper, like those of the ISI, serving as professional forums. Effectively, then,COINS pre-empted the role of developing and coordinating regional statistics that, in other parts of the world, eventually came to be played by the regional commissions of the United Nations. The bureau was an active and enthusiastic participant in the work of IASI from the start. This was almost certainly with the encouragement of the Department of Trade and Commerce, which was expanding commercial relations with Latin America during this time.[63] Coats was the institute's first treasurer, and Herbert Marshall served as president for several years.

The first postwar Conference of British Commonwealth Statisticians took place in Canberra in 1951. By comparison with the Ottawa conference of 1935 and its predecessor, the original London conference of 1920, there were important changes in its composition, reflecting changes in the Commonwealth itself. India and Ceylon were present as full members of the Commonwealth. Pakistan had been invited but declined on the grounds that "urgent internal statistical problems made it impossible ... to accept the invitation."[64] On the other hand, the Irish Free State of 1935 no longer existed, but its successor, the

Republic of Ireland, sent an observer. Canada was represented by Herbert Marshall, Nathan Keyfitz, and Frank Leacy. Marshall was the only delegate who had taken part in the 1935 meeting.

Under the chairmanship of S.R. Carver of Australia, the conference addressed a wide range of traditional topics, such as agriculture, trade, classifications, and census taking, as well as newer ones like national accounts and the application of sampling methods. Industrial and commodity classifications received a great deal of attention, probably because of recent United Nations initiatives in the establishment of an International Standard Industrial Classification, and of an International Standard Trade Classification in 1950. It was agreed that future conferences were desirable and should be held at least once every five years. Conferences were in fact held in London in 1956, Wellington in 1960, Ottawa again in 1966, and New Delhi in 1970. As former colonies in the West Indies, Africa, and Southeast Asia gained their independence during the 1950s and 1960s, they began to attend in their own right, rather than being represented collectively by the British Colonial Office. Correspondingly, the emphasis of the conferences' proceedings shifted towards the special problems encountered by developing countries in putting in place viable statistical systems.

During the 1950s, major technical assistance programs were launched under such auspices as the Truman Point IV Program of the United States, the Commonwealth's Colombo Plan, and the United Nations' Technical Assistance Plan. The establishment of viable statistical systems in recipient countries was considered a *sine qua non* for substantive assistance, and the bureau contributed to the development of statistical infrastructure and programs in many parts of the world through the provision of "hands-on" training in Ottawa, and by the secondment abroad of experts in various fields. Among the many bureau officers who undertook technical assistance assignments, none was more active than Nathan Keyfitz, who served in Burma in 1951, in Indonesia in 1953, and as director of the Bureau of Technical Cooperation for the Colombo Plan countries in 1956. Two years later he spent three months in Calcutta, India, with the International Statistical Education Centre. In 1958 these contributions won Keyfitz the Gold Medal of the Professional Institute of the Civil Service of Canada.

Marshall's Retirement

Marshall reached the age of sixty-five in November 1952 but was evidently determined not to "go gently into that good night." He received successive extensions on such grounds as the need to see the 1951 census through to a successful conclusion and "the continuing need for his services in connection with advancing the current program for improving procedures and techniques within the organization."[65] It was finally settled that he should retire on

31 December 1956. Even so, however, he had still been arguing during his last few months for a special postretirement appointment as adviser to the Dominion statistician (or International Statistical Liaison Officer, in a second version of the proposal), so that he would have official standing in continuing his duties as vice-president of the International Statistical Institute and president of the Inter-American Statistical Institute. Although he had some support from the minister C.D. Howe, the Treasury Board Secretariat insisted that "retirement was retirement," no doubt to the relief of his successor, Walter Duffett.

At his retirement party on 7 January 1957, Marshall was presented with a testimonial signed by some 1,700 colleagues, past and present, which began with a somewhat arcane quotation from Tennyson: "All experience is an arch wherethro' gleams that untravelled world, whose margin fades forever and forever when I move." The speaker went on to say: "These words, Mr Marshall, are an apt description of the spirit which lies behind your creative contribution to Canadian and international statistics. You leave behind you in the Bureau a tremendous awareness of your achievements as well as a warm appreciation of your personal qualities – of highmindedness, justice and consideration, which will not soon be forgotten by your fellow workers."[66]

It was a fitting tribute to thirty-five years of dedicated service. During the interwar years Marshall had made a remarkable contribution to the development of the bureau's program, notably in the areas of prices and statistics of distribution and international trade. In 1936, he was co-author of a pioneering study of reciprocal investment in the United States and Canada.[67] In 1939 his work in the area of international trade had been recognized by the award of the Gold Medal of the Professional Institute of the Civil Service of Canada. During the Second World War he had toiled mightily for the Wartime Prices and Trade Board and in setting up the regional manpower records for National Selective Service, to mention only two of his contributions, and his subsequent appointment as an Officer of the Order of the British Empire was but scant recognition of these services.

After the war Marshall took over, elaborated, and implemented Cudmore's plans for providing the statistical foundation on which Canada's postwar development could be based. It was perhaps not inappropriate that he should have fought so persistently for extra time to carry out the task that he apparently felt he alone was qualified to complete. Through his political skills,[68] and by continuing the rigorous development of the national accounts, fostering the application of scientific methodology, and paving the way for the use of computers, he left a bureau radically transformed from the organization he had inherited. Marshall's recruitment of a new crop of postwar graduates was an important factor in his success, and they provided the middle and senior management that sustained the bureau for much of the next three decades. Finally, he established for the bureau a high-profile role among the new and revived organizations of the international statistical community.

Marshall became a fellow of the Royal Society of Canada, president of the Canadian Political Science Association in 1952–53, president of the American Statistical Association in 1954, and an honorary fellow of the Royal Statistical Society in 1954. He served as vice-president of the International Statistical Institute from 1953 to 1960, and as president of the Inter-American Statistical Institute from 1955 to 1962. Immediately following retirement, he was for a time statistical advisor to what was then the West Indian Federation. In 1960 he came back to the bureau for six months in order to supervise compilation of the Balance of International Payments and related material for a volume of historical statistics.[69]

In 1967, with the bureau's fiftieth anniversary on the horizon, Marshall was commissioned to prepare material for a history of the bureau. But age was now catching up with him, and his plans for a detailed history of each subject-matter program proved to be too ambitious.[70] His last public appearance at the bureau was on the occasion of the formal opening of the R.H. Coats Building in Tunney's Pasture in May 1975. Marshall's legacy was not all statistical; he was as well known among Ottawa's ski enthusiasts as among those who used the bureau's data. A lifelong devotee of downhill skiing, he did much to develop the Ottawa Ski Club, of which he was president for many years, and which honoured him by naming after him one of the most popular ski hills at Camp Fortune, Quebec. Marshall died peacefully at his home in Ottawa on 1 October 1977 in his ninetieth year, survived by his wife of fifty-three years, the former Muriel Meek of St Thomas, Ontario.

CHAPTER THIRTEEN

1957–1972
The Duffett Years I: Administrative and Infrastructure Developments

Introduction

Walter Elliott Duffett took office as Dominion statistician on 1 January 1957 at the age of forty-six and served until 30 June 1972–a term longer than those of his two predecessors combined. He was the first outsider to head the bureau but had worked closely with its senior staff as well as with many of the user departments and was well versed in the statistical politics of the postwar era.

A native of Galt, Ontario, he was educated at the University of Toronto and the London School of Economics, and he had served as an economist with the Sun Life Insurance Company in Montreal before coming to Ottawa in 1942 to work with the Wartime Prices and Trade Board. In 1944 he had joined the research staff of the Bank of Canada and had at one point been considered for the task, subsequently assigned to George Luxton, of reshaping the bureau's work on statistics of national income. Since 1954 he had served as director of the Economics and Research Branch of the Department of Labour.

Had he remained in the bureau, Claude Isbister would have been a strong internal candidate for the position of Dominion statistician. Since his departure, Simon Goldberg had emerged as a dominant presence in the development of the national accounts and related research activities but was perhaps thought to be not yet sufficiently seasoned. J.T. Marshall was known to have been disappointed at being passed over,[1] but he had no background in economic statistics. Ironically, some of the most important program developments during the next decade and a half were in fact in areas of social concern.

The Duffett years were an era of sustained economic growth and unprecedented social development in Canada. Population grew by 6.2 million or thirty-one percent, fuelled for much of the time by the postwar baby boom and, except for a faltering in the early 1960s, by high levels of net migration. The labour force grew even more strongly, showing a forty-eight percent gain, much of which was the result of increased female participation. Unemployment rates, however, never again achieved the lows experienced between 1946 and 1956, averaging more than five percent per annum during the next sixteen years. Gross national product, measured in constant dollars, rose by 106 percent between 1956 and 1972, or at an annual rate of 4.6 percent. Annual increases in the consumer price index accelerated slowly during the 1960s, reaching a rate of 4.8 percent by 1972 but averaging only 2.5 percent per annum for 1957–72 as a whole. These, then, were years of high prosperity.

The federal government's budgetary expenditures were relatively stable during the early years of Duffett's tenure but increased very rapidly as the 1960s progressed, reflecting in large part major outlays on new social programs. Thus, a recurring theme in the annual reports of the Dominion statistician was the steady acceleration of demands for statistical services at both the federal and provincial levels, not only from long established users but also from newer ones, such as the Economic Council of Canada, the Special Planning Secretariat of the Privy Council, and bodies with responsibilities for regional development.[2]

These indications of new and elaborated demands were always bracketed with warnings of their resource requirements. In fact, the bureau's continuing staff increased from 1,449 on 31 March 1957 to 3,545 on 31 March 1972, with a strong shift towards a higher proportion of professionals. But strength in the key employee category of economist/statistician lagged behind the authorized establishment during Duffett's entire tenure. In the early years this was largely due to the classification and salary handicap under which the bureau operated. Later, when this anomaly had been rectified and the bureau could compete for professional staff on equal terms with other departments, all suffered from the continuing disparity between growth in the demand for such employees brought about by the universal expansion in government programs, and the restricted sources of new supply. During the last half dozen years of Duffett's tenure, turnover rates for all categories of bureau staff reached unprecedented levels, and this almost certainly had an effect on staff quality and, in consequence, program performance.

The defining event of the Duffett years was the scrutiny of the bureau's programs and management practices by the 1960 Royal Commission on Government Organization (the Glassco Commission). The commission's report was probably instrumental in bringing about the recognition, in 1965, of the bureau as a department in its own right. This in turn facilitated the resolution of the bureau's longstanding classification problems and paved the way for a major upgrading of the organizational structure in 1967.

Before the end of the decade, the bureau was involved in two further external scrutinies of its program activities. In November 1967 the Senate of Canada, concerned that the country was not developing its science and technology capability fast enough, set up a special committee to review and assess government science policy. The committee's mandate covered the human as well as the physical and life sciences, and the bureau was thus among the many federal departments and agencies that submitted briefs and took part in the hearings.

The experience was a positive one for the bureau, although the committee's report did not single it out for particular attention. By contrast, the Task Force on Government Information, appointed by the prime minister in August 1968 to examine the structure and activities of federal departmental information services, identified the bureau as an institution of which information was, as it were, "of the essence" and subjected it to a particularly close and careful study. Its findings were helpful and constructive, and although nothing came of them during the remaining years of the Duffett regime, they sowed a seed that came to fruition under his successor and gave a significantly higher profile to the information and marketing functions.

The most exciting and challenging development of the 1960s lay in the transformation of statistical technology. Computer power was harnessed if not altogether tamed and, in conjunction with probability sampling and related statistical disciplines, provided the basis for the revolutionary approach to survey design and implementation that became known as automation. However, the transformation from the bureau's traditional survey methodology to the new world of automation was by no means an easy or a speedy one, and its potential for quality improvement and cost saving was only partly realized during the Duffett years.

Towards the end of the 1960s the Treasury Board adopted a new approach to the allocation of budgetary resources among departments – the Planning, Programming, Budgeting System, or PPBS, (PPB in short). The bureau set up a central planning and programming function and began the difficult task of looking critically at its program activities and assessing how well they served the needs of users.

Duffett's final contribution as Dominion statistician was to plan and guide the passage through Parliament of a new Statistics Act. The act, conceived in response to the growing pressures for a reduction of response burden, came into force on 1 May 1971 and gave the bureau a new title – Statistics Canada, the minister's deputy for the purposes of the act being henceforth known as the chief statistician of Canada.

The Glassco Commission and After

On 16 September 1960 the Royal Commission on Government Organization was appointed under the chairmanship of J. Grant Glassco to "inquire into and report upon the organization and methods of operation of the Government of Canada, and to recommend the changes therein which they consider would best promote efficiency, economy and improved service in the despatch of public business."[3]

The Glassco Commission, as it came to be known, was specifically required to address such issues as the possible duplication and overlapping of services; the identification and elimination of unnecessary operations; the potential benefits of further decentralization of operations and administration; changes in the relative responsibilities of departments and agencies on the one hand, and the central agencies on the other; and the scope for improving managerial performance through the better use of budgeting, accounting, and other financial tools.

On the face of it, this was the opportunity to find its place in the sun that the bureau had been seeking since it lost the patronage of Sir George Foster some four decades earlier. In spite of the headway it had made with users in the policy departments through its successful development of the national accounts, statisticians were still seen as little more than hewers of wood and drawers of water.[4] This perception, that statisticians should confine their activities to gathering and compiling numbers and leave the functions of analysis and interpretation to others, was of long standing and by no means unique to Canada.[5] Finally, however, an objective study of the bureau's mandate, programs, and activities would surely demonstrate that there was more to statistics than the routine collection and compilation of numbers. Recognition of the planning and analytic dimension, together with the requirement for operational independence in the exercise of the bureau's mandate, would make possible the upgrading of the Dominion statistician to the rank of deputy minister and give him correspondingly greater leverage in recruiting and retaining professional staff.

Since Herbert Marshall's early postwar successes in creating new managerial positions and upgrading others, increasing difficulties had been encountered in staffing research and analytical positions. Many of Marshall's bright prospects had departed for greener pastures in academe and in other government departments.[6] Professional salary scales had remained virtually static during the 1950s, not only for the bureau but for other departments employing statisticians and economists and most probably for the universities too. The problem, then, was not one of absolute but of relative levels. As Goldberg wrote around this time: "Many professional people in the Bureau ... are underpaid compared to other government departments."[7] Thus, it was possible for individuals not only to qualify readily for higher paying positions elsewhere but subsequently to be promoted further. Pecuniary advantages apart, there were also gains associated with self-esteem and recognition by others. The salary disadvantages of taking a position with the bureau at a junior level were less obvious, but image was certainly an inhibiting factor. It was only a few years since the bureau had cheerfully allowed itself to be called a "figure factory."[8]

But the prospect of examination by a royal commission aroused apprehensions in the bureau as well as hopes. Over the years it had fought successfully to protect powers that it considered to be vested in it by the Statistics Act. But in matters relating to its internal administration, it could not be so confident. As the commission's work proceeded, problems in this area came to light.

The commission's staff work was divided among a number of project groups. That dealing with "Economic and Statistical Services," headed by Professor E.F. Beach of McGill University, soon made its information requirements known to the bureau. In a memorandum of 28 October 1960 to his directors,[9] Duffett set out a lengthy list of headings under which he was to report. These included the framework of each divisional statistical program, its beneficiaries and users, uses and financial costs; procedures and criteria for adopting, dropping, or changing the contents of surveys; practices in charging for special work; problems of respondents and what was done to address them; procedures for appraising or eliminating duplication within and between divisions and with other departments; the main forces accounting for growth over the previous five years, and the prospects for the next five. There were also questions relating to the adequacy and effectiveness of administrative facilities and procedures, and the arrangements for maintaining effective liaison with users, suppliers, and other government agencies.

An unsigned memorandum of 12 April 1961 documented, albeit cryptically, some of the reported findings. The bureau's administrative procedures were summarized as "simple and lacking in formality," with specific observations such as the following:

- Relations with Directors. No regular meetings prior to 1957. No specific delegation of functions. No regular review even now.
- No regular machinery for reviewing redundant surveys or activities.
- Absence of uniformity in procedures for staff appraisal, signing authority.
- Establishment review procedures varied and not set out on paper.
- No uniform administrative procedures within Divisions. We do not know what they are ourselves.
- Generally an arms-length relationship on administrative matters, although considerably closer on some conceptual matters.[10]

A second part of the memorandum listed "some of the reasons":

- The complicated and specialized nature of the Divisions' work. We cannot supervise details of their operations.
- Overloaded Directors and divisional staffs. A hesitation by the Executive to impose ... formal and time consuming procedures even though these would be useful.
- Lack of enough management interest and aptitude on the part of the Executive.
- The rapid and continuing postwar growth of the Dominion Bureau of Statistics ... [which] is still evolving but has not succeeded in either (a)

developing criteria which will limit its growth to its resources, and (b) getting enough resources to meet its obligations.

- With generally insufficient staff and Treasury Board pressures, priority given to survey resources rather than to management resources.
- Government courses on administration have been non-practical. Government has neither sought, developed nor paid for good administrators."[11]

Later that year, a rationalization of these loose administrative arrangements and the *de facto* independence enjoyed by directors argued that "the organizational problems of the Dominion Bureau of Statistics differ somewhat from those of other Government Departments, and the nature of [its] organizational requirements suggest an analogy to a university."[12]

Duffett was on firmer ground in the 23 May 1961 memorandum on statistical centralization and coordination that he prepared for Beach.[13] It noted that centralization was not an end in itself, although it could be shown to have many operational advantages. Rather, it was a means – one means – of ensuring statistical coordination. In countries like the United States and the United Kingdom, where the production of statistics was a by-product of the administration of program departments, coordinating mechanisms had had to be developed to ensure that statistics from the various sources were conceptually compatible and could be used jointly. It was probably not feasible to reverse a historical commitment to one or the other forms of organization, but as a matter of record, most of the new national statistical systems that had been put in place after the Second World War had in fact been centralized.

Duffett argued that centralization could not by itself ensure effective coordination. The sections of Canada's Statistics Act relating to coordination were an admirable statement of objectives but did not give the Dominion statistician the authority to achieve them. He was required to consult with and advise "the several departments of government," but there was no reciprocal obligation on them to collaborate with him. They were thus free to engage in statistical activities of their own without regard to the possibilities of their duplicating, overlapping, or being inconsistent with statistics already available from the centre.

Duffett quoted from a Treasury Board letter of 11 March 1957 that had attempted to bridge that gap. It was hoped, the board had said; "that departments and agencies will take the initiative in discussing their problems with the Bureau and no new statistical operations will be undertaken without this consultation ... It is the intention of the Board that any staff requirements arising out of statistical functions will be scrutinized during the meetings of Establishment Review Committees to ensure that this procedure has been carried out." But, wrote Duffett, "there is little or no evidence that this letter has influenced government departments or has produced any change in the situation."[14] He concluded with a plea for machinery to render effective the policy of statistical coordination.

Beach's draft report on the bureau was sympathetic, acknowledging its longstanding administrative problems and noting Duffett's efforts towards resolving them. On the issue of the underclassification of senior bureau staff, Beach remarked that he had no hesitation whatsoever in supporting the requests of the Dominion statistician that his directors be ranked as Senior Officers. "The whole status of the Bureau should be examined," he argued, adding that "the Bureau of Statistics has much more right to the status of a department than the Department of Insurance or the Queen's Printer."[15]

Beach's treatment of the bureau's relations with other federal departments and agencies, provincial governments, business and industry, and the public at large provided a lot of descriptive information, but no conclusions were drawn. In some areas, such as response burden and the adequacy of the bureau's publicity efforts, this was because the problems were of a general nature and under study by other project groups. The report took note of special problems in the relations between the bureau and three federal departments – Labour, National Health and Welfare, and Transport – and promised detailed assessments at a later date. Duffett's memorandum on centralization was attached as an exhibit to the Beach report, but its concerns with respect to statistical coordination were not otherwise addressed.

Volume three of the official Glassco Commission report, which contained its study of economic and statistical services, was published on 3 December 1962. On the issue of centralization, arguments for and against were reviewed, with the conclusion that "it is impossible to evaluate [them] ... on any basis that is not, fundamentally a matter of subjective judgment."[16] Nevertheless, the report opted for centralization, largely on the basis of what it judged to be the bureau's successful experience. It was thought to be neither necessary nor desirable that the statistical system be completely centralized. Departments should be free to collect and process certain kinds of statistics themselves, but where there was any substantial commitment of resources, their use should be subject to review by the Dominion statistician.

The commission's report agreed with Duffett that, whatever its virtues in other respects, the Statistics Act had been weak as an instrument of coordination. It noted that the Dominion statistician did not have the status of a deputy minister, and that this, in conjunction with the Civil Service Commission's "rather rigid and questionable distinction between those who participate in policy-making and those who do not," put the bureau's salary structure "a notch (or more) lower than that of other departments."[17] In consequence, many important statistical programs were understaffed. By way of example, it was pointed out how crucially the bureau's balance of international payments depended on the skills of two senior staff members.[18]

On the status question, a fundamental requirement was said to be that the statistical service should operate with unimpeachable integrity. Accordingly, "the status of the Dominion Statistician must be appropriate to his functions, conferring upon him the absolute freedom to refuse requests that might impair the objectivity of statistical operations." This could not be assured while he held office "during pleasure," and the report therefore recommended that he hold office "during good behaviour and be removable only for cause."[19]

To improve the effectiveness of statistical coordination, it was thought inappropriate, in view of the existing statutory responsibilities for statistical work, to confer direct powers of intervention on the Dominion statistician. Rather, he should be required to audit the statistical programs of all departments and agencies and to report annually to Parliament on the state of government statistical services. Coupled with this was the recommendation that the Dominion statistician screen all new requests from departments and agencies for the conduct of statistical surveys involving more than ten respondents[20] in order to avoid duplicating information that might already exist.

Other areas of the commission's report had referred to the need for better statistical information in the areas of management and policy formulation, and it was therefore recommended that the Treasury Board rely on the Dominion statistician for assistance in securing statistical data needed for management and policy decisions, and as the principal source of advice on all statistical programs and the employment of statisticians within the public service. Beach's draft report had alluded to special problems with respect to health, labour, and transport statistics, and the commission recommended that the programs be reviewed with a view to determining their appropriate allocation between the Dominion Bureau of Statistics and other departments and agencies.

The bureau's current staffing problems were dealt with by a recommendation that the remuneration of its professional and auxiliary staff be reviewed for compatibility with that of comparable personnel elsewhere in the public service. Finally, it was recommended that an advisory council be formed, comprising representatives of the principal users of statistics and other public bodies, to meet periodically with the Dominion statistician to discuss statistical programs and the problems of respondents, and to report annually to the responsible minister.

These were sympathetic recommendations, but that relating to the bureau's staffing problems was anticlimactic. Since 28 June 1962 a governmentwide freeze on staffing had been in force as part of a broader economy program. The bureau's staff complement was required to shrink by attrition to eighty-five percent of its authorized establishment of 1,863 continuing positions for 1962–63. As a concession to make up for the loss of specialists, one person from outside could be recruited for every ten lost. For several years the bureau's authorized establishment had been edging up, but actual strengths had lagged behind, so that a relaxation of the freeze would not have been helpful in itself. But the bureau took it as a challenge to the integrity of its programs and responded with a report to Treasury Board, assessing in very stark terms the consequences of the austerity measures.[21] Supporting the bureau's position were a great many letters of protest to the minister and the Dominion statistician from provincial authorities and business firms, expressing alarm at prospective cuts. This resulted in a directive from the Treasury Board exempting the bureau from the austerity regulations as of 2 January 1963 – the first government agency to be freed.[22]

In the meantime, a special committee to consider the Glassco recommendations with respect to statistical services had been set up under James A. Roberts, deputy minister of Trade and Commerce.[23] It reported in April 1963 and, with some qualifications, agreed with them all. In one instance it went further, suggesting that not only should professional and related salaries in the bureau be reviewed for compatibility with those of comparable personnel elsewhere but that the bureau's authorized establishment should also be reviewed in the light of the existing workload and prospective statistical developments.

Action on the recommendations was a different matter. In most instances, it would have been difficult for the Dominion statistician himself to take any initiative, and help could not realistically be expected from the Treasury Board when there was a potential encroachment on its own functions, as in the case of the recommendations that the bureau should scrutinize and advise on other statistical programs and serve as a source of statistical expertise for its management and policy decisions. It is difficult, too, to credit that the board would wish to get involved in jurisdictional disputes between the bureau and the Departments of Transport, Labour, and National Health and Welfare.

One step taken by the Treasury Board at little trouble to itself was to put in place a mechanism under which the bureau could administer a "ten respondent rule" as earlier described.[24] In practice, departments frequently neglected to advise the bureau of their proposed activities or did so after the fact, and the rule's impact on the overall problem of coordination was marginal at best during the remainder of Duffett's tenure.

In the matter of an advisory committee, the bureau itself seemed reluctant for action to be taken. Such a committee had been regularly urged by Coats, but there was now some faltering of nerve at the prospect of the bureau's overall program and priorities being the subject of external scrutiny. In December 1964 Duffett noted that "there is at present a network of 45–50 detailed subject-matter and other committees plus the Interdepartmental Committee on Economic Statistics, the Interdepartmental Committee on Financial Statistics, and the Federal-Provincial Committee on Economic Statistics." A study of this structure was said to be underway, completion of which "will place the government in a better position to judge what role an advisory council such as recommended by Glassco Commission could play and what its membership should be."[25] It was in fact two more decades before this issue was seriously addressed.

Symbolically, the most important consequence of the Glassco Commission for the bureau came on 25 January 1965 through Order in Council PC 1965–29, by which the bureau for legal and administrative purposes was designated as a department of the federal government, with the Dominion statistician as its deputy head. After almost half a century of tutelage by the Department of Trade and Commerce, the bureau had formally come of age. In practical terms, the effects of departmental status were hardly perceptible. Working relationships with Trade and Commerce had already improved immeasurably by comparison with those that had frustrated Coats so much during the 1920s and 1930s. And the bureau had consistently demonstrated its professionalism to the sophisticated community of users that had managed the wartime economy and postwar reconstruction.

Departmental status may have assisted indirectly in the resolution of the bureau's classification problems, but it was its own persistence that finally carried the day. A report prepared in February 1964 for the Civil Service Commission on the bureau's classification structure seems to have provided the basis for a breakthrough.[26] It drew extensively on the Glassco Commission's own observations of the continually growing demand for more and more statistical information as a consequence of the "maturing recognition that business decisions, public policies, and the discussion of public issues require soundly-based factual knowledge."[27] A serious obstacle to the bureau's ability to keep pace with growing demands for new, more sophisticated, and better integrated statistical information was the chronic shortage of professional manpower resulting from the Civil Service Commission's well-known position on the distinction between policy makers and those who merely served them.

It was pointed out that, twelve months earlier, the Treasury Board had exempted the bureau from the servicewide staffing freeze then in force. So the board was clearly "on side" and had in fact authorized substantial increases in the establishment of continuing positions for both 1963–64 and 1964–65. The report was seeking parallel recognition from the Civil Service Commission with respect to classification levels, without which the Treasury Board action would be of no avail.

The report further noted that previous submissions to the commission in respect of particularly urgent positions had resulted in "prolonged, time-consuming, repetitive and frustrating 'negotiations', and massive amounts of documentation."[28] In some cases, it was said, by the time the commission had agreed, the incumbent had left the position in question. The report concluded with the recommendation that, with the exception of the National Accounts and Balance of Payments Division, the Industry and Merchandising Division, and the Census Division where the directors' positions warranted a classification of Senior Officer 2, the positions of divisional directors should be classified at the level of Senior Officer 1. The three positions of assistant Dominion statistician should then be adjusted accordingly – presumably to the level of Senior Officer 3. The working level for professionals should be upgraded to Statistician 4, and highly qualified and experienced professionals should be able to aspire to the most senior level of the statistician category – Chief

Statistician 2 (one level below Senior Officer 1) – without needing to assume significant administrative responsibility.

As the year proceeded, the Civil Service Commission appeared still to be impervious to the bureau's arguments. However, an 18 December 1964 report by Duffett to the assistant Dominion statisticians referred to a meeting with commission officials that had concluded with the agreement that "changes along the lines proposed by the Dominion Bureau of Statistics would clearly have to be made by the Civil Service Commission."[29] The tide had thus turned, and over the next year or so most of the recommended reclassifications were implemented. As the bureau had predicted, there was a perceptible impact on recruitment. In the five fiscal years up to and including 1963–64, a total of 134 economists and statisticians had been recruited. During the next two years, 1964–65 and 1965–66, 124 were recruited.[30] Separations of economists and statisticians continued and indeed increased, but there was now a more comfortable margin of retention.

The bureau's competitive position with regard to recruitment would not be fully secured until other key categories, such as those involving computer programming skills where the majority of recruits came from outside government, were also brought into line. This had to await the work of the Bureau of Classifications Revision, set up in the late 1960s by the Public Service Commission, as the Civil Service Commission was by then called, to conduct a servicewide review of all occupational categories. During the remainder of the decade, however, there was a virtual explosion in federal government program expenditures that gave rise to unprecedented increases in staff levels. Between 31 March 1966 and 31 March 1971, the bureau increased the number of its continuing staff from 2,248 to 3,440. Quality was perhaps a different matter. During the year ended 31 March 1970, 1,127 continuing employees of all occupational categories were hired and 748 terminated – this on an average staff level for the year of some 3,000.

The market for economists and statisticians was now at its tightest ever. The bureau was diligently wooing new university graduates and sending recruiting teams to the United States and Europe in search of experienced candidates. One hundred and ten economists and statisticians were hired during 1969-70 and sixty-seven separated. On a basis of some 450 continuing positions, this was a lower rate of turnover than for the staff as a whole, but it was dangerously high from the standpoint of the continuity and stability of program management, which this category was expected to provide.

Appendix A illustrates some of the financial dimensions of the bureau's expansion during the 1960s. It tracks total budgetary expenditures (inclusive of census costs) between 1947–48 and 1971–72, as well as the corresponding figures for the total expenditures of the federal government and gross national product at market prices. For the quarter century covered, federal government expenditures as a proportion of GNP show remarkable stability. Bureau expenditures as a proportion of federal government expenditures were similarly stable up to the beginning of the 1960s, allowing for the peak census expenditures of 1951–52 and 1956-57. From 1960–61 on, however, this indicator increased steadily. The years 1961–62, 1966–67 and 1971–72 were again aberrations, but the trend was unmistakeable.

Organizational Restructuring

An organizational restructuring unique in the bureau's history took place on 1 January 1967, when its subject-matter divisions and supporting infrastructure were regrouped into seven branches, thereby adding another layer of management to the bureau's hierarchy. When Duffett was appointed there had been eleven subject-matter divisions, including the Special Surveys Division (primarily responsible for the labour force survey) and the Central Research and Development Staff, which looked after various embryo projects. A decade later the number of subject-matter divisions had grown to fifteen, some of which were ripe for further subdivision. Supporting services, too, had become more numerous and elaborate. All this amounted to a significant extension of the Dominion statistician's span of control and, given the historic propensity of divisional directors to go their own way, was clearly a threat to the integration of statistical programs and the effective management of the bureau as a whole.

At the time of the Glassco Commission, senior management had firmly rejected the notion of an extra layer of management between the Dominion statistician and divisional directors: "Such an arrangement has been seriously considered at times but has never had much appeal. The main reason is that the needs of the subject-matter divisions relate not to one another but to those facilities and controls which DBS provides in total. There is, in fact very little room for 'super-directors'; they would diminish the sense of responsibility of directors and would not be able to provide the sort of expert functional help which is now provided by the existing senior officials in the office of the Dominion Statistician."[31]

The latter part of this quotation appears to refer to the appointment, during the fiscal year 1959–60, of L.E. Rowebottom, formerly director of the Prices Division, as assistant to the Dominion statistician, with the objective of bringing about a closer liaison between bureau administration and the divisional directors. Four years later, in 1963–64, Rowebottom was designated assistant Dominion statistician – General Assignments. Whatever effect this may have had initially in relieving the management burden on Duffett, it had clearly become insufficient by the mid-1960s.

On 1 January 1967 it was announced that four new subject-matter branches, two infrastructure branches (Finance and Administration, and Operations and Systems Development), and an Integration and Development Branch were being created, interposing seven directors general[32] between the Dominion statistician and more than thirty organizational units, most of which had divisional status. Personnel and the Information and Year Book Division continued to report directly to the Dominion statistician. The reasoning advanced for the restructuring was curious. Hitherto, it was argued, "the main obstacle had been the availability of staff to man such an organization, but by 1966 it appeared that recruiting plus the development of DBS officers could provide the necessary staff."[33] This argument is difficult to understand. The recruitment of professional staff had begun to pick up by that time, but it was largely at junior levels. And while management training was beginning to be made available,[34] it could hardly be said to have been a *sine qua non* for many of the veteran directors who were fully capable of taking on further responsibility. The real reason was almost certainly related to the recent recognition of the bureau as a department in its own right, the long-overdue acknowledgement that senior professional positions had always been underclassified, and the potential thus opened up for higher classifications from the Dominion statistician down.[35]

The four new subject-matter branches were Economic Accounts, Financial Statistics, Economic Statistics, and Socio-Economic Statistics. The Economic Accounts Branch, under C.D. Blyth, split the former National Accounts and Balance of Payments Division into separate divisions for the Balance of Payments and Financial Flows, and for National Accounts, Production and Productivity.

The Financial Statistics Branch, under G.A. Wagdin, included the Governments Division,[36] the Corporations and Labour Unions Returns Act Administration Division (CALURA), the Business Finance Division, a Co-ordinator of Financial Statistics, and a Central Personnel Record System. V.R. Berlinguette became director general of Economic Statistics, with responsibility for the divisions of Labour, Prices, Transportation and Public Utilities, Manufacturing and Primary Industries,[37] Merchandising and Services, and External Trade, as well as for Input-Output Research and Development, which had been transferred from the Central Research and Development Staff. L.E. Rowebottom was appointed to head the Socio-Economic Statistics Branch, retaining his title of assistant Dominion statistician, with responsibility for the divisions of Census, Agriculture, Health and Welfare, Education, and Special Surveys (including the Regional Offices), as well as for Provincial Liaison and Consultative Services and Consumer Finance Research.

The various elements of the Central Research and Development Staff, now known as the Integration and Development Staffs, continued, under Simon Goldberg, to have bureauwide responsibility for Central Classifications; Research and Development; Sampling and Survey Research; Econometric Research; Regional Statistics, Research and Integration; Company-Establishment Integration;[38] Special Manpower Studies and Consultation; and the Consultant on Demographic Research. The Tabulating Services and Central Programming Divisions, together with a newly created Management Services

Section and the Central Registers Section, made up the Operations and Systems Development Branch under L.A. Shackleton. H.L. Allen continued to be responsible for what was now the Finance and Administration Branch.

Subject to two important changes, this was the organizational structure that carried the bureau through to the end of Walter Duffett's tenure. The first of these changes was the dismantling of the Operations and Systems Development Branch, and the second the establishment of a planning function. Both are described later in this chapter. Appendix F shows the organization as it stood on 31 March 1972.

The Senate Special Committee on Science Policy

In November 1967, concerned about the adequacy of Canada's science policy and activities in the face of the challenges of the late twentieth century, the Senate of Canada set up a special committee on science policy under the chairmanship of the Honourable Maurice Lamontagne. The committee's inquiry broke new ground by covering the human as well as the physical and life sciences, and the bureau jumped at the opportunity to submit a brief.[39] Predictably, it stuck to its own mandate and programs and offered no general recommendations. The Bank of Canada was more venturesome, arguing for an efficient scientific and technological information system and suggesting a role for the bureau: "The time would now seem to have arrived to carry the development of the nation's information systems further by undertaking (perhaps through the Bureau of Statistics) new initiatives to ensure that Canadians will in fact be able to benefit from the greatly improved access to economic and other information which the computer puts technically within our grasp."[40]

The relatively underdeveloped state of the humanities and social sciences in Canada *vis-à-vis* the situation in the United States was widely deplored in the many briefs that were submitted. Again, it was urged that none of the new needs that had been identified could be effectively met without the formulation of a coherent overall science policy and the creation of central machinery to implement it. The committee's recommendations – more than seventy of them – did not appear until 1972 and 1973,[41] and their subsequent disposition is a matter that goes beyond the scope of this history. In fact, none of them bore directly on the bureau, and most of those that might have had an indirect impact, such as the proposal for the special scrutiny of departmental science expenditure proposals and their assembly in a separate science budget, came to nothing.

The committee's mandate was just the kind of vehicle that Coats would have seized upon in the 1930s to showcase the bureau's capabilities and needs. In the circumstances of the late 1960s, however, there was little the committee could have done to help the bureau. Its professional reputation had been well established for two decades, and the Glassco Commission had finally conferred the accolade of administrative independence. Financial resources were flowing plentifully enough, and the committee could not have helped with what the bureau perceived at that time to be its principal problem, namely the recruitment of experienced professional staff.

Nevertheless, the committee's work fostered an interest in the bureau's existing program of science statistics and provided a stimulus for their further refinement and extension. The true legacy, however, came from the opportunity afforded the bureau, through the preparation of its brief, to take stock of the achievements of its first half century and to address the challenges that lay ahead of it. The brief was refreshingly free of the self-serving flavour that normally characterizes such documents and provided a fascinating window into the bureau of the late 1960s.

Two Looks at the Bureau's Information Function

In August 1968 a task force on government information was appointed with a mandate to examine the structure, operation, and activities of federal departmental information services. The bureau was one of four institutions selected for "a concentrated or vertical examination ... to follow the public information process ... from the policy level out to the people."[42] The bureau had frequently contended with studies of the overall government publishing function that threatened, on grounds of efficiency or rationalization, to take over or constrain its own distribution responsibilities. It had, however, always managed to fend them off, arguing from the high ground of the publishing mandate vested in it by the Statistics Act.

The 1968 task force apparently had no sinister intentions, but its findings relative to the bureau, while generally sympathetic, were critical in a number of areas. A user survey that the task force conducted registered many complaints about the bureau's marketing practices, including the timeliness, usefulness, clarity, and accessibility of data. Again, it was thought by many of those who were surveyed that, notwithstanding the bureau's new-found status as a department in its own right, its weak power base within the federal hierarchy and its perceived role as a purely service organization limited its potential for contributing to the development and assessment of national policy. Accordingly, a lead recommendation of the task force was that, in recognition of the bureau's "major and specialized information role," it be "transferred from its present position within a ministry which has its own special publics to one which would be more compatible with the bureau's central service functions, and that its autonomy be preserved."[43]

Most of the task force's recommendations for the bureau were aimed at improving the visibility and effectiveness of its Information Division. They were not acted upon at the time and will not be addressed here. But one general comment of the task force merits mention. On the matter of timeliness that the user survey had addressed, it found, to its astonishment, that for well over a year a bureau committee, headed by Simon Goldberg, had been working on the problem and had already achieved some impressive results. Strangely, however, no one outside the bureau seemed to be aware of this work. One senior bureau official told the task force that "DBS had considered 'doing a real publicity job' on the drive for better timeliness but decided against it for fear that public reaction might be 'about time!' or 'Why don't they speed up everything else?'"[44]

Some three years later, in the closing months of the Duffett regime, an internal bureau study group was constituted to examine what "image" the bureau should be projecting, and what action was needed to achieve the desired result. The group found a considerable imbalance between the bureau's production facilities and expertise and its marketing capability.[45] To correct this, the group recommended a strengthening of the bureau's marketing and communications activities through organizational restructuring and the injection of additional resources. Some forty specific recommendations were made in such areas as the use of paid advertising, the provision of editorial assistance to the authors of publications, an expansion of user advisory services in the regional offices, improved internal communication, and greater emphasis on the dissemination of information through media other than printed publications.

By the time the report could be made available, time had literally run out for its assessment and possible implementation. Walter Duffett retired at the end of June and his successor, Sylvia Ostry, chose to start with a clean slate. However, the reorganization task force that she immediately constituted observed the same imbalance between production and marketing,[46] and its recommendations eventually led to the creation of a Marketing Services Field, headed by an assistant chief statistician. This was clearly a ringing endorsement of the earlier report.

Mostly about Automation

Automation is essentially the marriage of scientific methodology and computer power to plan and carry out all the elements of a statistical operation from the specification of survey objectives and quality requirements of the end product through questionnaire design, sample design, data collection and processing, editing and imputation to quality assessment, analysis, and the provision of user access.

Computer power did not come on the scene until the early 1960s when it was used in the 1961 census, but scientific methodology had made its debut in the late 1940s when the bureau used probability sampling to develop a quarterly sample survey of the Canadian labour force. The survey was the responsibility of the Sampling Organization of the Central Research and Development Staff, which eventually acquired a separate identity as the Special Surveys Division. Within the division there was a Sampling and Analysis Section, which was effectively the cradle for all the methodological developments of the next four decades. From the late 1940s on, the division as a whole was occupied not only with its core responsibility for what soon became the monthly labour force survey but also with supplementary household surveys, based on the labour force sample, which were carried out with increasing frequency for other bureau divisions and external clients.

During the 1950s the activities of the Sampling and Analysis Section were extended beyond sampling methods to encompass such problems as errors of reporting, processing errors, editing errors, and so on, as well as their collective impact. The statistical operation was thus being looked at as a whole. An early example of this broader view was the quality check survey, conducted for the 1956 census of agriculture, which sought to provide estimates of the completeness of coverage and checks on the quality of selected variables. The three censuses conducted during the Duffett years benefited from progressively more sophisticated methodological inputs, and indeed, it was on the basis of intensive research into the problems of response error that the decision was made to use self-enumeration in the 1971 census. In the early 1960s the labour force survey was redesigned, partly in response to user demands for more data at finer levels of geographic aggregation and also in the light of shifts in the demographic characteristics of the population during the preceding decade and a half. Various technical studies never previously undertaken contributed to the redesign, a notable aspect of which was the shift from uniform national sampling to a system whereby smaller provinces were more heavily sampled so as to improve the reliability of provincial data.[47] Data from the 1961 census were used for the stratification of a new sample capable of modification for the purpose of different inquiries and with the flexibility for easy implementation of design changes and improvements when and where required. Newly developing modelling techniques permitted the costs and sampling variability of alternative samples to be evaluated.

During 1960–61, the visibility of the Sampling and Analysis Section was considerably enhanced by plucking it out from the Special Survey Division and assigning it to the Senior Mathematical Advisor under the title of the Sampling Research and Consultation Staff. By 1963–64, the staff had relocated to the central staffs under the assistant Dominion statistician – Integration. With Ivan Fellegi as director, it had a broader mandate covering other aspects of survey methodology as well as sampling and was now called the Sampling and Survey Research Staff. These moves were an attempt to target the bureau's wide range and large number of business and institutional surveys for methodological input. But while methodology was virtually an innate element of household surveys, the situation was very different elsewhere in the bureau and progress was slow.

This was in part due to the extreme compartmentalization of the field and the lack of common elements such as frame, or list, information and classification systems. The bureau's historical culture was also a factor. Coats had always paid lip-service to the integration of economic statistics, but in practice he gave the responsible directors a great deal of latitude. However, attitudes gradually began to change in light of the requirements of what later became known as the System of National Accounts. This provided the framework, hitherto lacking, for the integration of economic statistics. Thus, progress was gradually made. Early examples included the development of a new sample design for the monthly retail trade survey, based on 1961 census data, and revisions in the sample design, data processing, and estimation procedures for the motor transport survey. More ambitiously, the redesign of the monthly employment survey sought to use the computer to select the sample, handle the mailing, check the receipt of completed questionnaires, and prepare estimates from the sample using new methods of estimation. This was a major step towards full automation of the handling of a survey. Later in the decade, the job vacancy survey was the first example of a fully automated survey.

In addition to the automation of individual surveys, emphasis was also given to the development of general systems, applicable to the processing of more than one survey. During the closing years of Duffett's tenure, the most advanced developments along these lines were the Geographically Referenced Data Storage and Retrieval System (GRDSR) and the grandiloquently titled time series data bank, Canadian Socio-Economic Information Management System (CANSIM), described in the following chapter.

The bureau's computer facilities, located in the Tabulating Services Division, had initially been installed for the purposes of the 1961 census and could not be used to any great extent for noncensus work until well into the 1960s. Some work had in fact to be contracted out to computer facilities at other installations through the agency of the Central Data Processing Services Bureau. Many of the early applications were limited in scope, as with the census of manufactures, where computer processing was at first restricted to the tabulation and editing of principal statistics. This, then, was computerization in the narrower sense rather than the broader concept of automation outlined earlier. During 1963–64, a Scientific Section was established within the Central Programming Division to work with the Sampling and Survey Research Staff, the Research and Development Staff, and economists and statisticians in subject-matter divisions, to produce and modify programs for the analysis of tabulated data, for the seasonal adjustment of time series, and for perfecting sampling techniques and the design of sampling areas.

By mid-decade it was becoming clear that the bureau's computer facilities were incapable of handling prospective demands on them. This situation also affected the recruitment and retention of experienced programmers who were reluctant to work with outmoded equipment. Some relief was afforded when the Tabulating Services Division acquired an IBM 360/30 computer in 1966–67. This was substantially upgraded in the following year, but the equipment problem was not fully resolved until an IBM 360/65[48] system was installed in June 1969. Even so, the conversion or adaptation of ongoing computer work placed a heavy strain on systems and programming resources and hampered the development of new applications for an extended period.

But the most fundamental obstacles in the way of automation during the late 1960s were not equipment difficulties or shortages of working-level staff. Rather, they related to the inability to achieve the kind of interdisciplinary cooperation between subject-matter specialists, survey methodologists, computer programmers, and others to ensure that potential applications were looked at in their entirety rather than as collections of disparate elements some of which might benefit from computer power. This process had to start with common understandings at the management level in the subject-matter and functional areas concerned. Regrettably this took more than another decade to achieve fully. At this time, the Tabulating Services and Central Programming Divisions were part of an Operations and Systems Development Branch following the major restructuring of 1967. By the end of the decade, however, it seemed desirable to eliminate a major point of friction by putting survey methodology and computer programming under common management. Thus, the Operations and Systems Development Branch was effectively dismantled, with a new Methodology and Systems Branch under Ivan Fellegi taking responsibility for the Central Programming Division, renamed the Computer Systems Development Division, and the Sampling and Survey Research Staff.[49] For the time being, the Tabulating Services Division continued to report directly to the Dominion statistician.

The Advent of Formalized Planning

In the late 1960s the Treasury Board relinquished its annual establishment reviews for putting together departmental estimates in favour of a new system of program forecasts. These were to be prepared on the basis of a management philosophy developed by Robert McNamara while he served as US Secretary of Defense in the early 1960s. By requiring departments to identify their objectives and to consider alternative ways of achieving them, the Planning, Programming, Budgeting System (PPB) sought to remedy defects in existing budget-making processes, particularly the practice of "incrementalism," or simply tacking on additional funds to last year's budget. The system, which was to operate in Canada in the context of a five-year planning horizon (later shortened to three years), introduced new terminology to the management lexicon, notably the concept of cost-benefit analysis.

It did not matter, apparently, that PPB had already passed the peak of its usefulness in the US government, or that, in Canada, budgetary allocations could only be approved for one year at a time.[50] This was the system that prevailed into the mid-1970s. From the bureau's point of view, it seemed like the exchange of one bureaucratic procedure for another, but it did its best to play by the rules under what generally seemed like uncertain guidance from the Treasury Board

Secretariat. But money was flowing in any case, and the bureau always seemed to get its fair share.

It was against this background that, in 1969, the Treasury Board appointed Professor D.G. Hartle of the University of Toronto as deputy secretary – Planning, to bring some visible rationality into the process of resource allocation and to counterbalance the mechanistic application of program forecast procedures. At the bureau, Simon Goldberg, while as keen as any of his senior colleagues to secure additional resources, was nevertheless anxious to demonstrate that the best possible use was being made of them. Thus, largely at his urging, a management consultant from Montreal with no previous experience in the pubic service was appointed director of Central Planning and Programming in October 1968. In spite of my own appointment as assistant director to help the new director find his feet, he did not win the confidence and support of senior bureau management and returned to the private sector within two years. But there was more to the problem than bridging a cultural gap. I was subsequently appointed to the position and enjoyed the full support of Duffett, Goldberg, and other key figures but nevertheless found the job uphill work.

Ideally, the statistical program should be established by comparing the costs and expected benefits of each of its elements, existing and proposed, and then ranking them in the order of net benefit. In-house costs could be measured; an effective project and cost accounting system was put in place before the end of the decade. The burden on survey respondents also needed to be taken into account. But the appraisal of benefits was another matter, involving – again ideally – the determination of which statistical series played a part in which decisions, assessing the importance of those decisions, and the extent to which their quality was affected by the availability or absence of statistical information. In moving from individual projects to the combined and diverse programs of divisions and finally to the totality of activities, there were difficulties of comparability. How, for instance, could the benefits of more data on crime or health be assessed against those of more statistics on transportation or the balance of payments? In practice "incrementalism" could not be discarded. The pattern of statistical outputs at any one time, while by no means sacrosanct, reflected a fairly realistic appraisal of priorities by virtue of the known usefulness of its parts, both individually and as elements in higher aggregations. Trade-offs at the margin of this existing corpus were ultimately intuitive but were made on the basis of continuous and careful consultation with users.

The identification and assessment of federal needs would have been greatly assisted if the Dominion statistician could have had the access to cabinet documents afforded to most deputy ministers. This would have provided him with some insight into the government's longer-term thinking and what it regarded as current priorities. Unfortunately, such access did not come about for another decade or so.

Late in 1971 Duffett tried to get an overview of where and how the bureau should be moving by setting up an Interdepartmental Advisory Committee on Statistics to advise with respect to both the content of its statistical program as a whole and the more general aspects of its capacity to provide useful service, particularly from the standpoint of federal government users. Despite the senior standing of most of the members, which it was thought would guarantee some objectivity of approach, the committee soon developed into a lobby for promoting departmental interests and had lapsed by the time of Duffett's retirement.

A New Statistics Act

On 11 February 1971 royal assent was given to "An Act respecting Statistics of Canada,"[51] the first major revision of the Statistics Act since 1948 and only the second in the bureau's history. The process of drafting the revised act had begun in the mid-1960s under the general direction of a Statistical Legislation Committee chaired by L.E. Rowebottom, and extensive consultation with both provincial and federal departments took place.

The main objective of the revision was to reduce the level of response burden, which had become a matter of considerable public concern, and to forestall the further impositions on respondents to surveys that would have been inevitable, given the continuing pressures on the bureau for new and extended statistics. The provinces were part of both the problem and its solution. They had by this time become major users of economic statistics in particular and, in several cases, had the capability to collect statistics that they could not readily obtain from the bureau, thus potentially aggravating the overall response burden problem.

For the bureau's own purposes, the most important provisions were that the access to corporate income tax records granted to the Dominion statistician under his responsibility for the Corporations and Labour Unions Returns Act was now extended to his more general activities under the Statistics Act. Access to the tax returns of unincorporated businesses and individuals was also authorized. It was estimated at the time that this latter provision would immediately relieve 10,000 small businesses from the onus of response to the census of manufactures and eventually some 80,000 from a broader range of surveys. Cooperative arrangements for data sharing with the provinces were extended so as to minimize possible duplication in collection activities. In particular, data could now be shared with a provincial statistical agency, provided it had statutory confidentiality provisions similar to those of the bureau, simply by advising the respondent of the agreement.

Some needlessly restrictive confidentiality requirements were relaxed. Previously, there had been an absolute prohibition of disclosure of any information contained in an individual return. Now the prohibition applied only to identifiable information. Information obtained by the bureau from another agency would retain the degree of secrecy it had with that agency rather than, in some cases, acquiring a greater degree of secrecy because of its being passed on to the bureau. Also, the act allowed full disclosure of information relating to public institutions, such as hospitals, provided no attribution to individuals was possible. In addition, it permitted the publication of lists of organizations and the products or services they provided, as well as the names and addresses of individual establishments, firms, or businesses within certain employment size ranges.

Finally, in section 3(d) it was provided that the bureau should "promote the avoidance of duplication in the information collected by departments of government." This was a point of more symbolic than practical value, since there was still no reciprocal obligation for other departments to collaborate. The new act also changed the name of the bureau from "the Dominion Bureau of Statistics" to "Statistics Canada," and that of the minister's deputy for the purposes of the act from "Dominion statistician" to "chief statistician of Canada." Provision was made for a transitional period during which both old and new titles could be used. This accommodated the needs of the 1971 census, for which advertising and questionnaires had been printed before the passage of the new act.

During second reading of the bill, Bruce Howard, the minister's parliamentary secretary, argued that "the name of a department or organization is an important indication of the function and even the attitude of that group. In this light, we are proposing the name 'Statistics Canada.' En français 'Statistique Canada,' un nom simple et moderne, en Anglais ou Français un nom presque bilingue. In just two words, what it does and where it does it. It is an efficient, definite title, I think it will make a great improvement in the name we call our statistics agency."[52]

Traditionalist members of the House were not impressed. The Honourable D.S. Harkness replied: "I can see no good reason for this. It seems to be only a continuation of an attack which has been going on for some years on what we might call traditional titles, particularly those that use the term 'Dominion.' This is an honourable term and one which in this case has attained a particular status in the eyes of the public. I think it should be maintained."[53]

Within the bureau, the concern was more with the perceived inelegance of a name that could readily be contracted to "StatCan." An alternative that had been put forward at one time was "the Canadian Bureau of Statistics," but this came to nothing. Employees could, of course, legitimately continue to speak of "the bureau,"[54] as had long been their practice, and in fact both external and internal misgivings about the new name soon evaporated.

CHAPTER FOURTEEN

1957–1972
The Duffett Years II: Program and Related Developments

Introduction

The accident of timing exposed Walter Duffett to four censuses during his fifteen years as Dominion statistician. He inherited the residual tasks of the quinquennial census of 1956–final tabulations and the analysis and dissemination of findings – continued with the censuses of 1961 and 1966, and concluded with the planning, conduct, and preliminary tabulations of the decennial census of 1971. This latter was the most complex and expensive undertaking to date in Canadian census history. Apart from their informational value, Duffett's censuses were also important vehicles for the development of new statistical methodology.

Achievements in the bureau's other programs were significant, notably in the further development of the System of National Accounts, the various elements of which were brought to full fruition by the late 1960s. And starting in the middle of that decade, there was a major drive to improve the timeliness of bureau outputs, particularly, but by no means restricted to, the indicators bearing on economic conditions. One area of the bureau's responsibility that came under particularly close public scrutiny during the late 1950s related to the measurement of unemployment. This was a consequence of the steady growth of unemployment during those years, which focused what was, for the government of the day, embarrassing attention on differences in the two official concepts of the phenomenon and the statistical measures derived from them. The bureau played an important role in resolving this anomaly.

All through the Duffett years, the bureau continued to maintain a high profile in the international statistical community, although with less emphasis on technical assistance work. During the 1960s the bureau played host to two major intergovernmental statistical meetings and began to participate in the work of the Conference of European Statisticians. The 1960s also witnessed the gradual development of the government's policies and practices with respect to bilingualism in the public service. There was much that needed to be done to achieve an equitable balance between the use of the two official languages in the bureau's operations, and some progress was made. But the major impact of bilingualism during the 1960s was on the bureau's publication program.

THE 1961, 1966, AND 1971 CENSUSES[1]

In 1957 planning for the 1961 census began with the constitution of a Census Executive Committee, supported by a number of subject-matter and functional committees. Early in its work the committee determined that the prospective processing workload could not be handled by the system used in 1951. This consideration, together with a favourable assessment of the experience of the US Bureau of the Census with computers in its 1950 census, led to the decision that computer facilities would be used for the 1961 Census of Canada. The chosen configuration centred around an IBM 705 Mark III with ten tape drives and an auxiliary IBM 1401 with two tape drives. Information was to be collected in the field on "mark-sense" documents and then transferred by an optical document reader to magnetic tape for later computer processing.

The scope of the 1961 census was somewhat broader than that of 1951 as regards population and housing. In the basic population data collected from everyone, the only new question concerned the level of educational attainment. A twenty percent sample of households was used to collect additional information on internal migration, fertility, and income characteristics, and the same sample accommodated the housing census. The census of agriculture asked twenty-five percent fewer questions than its predecessor of 1951, and, partly because of definitional changes, fewer farms were covered. The year 1961 also saw the fourth decennial census of merchandising and services.

Enumeration of the population, housing, and agricultural censuses and initial processing of the first two were carried out by the bureau's eight regional offices. The enumeration process included a postal check covering sixty percent of Canadian households. Letter carriers in 170 urban areas checked enumerators' listings of addresses against their own. Subsequent follow-up of missed addresses added over 40,000 persons to the total population count. Similar checks were later used in the 1966 and 1971 censuses.

The lack of sufficient competent staff in Ottawa and the required office accommodation for such a large-scale but short-term undertaking made it necessary to devolve certain processing operations to the regions. Field processing consisted of checking documents for completion and consistency and the coding of occupations that had been written on the "mark-sense" documents. Initial processing of information from the census of agriculture which had been collected on conventional questionnaires, also included coding but mainly consisted of the transcription to mark-sense documents for later head office processing. This work was carried out in separate agricultural processing centres in Cornwall, Ottawa, and Winnipeg. Supervisory arrangements for the enumeration process were modified, the number of census commissioners being greatly increased, so that each was now responsible for an average of twenty-four enumerators as opposed to sixty-five in 1951.[2] At the same time, the positions of field supervisors, varying numbers of whom had hitherto assisted each census commissioner, were eliminated.

Head Office processing began with the transcription to magnetic tape of documents received from the field. The document reader wrote on low-density tapes that were then compressed into high-density tapes on the 1401 computer system. During the six months that this operation took, the document reader only ever achieved thirty to fifty percent of its rated speed. Tapes were computer edited on the 705 system for completeness and internal consistency, and errors greater than the program tolerances were followed up manually. Many rejections resulted from failure of the document reader to pick up mark-sense entries.

Computer tabulations began in early 1962 and, up to 1965, were addressed to the needs of the census publications. Subsequently, tabulations were carried out to meet special requests, including census monographs. The preparation of editing, tabulation, and other programs was a major challenge. Qualified programmers were a scarce resource in the late 1950s, and it was necessary to mount a crash training program. The 1961 census was the swansong of the veteran director of the Census Division, O.A. Lemieux, who had made his name in the census of agriculture of 1931. He was succeeded on an acting basis by J.L. Forsyth and, later in the decade, by W.D. Porter, formerly with the census of agriculture, after his return from a posting with the Organization for Economic Co-operation and Development (OECD).

In 1966 a mid-decade census for the whole of Canada was conducted for the second time under the authority of Order in Council PC 1965–449, dated 12 March 1965.[3] The collection and processing methods were largely patterned on those of 1961. The content of the population and housing questionnaire was similar to that of 1956, covering name, sex, age, marital status, relationship to Head of Household, and the structural type and tenure of dwelling. The agricultural questionnaire contained 138 questions, compared with 251 in 1961. The evaluation of the 1961 census had shown the need for better training and supervision of field staff. Accordingly, in 1966 sixty new appointments were made with the title of regional office representative (ROR). After being themselves instructed by master trainers from head office, the RORS were in turn able to provide more intensive instruction to the census commissioners.

The computer system used in the 1966 census was essentially the same as that of 1961. In 1967 an IBM 360/30 was installed and assisted in the later stages of processing. The 1961 document reader was used again in 1966, with some modifications to cope with problems encountered in 1961. Document reading was conducted in a temporary location away from the atmospherically controlled area of the computer facility. This gave rise to reading failures, and it was found necessary to test each work unit before accepting it for processing. Thus, once again, the reader worked at only a fraction of its rated capacity.

By 1966 the availability of qualified programmers had improved and census programming requirements were met with less difficulty. With fewer questions on the population questionnaire, the number of cross-classified tables was greatly reduced, and many tabulations could be generated from a single generalized program. A change in editing and correction procedures was made in 1966. In 1961 errors remaining after the first phase of editing and correction were corrected by the computer in a programmed procedure. In 1966 records in error were returned for manual examination and correction. This caused considerable delays and it was subsequently recommended that a return be made in 1971 to the procedure used in 1961.

The year 1971 marked the hundredth anniversary of the first census of the new Dominion of Canada. The census of that year will, however, best be remembered for its sharp break from tradition by the introduction of more methodological innovations than any of its predecessors. In addition, the content of the questionnaires was greatly enlarged. New questions on vocational education, language spoken in the home, full-time and part-time employment, place of work, and farm income were some of the major additions to the population questionnaire.[4] Environmental concerns gave rise to new agricultural questions on topics such as the use of sprays and dusts for pest and weed control and the use of fertilizers. Planning for the 1971 census was a more extended and complex process than ever before. This was reflected in the organizational arrangements, which included a Census Policy Committee, a Census Executive Group, a Census Management Group, and numerous committees, subcommittees, task forces, working groups, etc., filling out some sixty boxes on the Census Committee Structure Organization Chart.[5]

The Sampling Research and Consultation Staff had evaluated the quality of the 1961 census as well as relevant international experience and concluded that, among the various sources of error to which census statistics are subject, enumerator error was the most important. This consideration, together with the fact that the content of the 1971 census of population would be longer and more complex than ever before, led to the decision that the role of the enumerator should be minimized by the adoption of self-enumeration wherever possible. After appropriate testing, it was decided to use a "drop-off, mail back" questionnaire in urban areas, while in rural areas questionnaires were both dropped off and picked up by the census enumerators. The remainder of the population, living in northern regions, the coastal outports, institutions etc., were enumerated by traditional face-to-face canvassing.

Two questionnaires were used. The first, or "short" form, distributed to two-thirds of Canadian households, covered the basic population questions and nine housing questions. The remaining one-third received a "long" form containing the same questions as well as a further twenty housing and thirty socioeconomic population questions. The census of agriculture questionnaire contained 199 questions, down from 251 in 1961.

The larger population in 1971 and the increased complexity of the population and housing census necessitated a considerable increase in the number of census enumerators – some 41,000 as opposed to 30,000 or so in 1961. In view of the supervisory difficulties of 1961, there were not only census commissioners and regional office representatives as in 1966 but also senior RORs, ROR technicians, ROR administrative assistants, census commissioner assistants, and, in each regional office, a regional census officer responsible to the regional director for all census field operations within the office's jurisdiction. The arrangements were supported by a Field Information Reporting System, which scheduled all tasks in the census operation, monitored the expenditures and progress of all regional offices against plans, and provided regular reports to members of the Census Management Group and regional directors.

Temporary regional processing offices were set up to handle field processing operations, which were carried out by 3,000 clerks and 300 supervisors Much of the work consisted of hand-coding the write-in answers of the population and housing questionnaires, and further quality checks were conducted before the questionnaires were forwarded to head office. In addition, agricultural questionnaires were hand-matched with the corresponding population and housing questionnaires in preparation for the computerized linkage that later took place at head office.

Head office processing was radically different from that of 1966 and 1961, mainly as a consequence of dissatisfaction with the earlier document-reading arrangements. In 1971 processing of population and housing questionnaires began with their microfilming, which was carried out with twelve automatic table feed cameras provided by the US Bureau of the Census. Data were then transferred from film to magnetic tape by means of a new kind of document reader, the Film Optical Sensing Device for Input to Computer (FOSDIC), two of which were purchased from the US Bureau of the Census. These had been used in the 1960 and 1970 US censuses and tried out in Canada during a 1967 test and in the 1969 dress rehearsal, where their superior speed in transcribing data from microfilm rather than from the original documents had been satisfactorily demonstrated. Computer processing was carried out on an IBM 360/65, originally acquired in June 1969 and subsequently upgraded to double the core memory.

Most of the processing of census of agriculture questionnaires was manual, and after transcription of the data to machine-readable form, the subsequent preparation of tabulations proceeded more or less uneventfully. There were problems, however, with the population and housing census – particularly with the form 2B, or long sample questionnaires, where major delays were encountered in the computer editing of data and in preparing their tabulation programs. The sample data were to have been grossed up by a weighting system known as the Raking Ratio Estimation Procedure, but in the Dominion statistician's annual reports for two or three years after the census year, reference was still being made to the difficulties of validating the long questionnaire data base.

A different kind of problem occurred with the 1971 census of merchandising, which had been conducted by mail on the basis of a list of respondents compiled by special census representatives at the time of the population census – a practice followed since the Coats era. The inadequacies of this list gave rise to considerable difficulties and delays in the processing of the data. The recognition that satisfactory efforts in the future would depend on the successful outcome of ongoing efforts to develop a comprehensive and properly classified central list of business establishments caused plans for a 1976 census of merchandising to be cancelled.

Early in the planning of the 1971 census, research had begun on the development of a system to provide census data by small areas. This resulted in the Geographically Referenced Data Storage and Retrieval System (GRDSR), generally referred to as the Geocoding System. To facilitate the production of both standard and special tabulations from GRDSR, a generalized retrieval system, STATPAK, was set up. The Agriculture-Population Linkage program was a computerized operation that matched each agricultural questionnaire with the corresponding population and housing questionnaire (short or long form). The resultant data base of 130,410 linked documents opened up analytical possibilities not hitherto feasible.

The reverse record check of 1961, conducted by the Sampling Research and Consultation Staff, was an important innovation in census methodology. It sought to ascertain the undercoverage of a sample of 6,000 persons drawn from the 1956 census of population, updated by birth and immigration records and therefore independent of the 1961 census. The success of the experiment led to its repetition in subsequent censuses and its international recognition as one of the most reliable methods of evaluating census undercoverage. Another smaller study, using the technique of re-enumeration, analyzed the effect of errors in response on the final census estimate and was an important factor in the later decision to adopt self-enumeration. A quality check of the 1961 census of agriculture was also carried out to provide regional and national measures of the accuracy of census results for certain items, an outline of the characteristics of farm holdings completely missed by the census, and an estimate of the magnitude and direction of errors in census reporting at the individual farm level.

In 1966 a reverse record check, using a sample four times larger than that of 1961, was again conducted to estimate the proportion of persons not enumerated in the census of population. A second quality check at that time was the labour force/census match, designed to obtain estimates of under- and overenumeration of households in the census, as well as estimates of content error. This compared data collected in May 1966 from approximately half of the labour force survey households with corresponding data from identical census households. A third project was again a quality check of the census of agriculture based on the re-enumeration of a sample of area segments, and farms within those segments.

The reverse record check carried out in 1971 used an even larger sample than that of 1966. This permitted the estimates of persons missed to be broken down by age and province. Information was also collected that permitted the characteristics of missed persons to be analyzed and the impact of coverage errors on census tabulations to be estimated. In order to validate the correctness of the decision to use self-enumeration in the 1971 census, a national-level response variance study was carried out. A final undertaking in 1971 by what was now called the Sampling and Survey Research Staff was a greatly elaborated agriculture quality check program, which included the collection by sample of additional information that was required at national and provincial levels by some users but that was not covered by the census proper.

All three censuses – 1961, 1966, and 1971 – were the object of considerable publicity efforts to ensure public awareness of the events and an understanding of their importance as a basis for full participation and accuracy of the information. The introduction of self-enumeration in 1971 gave rise to the slogan "Count Yourself In" in an effort to foster personal identification with the objectives of the census. Other special efforts in 1971 included the preparation of a thirty-minute film, "On a Clear Day You Can Count Forever," the issuance of a commemorative stamp on 1 June, and the use of census cancellation dies in the post offices of two hundred cities across Canada.

Perhaps the most imaginative publicity project in 1971, however, was the conduct of a student census, involving one million students from 6,000 elementary and secondary schools, carried out during the last two weeks of May. This sought to familiarize students with the purpose and value of the census and thus enable them to acquaint their parents with the self-enumeration methodology.

Publication arrangements followed the same basic plan in each of the three censuses. Population totals by municipality, based on manual counts from visitation records, were the first information to appear–generally within three months or so of census day. Municipalities were given the opportunity of challenging these figures before they were made public. The small number of municipalities that submitted formal challenges was attributed in major part to the effectiveness of the postal check.

In the publication program proper, the Advance Series appeared first, providing early basic information on the demographic, social, housing, family, and economic characteristics of the population, and on agriculture. This information was followed by publication of the definitive Volume Series – generally a more extended process – providing the main body of data with extensive cross-classifications for all subject fields. In the 1961 census, the final volume contained an analysis of the statistics published in other volumes and included a number of separate reports covering a wide variety of topics such as population, labour force, housing and families, agriculture, merchandising, etc. In the 1971 census, the Volume Series again provided the main body of cross-classified data relating to all subject fields, as well as profile studies demonstrating major trends and patterns in the areas of population growth and general demographic characteristics, economic characteristics of the adult population, and families, housing, and agriculture. A third element of the publication program was the Special Series covering basic information, not included in the regular Volume Series, relating to more specialized subject classifications and in some cases providing more detailed area breakdowns. Finally, the Census Tract Series provided basic population, housing, and labour force characteristics[6] for statistical units (i.e. census tracts) within larger cities and census metropolitan areas.

In the 1971 census, a large number of other tables were produced as computer printouts and then microfilmed for subsequent distribution to users. There was also a census user summary tape program designed to satisfy user demand for aggregated data in machine-readable form, and public-use sample tapes provided, with appropriate confidentiality safeguards, data disaggregated back to their original reporting units, so that they could be resummarized and tabulated to meet particular research needs. The distribution of census data from these new sources was channelled through a Data Dissemination Section, which was particularly oriented towards provincial needs and which used the provincial statistical bureaux as secondary distributors.

The crowning glories of both the 1961 and 1971 censuses were their monograph programs, which paralleled in numbers and quality of analysis those associated with the 1931 census. There were fifteen in 1961 covering such topics as Canadian marketing trends, unemployment, incomes, internal migration, urban development, female workers, etc. and bringing to the foreground a new generation of in-house authors that included Frank Denton, Sylvia Ostry, Leroy Stone, M.V. George, and Jenny Podoluk. The 1971 monographs, which were actually described as Census Analytical Studies, numbered fourteen and were mostly the work of academics who had been invited to submit research proposals.

Census taking became a costly activity during the Duffett years. As Appendix B demonstrates, current-dollar costs increased by 108 percent between 1951 and 1961, and by 137 percent between 1961 and 1971. Population increases of thirty percent and eighteen percent respectively explain only small proportions of the increases, which must relate to the extended and more complex nature of census operations in 1961 and 1971. Appendix B converts costs from 1871 to 1971 into constant dollars and calculates constant-dollar cost per head of population for each census. This rather crude measure shows that, with the exception of 1901, costs from 1871 to 1951 remained remarkably stable. The increases of thirty-five percent between 1951 and 1961 and of forty-five percent between 1961 and 1971 clearly indicate that a new era of more complex censuses had arrived.

The System of National Accounts

Other than the conduct of the censuses of 1961, 1966, and 1971, the bureau's major program development during the Duffett years was the full articulation, under the leadership of Simon Goldberg, of what came to be called the System of National Accounts.[7] The core elements of the system were the quarterly national income and expenditure accounts, first published in 1945. These underwent two historical revisions, the first completed in the late 1950s and the second a decade later. In 1961-62 the quarterly accounts were elaborated by the development of seasonally adjusted constant-dollar data.

Organizationally, this work had originally comprised a section within the Central Research and Development Staff, but during 1960-61 it was given separate status as the National Accounts Division, at the same time absorbing the work on current business indicators and industrial output. These latter two areas had hitherto been the responsibility of the Business Statistics Section of Central Research and Development, which now disappeared. The current business indicators, published each month in the *Canadian Statistical Review*, were seasonally adjusted at an early stage, as one of the bureau's first ventures into computerization. The major development in the industrial output work occurred in the early 1960s with the extension of the coverage of the index of industrial production to provide quarterly measures of real output by industry of origin for the economy as a whole. This work was particularly useful as an independent check on the theoretically equivalent measures of national income and expenditure and also provided a basis for the bureau's work on the measurement and analysis of productivity change.

Continually unsettled conditions in the international exchange and money markets, as well as recurring balance of payments deficits in some of the principal countries of the world, kept the spotlight on Canada's balance of payment statistics.[8] In 1961–62 these were transferred from the International Trade Division to the National Accounts Division, which now became the National Accounts and Balance of Payments Division under C.D. Blyth. The residual elements of the International Trade Division, responsible for the compilation of import and export statistics, continued as the External Trade Division. During the 1960s more data were provided on short- and long-term capital movements, and in 1969 work that had begun under the auspices of the Gordon Commission finally resulted in the publication of financial flow accounts, linking changes in the stocks of financial claims within various sectors of the economy to the production of goods and services.

The 1949 input-output table had been developed as a relatively modest undertaking of the Special Projects Section of the Central Research and

Development Staff. After its publication in 1956 and the departure soon after of its author, J.A. Sawyer, to the University of Toronto, the input-output work temporarily languished. However, following the appointment in 1962 of Terry Gigantes as Sawyer's successor, plans were laid for a 1961 table that would embody important conceptual refinements and distinguish more industry and commodity detail and sectors of final demand. This was published before the end of the decade, by which time a full-blown Input-Output Research and Development Division had emerged as part of the Economic Statistics Branch in the major reorganization of 1967. In the early 1960s work was also initiated under T.K. Rymes on the development of measures of the gross and net stock of fixed capital in current and constant dollars by the perpetual inventory method. There were important precedents for this work in the United States where, for instance, such measures had been used in unofficial but nonetheless highly regarded estimates of changes in "total factor productivity," i.e., the change in real output not accounted for by changes in the quantity of labour and capital inputs.[9]

Since the immediate postwar years, when US technical know-how was being injected into the war-ravaged British economy through the agency of the Anglo-American Productivity Council and later disseminated through the European Recovery Program to a broader range of European countries, the Government of Canada had also been keenly interested in the topic. An Interdepartmental Advisory Committee on Labour Statistics, which functioned in Ottawa during the late 1940s and early 1950s, had a subcommittee on productivity measurement on behalf of which the bureau carried out experimental work from time to time. Governmental interest did not, however, translate into political commitment until December 1960 when the National Productivity Council was established under George de Young. This body had a mandate to strengthen Canada's competitive position in export and domestic markets by improving the productivity of primary and secondary industry. As constituted, it could do little direct work towards this end and functioned, during its three years of existence, mainly as a clearing house for the assembly and dissemination of information aimed at improving public awareness and understanding of the topic. In August 1963 – some twenty-seven years after the demise of its 1930s namesake – a new Economic Council of Canada was established. This body, chaired by John Deutsch, took over the functions of the National Productivity Council, which was disbanded.

The bureau formally launched a program of productivity measurement in the late 1950s, modelling it on that of the US Bureau of Labor Statistics, which had long been conducting studies of individual manufacturing industries but did not publish measures for the total private economy until 1959. The program had its start in Central Research and Development but was soon moved to the industry side of the Industry and Merchandising Division, where it remained until it was transferred to the new National Accounts, Production and

Productivity Division in 1967. Work at the bureau started at both the industry and aggregate levels simultaneously and by 1970 seven individual industry studies had been published. At that time, however, this work was judged to be no longer cost effective and was discontinued. At the aggregate level, indexes of annual productivity change from 1947 were published for the commercial nonagricultural industries in 1965. Later, the coverage of the measures was extended to include agriculture.

During the winter of 1962–63, Simon Goldberg organized a first of its kind for the bureau – an interdepartmental seminar on productivity and related topics at which some twenty papers were presented and discussed.[10] Participants from departments other than the bureau included several who subsequently joined the research staff of the Economic Council, among them D.J. Daly and D.A. White of Trade and Commerce, and B.J. Drabble and D.L. McQueen of the Bank of Canada. The seminar's work was useful to the Economic Council in its first major research project – the estimation of potential output to the year 1970, but the conservative approach of the bureau's program could not help the council with its plans for a more sophisticated analysis of the factors determining productivity growth. Instead, it looked to the work of Edward F. Denison who, in the context of an international comparison between the United States and various European countries, took into account such factors as qualitative differences in labour inputs – including those caused by education, resource shifts between different sectors of the economy, and economies of scale.[11] This work inspired a study by Dorothy Walters of the council's research staff, who developed comparable Canadian data.[12]

The bureau stuck with its conceptually simpler approach. It was frequently urged to develop subannual measures of aggregate productivity change, but too many of the quarterly output measures were measures of labour input adjusted for assumed productivity change. The construction of annual aggregate measures has continued with essentially the original methodology but with minor analytical refinements such as the calculation of unit labour costs.

CALURA – A New Task for the Bureau

Among other highlights of the noncensus statistical program, the Corporations and Labour Unions Returns Act was enacted in April 1962 for the purpose of providing financial and other information on the affairs of corporations and labour unions operating in Canada. Such information was thought necessary to evaluate the extent and effects of nonresident ownership and control of corporations in Canada, and also of the association of Canadians with international labour unions. Although its operations were logically distinct from those carried on under the Statistics Act, the administration of CALURA, as it came to be known, was made the responsibility of the Dominion statistician.[13] The reporting requirements for corporations were onerous and duplicated in large measure the information provided in corporate income tax returns. Accordingly, the legislation was amended in 1964 to relieve them of the obligation of reporting if they had filed financial statements under the Income Tax Act. At the same time, access to corporate income tax returns was accorded to the Dominion statistician. This proved to be a valuable precedent for later initiatives to reduce, or avoid further, response burden in other areas of bureau activity by accessing the tax returns of unincorporated businesses and private individuals.

Developments in Primary Statistics

By the early 1960s the Industry and Merchandising Division had grown into the bureau's biggest subject-matter grouping, and in 1963-64 it was divided into two separate divisions, the Industry Division and the Merchandising and Services Division. The former then assumed complete responsibility for energy statistics including those of pipelines and electric and gas utilities, which were transferred from the Public Finance and Transportation Division.

In September 1958 the Labour and Prices Division was also split into two separate divisions, each of which, during the next decade or so, took on extensive new program commitments. Concerns about inflationary pressures and international competitiveness gave rise to such developments as industrially classified price indexes for manufacturing industries and price indexes related to capital expenditures in residential and nonresidential building as well as in engineering construction. Again, the development of spatial consumer price indexes for major urban centres contributed to policy formulation and program operation in the fields of welfare, income maintenance, and area development. Early in the 1960s the Labour Division initiated a new sample survey of employment in small firms, and the collection of employment data in the growing noncommercial sector was extended. This new information, in conjunction with that from the regular employment survey of large commercial establishments, made possible the estimation of measures of total employment by province for major industries. Later, in conjunction with the Department of Employment and Immigration, work began on the development of an occupational job vacancy survey, designed to provide information on the demand side of the labour market paralleling that of the labour force survey on the supply side.

The biennial program of household-based sample surveys to estimate the size distribution of nonfarm family incomes began to be supplemented in the late 1950s by statistics of consumer assets and indebtedness. Later, the scope of the surveys was expanded to include farm families, and additional topics, such as stock ownership, work history, and the economic and demographic characteristics of income recipients, were covered. Increase of the sample size made possible better regional analysis of income characteristics. This work, originally located in the Central Research and Development Division, was assigned to a separate Consumer Finance Research Division within the Socio-Economic Statistics Branch in the organizational restructuring of 1967.

The 1960s witnessed a doubling of elementary and secondary school enrolment in Canada and a quadrupling of university enrolment, as well as the emergence of new kinds of postsecondary educational institutions. This necessitated the reassessment of statistical programs in the postsecondary area and the development of new ones. Programs to measure cultural facilities, libraries, museums, art galleries, theatres, etc. and their use, were also initiated. Judicial and health statistics were greatly expanded during the Duffett years. Growing public concerns with the consequences of crime and delinquency, and developments in the correctional field such as the establishment of a National Parole Board, set in motion work on the establishment of common definitions, records, and reporting procedures among the various jurisdictions, leading to new developments such as the Uniform Crime Reporting System. In 1969 the Judicial Section of the Health and Welfare Division became a division in its own right. Again, the advent of a joint federal/provincial hospital insurance program in the late 1950s called for more precise information on the operation and utilization of hospital services. At this time, the results of the pioneering Canadian Sickness Survey, conducted in 1950–51, were released. As universal health care became a reality later in the 1960s, health statistics were further elaborated through such initiatives as the surveys of health manpower.

Provincial and Small Area Data

The interest in provincial and subprovincial data increased substantially during Duffett's time, partly due to the local orientation of many federal programs, but more importantly as a consequences of the provinces' greater involvement in economic and social planning and development. Following a recommendation of the 1962 Dominion/provincial Conference on Economic Statistics, a Regional Statistics Research and Integration Staff was set up and made responsible for studying provincial statistical needs and developing data to supply them. One approach that came to full fruition when the Statistics Act was later revised was the development of arrangements for the sharing, or joint collection, of data with the provinces. A related organizational development was the establishment of a Provincial Liaison and Consultative Services Staff, responsible for initiating and coordinating the bureau's contacts with provincial departments in their capacity as producers and users of statistics.

What Is the Best Measure of Unemployment?

As unemployment perceptibly increased during the late 1950s, public concerns were compounded by the apparent inability of official statisticians to provide a single definitive measure of the phenomenon. Each month, the Department of Labour published figures of current registrations at National Employment Service (NES) Offices, made up of unemployment insurance beneficiaries and voluntary registrants, while the Dominion Bureau of Statistics' monthly labour force survey yielded, *inter alia*, the number of persons without jobs and seeking work. The former figures were consistently and appreciably higher than the latter, and the decision by the two departments in 1954 to release them simultaneously in a joint press release with appropriate explanations did not, unfortunately, resolve the difficulty. Parliamentary questions were asked with increasing frequency. The Honourable Lester B. Pearson, for example, when speaking of the two measures on 19 July 1958, noted that "over the years there has been confusion inside and outside the House as to the relationship between the two and what they stand for" and called for "a detailed report on the exact meaning and significance of the bureau of statistics figures on unemployment compared with the figures collected by the Department of Labour."[14] The Honourable Gordon Churchill, minister of Trade and Commerce, replied that "the head of the Dominion Bureau of Statistics has studied this problem with painstaking care and has prepared a report which I think he has now attempted to bring to the attention of one government or another on 3 different occasions ... I have been considering asking Mr Duffett to bring the report forward again."[15]

Such a report had indeed been prepared by the bureau in conjunction with the Department of Labour.[16] It described the characteristics of the two sources of information on unemployment and explained the different levels of the measures they provided.[17] The two series, it said, "differ in what they attempt to measure. They differ in the method of measurement. They differ in the periods to which they refer."[18] And while it was recognized that the NES registrations data provided such valuable information for labour market analysis as occupational and geographical detail, the labour force survey data were nevertheless thought to provide the only satisfactory information on the extent of employment and unemployment on a national and broad regional basis. A difficulty with the labour force survey from the user's standpoint was that it did not produce a single figure called "unemployment" but rather a range and variety of information, making it possible to define the term in a number of ways. The report concluded with the suggestion that the measure of persons "without jobs and seeking work" might command the broadest measure of public support.

The report was not published, as Churchill had suggested it might be, and so the parliamentary questioning continued. In March 1960, however, the Honourable Michael Starr, minister of Labour, in conjunction with the minister of Trade and Commerce, set up a committee to look into the matter. Under the chairmanship of A.H. Brown, deputy minister of Labour, assisted by Duffett and Goldberg from the bureau, and with senior luminaries from Labour and other departments, the committee was required to: "(1) consider the most appropriate basis for the official national measure of unemployment in Canada and to recommend accordingly; (2) to review the adequacy of existing statistics for this purpose; and (3) consequent therein, to consider the changes required in the joint Department of Labour/Dominion Bureau of Statistics monthly employment release. The Committee is required to submit its report to the undersigned ministers as soon as possible."[19]

The report was submitted on 5 August 1960 and publicly released on 7 October 1960, its recommendations having been endorsed by the two ministers. It favoured a definition of unemployment that included people without work and seeking work, as well as workers on temporary layoff, as reported by the bureau's monthly labour force survey. This definition was similar to that in use in the United States and fully consistent with the recommendations of the International Labour Organization in this area.

The statistics that resulted from the operations of the Unemployment Insurance Act and the National Employment Service were found to have serious limitations as measures of unemployment, and it was recommended that they no longer be included in the monthly press release. A simplified release based on the bureau's monthly publication *The Labour Force*[20] would be adopted and the analysis prepared by the Department of Labour. The report also recommended the establishment of a continuing interdepartmental advisory committee on labour force research. This body was instrumental in bringing about the more extensive exploitation of data, available or readily collectable, on the labour force, such as familial characteristics, the occupational and industrial distribution of the employed, educational characteristics, and gross and net flows in and out of employment.

New Classification Systems

It was realized early in the 1960s that the emphasis being placed on integrated economic statistics would be mere lip-service without up-to-date, unambiguous, and consistently applied classification systems – industrial, commodity, occupational, and geographic. In 1963 N.L. McKellar was appointed director of a newly formed Central Classifications Staff, and there ensued a period of sustained work on the development or revision of such systems and their application in areas like the decennial census, statistics of external trade and employment, and the census of industry. In the latter, a new definition of "establishment" was adopted. This required that all the activities of the establishment be covered in a single report, classified to the industry of the major activity. A related infrastructure project was the development of a central list of companies and establishments to provide comparable coverage between different business surveys, and the relationship between the statistical records of companies and their constituent establishments was explored through detailed profiling studies.

Time Series and Model Building

In the late 1960s the bureau collaborated with the Economic Council of Canada and others in the construction of a medium-term model, CANDIDE–a somewhat forced acronym for the Canadian Disaggregated Inter-departmental Econometric project. This model, embodying some 1,600 equations and for the most part using the bureau's time series data, could focus on the operation of a single market or the functioning of the economy as a whole and was subsequently used as the basis for all the council's projections. The bureau participated through the econometrics capability that Simon Goldberg had established a year or two earlier. Following the organizational restructuring of 1967, it was given divisional status within the Integration and Development Branch. CANDIDE also provided the initial impetus for the development of the bureau's computerized time series data bank, CANSIM.

Another major econometric model development at that time was the Bank of Canada's RDX (Research Department Experimental) model. RDX2, as it was eventually known, was a quarterly model and thus was particularly well served by the gains in timeliness that the bureau was then effecting in its array of subannual economic statistics and indicators. Partly through problems in the conversion to new classification systems, timeliness had been slipping for some time. Initial targets included statistics of employment and payrolls, imports and exports, and retail trade, as well as the index of industrial production, where, through forceful action, significant gains were eventually realized.

Earlier in the decade an important collection of historical time series had resulted when the bureau collaborated with Professors M.C. Urquhart and K.A.H. Buckley in the compilation of a 672-page volume covering the period 1867 to 1960.[21] Section chiefs, mostly academics, worked with specialist panels to assemble and describe the component series in twenty-one subject-matter areas.

Bilingualism

Policies and practices with respect to bilingualism in the Public Service of Canada had their origins in the recommendations of the Royal Commission on Bilingualism and Biculturalism of 1963. These were not formally adopted until the passage of the Official Languages Act in 1969, but their essence was graphically summarized by the prime minister, the Rt. Hon. Lester B. Pearson, in his statement of 6 April 1966: "an atmosphere [must] be created within the Public Service wherein public servants of English or French expression may be able to work together towards common goals, each applying the cultural values of his ethnic language group while understanding those of the other. Public servants must be free to choose the language to be used in oral or written communication, knowing that they will be understood. Further, when a supervisor has under his orders persons of a language different from his own, he must be able to give effective direction to these persons."[22]

Until later in the decade, however, the bureau's most visible and productive efforts were addressed to the related goal of providing its publications to users in the language of their choice.

From his earliest days as Dominion statistician, Coats had had a translation staff, headed by Omer Chaput, who served until 1942. Their duties had centred around the translation of census reports and the *Canada Year Book*, which had *de jure* status as bilingual publications. In the early 1930s the new *Canada Handbook* was accorded similar status. In 1926 a *Monthly Review of Business Statistics* (later the *Canadian Statistical Review*) had been launched, and this was published in both French and English because of its primarily commercial audience.

Coats's minister in 1933, the Honourable H.H. Stevens, made a modest reputation as a champion of bilingualism by insisting that the new *Daily Bulletin* appear in French as well as in English. In commenting on this, Montréal's *Le Devoir* noted, on 7 October 1933, that "it is the same Minister who saw to it that the *Annuaire* and the *Year Book* should appear simultaneously." On 10 October *Le Droit* in Ottawa exulted that "bit by bit, after many requests, protests and urgings, official bilingualism is gaining ground." This optimism was premature. Some thirty years later, such staple publications as the monthly employment and prices reports, the quarterly national accounts, and the annual census of manufactures reports were still not available in French.

But attitudes and practices were slowly changing. By the early 1960s many new reports and statistical series were being voluntarily planned as bilingual publications. In January 1967 Mr J.C. Cantin, parliamentary secretary to the minister of Trade and Commerce, declared in response to a question in the House that "it is the policy of the Dominion Bureau of Statistics to produce as many reports as possible in both languages, bearing in mind the amount of translation resources available. In increasing the number of bilingual reports, an effort is made to give priority to the translation of those with the greatest known demand."[23]

This was to be no small task. Out of some one thousand publications per year of varying periodicities, about two-thirds were still English only. Apart from the limitations on translation facilities and the priorities imposed by market demand, the need for translation staff to master the widely different technical vocabularies in the various subject-matter divisions had also to be considered. This generally made it preferable for translators to exhaust the publications of one division at a time rather than work on all divisions simultaneously. In any case, progress was made. In 1965 there were five publications in separate English and French editions and 350 with side-by-side English and French, which was the most economical way of formatting texts with extensive tabular and graphics material common to both versions. By 1969 these figures had improved to eighty-five and 707 respectively. As percentages of all publications, however, the improvement was less marked, because the total number of publications had increased from 965 to 1,525[24] as a consequence of the buoyant program activity between 1965 and 1969.

Less attention was given to the broader aspects of bilingualism until, towards the end of the decade, an Adviser on Bilingual Development was appointed to assist with the implementation of those provisions of the Official Languages Act relating to the Public Service. At this time, some nine hundred of approximately 2,700 employees in the bureau were classified as bilingual.[25] However, these were mostly in clerical and lower-grade administrative positions, and in the absence of any program to designate the bilingual requirements of positions, there was no way of knowing whether this linguistic capability was being effectively used. A more telling statistic was that, of some forty-one public servants earning more than $17,000 per annum in 1969 – a group corresponding to director, directors general, and persons of equivalent seniority, only eight were bilingual.[26] Given the low rates of turnover in the bureau, particularly at more junior levels, the key to improving the proportion of bilingual employees had to be language training. The Public Service Commission was at this time engaged in a major expansion of its language training facilities, but even so, the bureau was required to give careful attention to its priorities, which in the first instance centred around the Executive category and first-line supervisors in the Administrative and Foreign Service, and Scientific and Professional categories. The Dominion statistician's annual report for the year ended 31 March 1970 noted that 242 employees were designated for language training during the year. Progress fell off somewhat as the 1971 census approached and many employees were obliged to withdraw temporarily from the program.

International Activities

During the Duffett years the bureau maintained its high profile in the international statistical community, although with less emphasis on technical assistance work. A new intergovernmental body, the Organization for Economic Co-operation and Development, was formed in 1960, essentially as an extension of the former Organization for European Economic Co-operation, which had administered the postwar Marshall Plan. The consultative functions of the OECD, which centred around the achievement of sustainable growth, high employment, and the maintenance of financial stability among member countries, depended heavily upon the availability of relevant and comparable international statistics, and the bureau quickly became involved in their planning and supply. Canada also maintained its tradition of service on the United Nations Statistical Commission through the 1960s. In 1953 the Conference of European Statisticians had been set up as a subsidiary body of the UN's Economic

Commission for Europe. While Canada did not join the latter until 1974, Duffett attended the 1966 conference meeting as an observer, and the bureau thereafter participated actively, although informally, in its work.

Duffett followed in Marshall's footsteps by continuing Canada's leadership role in the Inter-American Statistical Institute, and bureau staff regularly took part in its meetings and the concurrent sessions of the Committee on the Improvement of National Statistics. In August 1963 the Government of Canada acted as host to the thirty-fourth Session of the International Statistical Institute. Held in Ottawa and attended by 780 registrants, the session was organized entirely by the bureau. Later in the decade, the bureau could claim eight active or retired officers – the highest figure in its history – as members of this most prestigious nongovernmental international statistical organization.

In September 1966 the Sixth Conference of Commonwealth Statisticians was held in Ottawa. It was attended by twenty-two delegates from fifteen countries and a number of observers from United Nations organizations and elsewhere. As with earlier postwar conferences, the agenda included topics of interest to both the older and the developing Commonwealth countries. In 1970 India hosted the Seventh Conference and the bureau sent a strong delegation.

Duffett Steps Down

Walter Duffett retired on 30 June 1972. At the age of sixty-two he could conceivably have carried on, as did his predecessors, Coats and Marshall, until the age of sixty-five or beyond. By the late 1960s the practice of playing musical chairs with deputy ministerial appointments had become established, but few within the bureau would have thought it applicable to a politically neutral, professional appointment like that of the chief statistician of Canada. The most probable explanation may have derived from the concerns of the Privy Council Office, the Treasury Board Secretariat, and other departments that, in spite of the additional resources channelled to the bureau in recent years, the statistical requirements of the government were not being adequately met, and that insufficient attention was being given to the anticipation of future demands for statistics. Thus, without necessarily reflecting on Duffett, the times were perhaps "ripe for a change." This view is given credence by the central recommendations of a new-broom report by Duffett's successor in January 1973, which proposed to:

1. Sharpen approaches for establishing Statistics Canada's priorities on the use of statistical resources.
2. Make statistical information more accessible.
3. Produce statistics important for policy with better quality and timeliness.
4. Tie some statistical activities closer to user departments.[27]

The only feasible internal candidate to follow Walter Duffett as chief statistician was Simon Goldberg, who was widely respected for his work in bringing the System of National Accounts to full fruition and enjoyed immense popularity within the bureau. Four years younger than Duffett, he could have served long enough to make a real impact on a mandate such as that outlined above. But his Achilles' heel was loyalty. He had served Duffett steadfastly for fifteen years and, for better or worse, was inescapably associated with his track record. Instead, the appointment went to Sylvia Ostry, most recently a director of the Economic Council of Canada. Her academic qualifications were impressive, with doctoral studies at McGill and Cambridge and teaching experience at Oxford and McGill. Earlier in the 1960s Goldberg had brought her in as director of Special Manpower Studies at the bureau and she had been responsible, as author or co-author, for no fewer than seven of the 1961 census monographs.

Soon after Ostry took office, Goldberg was appointed, virtually by international acclamation, director of the Statistical Office of the United Nations, where he served until 1979 . In this position he substantially strengthened the professional capability of the office and led it to heightened achievements in international statistics and statistical standards. He conceived and became the driving force in the implementation of the worldwide United Nations National Household Survey Capability program, aimed at providing developing countries with the capability for taking household surveys on a continuing basis. Following his formal retirement as director in 1979, Goldberg served for four years as coordinator of this program. From 1983 until his sudden death in 1985, he continued to make his talents available as an international consultant and, in this capacity, came back to Statistics Canada on more than one occasion.

After his retirement from Statistics Canada, Walter Duffett accepted an appointment as vice-president of the Conference Board of Canada. Later in the decade he relinquished this position to spend more time with an international organization for which he had long had a soft spot – the Inter-American Statistical Institute. He was a vice-president of the institute from 1974 to 1979 and, on 1 January 1980, he became president, a position that he held at the time of his death in Ottawa in 1982. He was survived by his wife, the former Isabel Rothney, and two daughters.

The Duffett Years – A Tentative Assessment

Until the government archives for the late 1960s and early 1970s are opened to the public, it would be rash to attempt any definitive assessment of Walter Duffett's contribution to Canadian statistics. Even a tentative assessment is rendered difficult by the fact that, unlike his predecessors, Coats and Marshall, who never shunned the limelight, he was austere and reserved and thus not an easy man to know or understand. The divisional directors met with him regularly, but many senior professional staff took their cues from Simon Goldberg. The bureau was in fact run as an unspoken, but no less real, partnership.

Duffett got on well with the succession of ministers under whom he served and was popular with the parliamentarians he met on estimates committees. Prior to the Trudeau era, most deputy heads were of the same age and background as Duffett and regarded him as a safe and steady hand. Goldberg sought the cooperation of those in other departments and elsewhere who could assist him in the task of program development. An interesting case in point was the relationship he developed with Senator Maurice Lamontagne in the late 1960s after he had determined that the latter's inquiry into science policy could be useful in focusing political and public attention on the bureau's role and capabilities.

In addition to his central role in extending and elaborating the System of National Accounts and its supporting body of primary statistics, Goldberg worked continually at building a methodological capability and other elements of infrastructure such as classification systems. In this connection, he involved himself directly in what he regarded as the key staff appointments. No other senior officer in the bureau's history, before or since, has enjoyed such managerial and professional freedom, and it is greatly to Duffett's credit that, although he no doubt imposed checks from time to time, he was wise enough to allow Goldberg plenty of latitude.

One fact is indisputable. Duffett presided over the greatest expansion of the bureau's resources in the almost eighty years of its operation. Authorized person-years more than doubled in fifteen years, increasing at an accelerating rate as the 1960s progressed. So, much was given. At the same time, as this chapter has shown, much was achieved. A specific and highly visible area where success was not achieved was computerization. But the bureau's difficulties were by no means unique. In the private sector and in other areas of government, intrinsically simpler applications were causing problems. The bureau had set its sights much higher and was trying to harness computer power with new statistical methodology in the process it called automation. The greater part of the 1970s was to elapse before the problem was fully resolved.

Duffett was at the helm when, as a result of the work of the Glassco Commission in the early 1960s, the bureau was finally recognized as a department in its own right, no longer accountable to the deputy head of another department. This, however, was an essentially fortuitous occurrence for which neither Duffett nor his senior colleagues could take credit. And it was little more than a formality that simply legitimized the *de facto* independence that had been won inch by inch since the early days of the Coats regime.

The real problem in the final years of Duffett's tenure was, in my view, the almost prodigal increase in the resources afforded to the bureau. This had two serious consequences, neither of which would have been conceded at the time.

The first was the dilution in the quality of staff that resulted from the abnormally high recruitment rates, mainly, but not exclusively, in the professional categories. People who were qualified on paper but lacked experience could not be absorbed into the bureau's culture as quickly as they would have been under more normal circumstances. This situation persisted well after Duffett's retirement and even manifested itself at the most senior levels of appointment.

The second consequence was the blurring in the focus of program priorities that occurred when it seemed that the bureau could do almost anything it set its mind to. Projects were proposed, and in some cases attempted, that would never have survived scrutiny in a more rigorous budgetary climate. It would be futile and inappropriate to assign blame within the bureau for this state of affairs. It affected other departments of government also, and the bureau was simply swept along by the tide. The effects of these two phenomena on the bureau – staff dilution and fuzzy priorities – were slow to manifest themselves and difficult to eradicate. The epilogue to this history sketches some of the developments of the 1970s and shows how the tide was eventually turned.

EPILOGUE

1972–1995

The preface to this history explained why I did not think it desirable, or even feasible, to pursue the story of Canada's central statistical office beyond Walter Duffett's retirement. Nevertheless, I am sure that many readers will feel disappointed, if not cheated, to have been left stranded in mid-1972. So, notwithstanding my reservations about the difficulties of adequately documenting subsequent events and of assessing them objectively, it may still be useful to recall briefly and tentatively how the bureau has fared during the quarter century since Duffett stepped down.

As noted earlier, since the late 1960s there had been growing concerns in the Privy Council Office and elsewhere that, in spite of the additional resources being channelled to the bureau, the statistical requirements of the government were not being adequately met, and that insufficient attention was being paid to the anticipation of future demands. Duffett's successor as chief statistician of Canada, Sylvia Ostry, set up a study group soon after her appointment to evaluate the state of Canada's statistical system. Early in 1973 its report identified three major challenges facing the system: statistics had to be made more usable and useful; the nation's overall statistical capability needed to be upgraded over the long haul; and more attention had to be paid to maintaining public support. As the major component of the national statistical system, the onus of these challenges fell largely on the bureau itself, but they also implied a more visible leadership role for it *vis-à-vis* the other players in the system, including more effective coordination of their activities.

The report's recommendations included the development and continuous updating of a medium-term plan, improved consultative arrangements, and an internal program evaluation capability that, *inter alia*, could distinguish between those activities of national scope, which could appropriately be funded from Statistics Canada's budget, and the production of special interest statistics, the cost of which ought to fall upon the beneficiaries. There also needed to be stronger and more visible efforts to keep reporting burden to a minimum, protect confidentiality in the face of growing demands for microdata, improve timeliness, and facilitate access to the data available in all parts of the statistical system.

An organizational restructuring was also recommended with a new level of management–assistant chief statisticians – to be interposed between the chief statistician and the directors general. Following approval of this strengthened managerial complement, a drive was undertaken to bring in new blood. Those appointed from outside to the new assistant chief statistician and director general positions brought with them important new talents, but none were familiar with the culture and operation of a central statistical office. Thus, the collective pool of experience among senior management was significantly diluted.

During the Ostry tenure, which lasted for two and a half years, resources were still flowing freely. In 1973–74 and 1974–75, the bureau's noncensus program benefited from an additional 855 person-years. Following on the increase of 637 in the two previous years, this represented an increase of forty-eight percent over the 1970–71 total of 3,135, and there must surely have been considerable difficulty in effectively absorbing such an increase. In fact, many new positions remained unfilled.

Nevertheless, the annual reports of those years speak of significant improvements in and extensions of the statistical program. Some progress was being made in the automation of the bureau's great many noncensus surveys, but it remained uphill work. There continued to be difficulties in bringing about fruitful collaboration between subject-matter specialists on the one hand and methodologists and computer systems people on the other, but these cannot be dismissed as irrational. They were the consequence of simultaneous and revolutionary changes in two critically important domains: in statistical methodology because of the development of modern sampling and related techniques; and in the dramatic transformation of processing by the introduction of computer technology, and the bewideringly rapid pace at which it was developing. These latter difficulties were by no means unique to the bureau. Other government departments as well as the private sector were also floundering, often with applications far less complex than those being attempted by the bureau.

Early in 1975 Sylvia Ostry was appointed deputy minister, Corporate and Consumer Affairs. She was succeeded by Peter Kirkham, whom she had brought in two years earlier from the University of Western Ontario's School of Business Administration to serve as assistant chief statistician – Economic Accounts and Integration.

In the year following Kirkham's appointment, the steady growth of Statistics Canada's program resources came to a halt, and in 1978, as part of a governmental restraint program, an actual cut was imposed. This was a new and almost unimaginable experience for program managers, even the older ones, who had come to rely on an annual budgetary increment to cope with the constant demands of users for more and better statistics. The 1978 cuts had to be "delivered" at short notice and no guidance was offered as to where they might best take place, except that"critical national economic series" should be preserved. This would certainly have happened in any case. But the systems and procedures of a decade later by which an optimal response to the cuts could have been worked out and implemented were not in place. Two casualties of the 1978 cuts that, in the view of many, had not lived up to their original promise were the occupational employment and job vacancy surveys. On the other hand, there was definite evidence that the Canada health survey, which had just become fully operational, was going to meet an important need, but this too was cancelled. By the last year of Kirkham's tenure, 1979–80, the person-year allocation for the bureau's noncensus program and its core census activity had been scaled down to fewer than four thousand.

In 1978 Kirkham dismantled the Statistical Services Field, allocating the various specialized methodological divisions to the corresponding subject-matter fields. The rationale for this decentralization was that direct integration of the divisions into the management structures of their clients would improve responsiveness and result in more effective collaboration. Coming at a time when Statistics Canada's programs and management practices were being severely criticized in Parliament and the media, it was perhaps thought that the move would soften this criticism. Of course, it was not looked upon kindly by the methodologists, who argued that in a working environment where the typical project manager was a subject-matter expert with understandably limited knowledge of methodology, they had been deprived of a line of professional appeal. Furthermore, it was thought that there could no longer be an overview of the function as a whole, that central research and training would suffer, and so on.

In retrospect, neither the hopes nor the fears were justified. Mutual understanding and cooperation between subject-matter and methodological staffs was a function of more profound considerations than organizational arrangements. Progress towards automation continued to be made, albeit slowly. The centralized mainframe computer increased exponentially in power and was eventually supplemented by a capacity for flexible decentralized operations made possible by so-called micro- and minicomputers. At the same time, a new generation of computer-literate subject-matter specialists who did not see automation as a threat was emerging.

A different organizational change initiated by Kirkham somewhat earlier seems to have had merit. A separate Census Field, with its own assistant chief statistician, had been created in Sylvia Ostry's 1973 reorganization and had subsequently grown very rapidly, acquiring data processing and dissemination capabilities rivalling those of the centre. Kirkham's initiative deflated this structure appreciably and combined it with the Household Surveys Branch, which was transferred from the Household and Institutional Statistics Field. At the same time, the Census of Agriculture Division was transferred, along with the Agriculture Division from the Business Statistics Field, to what now became the Institutions and Agriculture Statistics Field. Ivan Fellegi, who had been on leave of absence in Washington, DC, was appointed to head the new Census and Household Surveys Field and did much to reintegrate the census with general bureau operations, from which it had gradually become alienated.

Some things failed to happen. For a quarter century prior to 1972, the continued development and refinement of the System of National Accounts, under the strong leadership of Simon Goldberg, had served as the framework for an integrated body of economic statistics and as a measure of their quality. During the 1970s, in spite of the importance nominally ascribed to this function in the new organizational structure, it appeared to lose much of its impetus, contributing without doubt to the growing criticisms of the bureau's statistical products and management practices, which began in 1976. These criticisms were grossly prejudicial to the image of the bureau, which appeared to have no effective way of countering them.

In December 1979 the minister responsible for Statistics Canada commissioned external inquiries into the statistical methodology used in key economic series, and into the bureau's management and communications practices. Heading the statistical inquiry was Sir Claus Moser, a former director of the Government Statistical Service of the United Kingdom. Price Waterhouse Associates were asked to study "the management, organization, personnel and communication processes in the Agency." Before either group delivered its report, Kirkham resigned as chief statistician to take a senior appointment with the Bank of Montreal. Larry Fry, deputy minister of Supply and Services, accepted a parallel appointment as chief statistician pending the appointment of a "regular" incumbent.

Moser was assisted by US specialists of international reputation in the areas of national accounts, the consumer price index, labour statistics, and quality assurance. Their report professed some surprise that the need to assess public confidence in Statistics Canada had even arisen. They emphasized the high – "almost uniquely high" – reputation that the agency had built up both nationally and internationally in the postwar decades. In the course of their subsequent assessment, they found no evidence of any lack of integrity or impartiality. With reference to data quality, they were impressed by the high professional standards they found in most of the areas examined. Thus, most of the public criticisms were, in their view, ill founded or exaggerated. There were, they conceded, technical defects and development needs in many series, but this was frequently the case with comparable series abroad.

More important than the occasional error or technical gap in a series, however, was what the team called the rundown in the "methodological stock" of Statistics Canada. They cited the loss of outstanding people, the deterioration of sample frames, the disbanding of a central concern for methodology, and the apparent "demotion" of the central integration function through the national accounts. The main concern of the report, therefore, was that such problems, if not addressed, would lead to a more serious deterioration of statistics in the future.

The report had a great many specific recommendations that cannot be described here. Its most remarkable consequence was that its blue ribbon authorship and generally supportive tone seemed almost immediately to have a cathartic effect. There was promise for what the report called "a more encouraging government and public context within which the agency can operate."[1]

The Moser report overshadowed the companion report by Price Waterhouse Associates. The latter listed forty-eight recommendations across its mandated areas of inquiry. All were carefully studied and some subsequently acted upon, but they lacked a collective focus and impact. In some cases, the recommendations were based on the premise that there should be separate streams of progression for professional and managerial employees. It was argued that the responsibilities of the chief statistician were primarily managerial and that the next appointee should have "proven executive management competence." There should also be an assistant chief statistician – Planning and Development, who would be the senior professional officer and would "provide technical leadership ... work in close collaboration with the managerially oriented Chief Statistician, and be the Agency's chief representative in international statistical affairs and with technically oriented users."[2] Such recommendations were, of course, a difficult sell and understandably withered on the vine.

Another recommendation was for the establishment of a national statistics council. Such a body was in fact established some years later but not on the basis of the obviously inappropriate model suggested by Price Waterhouse–the Economic Council of Canada.

Later in 1980 Dr Martin Wilk was appointed chief statistician of Canada. A Canadian, he had a PhD in statistics, a strong research background, and managerial experience at a senior level in American Telephone and Telegraph in the United States. He was in fact the first formally qualified statistician to head Statistics Canada or its forerunner organizations.

Wilk immediately began the work of restoring the image of Statistics Canada with government and the public, and of rebuilding staff morale, which had suffered badly during the previous decade. Some of the first steps taken to these ends are documented in the popular history of 1993 under the apt title of "*Setting a Course for Recovery*."[3] The auditor general published the findings of a major review of Statistics Canada in his 1983 report, a lead statement of which was that "the Agency has now stabilized and there is a renewed sense of direction and purpose."[4] From a somewhat different perspective, the Ministerial Task Force on Program Review of 1985 commented that "Statistics Canada, having been pressured since 1978 to develop proper management, has responded and is now a tightly managed agency of government."[5]

One of Wilk's most visible achievements was the plan he developed to reverse the government's decision that, as a cost-cutting measure, the 1986 census of population and agriculture should be scaled down to minimal constitutional requirements. The first step was to rally the support of major governmental users of census data to demonstrate the grave consequences that would ensue from the loss of planned 1986 outputs. This process, by the way, admirably exemplified the tradition of a stronger client orientation that Wilk had sought to build from the beginning of his tenure. Subsequently an agreement was negotiated whereby, in return for the restoration of census funding, the bureau would commit itself over the next five years to a substantial reduction of program costs and related person-years, as well as an increased emphasis on cost recovery through the sale of statistical products.

Less obviously, through marginal organizational changes and such initiatives as the more frequent rotation of senior managers (including cross-appointments of methodologists and subject-matter specialists) and the establishment of a broadly-based and transparent internal planning system and related management committees, Wilk fostered a strong sense of interdependence and collegiality within the bureau. Apart from the obvious effect on staff morale, this contributed appreciably to the effectiveness of bureau operations. Again, he strengthened the bureau's consultative arrangements by putting in place a network of external advisory committees in specific subject-matter areas to provide professional stimulus and at the same time to serve as a support network.

The 1986 census experience provided valuable lessons for dealing with the further budgetary cuts imposed on the bureau as the decade progressed. Actual program cuts were minimized by the greater productivity resulting from initiatives such as the decentralization of data collection, the centralization of operations like coding and editing in specialized service divisions, and the contracting out to the private sector of others like publications composition and data entry.

During the 1980s the use of computer services more than doubled and the number of staff interacting with computer technology increased correspondingly, resulting in a more productive work force. The use of general-purpose computer programs and modular systems put an end to the wasteful use of resources for programs tailored to the needs of particular surveys. Thus the labour-saving and efficiency potential of computers that had so long eluded the bureau was now a reality. In total, taking the savings in person-years associated with the 1986 census and a further phased reduction announced in the May 1985 budget, the bureau was managing with some five hundred person-years fewer by the end of the decade.

The computer made possible a new range of electronic data products. At the same time, a greater emphasis was placed on analysis, so that the bureau would be communicating information rather simple data. And a more aggressive marketing strategy was adopted for those publications with high sales potential.

In 1985, after five eventful years in office, Wilk retired. He was succeeded by Ivan Fellegi, who had served as deputy chief statistician since 1984. Just as Wilk had been the first formally qualified chief statistician, so Fellegi was an even more remarkable "first" – the first formally qualified chief statistician to have worked his way up from the bottom ranks of the bureau. The transition was a smooth one, and the policy thrusts of the first half of the 1980s were given even greater impetus.

Soon after Fellegi's appointment, the bureau's consultative arrangements were further strengthened. In 1986, on the recommendation of the Ministerial Task Force on Program Review referred to earlier, the minister responsible for Statistics Canada established a National Statistics Council. Under the chairmanship of Professor Thomas H.B. Symons (who still holds that appointment), some forty members from a variety of backgrounds, serving in a personal rather than a representative capacity, advise the chief statistician on broad issues of policy and program priorities.

Fellegi was a veteran of almost thirty years in the bureau and had been responsible for virtually all of the developments in its statistical methodology since the 1961 census. This had established him not only as a dominant figure among Canadian statisticians but also as a major player in the international statistical community. He had long been a member of the prestigious International Statistical Institute and in 1987 was elected its president for a two-year term–the first Canadian to be accorded this honour. In 1992 he was appointed to the Order of Canada.

Many hallmarks of Fellegi's tenure as chief statistician can be cited. One is the continuing development of cooperative relations with key federal departments beyond the minimal and grudging levels at which they had sometimes stagnated in earlier years, and similarly with provincial departments in respect of their statistical activities. Again, the needs of clients in the business sector are being more effectively served by innovative marketing practices. The bureau's traditional role of monitoring social, economic, and environmental phenomena has been elaborated by a deeper level of analysis that seeks to understand the factors at work and how they interact. The greater frequency and improved quality of media coverage suggest that the bureau is doing an effective job of communication, resulting in a public that is better informed about its work and better able to exercise its electoral responsibilities.

Finally, recalling the concerns of the Moser Commission about the rundown of methodological stock, Fellegi has been firm about the need to strengthen, in spite of serious budgetary pressures, the statistical infrastructure on which the quality of bureau outputs crucially depends: business registers, classifications systems, methodological capability, a strong regional presence, computing and communications capacity, staff training and development, etc.

In September 1991 the influential London weekly *The Economist* published the "Good Statistics Guide," an assessment by an international panel of statistical experts of the perceived reliability of official statistics in ten large OECD countries. Using criteria reflecting the coverage and reliability of the statistics, the methodology used, and the integrity and objectivity of the statistical systems, the panel declared Canada the winner. Two years later a similar assessment of thirteen industrial economies again saw Canada come out in top place.

This was a well-deserved tribute to more than a decade of patient work by Wilk and Fellegi in restoring Statistics Canada to good health. All indications are that, whatever problems the twenty-first century may bring, the bureau will be confidently looked to by all Canadians for information on their dimensions and possible resolution.

APPENDICES

APPENDIX A

BUDGETARY EXPENDITURES, DOMINION BUREAU OF STATISTICS 1947–48 TO 1971–72

Year	(1) Budgetary Expenditures DBS, Inc. Census ($ Thousands)	(2) Budgetary Expenditures Federal Government ($ Millions)	(3) GNP at Market Prices ($ Millions)	(1) divided by (2) = (4) (%)	(2) divided by (3) = (5) (%)
1947-48	3,420	2,196	13,473	0.16	16.3
1948-49	3,650	2,176	15,509	0.17	14.0
1949-50	3,868	2,449	16,800	0.16	14.6
1950-51	4,396	2,901	18,491	0.15	15.7
1951-52	10,624	3,733	21,640	0.28	17.3
1952-53	5,670	4,337	24,558	0.13	17.7
1953-54	5,339	4,396	25,833	0.12	17.0
1954-55	5,536	4,275	25,918	0.13	16.5
1955-56	6,046	4,483	28,528	0.14	15.5
1956-57	10,051	4,849	32,058	0.21	15.1
1957-58	7,478	5,087	33,513	0.15	15.2
1958-59	7,717	5,364	34,777	0.14	15.4
1959-60	8,326	5,704	36,846	0.15	15.5
1960-61	10,406	5,958	38,359	0.17	15.5
1961-62	24,621	6,521	39,646	0.38	16.4
1962-63	11,883	6,571	42,927	0.18	15.3
1963-64	12,299	6,872	45,978	0.18	14.9
1964-65	13,493	7,218	50,280	0.19	14.4
1965-66	15,592	7,735	55,364	0.20	14.0
1966-67	26,635	8,798	61,828	0.30	14.2
1967-68	22,475	9,872	66,409	0.23	14.9
1968-69	24,673	10,767	72,586	0.23	14.8
1969-70	32,393	11,931	79,815	0.27	14.0
1970-71	39,036	13,182	85,685	0.30	15.4
1971-72	69,185	14,841	94,450	0.47	15.7

Sources: Cols. (1) and (2) - Public Accounts of Canada
Col. (3)–Series F 13, *Historical Statistics of Canada,* 2d ed.

Note: In 1961–62, and intermittently thereafter, DBS Budgetary Expenditures included major capital expenditures related to computer acquisitions.

APPENDIX B

DECENNIAL CENSUS COSTS, 1871–1971

Year	Current costs $(000)[1]	Composite Price Index (1900=100)[2]	GNE Implicit Price Index (1971=100)[3]	Costs in 1971 $(000)	Population (000)[4]	Per Capita Costs (1971$)
1871	511	107		2,691	3,689	0.73
1881	453	108		2,345	4,325	0.54
1891	550	104		2,957	4,833	0.61
1901	1,185	101		6,617	5,371	1.23
1911	1,303	126		5,843	7,207	0.81
1921	2,008	226		4,996	8,788	0.57
1926	n/a	205	37	n/a	n/a	n/a
1931	2,828		33	8,510	10,377	0.82
1941	3,645		36	10,211	11,507	0.89
1951	8,292		61	13,593	14,009	0.97
1961	17,258		72	23,837	18,238	1.31
1971	40, 866		100	40,866	21,568	1.90

1 1871-1911, Report of the Dominion Statistician, 1918-1919; 1921-1971, Various Census Administrative Reports.

2 Table 2.9, M.C. Urquhart, "New Estimates of Gross National Product, Canada, 1870-1926", published in vol. 51 of the National Bureau of Economic Research, *Studies in Income and Wealth*.

3 Series K172, *Historical Statistics of Canada,* 2d ed.

4 Series A2, Ibid

APPENDIX C

FIRST ORGANIZATION CHART, DOMINION BUREAU, 1919–1920

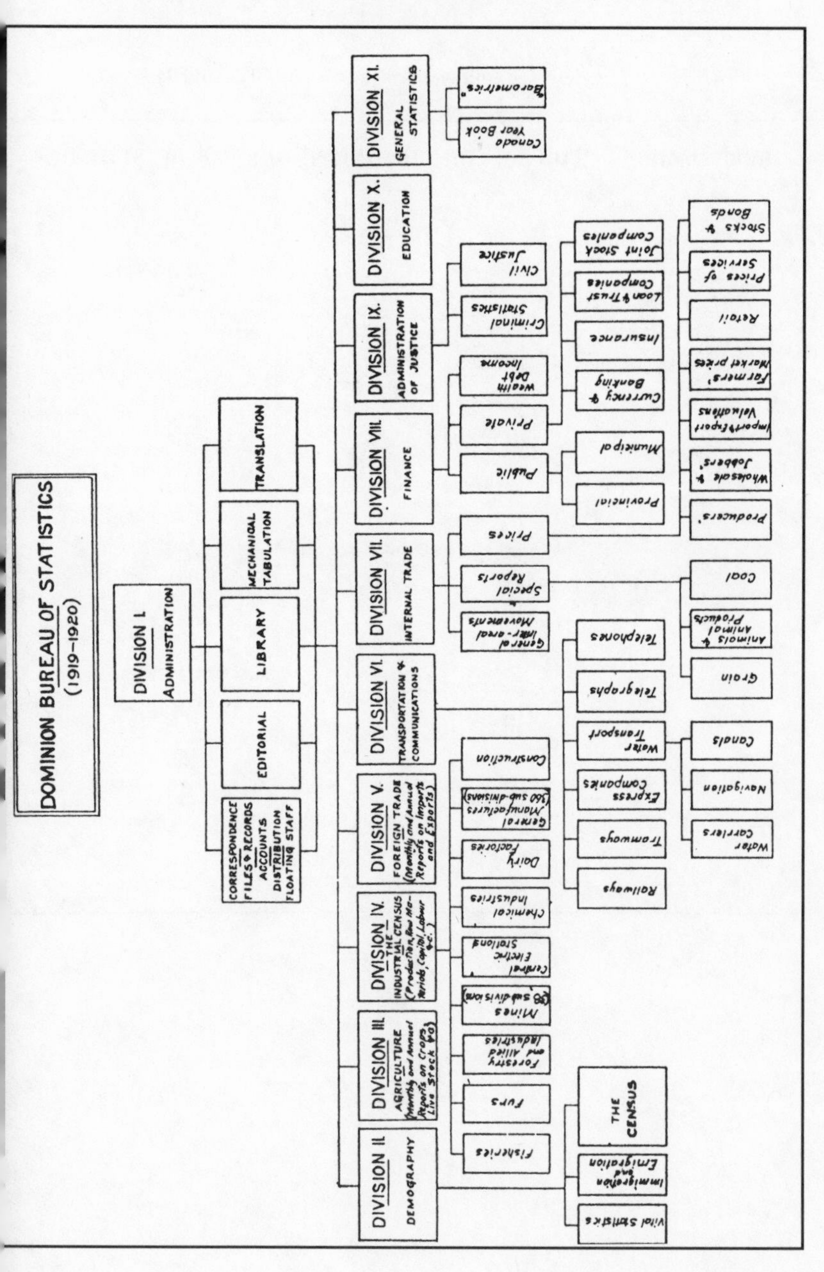

Appendix D

Organization Chart, of the Dominion Bureau of Statistics, 31 March 1935

(Overview, see following pages for parts 1,2, and 3)

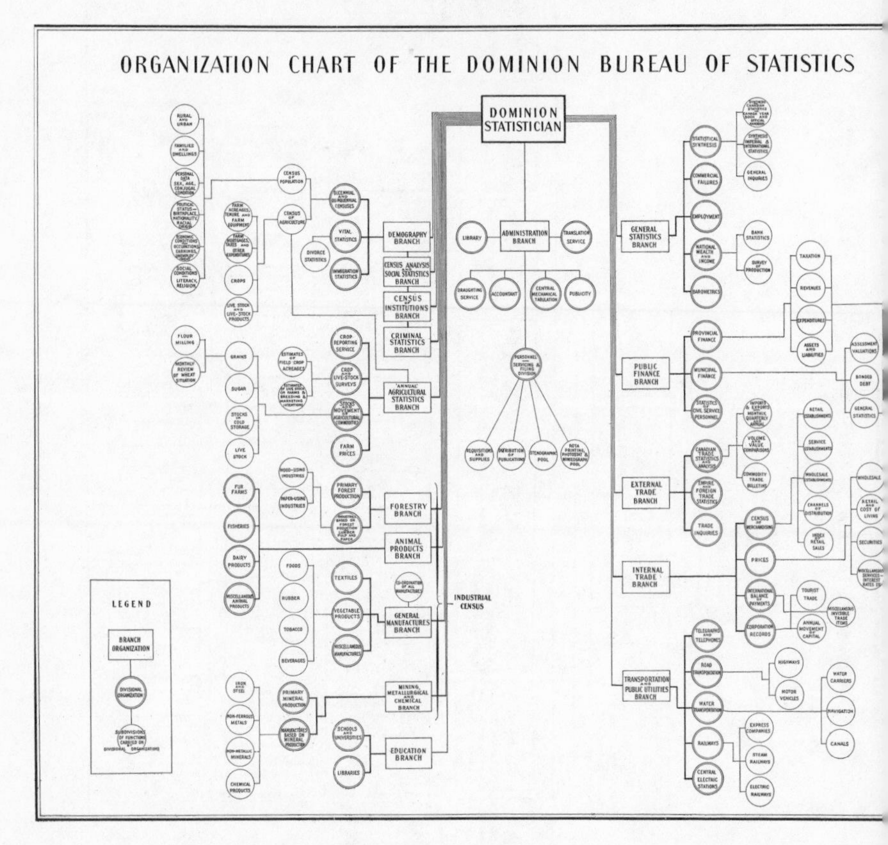

APPENDIX D
PART 1

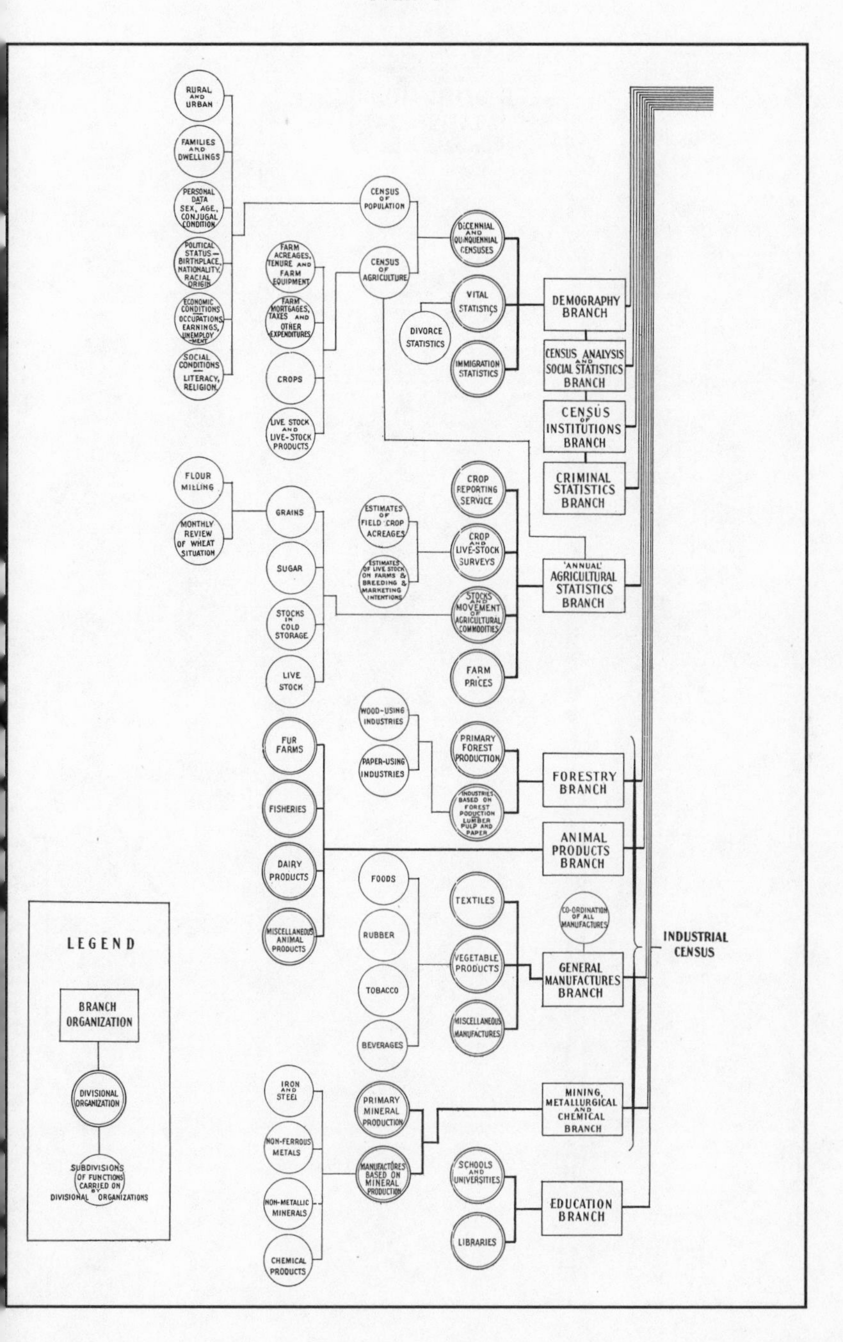

Appendix D
Part 2

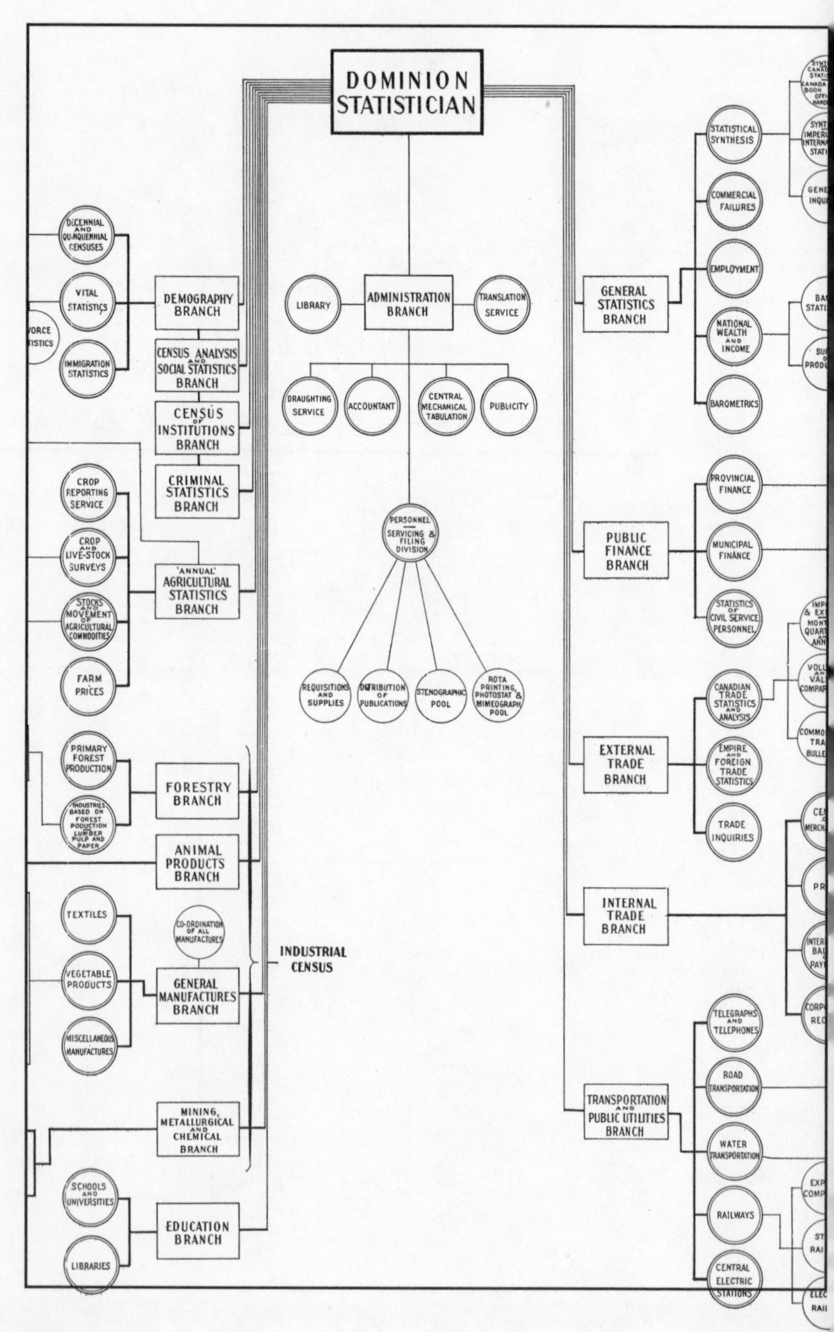

APPENDIX D
PART 3

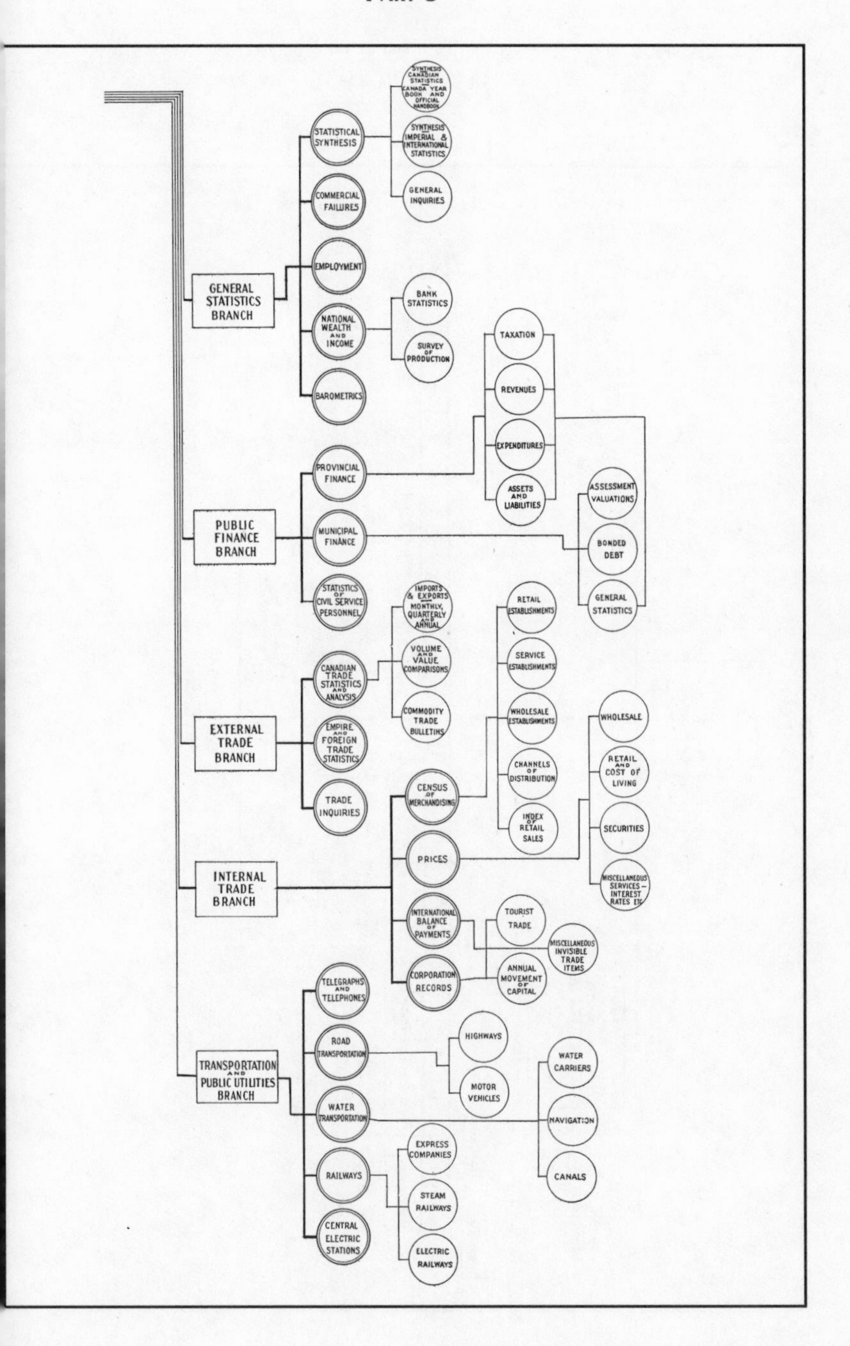

Appendix E

General Organization, Dominion Bureau of Statistics, 31 March 1955

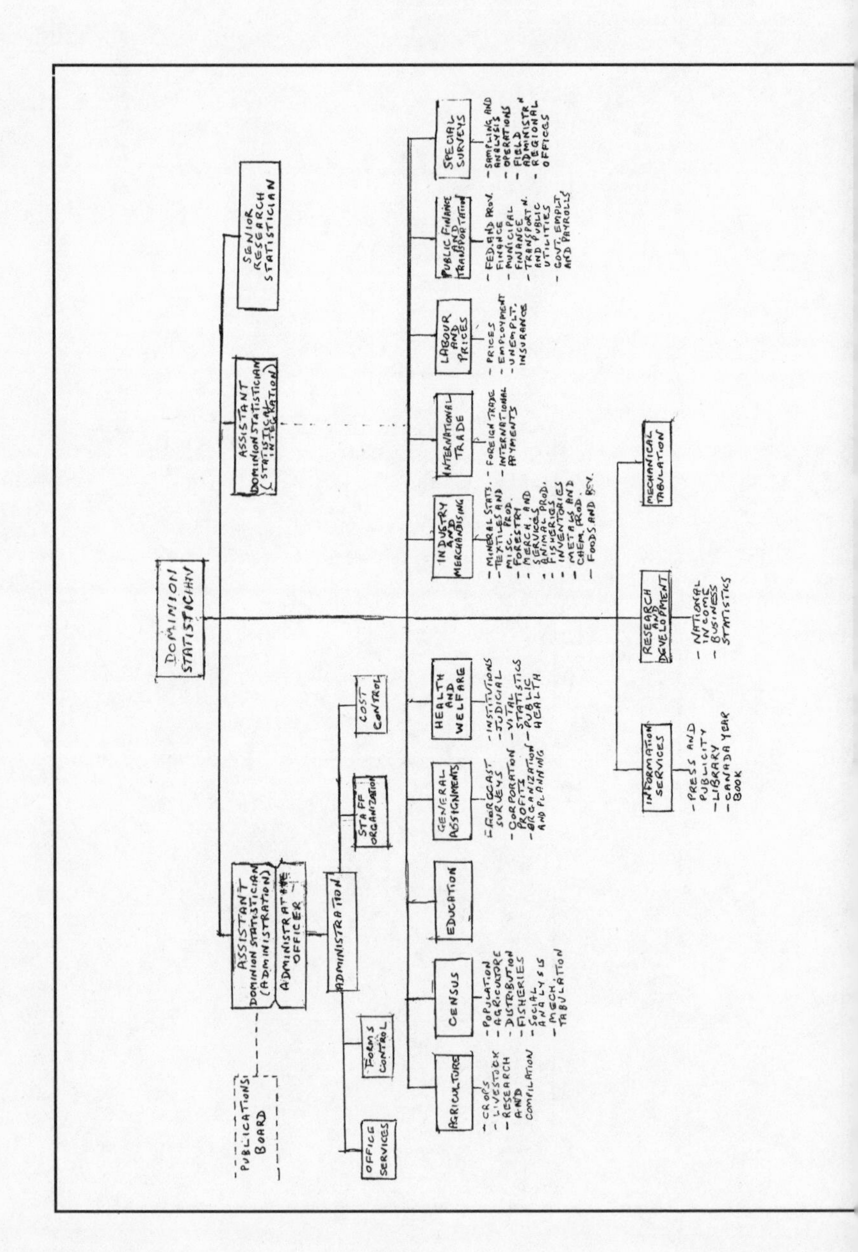

APPENDIX F

ORGANIZATION CHART, STATISTICS CANADA, 31 MARCH 1972

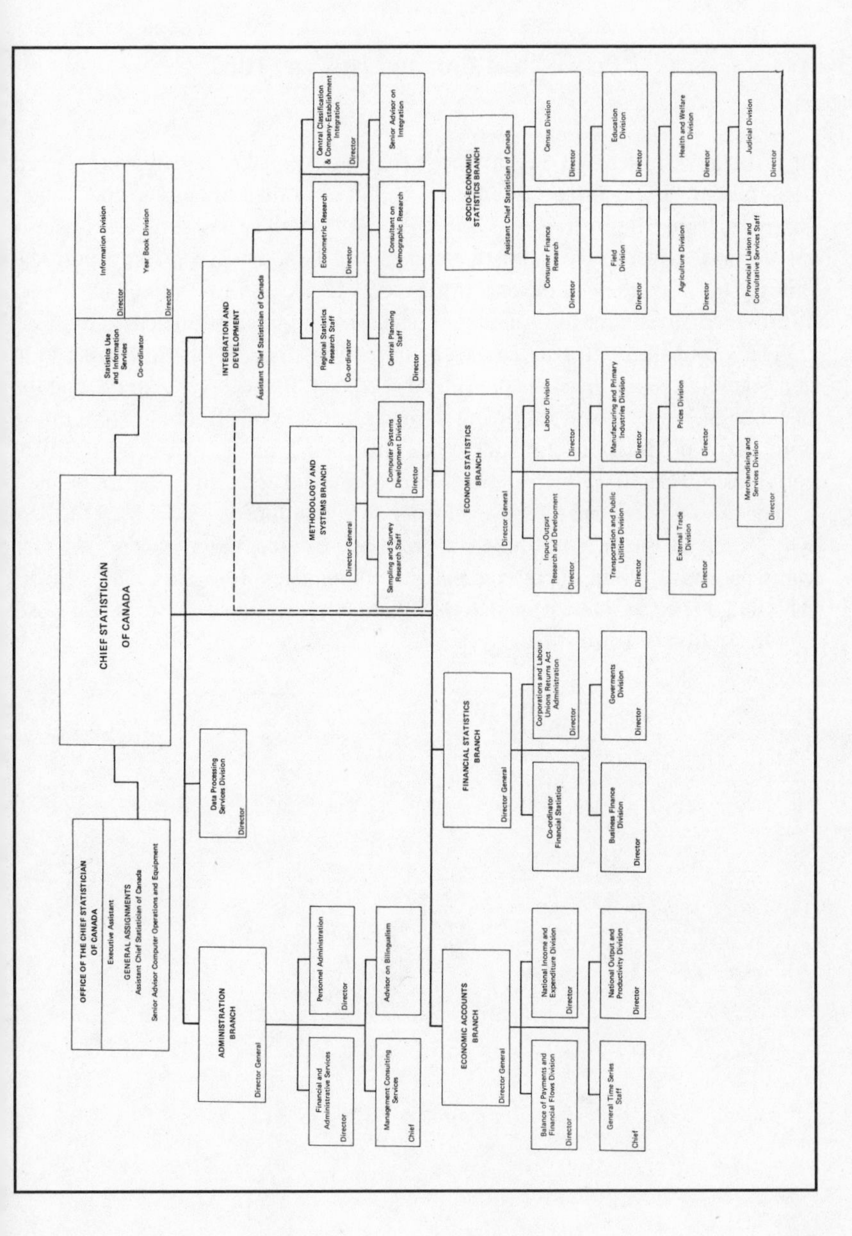

Appendix G

Ministries and Ministers Responsible for Statistics: 1841 to 1972

Province of Canada, 1841 to 1867

In the twenty-six years of the Province of Canada's existence, there were sixteen dual ministries, the longest of which was that of Louis LaFontaine and Robert Baldwin, from March 1848 to September 1854. In the early struggles towards responsible government, statistics can hardly have been a leading political priority, but nevertheless, the enactments of 1847 and 1852, described in chapter 1, provided a basis for the conduct of censuses and other statistical activities.

The responsibility for statistics was at first vested in a Board of Registration and Statistics, made up of the provincial secretary, the receiver general, and the inspector general. Later, following the establishment of a Board of Agriculture with its own Minister, statistics were absorbed into his broad portfolio of activities relating to immigration, colonization, and economic development.

The most notable and effective minister of Agriculture was T. D'Arcy McGee, who served for the three or four years preceding Confederation in 1867. McGee was responsible for the appointment as deputy minister of Joseph Charles Taché, who had a special interest in statistics and later conducted the first two post-Confederation censuses.

Dominion of Canada, 1867-1972

Prime Ministers	Party	Dates of Administration	Ministers Responsible for Statistics[1]
Sir John A. Macdonald	C	1 July 1867 to 5 November 1873	J.C. Chapais C. Dunkin J.H. Pope
Alexander Mackenzie	L	7 November 1873 to 9 October 1878	L. Letellier R.W. Scott (Acting) C.A.P. Pelletier
Sir John A. Macdonald	C	17 October 1878 to 6 June 1891	J.H. Pope John Carling
Sir John J.C. Abbott	C	16 June 1891 to 24 November 1892	John Carling
Sir John S.D. Thompson	C	5 December 1892 to 12 December 1894	A.R. Angers
Sir Mackenzie Bowell	C	21 December 1894 to 27 April 1896	A.R. Angers J.A. Ouimet (Acting) W.H. Montague
Sir Charles Tupper	C	1 May 1896 to 8 July 1896	W.H. Montague
Sir Wilfred Laurier	L	11 July 1896 to 6 October 1911	Sydney A. Fisher
Sir Robert L. Borden	C	10 October 1911 to 12 October 1917	Martin Burrell Sir George E. Foster
Sir Robert L. Borden	U	12 October 1917 to 10 July 1920	Sir George E. Foster
Arthur Meighen	U	10 July 1920 to 29 December 1921	Sir George E. Foster H.H. Stevens
W.L. Mackenzie King	L	29 December 1921 to 28 June 1926	James Robb Thomas A. Low James Robb (Acting)
Arthur Meighen	C	29 June 1926 to 25 September 1926	J.D. Chaplin
W.L. Mackenzie King	L	25 September 1926 to 6 August 1930	James Malcolm
Richard B. Bennett	C	7 August 1930 to 23 October 1935	H.H. Stevens R.B. Hanson

Dominion of Canada, 1867-1972

Prime Ministers	Party	Dates of Administration	Ministers Responsible for Statistics[1]
W.L. Mackenzie King	L	23 October 1935 to 15 November 1948	W.D. Euler J.A. MacKinnon
Louis St. Laurent	L	15 November 1948 to 21 June 1957	C.D. Howe
John G. Diefenbaker	C	21 June 1957 to 22 April 1963	Gordon Churchill George Hees
Lester B. Pearson	L	22 April 1963 to 20 April 1968	Mitchell Sharp R.H. Winters
Pierre E. Trudeau	L	20 April 1968 -	R.H. Winters J.-L. Pépin

1 From 1 July 1867 to 31 March 1912 – ministers of Agriculture; from 1 April 1912 to 27 March 1969 – ministers of Trade and Commerce; and from 28 March 1969 to 30 June 1972 – ministers of Industry, Trade and Commerce.

APPENDIX H

8-9 GEORGE V.

CHAP. 43.

An Act respecting the Dominion Bureau of Statistics.

[*Assented to 24th May, 1918.*]

HIS Majesty, by and with the advice and consent of the Senate and House of Commons of Canada, enacts as follows:— R.S., c. 68.

1. This Act may be cited as *The Statistics Act.* Short title.

INTERPRETATION.

2. In this Act, unless the context otherwise requires,— Definitions.

(*a*) "Minister" means the Minister of Trade and Commerce;

(*b*) "Bureau" means the Dominion Bureau of Statistics;

(*c*) "Transportation Company" means any railway, telegraph, telephone and express company and any carrier by water;

(*d*) "Regulation" means any regulation made under the provisions of this Act or any order of the Governor in Council made under the authority of this Act.

GENERAL.

3. There shall be a bureau under the Minister of Trade and Commerce, to be called the Dominion Bureau of Statistics, the duties of which shall be to collect, abstract, compile and publish statistical information relative to the commercial, industrial, social, economic and general activities and condition of the people, to collaborate with all other departments of the Government in the compilation and publication of statistical records of administration according to the regulations, and to take the Census of the Dominion as hereinafter provided. Dominion Bureau of Statistics.

4. (1) The Governor in Council may appoint an officer to be called the Dominion Statistician, who shall hold office during pleasure, whose duties shall be, under the direction Dominion Statistician appointment and duties.

direction of the Minister, to prepare all schedules, forms, and instructions, and generally to supervise and control the Bureau, and to report annually to the Minister with regard to the work of the Bureau during the preceding year.

Officials.

(2) Such other officers, clerks and employees may be appointed as are necessary for the proper conduct of the business of the Bureau, all of whom shall hold office during pleasure.

Commissioners, enumerators, and agents.

5. The Minister may employ from time to time, subject to the provisions of the *Civil Service Act*, such commissioners, enumerators, agents or persons as are necessary to collect statistics and information for the Bureau relating to such industries and affairs of the country as he deems useful and in the public interest, and the duties of such agents or persons shall be such as the Minister determines.

Oath of office.

6. (1) Every officer, census commissioner, enumerator, agent and other person employed in the execution of any duty under this Act or under any regulation made hereunder, before entering on his duties, shall take and subscribe the following oath:—

I.................................solemnly swear that I will faithfully and honestly fulfil my duties as ...., in conformity with the requirements of the Act and of all proclamations, orders in council and instructions issued in pursuance thereof, and that I will not, without due authority in that behalf, disclose or make known any matter or thing which comes to my knowledge by reason of my employment as such..........................

....

Attestation.

(2) The oath shall be taken before such person, and returned and recorded in such manner, as the Minister prescribes.

Rules, regulations and forms.

7. The Minister shall make and prescribe such rules, regulations, instructions, schedules and forms as he deems requisite for conducting the work and business of the Bureau, the collecting of statistics and other information and taking of any census authorized by this Act; he shall prescribe what schedules, returns and information are to be verified by oath, the form of oath to be taken, and shall specify the officers and persons by and before whom the said oaths are to be taken.

No discrimination.

8. The Governor in Council shall not, nor shall the Minister, in the execution of the powers conferred by

this

this Act, discriminate between individuals or companies to the prejudice of any such individual or company.

9. (1) The Minister may enter into any arrangement with the government of any province providing for any matter necessary or convenient for the purpose of carrying out or giving effect to this Act, and in particular for all or any of the following matters:—

Arrangements with provincial governments.

(*a*) The execution by provincial officers of any power or duty conferred or imposed on any officer under this Act or the regulations;

(*b*) The collection by any provincial department or officer of any statistical or other information required for the purpose of carrying out this Act; and,

(*c*) The supplying of statistical information by any provincial department or officer to the Dominion Statistician.

(2) All provincial officers executing any power or duty conferred or imposed on any officer under this Act or the regulations, in pursuance of any arrangement entered into under this section, shall, for the purposes of the execution of that power or duty, be deemed to be officers under this Act.

Provincial officers.

10. Every person who has the custody or charge of any provincial, municipal or other public records or documents, or of any records or documents of any corporation, from which information sought in respect of the objects of this Act can be obtained, or which would aid in the completion or correction thereof, shall grant to any census officer, commissioner, enumerator, agent or other person deputed for that purpose by the Dominion Statistician, access thereto for the obtaining of such information therefrom.

Access to public records.

11. The Minister may, by special letter of instruction, direct any officer, census commissioner or other person employed in the execution of this Act, to make inquiry under oath as to any matter connected with the taking of the census or the collection of statistics or other information, or the ascertaining or correction of any supposed defect or inaccuracy therein; and such officer, census commissioner or other person shall then have the same power as is vested in any court of justice, of summoning any person, of enforcing his attendance and of requiring and compelling him to give evidence on oath, whether orally or in writing, and to produce such documents and things as such officer, census commissioner or other person deems requisite to the full investigation of such matter or matters.

Inquiries under oath.

Evidence of appointment, removal for instructions.

12. (*a*) Any letter purporting to be signed by the Minister or the Dominion Statistician, or by any other person thereunto authorized by the Governor in Council, and notifying any appointment or removal of or setting forth any instructions to any person employed in the execution of this Act; and,

(*b*) Any letter signed by any officer, census commissioner, or other person thereunto duly authorized, notifying any appointment or removal of or setting forth any instructions to any person employed under the superintendence of the signer thereof;

shall be, respectively, *prima facie* evidence of such appointment, removal or instructions, and that such letter was signed and addressed as it purports to be.

Presumption.

13. Any document or paper, written or printed, purporting to be a form authorized for use in the taking of census, or the collection of statistics or other information, or so set forth any instructions relative thereto, which is produced by any person employed in the execution of this Act, as being such form or as setting forth such instructions, shall be presumed to have been supplied by the proper authority to the person so producing it, and shall be *prima facie* evidence of all instructions therein set forth.

Remuneration.

14. (1) The Minister shall, subject to the approval of the Governor in Council, cause to be prepared one or more tables setting forth the rates of remuneration or allowances for the several census commissioners, enumerators, agents and other persons employed in the execution of this Act, which may be a fixed sum, a rate per diem, or a scale of fees, together with allowances for expenses.

Voted by Parliament.

(2) Such remuneration or allowances and all expenses incurred in carrying this Act into effect shall be paid out of such moneys as are provided by Parliament for that purpose.

Condition of payment.

(3) No remuneration or allowance shall be paid to any person for any service performed in connection with this Act until the services required of such persons have been faithfully and entirely performed.

SECRECY.

No individual return to be published or divulged.

15. (1) No individual return, and no part of an individual return, made, and no answer to any question put, for the purposes of this Act, shall, without the previous consent in writing of the person or of owner for the time being of the undertaking in relation to which the return or answer was made or given, be published, nor, except for the purposes of a prosecution under this Act, shall any

person

person not engaged in connection with the Census be permitted to see any such individual return or any such part of any individual return.

(2) No report, summary of statistics or other publication under this Act shall contain any of the particulars comprised in any individual return so arranged as to enable any person to identify any particulars so published as being particulars relating to any individual person or business.

No report to reveal individual particulars.

CENSUS OF POPULATION AND AGRICULTURE.

16. The Census of population and agriculture of Canada shall be taken by the Bureau, under the direction of the Minister, on a date in the month of June in the year one thousand nine hundred and twenty-one, to be fixed by the Governor in Council, and every tenth year thereafter.

Census of population and agriculture every tenth year.

17. A census of population and agriculture of the Provinces of Manitoba, Saskatchewan and Alberta shall be taken by the Bureau, under the direction of the Minister, on a date in the month of June in the year one thousand nine hundred and twenty-six, to be fixed by the Governor in Council, and every tenth year thereafter.

Manitoba, Saskatchewan and Alberta.

18. The Governor in Council shall divide the country in respect of which the census is to be taken into census districts, and each census district into subdistricts to correspond respectively, as nearly as may be, with the electoral divisions and subdivisions for the time being, and, in territories not so defined or so situated as to admit of adhering to boundaries already established, into special divisions and subdivisions, for the purpose of the census.

Census districts.

19. Each census of population and agriculture shall be so taken as to ascertain with the utmost possible accuracy for the various territorial divisions of Canada, or of the provinces of Manitoba, Saskatchewan and Alberta as the case may be,—

Details.

(*a*) their population and the classification thereof, as regards name, age, sex, conjugal condition, relation to head of household, nationality, race, education, wage-earnings, religion, profession or occupation and otherwise;

(*b*) the number of houses for habitation, whether occupied or vacant, under construction or otherwise, the materials thereof and the number of rooms inhabited;

(*c*) the area of occupied land and its value, and its condition thereof as improved for cultivation, in fallow, in forest, unbroken prairie, marsh or waste land, and otherwise; the tenure and acreage of farms and the value of farm buildings and implements;

 (*d*)

(*d*) the products of farms, with the values of such products, and the number and value of domestic animals within the preceding census or calendar year;
(*e*) the municipal, educational, charitable, penal and other institutions thereof; and,
(*f*) such other matters as may be prescribed by the Governor in Council.

Census of Industry—Mines, Fisheries, Forestry, Manufactures, Etc.

Census of industry.

20. A census of the products of industry shall be taken for the year one thousand nine hundred and eighteen, and subsequently at such intervals as may be determined by the Minister, which census shall be taken so as to ascertain with the utmost possible accuracy,—
(*a*) the products of all mines and quarries, fisheries, forests, manufacturing establishments, and the number and kind of buildings and other works of construction used in connection with the same;
(*b*) any other trade and business which may be prescribed, with the quantity of real estate and the number and kind of buildings and plant used in connection therewith; and
(*c*) any other matters that may be prescribed by the Minister.

Schedules of details.

21. (1) The Dominion Statistician shall, under the direction of the Minister, prepare a form for the collection of such data as may be, in his judgment, desirable for the proper presentation of industrial statistics, and the said form shall embody inquiries as to (1) the name of person, partnership or corporation; (2) kind of goods manufactured or business done; (3) capital invested; (4) principal stock or raw materials used, and total value thereof; (5) gross quantity and value of articles manufactured; (6) number of persons employed, distinguished as to sex, adults and children; (7) the power used or generated; (8) total wages and salaries paid; (9) number of days on which it was carried on; and (10) any other specified matter.

Distribution and returns.

(2) The said schedule shall be sent by mail to the owner, operator or manager of each industrial concern with respect to which information is desired, and such owner, operator, or manager, or any other person to whom this schedule or blank form is sent shall answer the inquiries thereon and return the same to the Bureau, properly certified as to its accuracy, not later than the time prescribed thereon, provided, however, that the Minister may, in his discretion, extend the time for returning the schedules, and provided that when deemed expedient, the Minister may employ agents or other persons for the collection of these statistics.

Statistics of Trade and Commerce.

22. (1) The Dominion Statistician shall, under the direction of the Minister, annually prepare a report on the statistics of Commerce and Navigation of Canada with foreign countries. Such reports shall comprehend all goods, wares and merchandise exported from Canada to other countries, all goods, wares and merchandise imported into Canada from other countries, and all navigation employed in the foreign trade of Canada, which facts shall be stated according to the principles and in the manner defined in the regulations.

Statistics of Commerce and Navigation.

(2) The Department of Customs shall send to the Dominion Statistician, in such manner and form and at such periods as the Governor in Council may prescribe, returns of imports from and exports to foreign countries arriving at or leaving Canada by water or by rail, and of the navigation employed in the foreign trade of Canada.

Returns of imports and exports from Customs.

23. The annual report of the Statistics of Commerce and Navigation shall state the kinds, quantities and values of the merchandise entered and cleared coastwise into and from the customs collection ports of Canada.

Contents of annual report,

24. The Dominion Statistician shall, under the direction of the Minister, prepare and publish monthly reports of the exports and imports of Canada, including the quantities and values of accounts drawn from the warehouse and such other statistics relative to the trade and industry of the country as the Minister may consider expedient.

Monthly reports.

25. The Dominion Statistician shall prepare and make a report annually containing the results of any information collected during the preceding year upon the domestic trade of Canada.

Domestic trade.

Transportation.

26. (1) Every transportation company shall annually prepare returns in such form as may be prescribed by the Governor in Council with respect to its capital, traffic equipment, working expenditure, and such other information as the Governor in Council may prescribe.

Annual transportation returns.

(2) Such returns shall be dated and signed by and attested upon the oath of the secretary or some other chief officer of the company, and shall also be attested upon the oath of the president, or, in his absence, of the vice-president or manager of the company.

Attestation.

(3) Such returns shall be made for the period beginning from the date to which the then last yearly returns made by the company extended, or, if no such returns have been

Period included.

previously made, from the commencement of the operation of the company and ending with the last day of June in the then current year.

Date of forwarding.

(4) Such returns, dated, signed and attested in manner aforesaid, shall be forwarded by such company to the Dominion Statistician within one month after the first day of July in each year.

Traffic returns. monthly.

27. (1) Every transportation company shall prepare returns of its traffic monthly, that is to say, from the first to the close of the month inclusive. Such returns shall be in accordance with the form prepared by the Dominion Statistician and approved by the Minister.

Copies forwarded.

(2) A copy of such returns, signed by the officer of the company responsible for the correctness of such returns, shall be forwarded by the company to the Dominion Statistician within seven days from the day to which the said returns have been prepared.

Returns to be privileged.

28. All returns made in pursuance of any of the provisions of the two sections of this Act immediately preceding this section shall be privileged communications and shall not be evidence in any court whatever, except in any persecution for,—

(*a*) default in making such returns in accordance with the requirements of this Act;

(*b*) perjury in making any oath required by this Act in connection with such returns;

(*c*) forgery of any such return; or

(*d*) signing any such return knowing the same to be false.

CRIMINAL STATISTICS.

Courts to furnish criminal statistics.

29. The clerk of every court or tribunal administering criminal justice, or in case of there being no clerk, the judge or other functionary presiding over such court or tribunal, shall, before the end of October in each year, fill up and transmit to the Dominion Statistician, for the year ending the thirtieth day of September preceding, such schedules as he receives from time to time from the Dominion Statistician relating to the criminal business transacted in such court or tribunal.

Wardens and sheriffs.

30. The warden of every penitentiary and reformatory and the sheriff of every county and district shall, before the end of October in each year, fill up and transmit to the Dominion Statistician, for the year ending the thirtieth day of September preceding, such schedules as he receives from time to time from the Dominion Statistician relating to the prisoners committed to the penitentiary, reformatory or jail.

31. Every person required to transmit any such schedules shall from day to day make and keep entries and records of the particulars to be comprised in such schedules. **Records.**

32. Every officer required to transmit to the Minister of Finance true copies of returns made by justices of the peace shall, before the end of October in each year, transmit to the Minister true copies of all such returns for the year ending the thirtieth day of September next preceding. **Copies of returns.**

33. The Secretary of State shall, before the end of October in each year, cause to be filled up and transmitted to the Dominion Statistician such schedules for the year ending the thirtieth day of September next preceding, relative to the cases in which the prerogative of mercy has been exercised, as the Minister may prescribe. **Pardons.**

GENERAL STATISTICS.

34. Subject to the direction of the Minister, the Bureau shall collect, abstract and tabulate annually statistics in relation to all or any of the following matters: (*a*) Population; (*b*) Births, deaths and marriages; (*c*) Immigration and Emigration; (*d*) Agriculture; (*e*) Education; (*f*) Public and Private Finance; (*g*) any other matters prescribed by the Minister or by the Governor in Council. **General statistics.**

35. The Governor in Council may authorize the Minister to have any special statistical investigation made that is deemed advisable, and may prescribe the manner and by what means such investigation shall be made. **Special statistics.**

OFFENCES AND PENALTIES.

36. Every person employed in the execution of any duty under this Act or any regulation who,—

(*a*) after having taken the prescribed oath, shall desert from his duty, or wilfully makes any false declaration, statement or return touching any such matter; or **Desertion or false declaration.**

(*b*) in the pretended performance of his duties thereunder, obtains or seeks to obtain information which he is not duly authorized to obtain; or **Unlawful information.**

(*c*) shall not keep inviolate the secrecy of the information gathered or entered on the schedules and forms, and who shall, except as allowed by this Act and the regulations, divulge the contents of any schedule or form filled up in pursuance of this Act or any regulation, or any information furnished in pursuance of this Act or any regulation; **Improperly divulging information.**

shall be guilty of an offence and shall be liable, on summary conviction, to a penalty not exceeding three hundred dollars **Penalty.**

dollars and not less than fifty dollars, or to imprisonment for a period not exceeding six months and not less than one month, or to both fine and imprisonment.

Refusal to answer or false answer.

37. Every person who, without lawful excuse,—

(*a*) refuses or neglects to answer, or wilfully answers falsely, any question requisite for obtaining any information sought in respect of the objects of this Act or any regulation, or pertinent thereto, which has been asked of him by any person employed in the execution of any duty under this Act or any regulation; or

Refusal or neglect, false information or deception.

(*b*) refuses or neglects to furnish any information or to fill up to the best of his knowledge and belief any schedule or form which he has been required to fill up, and to return the same when and as required of him under this Act or any regulation, or wilfully gives false information or practises any other deception thereunder;

Penalty.

shall, for every such refusal or neglect, or false answer or deception, be guilty of an offence and liable, upon summary conviction, to a penalty not exceeding one hundred dollars and not less than twenty dollars, or to imprisonment for a period not exceeding three months and not less than thirty days, or to both fine and imprisonment.

Wilful refusal or neglect to grant access to records.

38. Every person who has the custody or charge of any provincial, municipal or other public records or documents, or of any records or documents of any corporation, from which information sought in respect of the objects of this Act or any regulation can be obtained, or which would aid in the completion or correction thereof, who wilfully or without lawful excuse refuses or neglects to grant access thereto to any census officer, commissioner, enumerator, agent or other person deputed for that purpose by the Dominion Statistician, and every person who wilfully hinders or seeks to prevent or obstruct such access, or otherwise in any way wilfully obstructs or seeks to obstruct any person employed in the execution of any duty under this Act or any regulation, is guilty of an offence and shall be liable, upon summary conviction, to a penalty not exceeding three hundred dollars and not less than fifty dollars, or to imprisonment for a period not exceeding six months and not less than one month, or to both fine and imprisonment.

Penalty.

Leaving notice at house.

39. The leaving by an enumerator, agent or other person employed in the execution of this Act or any regulation, at any house or part of a house, of any schedule or form purporting to be issued under this Act or any regulation, and having thereon a notice requiring that it be filled

up

up and signed within a stated time by the occupant of such house or part of a house, or in his absence by some other member of the family, shall, as against the occupant, be a sufficient requirement so to fill up and sign the schedule, though the occupant is not named in the notice, or personally served therewith.

40. The leaving by an enumerator or agent or other person employed in the execution of this Act at the office or other place of business of any person or firm or of any body corporate or politic, or the delivery by registered letter to any person, firm or body corporate or politic or his or its agent, or any such schedule or form having thereon a notice requiring that it be filled up and signed within a stated delay, shall, as against the person or the firm and the members thereof and each of them or the body corporate or politic, be a sufficient requirement to fill up and sign the schedule or form, and if so required in the notice, to mail the schedule or form within a stated time to the Bureau.

Leaving notice at office.

41. Any fine imposed and recovered for any offence under this Act shall belong to His Majesty for the public uses of Canada, but the Minister may authorize the payment of one-half of any such fine to the prosecutor.

Application of fines.

42. The *Census and Statistics Act*, chapter sixty-eight of the Revised Statutes of Canada, 1906, is hereby repealed.

Repeals.

OTTAWA: Printed by JOSEPH DE LABROQUERIE TACHÉ, Law Printer to the King's most Excellent Majesty.

NOTES

Chapter One

1 1847, 10 and 11 Vict., cap. 14.

2 Ibid.

3 In addition to collecting continuing data on taxes and public debt, it also had a schedule of social questions covering crime, pauperism, public libraries, newspapers, and periodicals, as well as religion, wages, and prices.

4 See A. Ross Eckler, *The Bureau of the Census* (New York: Praeger, 1972).

5 *First Report of the Secretary of the Board of Registration and Statistics on the Census of the Canadas from 1851–52*, (Quebec: John Lovell, 1853), vi.

6 Ibid., iv.

7 Under An Act to provide for the establishment of a Bureau of Agriculture, 10 November 1852, 16 Vict., cap. 11; subsequently amended and updated in respect of its statistical provisions in two parallel enactments: An Act respecting the Bureau of Agriculture and Agricultural Societies, and An Act respecting the Board of Registration, and the Census and Statistical information, 10 June 1857, 20 Vict., caps. 32 and 33 respectively.

8 Ibid.

9 *Public Accounts of the Province of Canada, for the year 1861* (Quebec, 1862).

10 The first volume – the so-called personal census – had been published on 11 August 1863; the second volume, covering agricultural produce, mills, manufactories, housing, etc., appeared on 1 February 1864 with the apology that, "from circumstances which this Department could not control, the publication of this volume has been delayed much beyond the time anticipated." *Census of the Canadas, 1860–61*, vol. 2 (Quebec, 1864), n.p. The quote is from the letter of transmittal by the assistant Secretary of the Census Department, Evelyn Campbell, to the members of the Board of Registration and Statistics. A promised administrative report did not appear at all.

11 *Report of the Minister of Agriculture and Statistics of the Province of Canada for the year 1862*, (Quebec, 1863), xxix.

12 Ibid., xxx. A recommendation exactly opposite to that for the integration of statistical and agricultural functions that had been successfully argued by the then secretary of the Board of Registration and Statistics in 1855.

13 *Report of the Minister of Agriculture and Statistics of the Province of Canada for the year 1863* (Quebec, 1864), v.

14 *Report of the Minister of Agriculture of the Province of Canada for the year 1864* (Quebec, 1865), 2. At no point in the reports of the 1860s is it acknowledged that a too-rapid turnover of ministers might also have contributed to the problem.

15 Ibid., 2.

16 Ibid.

17 Ibid.,4.

18 Seventeen years at the time Taché wrote.

19 "Memorial to the Board of Registration and Statistics," *Report of the Minister of Agriculture of the Province of Canada for the year 1865* (Ottawa, 1866), 25.

20 Ibid., 26.

21 Ibid. The emphasis is Taché's. Without detracting from the merits of Taché's critique, it may have owed something to an assessment by John Langton, auditor for the Province of Canada (and deputy minister of Finance after Confederation), that was read before the Literary and Historical Society of Quebec in March 1864. See notes to section A: "Population and Migration," in M.C. Urquhart and K.A.H. Buckley, eds., *Historical Statistics of Canada* (Toronto: MacMillan, 1965).

22 "Memorial," *Report of the Minister of Agriculture*, 1865, 27.

23 Ibid., 28.

24 Ibid., 27.

25 Ibid., 28.

26 Ibid., 29.

27 Composed at that time of Sir E.P. Taché, Hon. T. D'Arcy McGee, and Hon. Wm. McDougall.

28 On 16 March 1865 two second-class clerks, S. Drapeau and W.H. Johnson, were appointed to the Bureau of Agriculture at annual salaries of $1,000 each (Taché's own salary at the time was $2,600 a year). The Reverend C. Tanguay was also temporarily appointed as "Attaché for special statistics," i.e., to review historical material relating to Quebec. To put these appointments in perspective, the bureau, which served as the headquarters component for the ministry as a whole, was shown under the "Civil Government – Departmental Salaries" heading of the Public Accounts as having a staff of only seventeen, ranging from the minister down to a functionary described as the woodcutter.

29 *Report of the Minister of Agriculture*, 1865, 17.

30 "Report of the Select Committee of the Legislative Assembly on the Registration of Births, Marriages and Deaths in Upper Canada, 1865," appendix to the *Report*

of the Minister of Agriculture of the Province of Canada for the year 1866 (Ottawa, 1867), 107.

31 While marriages were mostly religious ceremonies, the baptisms and burials performed by the various denominations did not by any means account for all the births and deaths.

32 "Report of the Select Committee, 1865," appendix to *Report of the Minister of Agriculture*, 1866, 107.

33 A requirement imposed by the British Colonial Office.

34 *Report of the Minister of Agriculture*, 1864, 14.

35 *Report of the Minister of Agriculture*, 1866, xi.

36 *Miscellaneous Statistics of Canada for the year 1863*, Part i, submitted by Arthur Harvey, statistical clerk to Hon. Luther Hamilton, minister of Finance, contained information on: the area, population, debt, revenue, expenditure, imports and exports of Canada; capital, assets and liabilities of banks acting under charter; savings banks, building societies, hospitals receiving government grants; lunatic asylums; asylums and miscellaneous charitable institutions receiving aid from the province; coroners' inquests; fire insurance; electric telegraphs; boards of arts and manufactures for Upper and Lower Canada; allocation of the government grant to the agricultural societies of Lower Canada. Part ii of the same publication, submitted by John Langton, auditor, to Hon. A.T. Galt, minister of Finance, provided summaries of municipal returns for Upper and Lower Canada covering the number of acres assessed, the number of rate payers assessed, assets, liabilities, revenues, and expenditures.

37 "Memorial," *Report to the Minister of Agriculture*, 1865, 20.

38 *Report of the Minister of the Agriculture of the Province of Canada for the First Six Months of the Year 1867, Preceding the Confederation* (Ottawa, 1869).

39 Ibid., 11, 12.

40 *Censuses of Canada, 1665 to 1871*, vol. 4 of *Statistics of Canada* (Ottawa, 1876).

41 See chapter 2.

42 The most illustrious single delegate was probably Florence Nightingale.

43 It is not clear whether Galt, whose department had a keen interest in statistics, traveled to London especially for the congress, or whether he was there anyway on other business.

Chapter Two

1 British North America Act, 1867, section 91.

2 R.H. Coats, "Beginnings in Canadian Statistics," *Canadian Historical Review*, 27, no. 2 (Toronto, June 1946): 117.

3 See, for example, *Report of the Departmental Commission on the Official Statistics of Canada* (Ottawa, 1913), 8.

4 An Act for the Organization of the Department of Agriculture, 1868, 31 Vict., cap. 53.

5 *Report of the Minister of Agriculture of the Dominion of Canada for the Half Year of 1867 and for 1868* (Ottawa, 1870), 11.

6 An Act respecting the First Census, 33 Vict., cap. 21. This was an *ad hoc* enactment, making no provision for future censuses. The 1871 census was not in fact the first to be conducted under Dominion auspices. A census had been taken in Manitoba in 1870 for the purpose of dividing the province into its four original electoral districts. It was authorized merely by administrative instruction from the secretary of state.

7 *Report of the Minister of Agriculture of the Dominion of Canada for the Year 1870* (Ottawa, 1871), 15.

8 *Report of the Minister of Agriculture, 1867–68*, 12.

9 See "Introduction," *Census of Canada, 1870–71*, vol. 1 (Ottawa, 1873), x.

10 House of Commons, *Debates*, 24 February 1885, 213.

11 Introduction to vol. 1, *Census of Canada, 1890–91* (Ottawa, 1893).

12 The 1871 census findings proper were made up of three volumes, the first two of which, comprising the personal census, were published in 1873, while the third volume, covering agriculture, industrial, and other economic topics, appeared in 1875. The 1861 census, by contrast, had appeared long after the promised deadline and contained no analytical or descriptive text.

13 Following the establishment of the Canadian Archives in 1871 and their subsequent development, important new source material relevant to the purposes of volume four became available. Consequently, the 1931 census of Canada presented a revised and extended list of census documents and modified the historical commentary accordingly. See *Seventh Census of Canada, 1931*, Volume I – Summary (Ottawa, 1936), 133.

14 *Census of Canada, 1870–7*1, vol. 5, xxx.

15 Ibid., xlvi.

16 The two distinct sections of 42 Vict., cap. 21 were eventually regularized as separate acts – chapters 58 and 59 respectively of the Revised Statutes of Canada, 1886, under the titles of An Act Respecting the Census (the Census Act), and An Act Respecting Statistics.

17 *Census of Canada, 1880–81* (Ottawa, 1885), vol. 4, xii.

18 Ibid., x.

19 An Act to provide for the taking of a census in the province of Manitoba, the North-West Territories and the District of Keewatin, 48–49 Vict., cap. 3.

20 See ministerial reports for 1880 to 1885 under such headings as "Report on Alleged Exodus to Western United States at Port Huron." The concerns were for the detrimental effect on the confidence of potential migrants from the United Kingdom to Canada in the desirability of settling in a country from which such large numbers apparently left every year from a single port.

21 Johnson's standing in the departmental hierarchy was immediately below the deputy minister and on a par with the secretary of the department, the archivist, and the registrar of copyrights.

22 F.A. Walker, "The Eleventh Census of the United States," *Quarterly Journal of Economics*, 2 (1888): 150.

23 *Report of the Minister of Agriculture for the Dominion of Canada for the calendar year 1890* (Ottawa, 1891) xli.

24 *Report of the Minister of Agriculture for the Dominion of Canada for the calendar year 1891* (Ottawa, 1892), xlii.

25 Detailed cost information on decennial censuses from 1871 through 1911 is provided in *First Annual Report of the Dominion Statistician, 1918–19* (Ottawa, 1919).

26 *Report of the Minister of Agriculture for the Dominion of Canada for the year ended Occtober 31, 1901* (Ottawa, 1902) viii.

27 See below in this chapter.

28 NA, RG 31, Vol. 1301, John Cameron to Hon. Sydney A. Fisher, 7 April 1900.

29 Ibid., Hon. Sydney A. Fisher to Archibald Blue, 18 July 1900.

30 See paper by M.C. Urquhart, "New Estimates of Gross National Product, Canada, 1870 to 1926: Some Implications for Canadian Development", in *Long-Term Factors in American Economic Growth*, vol. 51 of Conference on Research in Income and Wealth, *Studies in Income and Wealth* (Chicago and London: University of Chicago Press, 1986).

31 The government had the power to convene central boards of health with sweeping emergency powers "whenever this Province ... appears to be threatened with any formidable epidemic, endemic or contagious disease." An Act respecting the Preservation of the Public Health, cap. 38, *Consolidated Statutes of Canada*, 1859.

32 "The Board ... adopted blank forms for the collection of such Statistics, intending to have them printed and distributed, and to be filled up by health officers, medical men, clergymen and other persons connected with the service of the sick. Those forms, however, have neither been distributed nor even printed, because the Board, in order to avoid creating unnecessary fears on the one hand and useless expenditure on the other, had determined to wait until the moment of absolute need, which happily did not come." "Report of the Central Board of Health of Canada," appendix to *Report of the Minister of Agriculture*, 1866, 97.

33 Including the months of deaths, so as to provide a detailed basis for checking against current registration records. Curiously, a question was asked as to the occupation followed during the lifetime of the deceased, the choices being agricultural, commercial, domestic, industrial, and professional. In Ontario, out of a total of 18,063 reported deaths, only 3,829 could be coded among these headings.

34 *Census of Canada, 1901* (Ottawa, 1906) vol. 4, 228.

35 *Report of the Minister of Agriculture of the Dominion of Canada for the calendar year 1871* (Ottawa, 1872), 22.

36 Ibid., 23.

37 *Report of the Minister of Agriculture of the Dominion of Canada for the calendar year 1872* (Ottawa, 1873), 17.

38 House of Commons, *Debates*, 10 April 1873, 149.

39 As noted earlier, statistics had hitherto been disregarded as an element in preventative public health measures.

40 *Report of the Minister of Agriculture for the Dominion of Canada for the calendar year 1882* (Ottawa, 1883), xliii.

41 Ibid., xliv.

42 No further explanation for this cessation was offered, but it seems clear that the municipalities were becoming less and less willing to serve two masters as the provincial systems gradually became operational. See *Report of the Minister of Agriculture*, 1891, xli–xlii.

43 "Conference of Provincial Representatives on Maritime and Provincial Sanitation and Health Statistics," convened by the minister of Agriculture, 31 January-1 February 1893. The Conference was reported on in *Report of the Minister of Agriculture for the Dominion of Canada for the calendar year 1892* (Ottawa, 1893), 108.

44 See *Vital Statistics, 1921: First Annual Report* (Ottawa: Dominion Bureau of Statistics, 1923).

45 *Report of the Minister of Agriculture for the Dominion of Canada for the calendar year 1877* (Ottawa, 1878), xi–xii.

46 *Report of the Minister of Agriculture for the Dominion of Canada for the calendar year 1879* (Ottawa, 1880), ix.

47 House of Commons, *Debates*, 19 February 1880, 102–3.

48 Arthur Harvey was one of the earliest Canadian fellows of the Statistical Society of London, if not the first. In putting together a compendium of Canadian statistics, he may have been inspired by the example of the Statistical Department of the British Board of Trade, which, since its formation in 1832, had gradually developed a set of annual publications on trade and related topics. His pre-Confederation publication continued until 1873, with the agreement of the provinces as far as its coverage of municipal returns was concerned. But in the 1867 edition, it had been warned that "unless the Governments and Legislatures of the Provinces lend both pecuniary and moral support to the work, it cannot long be continued" (Letter of Transmittal by John Langton, Auditor, to the Minister of Finance, Hon. John Rose, in *Miscellaneous Statistics of Canada, 1867* [Ottawa: Hunter, Rose and Co., 1869]). This probably accounted for the otherwise unexplained demise of *Miscellaneous Statistics of Canada* after the 1873 edition.

49 Arthur Harvey, ed., *Year-Book and Almanac of British North America for 1867; Being an Annual Register of Political, Vital, and Trade Statistics, Customs Tariffs, Excise and Stamp Duties; and Public Events of Interest in Upper and Lower Canada, New Brunswick, Nova Scotia, Prince Edward Island, Newfoundland, and the West Indies* (Montreal: Lowe and Chamberlin, 1867).

50 Coats, "Beginnings in Canadian Statistics," 126.

51 George Johnson, *Canada: Its History, Production and Natural Resources*, (Ottawa: Department of Agriculture of Canada, 1886)

52 See, for example, Johnson's *Graphic Statistics* (Ottawa: Department of Agriculture, 1887), which honoured Queen Victoria's jubilee and twenty years of Canadian Confederation; *Crime in Canada* (Ottawa: Queen's Printer, 1893); and *Alphabet of First Things in Canada (A Ready Reference Book of Canadian Events)* (Ottawa: Mortimer, 1897).

53 Johnson, *Canada*, Introduction, n.p.

54 The newly completed transcontinental rail link.

55 Coats, "Beginnings in Canadian Statistics," 126.

56 No such explanation had ever been offered while the yearbook was actually called a Statistical Abstract and Record.

57 *Report of the Minister of Agriculture for the Dominion of Canada for the calendar year 1896* (Ottawa, 1897), xxxiv.

58 *Statistical Year-Book for Canada of 1896* (Ottawa: Government Printing Bureaau, 1897), Introduction.

59 See annual auditor generals' reports for the Department of Agriculture.

60 From the *Canadian Gazette*, London, England, in *Report of the Minister of Agriculture for the Dominion of Canada for the calendar year 1897*, (Ottawa, 1898), 33.

61 See British Association for the Advancement of Science, *Canadian Economics*; papers prepared for reading before the association's Economical Section, Montreal, 1884 (Montreal: Dawson Bros., 1885), xxii.

62 Ibid., xxx.

63 In ibid., 195–224.

64 See, for example, series C1–35 in Section C; "The Labour Force," in Urquhart and Buckley, eds., *Historical Statistics of Canada*.

65 The summary classification for 1891 included a "Non-Productive" category, within which, *inter alia*, were included "Indian Chiefs" and "Members of Religious Orders."

66 "Occupation, whether employer or wage earner and, if wage earner, whether employed during the week preceding the Census." See "Introduction," vol. 1, *Census of Canada, 1890–91*, xii.

67 The *Report of the Minister of Agriculture for the Dominion of Canada for the calendar year 1889* (Ottawa, 1890), xiv, noted that "a list of prices of provisions, and rates of wages in the various Districts where Immigration Agencies exist will be found in the appendices, and for reference and comparison, as well as for the information of intending settlers, they will prove very useful."

68 See the (first) *Annual Report of the Bureau of Industries for the Province of Ontario, 1882* (Toronto, 1883). The wording quoted was identical with that of the provision of the Province of Canada enactment of 1852, 16 Vict. cap. 11, which outlined the statistical mandate of the newly established Bureau of Agriculture.

69 Blue's appointment was undoubtedly the consequence of his report on agricultural statistics to the commission, which in 1880 had studied the operations of the Bureau of Agriculture "with a view to giving it increased efficiency" through the imposition of such new duties as the collection of statistics and periodic crop reports. See appendix G, "Agricultural statistics: Their Value, History, Scope and System," *Annual Report of the Commissioner of Agriculture and Arts for the Province of Ontario, 1881* (Toronto: C. Blackett Robinson, 1882).

70 But only 919 of the 5,838 establishments to which "circulars" were sent provided responses.

71 *Annual Report of the Bureau of Industries for the Province of Ontario, 1883* (Toronto, 1884) 2.

72 The Public Accounts of Ontario show that S.A. Cudmore, who later pursued a distinguished career with the Dominion Bureau of Statistics, earned eighty-four dollars in 1904 and forty-six dollars in 1905 for work in tabulating agricultural statistics – presumably as a summer student.

73 *Report of the Royal Commission on the Relations of Labor and Capital in Canada* (Ottawa: Queen's Printer, 1889), 14. Among those providing evidence to the Commission in its public hearings was Archibald Blue, then secretary of the Ontario Bureau of Industries. Blue also argued that the decennial census should be moved back a year to coincide with that of the United States.

74 An Act to provide for the Collection and publishing of Labor Statistics, 1890, 53 Vict., cap. 15.

75 There had been on the Dominion statute books since 1885 an Act to restrict and regulate Chinese Immigration into Canada, 48–49 Vict., cap. 71 which, among other provisions, established the notorious poll tax.

76 *Report of the Minister of Agriculture*, 1871, 21.

77 See various references in Bureau of the Census, chapter K "Agriculture," *Historical Statistics of the United States, Colonial Times to 1970, Part 1*, (Washington, DC: Bureau of the Census, US Department of Commerce, 1975).

78 *Report of the Minister of Agriculture for the Dominion of Canada for the calendar year 1883* (Ottawa, 1884), xi.

79 *Report of the Minister of Agriculture for the Dominion of Canada for the calendar year 1884* (Ottawa, 1885), xii.

80 *Report of the Minister of Agriculture*, 1890, xli.

Chapter Three

1 Coats, "Beginnings in Canadian Statistics," 117.

2 Census and Statistics Act, 4–5 Edw. VII, cap. 5. The act consolidated the previous legislation relating to census, general, and criminal statistics (chapters 58, 59 and 60 respectively, *Revised Statutes of Canada*, 1886).

3 House of Commons, *Debates*, 7 February 1905, 626.

4 Ibid., 628.

5 NA, RG 32, Vol. 137, Personnel File of George Johnson.

6 Ibid.

7 NA, RG 31, Accession No. 1989–90/133, Box 8, File 834, "Statistical Reorganization," Memorandum to File, February 1917.

8 The auditor general's report for the year ended 30 June 1906 showed Archibald Blue and E.H. St Denis as the office's senior managers, together with three other principal officers and a permanent clerical staff of sixteen. This was in contrast with the situation of three years earlier when the officials and permanent clerks associated with statistical functions numbered fewer than ten.

9 All three inquiries were conducted by post. They were completed in about a year in each case and published in a new Bulletin series as nos. II, VII, and V respectively.

10 Coats, "Beginnings in Canadian Statistics," 121.

11 A fuller account of these developments was provided many years later by E.H. Godfrey, recruited from the UK at the time of the 1905 expansion and later chief of the Agricultural Branch of the Dominion Bureau of Statistics, in *Progress in the Collection of Annual Agricultural Statistics and of Crop Reports during Growth in the Dominion of Canada*, vol. 41, Revue de l'Institut International de Statistique (La Haye: 1936).

12 A.E. Thornton and F. Bélisle, both of whom went on to work in the Dominion Bureau of Statistics for a great many years. There had been experimental use of mechanical tabulating equipment in the 1891 census, but the records of the 1901 census make no reference to its use.

13 Coats, "Beginnings in Canadian Statistics," 118.

14 Ibid., 116, 124.

15 *Report of the Departmental Commission on the Official Statistics of Canada* (Ottawa: King's Printer, 1913), 11.

16 M.C. Urquhart, "Three Builders of Canada's Statistical System," *Canadian Historical Review*, 68, no. 3 (1987): 423.

17 See for instance, N.a., *Dominion Bureau of Statistics: History, Foundation, Organization* (Ottawa: Queen's Printer, 1958), 9.

18 Coats, "Beginnings in Canadian Statistics," 124.

19 Quoted in John Cummings, "Statistical Work of the Federal Government of the United States," in *The History of Statistics: Their Development and Progress*, edited by John Koren (New York: Macmillan, 1918), 678–9.

20 *First Annual Report of the Dominion Statistician for the Fiscal Year Ended March 31, 1917*, (Ottawa: King's Printer, 1919). The emphasis was Coats's. The annual report for 1918–19 is also described as the "First Annual Report," but that was the first report to be made under the provisions of the Statistics Act of 1918.

21 John Cummings, "The Permanent Census Bureau: A Decade of Work," *Journal of the American Statistical Association* 13 (December 1913), 607.

22 The observation of a contemporary US statistician and economist, Francis A. Walker, to the effect that official statistics in the US developed under the leadership of

amateurs – albeit gifted amateurs – was equally applicable to Canada. See Joh Cummings, "Statistical Work."

23 Coats, "Beginnings in Canadian Statistics," 129.

24 House of Commons, *Debates*, 10 June 1887, 862.

25 *Report of the Departmental Commission on the Official Statistics of Canad* (Ottawa: King's Printer, 1913), 18.

26 Letter of Transmittal by deputy minister, in *Report of the Department of Trad and Commerce for the Fiscal Year ended 30 June 1893* (Ottawa: Queen's Printer 1894), ix.

27 Letter of Transmittal by deputy minister, in *Report of the Department of Trad and Commerce for the Fiscal Year ended 30 June 1905* (Ottawa: Queen's Printer 1906), ix.

28 "The trade of Canada during the last decade has grown to such proportions, that on a per capita basis, she holds third position among the commercial nations o the world. Today it is evident that Canada is on the threshold of vast and numerou changes – commercial, industrial and other – and that with her geographica position; her unlimited resources in fisheries, forests and mines; her large area o productive land; her intelligent and patriotic citizens; she is destined to prove he fitness to work out her own destiny as a self-governing over-sea dependency o the British Crown." Department of Trade and Commerce, *Statistical Record o the Progress of Canada – Published on the Occasion of the Seventh Triennia Meeting of the Congress of Chambers of Commerce of the British Empire, at Sydney Australia, Sept. 24 1909* (Ottawa: Government Printing Bureau, 1909), Preface n.p.

29 See *Conférence Internationale de Statistique Commerciale, Bruxelles, 1913 Documents et Procès-Verbaux* (Brussels: Etablissements Généraux d'Imprimerie 1914). The five categories were: "Animaux Vivants," "Objets d'Alimentation e Boissons," "Matières Brutes ou Simplement Preparées," "Produits Fabriqués,' and "Or et Argent Non Ouvrés et Monnaies d'Or et d'Argent."

30 Section 10, An Act to aid in the prevention and settlement of trade disputes, an to provide for the publication of statistical industrial information (the Conciliatio Act), 63–64 Vict., cap. 24.

31 House of Commons, *Debates*, 17 June 1900, 8,399. The United States Departmen of Labor, although established in 1884, did not initiate a regular gazette-typ publication (now known as the *Monthly Labor Review*) until 1915.

32 King's credentials had been established through his investigation for Mulock o the practice of "sweating" in the carrying out of Post Office clothing contracts His recommendations resulted in regulations for the payment of fair wages an the provision of proper sanitary conditions for such work. NA, King Papers Report to the Honourable the Postmaster General of the Methods Adopted i Canada in the Carrying out of Government Clothing Contracts, January 1898.

33 The first issue of the *Gazette* described a parallel initiative in Ontario for th collection and publication of labour statistics through the establishment of a Burea of Labour under the Public Works department, with a mandate broadly similar t

that of the Dominion department. The province's Bureau of Industries had developed some useful labour statistics during the 1880s, but the work was eventually discontinued.

4 Harper was a close personal friend of King, who was greatly moved by his act and later published a tribute to Harper's memory, *The Secret of Heroism*, (New York: Revell, 1906). He was also the prime mover behind the erection, by public subscription, of the "Sir Galahad" statue, near Parliament Hill in Ottawa.

5 They had been contemporaries at the University of Toronto, both had worked on the Toronto *Globe*, and King had written a letter of condolence on the occasion of the death of Coats's brother-in-law in November 1900. NA, King Papers, Series 6, 1,604.

6 Ibid., 2,658–67. The reference to Coats's health is surprising, given the remarkable energy that he brought to his new duties from the very start.

7 Ibid., 2,686–7.

8 NA, AG 27, Department of Labour Records, Vol. 48, File 4: Collection and Publication of Statistics – Policy, 1904–09.

9 Ibid.

0 Ibid.

1 He was a graduate of University College, Toronto, in classics and political science and had won a Banker's Scholarship in economics during his second year.

2 NA, AG 27, Department of Labour Records, Vol. 48, File 4: Collection and Publication of Statistics – Policy, 1904–09.

3 Ibid.

4 Years later, in advising the deputy minister of Trade and Commerce as to the availability of wholesale prices to assist the work of a proposed wartime Trade Commission, Coats noted that "the Department of Labour went into wholesale prices in the first instance from a purely 'cost of living' point of view. Wholesale prices are of course a barometer rather of trade conditions than of cost of living, but they are so much easier to collect and handle that the Labour Department selected them for their first action in this connection." NA, RG 31, Accession No. 1989–90/133, Box 9, File 854, Pt. II, R.H. Coats to F.C.T. O'Hara, 31 March 1917.

5 NA, AG 27, Department of Labour Records, Vol. 48, File 4: Collection and Publication of Statistics – Policy, 1904–09.

6 Ibid.

7 Coats was secretary of the association, which in January 1909 presented him with a gold watch and chain in recognition of special services on its behalf.

8 *Report of the Department of Labour for the Fiscal Year ended March 31, 1909*, (Ottawa, 1909), 12.

9 House of Commons, *Debates*, 15 May 1909, 6,726.

0 Ibid.

1 Ibid., 7 April 1909, 4,121.

52 *Labour Gazette* 10 (February 1910): 894.

53 Ibid., 892.

54 Ibid., 915. From 1910 on, the wholesale prices data were updated in a new annua publication, of which the 1911 and subsequent editions contained an appendix o retail prices that provided budgetary calculations and comparisons.

55 Ibid., 893.

56 NA, AG 27, Department of Labour Records, Vol. 48, File 1, Prices Investigatior

57 R.H. Coats, *Wholesale Prices in Canada, 1890–1909*, (Ottawa: Governmen Printing Bureau, 1910).

58 *Labour Gazette* 11 (July 1910): 47.

59 "Memorandum of the Construction of an Index Number of Commodity Prices with a Review of Important British and Foreign Index Numbers, and a Statemen Relating to the Causes and Effects of Variations in Prices," in Coats, *Wholesal Prices in Canada*, 433–47.

60 Ibid., 443–4.

61 Ibid.

62 Ibid., 12. No details of Coats's adaptation of the BAAS schema were provided

63 Coats, *Wholesale Prices in Canada*, 12.

64 *Report of the Department of Labour for the Fiscal Year ending March 31, 191* (Ottawa, 1911), 144.

65 The report provided a detailed elaboration, in both narrative and graphic form, o the main features of what were seen as the responsibilities of the new branch. Se ibid., 144–5.

66 R.H. Coats, *Wholesale Prices in Canada*, 483.

67 In ibid., 1.

68 PC 3195, 20 December 1913; supplemented by PC 194, 22 January 1914, and letter, Rt. Hon. R.L. Borden to John McDougald, 8 January 1914.

69 *Report of the Board of Inquiry into the Cost of Living*, 2 vols. (Ottawa: King' Printer, 1915). It was not formally tabled in the House of Commons until 1 February 1916.

70 John McDougald, commissioner of Customs (chairman), C.C. James, Agricultura Commissioner, and J.U. Vincent, deputy minister of Inland Revenue.

71 NA, RG 31, Vol. 1417, R.H. Coats, Memo for Minister of Labour re Cost of Livin Report, 25 June 1915.

72 Ibid., R.H. Coats to John McDougald, 24 February 1915.

73 Ibid., 26 February 1915.

74 This material appeared as appendices one to seven in volume one of the publishe report.

75 NA, RG 31, Vol. 1417, R.H. Coats to John McDougald, 4 March 1915.

76 Ibid., R.H. Coats to T.W. Crothers, 9 March 1915.

77 Ibid., R.H. Coats to Hon. A. Meighen, 8 November 1915. Coats and Meighen ha been classmates at the University of Toronto, and the apparent impropriety of

relatively junior official writing directly to the minister of another department would not have been considered remarkable in the closely knit official circles of those days.

78 Without some knowledge of these background circumstances, the structure of the published report defies rational explanation.

79 Board of Inquiry into the Cost of Living, *Report of the Board.* Vol. 1, Introductory exhibit by R.H. Coats (Ottawa: King's Printer, 1915), 53.

80 Board of Inquiry into the Cost of Living, *Report of the Board*, Vol. 1 (Ottawa: King's Printer, 1915), 12. It was noted as "startling" that fewer than ten percent of these vehicles were for industrial use.

81 NA, RG 31, Vol. 1434, quoted by Herbert Marshall in Section C, chapter 2, Part 1 of his 1967 draft history of the Dominion Bureau of Statistics (no date provided but probably April/May 1916).

Chapter Four

1 Only a few months earlier, the Department of Labour, no doubt at the instigation of Coats, had argued that "the amalgamation with this Department of the Census Branch of the Department of Agriculture would appear to be decidedly in the interests of efficiency ... There is at present no bond other than that of a common administration between the Census and the Department to which it is attached, whereas the points of contact between the work of the branch and the statistical work of this Department are numerous and intimate." NA, RG 31, Accession No. 1989–90/133, Box 15, File 904, Pt. 3.

2 Its full title was the Royal Commission on the Natural Resources, Trade and Legislation of Certain Portions of His Majesty's Dominions. The United Kingdom, Canada, Australia, the Union of South Africa, New Zealand, and Newfoundland were represented on the commission. One of the UK members was Sir H. Rider Haggard who, in addition to being a public servant with expert standing on agricultural and social conditions in England and on colonial migration, was also famous as the author of such novels as *King Solomon's Mines*.

3 UK, Colonial Office, Dominions Department, *Report for 1911–12 Relating to the Self-Governing Dominions*, Cd. 6091 (London: His Majesty's Stationery Office, May 1912), 5.

4 "Self-governing" was a term that applied largely to domestic affairs. In many aspects of external relations, the colonies were still tied to the apron strings of the mother country. O. Mary Hill notes, for instance, that "until 1879 the British colonies had been included automatically in trade agreements that the United Kingdom made with other countries." *Canada's Salesman to the World: The Department of Trade and Commerce, 1892–1939* (Montreal and London: McGill-Queen's University Press, 1977), 73.

5 At the 1907 imperial conference, Canada had indicated its concurrence with the suggestion of the UK Board of Trade that each country should distinguish in its

statistics between trade with the UK, with British possessions, and with foreign countries.

6 Hill, *Canada's Salesman to the World*, 101, reports Borden's displeasure that Foster had gone on this long trip without his code book, so that cables had to be sent to him *en clair*.

7 UK, Dominions Royal Commission, *Second Interim Report*, Cd. 7210, (London: His Majesty's Stationery Office, January 1914).

8 Ibid., 53.

9 UK, Dominions Royal Commission, *Minutes of Evidence, Central and Western Provinces of Canada*, Cd. 8458 (London: His Majesty's Stationery Office, 1916).

10 UK, Dominions Royal Commission, *Final Report*, Cd. 8462 (London: His Majesty's Stationery Office, March 1917).

11 W.Stewart Wallace, *The Memoirs of the Rt. Hon. Sir George Foster, PC, GCMG*, (Toronto: Macmillan, 1933), 185.

12 UK, Dominions Royal Commission, *Final Report*, 148.

13 *Imperial War Conference: Minutes and Proceedings of Papers laid before the Conference*, Cd. 9177 (London: His Majesty's Stationery Office, 1918).

14 Ibid.

15 The commission was originally required to report on 15 September 1912, but this deadline was subsequently extended to 1 December 1912. The hearings that did take place were not always plain sailing. When Grigg met with the Canadian Manufacturer's Association on 3 July 1912, a Mr Beer asked "whether the Government has up their sleeve a design to use figures to the disadvantage of manufacturers." NA, RG 20, B1, Vol. 1, File A 70.

16 *Report of Departmental Commission on the Official Statistics of Canada, with Appendix Consisting of Notes of Evidence*, (Ottawa: King's Printer, 1913), 8.

17 Ibid.

18 Ibid., 9.

19 Arthur L. Bowley, "The Improvement of Official Statistics," *Journal of the Royal Statistical Society*, 81, Part 3, (30 September 1908), 478.

20 In respect of all these organizational arrangements, the experience of Australia, which, at federation in 1900, had added a centralized Commonwealth statistical bureau to the various state bureaux already in existence, was favourably commented upon.

21 *Report of Departmental Commission*, 11.

22 Ibid.

23 Ibid., 13.

24 The section of the report dealing with this topic emphasized "the great importance to Canada – whose main economic problem is the development of an immense and varied source of natural wealth – of complete and accurate statistics of trade, external and internal, which is based upon the possession of that wealth." See *Report of the Departmental Commission*, 17.

25 Ibid., 18.

26 Ibid., 21.

27 Ibid., 22.

28 Ibid., 24.

29 Provincial statistics had been dropped from the *Canada Year Book*, Second Series, in 1905.

30 At about this time Godfrey also elevated the international profile of Canadian statistics by being the first Canadian delegate to attend a session of the International Statistical Institute. This was in September 1913 in Vienna, where he delivered a descriptive paper on the organization of official statistics in Canada. Godfrey, who was away for two months including twenty-one days of statutory leave, submitted a travel claim for $566.82.

31 NA, RG 31, Vol. 1419, Statistics Commission Correspondence, File A–70, Part 5, 1913.

32 Ibid.

33 Ibid.

34 More than once in the 1913 correspondence, reference was made to the revision of statistics then under way in Québec, and, with what later could be seen as unwarranted alarm, to the fact that other provinces might soon follow Québec's example. "It is only while such reorganizations are in a formative state that a plan of co-ordination can be arranged." NA, RG 31, Vol. 1419, Statistics Commission Correspondence, File A–70, Part–5, 1913, R. Grigg to Hon. G. Foster, 20 November 1913.

35 These inquiries are described in a letter of 26 June 1912 from Foster to Grigg written from London, in Griggs's reply of 6 July, and in a letter of the same date from Grigg to Percy Ashley in London. NA, RG 20, B1 Vol. 1, File A70.

36 In a letter dated 10 February 1913 to Foster, Grigg had stated how impressed he was "with the capacity for usefulness in statistical work of Mr Coats of the Labour Department." He went on to argue that Coats would be a better choice because "he would be content with far less salary than Mr Knibbs and he would be free from the reproach of being an importation." Foster later met Knibbs during his travels to New Zealand and Australia with the Dominions royal commission. UK, *Dominions Royal Commission, Minutes of Evidence, Australia*, Command Papers 7171 and 7172 (London: His Majesty's Stationery Office, 1913).

37 Foster Papers, NA, MG 27, II D7, Vol. 19, File 2464, Mackenzie King to R.H. Coats, 24 June 1915. King at this time was in political exile, having lost his seat in Parliament in the Liberal debacle of 1911.

38 NA, RG 31, Accession No. 1989–90/133, Box 8, File 834. The emphasis is Foster's.

39 Ibid. The emphasis is Coats's.

40 M.C. Urquhart and K.A.H. Buckley, eds., *Historical Statistics of Canada* (Cambridge: Cambridge University Press; Toronto: Macmillan, 1965), 456

41 NA, RG 31, Accession No. 1989–90/133, Box 11, File 889.

42 Ibid.

43 An important methodological innovation in this census was the use of individual

schedules to provide the complete agricultural record for each farm. Hitherto, the schedules had been designed to contain the records of one hundred farms, with separate schedules for the various items of information. See Introduction, *Census of Prairie Provinces, Population and Agriculture – Manitoba, Saskatchewan and Alberta, 1916* (Ottawa: King's Printer, 1918), 13.

44 NA, RG 31, Accession No. 1989–90/133, Box 8, File 834, Statistical Reorganization, R.H. Coats, "A National System of Statistics for Canada – Centralization, Reorganization and Enlargement of Canadian Statistics," 25 August 1916, 5.

45 Ibid.

46 Ibid., 6

47 Ibid., 7.

48 Ibid. These were census of population and agriculture, vital statistics, agriculture, the industrial census, statistics of trade and commerce, transportation, municipal statistics, criminal statistics, and editorial branch.

49 Ibid., 8.

50 Already, at the time of Coats' writing, this work had been initiated, including the drafting of a model Bill and Order in Council for use by the provinces.

51 The Commission had obviously given considerable weight to the sensibilities of the Customs Department.

52 Coats, "A National System of Statistics," 11.

53 Ibid., 11, 12.

54 Ibid., 13.

55 Ibid., 14.

56 The value of the 1905 act as a basis for facilitating collaboration with other departments was almost certainly overestimated, as Coats was soon to point out. Some obligation on their part to collaborate with the Census and Statistics Office in the collection and publication of general statistics in intercensal years could be inferred from sections 15 and 17, but there was nothing as explicit as the provisions of section 16 for collaboration with the provinces.

57 NA, RG 31, Accession No. 1989–90/133, Box 8, File 834, R.H. Coats, Memorandum for the minister, "Statistical Reorganization," 28 October 1916.

58 Ibid., F.C.T. O'Hara, Memorandum for the minister, "Statistical Reorganization," 14 November 1916. The staffs referred to by O'Hara had not been taken over by the Census and Statistics Office when the latter was transferred to the department in 1912.

59 Ibid.

60 Ibid., R.H. Coats, Memorandum to the deputy minister, "Statistical Reorganization," 9 December 1916.

61 Ibid., R.H. Coats, Memorandum, "Statistical Reorganization," 31 January 1917.

62 Ibid.

63 NA, RG 31, Accession No. 1989–90/133, Box 8, File 835. H. Michell to R.H. Coats, 21 May 1917.

64 NA, RG 31, Accession No. 1989–90/133, Box 8, File 834, R.H. Coats to Sir George Foster, 26 May 1917.

65 Ibid. The emphasis is Coats's.

66 Ibid.

67 NA, RG 31, Accession No. 1989–90/133, Box 7, File 830, R.H. Coats to Hon. Arthur Meighen, KC, solicitor general, 24 July 1917.

68 Ibid., R.H. Coats to Sir George Foster, 29 January 1918.

69 House of Commons, *Debates*, 4 April 1918, 337.

70 The most noteworthy comment was the observation of one wag who suggested that, for information relative to the social activities of the people, the best source was the gossip columns of the newspapers.

71 Sections 20 to 33 inclusive. The requirement for criminal statistics had already been spelled out in the Census and Statistics Act of 1905, and the provisions for transportation returns were adapted from the statistical provisions of successive Railway Acts.

72 NA, RG 31, Accession No. 1989–90/133, Box 7, File 830.

73 Ibid.

74 Coats, "A National System of Statistics," 6.

75 NA, RG 31, Accession No. 1989–90/133, Box 8, File 834, R.H. Coats to F.C.T. O'Hara, 3 January 1917.

76 Ibid., File 830, R.H. Coats to F.C.T. O'Hara, 28 June 1918, and F.C.T. O'Hara to R.H. Coats, 2 July 1918. Foster, now seventy years old, had still not fully recovered from an accident late the previous year, which had put him in hospital for more than a month.

77 Ibid., R.H. Coats to F.C.T. O'Hara, 2 July 1918.

78 Ibid.

Chapter Five

1 *Report of the Dominion Statistician for the Fiscal Year ended March 31 1922* (Ottawa, 1923), 8.

2 Ibid, 9.

3 This department had been spun off from the Department of the Interior in 1907 under legislation that authorized it to collect and publish statistics. Coats frequently cited this as a lost opportunity on the part of the then recently established Census and Statistics Office to assert its coordinating powers.

4 In *DBS Staff News, 40th Anniversary Issue*, 1958, 7.

5 Taking over from E.H. Godfrey who was then able to work full time on agriculture statistics.

6 His academic career had been interrupted by military service during the First World War.

7 It was held to be a unique Canadian example of the so-called "Chicago School."

8 It was often referred to as the SCR Building, these initials standing for "Soldiers' Civil Re-establishment," the function it had previously housed.

9 Staff magazine, *Stat Monthly* (April 1955): 3.

10 NA, RG 31, Accession No. 1989–90/133, Box 13, File 894.

11 After the provision of assurances for the protection of the confidentiality of individual data.

12 NA, RG 31, Accession No. 1989–90/133, Box 13, File 894, R.H. Coats to Sir George Foster, 14 January and 8 February 1921.

13 NA, RG 31, Accession No. 1989–90/133, Box 8, File 834, Statistical reorganization, R.H. Coats, "Memorandum on the Establishment of a National System of Vital Statistics," 14 February 1916. The approaches described had been recommended some twenty-five years earlier by the Dominion/provincial conference which followed the failure of the mortuary statistics program that had operated during the 1880s.

14 One of these was Professor S.A. Cudmore of the University of Toronto. This was perhaps the first occasion on which he and Coats met.

15 NA, RG 31, Accession No. 1989–90/133, Box 12, File 891, R.H. Coats to Sir George Foster, June 25 1918.

16 Ibid., Dominion Statistician, "Memorandum for Information of Council Re Vital Statistics," 11 April 1919.

17 Ibid.

18 After further skirmishing with the provinces, a rate of four cents per transcript was finally agreed upon. This rate was still in force in the early 1940s. The bureau also arranged with the Post Office for free franking privileges in the mailing of transcripts to Ottawa.

19 The Department of Health Act, 9–10 Geo. V, cap. 24.

20 *Administrative Report on the Census of Population and Agriculture, 1921* (Ottawa: King's Printer, 1924), x.

21 Ibid., xiv.

22 There was public concern during the conduct of the census about persons of native-born Canadian stock not being recorded as "Canadians." It came about because the answer "Canadian" was not accepted in reply to the question on racial origin and prompted a lengthy explanation of "the census questions and nationality, birthplace, language and racial origin respectively, their relationship inter se, and their bearing upon the recording of "Canadians" (ibid., 14 n. 9). The issue was important because Canada's participation in the Peace Treaty and in the League of Nations had necessitated for the first time an official definition of Canadian nationality.

23 See below, in this chapter.

24 1921 Census, *Administrative Report*, xii.

25 See *Instructions to Commissioners and Enumerators*, 1921 Census, 8.

26 1921 Census, *Administrative Report*, xxi.

27 Volume three, *Population (Dwellings, Families, Conjugal Condition of Family Head, Children, Orphanhood, Wage Earners)*, was published on 12 February 1927, and volume four, *Occupations*, on 12 January 1928. Delays with volume four were said to have been due to problems with the quality of the occupational data collected, and in implementing the classification system.

28 1921 Census, *Administrative Report*, xv.

29 *First Annual Report of the Dominion Statistician, 1918–19*, (Ottawa, 1920), 26.

30 Ibid., 27.

31 Not all provinces participated in the program, and among those that did, rates of return varied considerably. For further details, see reports of the Dominion statistician for the years ended 31 March 1924, 1925, and 1927.

32 N.a., *The Dominion Bureau of Statistics: Its Origin, Constitution and Organization*, (Ottawa: King's Printer, 1935), 26, 27.

33 *First Annual Report of the Dominion Statistician*, 1918–19, 36.

34 Ibid., 36.

35 NA, RG 31, Accession No. 1989–90/133, Box No. 14, File 901, R.H. Coats to F.C.T. O'Hara, 24 October 1919.

36 NA, RG 31, Accession No. 1989–90/133, Box 11, File 889, Everett Bristol to Rt. Hon. Sir George Foster, 28 October 1920.

37 Ibid., Thomas J. Coonan to Secretary, Department of Justice, 30 March 1921.

38 Ibid., Memorandum from J.A. Schryburt to R.H. Coats, undated (probably late 1923).

39 Ibid., (Further) memorandum from J.A. Schryburt to R.H. Coats, undated (also 1923).

40 Ibid.

41 This term gradually went out of use. The responsible organizational unit after 1918 was the External Trade Branch.

42 NA, RG 31 Accession No. 1989–90/133, Box 7, File 830, R.H. Coats to Hon. A.K. MacLean, MP, 19 December 1918.

43 *First Annual Report of the Dominion Statistician*, 37–8.

44 See, for example, Dominion Bureau of Statistics, Department of Trade and Commerce, *Trade of Canada, Fiscal Year Ended March 31, 1921*, (Ottawa: King's Printer, 1922).

45 The bureau carried this work back to 1890 and it was subsequently extended to 1869 by K.W. Taylor in *Statistics of Foreign Trade, 1869 to 1915*, volume 2 of *Statistical Contributions to Canadian Economic History*, (Toronto: MacMillan, 1931).

46 *Report of the Dominion Statistician for the Fiscal Year Ended March 31, 1925*, 12. The statement in question was not strictly correct. Customs continued to publish an annual report as required by the Customs Act but purged of the statistical detail previously provided.

47 NA, RG 31, Vol. 1417, Trade Material, "Memorandum by the Dominion Statistician on Statistics of Trade (Exports and Imports) and Navigation, 1936."

48 Ibid.

49 In 1965 J.L. McDougall of Queen's University wrote that "the statistics of the early years should be received with gratitude because data for that period are so scarce, but they should also be treated with caution." For further details, see Urquhart and Buckley, eds., *Historical Statistics of Canada*, Section S, Transportation and Communication, General Note – Rail Transport, 516.

50 NA, RG 20, Vol. 989, File 12–20, F.C.T. O'Hara to R.H. Coats, 22 February 1922.

51 Ibid., J.L. Payne to F.C.T. O'Hara, 15 November 1920.

52 Ibid., 24 March 1921.

53 NA, RG 31, Accession No. 1989–90/133, Box 19, File 1378, "Memorandum on the Organization of Transportation Statistics" (undated), 1.

54 Ibid., 2.

55 Ibid., 4.

56 *Report of the Royal Commission on Railways and Transportation*, Terms of Reference – PC 2910, 20 November 1931 (Ottawa: King's Printer, Ottawa, 1932), 5.

57 Ibid., para. 168, 5.

58 *Report of the Royal Commission on Dominion-Provincial Relations, Book II* (Ottawa, 3 May 1940), 219

59 NA, RG 31, Accession No. 1989–90/133, Box 7, File 830, Pt. II, G.S. Wrong to S.A. Cudmore, Memorandum of 14 May 1942.

60 F.H. Leacy, ed., *Historical Statistics of Canada,* 2nd ed., Statistics Canada (in joint sponsorship with the Social Science Federation of Canada), Ottawa 1983, Section 1, Transportation and Communication, General Note to Series T142–194.

61 NA, RG 31, Accession No. 1989–90/133, Box 9, File 854, Pt. II. This was undated and unsigned but appears to have been written by Watson Griffin, superintendent of the Commercial Intelligence Branch of Trade and Commerce.

62 Ibid., R.H. Coats to F.C.T. O'Hara, 26 March 1917.

63 The Grain Statistics Branch of the Department of Trade and Commerce, which had eluded absorption by the Census and Statistics Office in 1917, had finally been taken over.

64 Dominion Bureau of Statistics, *Census of Trading Establishments, 1924* (Ottawa: King's Printer, 1928), 5.

65 It was officially known as the Census of Merchandising and Service Establishments, 1931, and covered the year 1930.

66 N.a., *The Dominion Bureau of Statistics: Its Origin, Constitution*, 46–7.

67 Jacob Viner, *Canada's Balance of International Indebtedness, 1900–1913* (Cambridge: Harvard University Press, 1924). In this study, Viner took a more charitable view of the Customs department's statistics than Coats did in "A National System," saying of them (page 27) that "For the items they cover [they] are probably as close to accuracy as is reasonably to be expected of any comprehensive statistics. An exceptionally efficient Customs Department collects with great care the data for both import and export statistics."

68 H. Marshall, F.A. Southard, and K.W. Taylor, *Canadian American Industry*, (New Haven and Toronto: Yale University Press and Ryerson Press, 1936). The volume was one of a series on the relations of Canada and the United States, prepared under the auspices of the Carnegie Endowment for International Peace.

69 Coats, "A National System of Statistics," 8.

70 Page 48.

71 *Historical Statistical Survey of Education in Canada*, Dominion Bureau of Statistics, 1921, Cat. No. 81–D–65.

72 *Report of the Dominion Statistician*, 1921–22, 22.

73 Catalogue No. 81–D–20E. Most Bureau publications of this era, other than those of the Census and the yearbook, were produced and distributed directly by the Bureau and can generally be cited merely by catalogue number. Branch names were not normally used in the title pages.

74 *Report of the Departmental Commission*, 12.

75 *Report of the Dominion Statistician for the Fiscal Year ended March 31, 1925* (Ottawa, 1925), 6.

76 Coats, "A National System of Statistics for Canada," 13.

77 *Report of the Dominion Statistician*, 1921–22, 22.

78 *Report of the Departmental Commission*, 13.

79 Ibid., 34.

80 Coats, "A National System of Statistics for Canada," 13.

81 Its staff during the early years averaged four.

82 See chapter 6.

83 NA, RG 31, Accession No. 1989–90/133, Box 20, File 1415, Dominion-Provincial Conference, Ottawa, 17–19 January 1933, Agenda Item 8, Uniform Statistical Information.

84 Coats, "A National System of Statistics for Canada", 7.

85 Cat. No. 11–D–51.

86 NA, RG 31, Vol. 1409, File 1476, J.G. Parmelee to R.H. Coats, 18 January 1936.

87 *First Annual Report of the Dominion Statistician, 1918–19*, 50.

88 In addition, the bureau assumed full responsibility for the field of price statistics. The Department of Labour retained statistics of trade disputes, labour organizations, and industrial accidents, as well as statistics of applications, vacancies, and placements by the Employment Service of Canada. It also continued the annual collection and publication of rates of wages and hours of labour in typical trades and occupations across the country. This arrangement continued for many years.

89 Such was the stature she eventually achieved that, for many years after her retirement, the series was still known as "the Roughsedge index."

90 This was probably the first bureau publication to be charged for. Even census publications were free until 1931.

91 *Monthly Review of Canadian Business Statistics*, 1, no. 1 (January 1926), 2.

92 NA, RG 31, Accession No. 1989–90/133, Box 10, File 877, R.H. Coats, "National Wealth and Income of Canada," undated (but probably written in December 1916).

93 *Canada Year Book*, 1922–23, 806–7.

94 This account of interwar developments in the estimation of national income draws upon S.A. Goldberg, "The Development of National Accounts in Canada," *Canadian Journal of Economics and Political Science* (February 1949).

Chapter Six

1 Much of what follows is drawn from materials in the form of letters, draft memoranda, and notes for file (many undated) making up a loose appendix to a document, "Valedictory Report," dated 10 November 1941, that Coats prepared just before his retirement. A special chapter was addressed to "Status of the Bureau," under the general heading of "Constitutional and Administrative Machinery."

2 NA, RG 31, Vol. 1301, R.H. Coats to Hon. Sir G. Foster, 19 May 1915.

3 See below, in this chapter.

4 Coats, "Valedictory Report," 15. Coats did not provide a date for the report of this commission, but it would have been in the early 1920s.

5 NA, RG 31, Accession No. 1989–90/133, Box 7, File 830, Part II.

6 Coats, "Valedictory Report," Appendix on Status of the Dominion Statistician, 1.

7 "Central statistical organizations in other countries never bear any Departmental imprimatur (vide Australia, New Zealand, South Africa, Holland, Sweden, Germany)," wrote Coats in the "Valedictory Report", 14 fn.

8 Coats, "Valedictory Report," appendix on Staff Administration of the Dominion Bureau of Statistics.

9 Foster's official biographer recorded that, at the time of leaving office, Foster looked back on his ten years of responsibility for the Department of Trade and Commerce, noting that "the Statistics Branch, which was but a myth, [is] now strong and inclusive." Wallace, *The Memoirs of the Rt. Hon. Sir George Foster*, 211.

10 Coats, "Valedictory Report," appendix on Status of the Dominion Statistician, 2.

11 The Civil Service Commission, through its Regulation 105 dated 10 December 1923, later ruled that "only one officer in each Department is authorized to conduct negotiations with the ... Commission."

12 Coats, "Valedictory Report," appendix on Staff Administration, 3.

13 NA, RG 31, Accession No. 1989–90/133, Box 17, File 1338, Pt. II, R.H. Coats to F.C.T. O'Hara, 13 August 1930.

14 Ibid., F.C.T. O'Hara to R.H. Coats, 21 August 1930.

15 Coats, "Valedictory Report," appendix re Imprimatur on Reports of the Dominion Bureau of Statistics, J.G. Parmelee to R.H. Coats, 28 February 1938.

16 Section 5, the Civil Service Amendment Act, 7–8 Edw. VII, c. 15.

17 See J.E. Hodgetts, William McCloskey, Reginald Whitaker, V. Seymour Wilson, *The Biography of an Institution: The Civil Service Commission of Canada, 1908–1967*, (Montreal and London: McGill-Queen's University Press, 1972), 66 et seq.

18 NA, RG 31, Accession No. 1989–90/133, Box 17, File 1338, Pt. II. R.H. Coats to W.C. Ronson, Royal Commission on Professional and Technical Salaries, 13 December 1929.

19 Ibid., "Memorandum on the Technical and Professional Classes in the Statistical Service," for the Royal Commission on Technical and Professional Services, Dominion Statistician, 31 July 1929.

20 Ibid., R.H. Coats to Professor Gilbert Jackson, University of Toronto, 21 December 1929.

21 *Report of the Royal Commission on Professional and Technical Services*, February 1930 (Ottawa: King's Printer, 1930).

22 This and later comments on the Beatty Commission recommendations appear in an undated document, "Memorandum on Appendix A of the Report of the Beatty Commission as Applied to the Dominion Bureau of Statistics," sent by Coats with a letter to Professor Jackson dated 10 March 1930. NA, RG 31, Accession No. 1989–90/133, Box 17, File 1338, Pt. II.

23 Ibid.

24 "A Reorganization Plan for the Dominion Bureau of Statistics," put forward on 12 July 1937, explained that "due to unusual demands made on the Bureau of Statistics by the Government and other bodies, the staff available from the 1931 Census was retained after the year 1933 when, in ordinary circumstances, this staff would have been disbanded." NA, RG 31, Vol. 1408, File 1474.

25 Ibid., File 1473, R.H. Coats to J.G. Parmelee, 3 September 1935.

26 In a typical instance, a claim by N.R. Bouton of the branch's Investigating Staff that "no new work has been undertaken in the past three years" by the Agricultural Statistics Branch prompted a twelve-page rebuttal from T.W. Grindlay, the chief. NA, RG 31, Vol. 1408, File 1474, letter of 15 September 1937.

27 Ibid., J.G. Parmelee to R.H. Coats, 23 July 1936.

28 Ibid., R.H. Coats to J.G. Parmelee, 17 August 1936.

29 Hodgetts et al., *The Biography of an Institution*, 153, compared this statement of management philosophy with that attributed to an American capitalist in the 1920s: "The greatest spur to efficiency on the part of workers is a long line of unemployed outside the factory gate."

30 Parmelee, who liked to be called "Major" and was the son of the department's first deputy minister, had been no more successful in understanding Coats than his predecessor, O'Hara. In 1923 friction between Coats and O'Hara had exasperated Mackenzie King to the point where he threatened to transfer the statistical work to some other department if the two men could not compose their differences.

31 Coats, "Valedictory Report," appendix on Administrative Machinery of the Dominion Bureau of Statistics.

Chapter Seven

1 See below, in this chapter.

2 A phrase borrowed from Coats's sometime Australian counterpart, George Knibbs.

3 This proposal, first advanced by Coats in the 1916 blueprint, became a standard feature of subsequent memoranda outlining the bureau's program plans.

4 *Report of the Dominion Statistician*, 1924–25, 5. He noted, *inter alia*, that the section on general construction in the industrial census had been discontinued.

5 See below, in this chapter.

6 D.C. MacGregor, "External Forces Governing the Development of the Bureau," Part II of an undated and untitled document that also included sections on "Position of Statistics in the Universities" (Part I), "Limitations of the Work of the DBS from the Standpoint of Economic Research" (Part III), and Personnel (Part IV): NA, RG 31, Vol. 1418, File: Miscellaneous, Pt. I.

7 Ibid., 7.

8 Ibid., 2.

9 Herbert Marshall, "The Role of the Dominion Bureau of Statistics in the Post-War World," presidential Address at the joint meeting of the Canadian Historical Association and the Canadian Political Science Association, London, 4 June 1953, published in the *Canadian Journal of Economic and Political Science*, 19, no. 3 (August 1953).

10 NA, RG 31, Vol. 1304. It was updated and resubmitted several times during the 1930s and is recognizable as the basis for much of the argument in Coats's 1941 "Valedictory Report."

11 Ibid.

12 But he did acknowledge census publications "as in many ways the closest approach to good scientific work that the Bureau has to its credit." MacGregor, "Limitations of the Work of the DBS," 5.

13 These were conducted separately from, and later than, the censuses of population and agriculture, but the enumerators for the latter were used to collect identifying information for the institutions and establishments concerned.

14 One new question in the census was "Do you own a radio?." A special press release was thought necessary to assure respondents that its purpose was not to locate persons who may not have paid their licence fees, or to assist manufactures in making sales by letting them know which families did not own radios.

15 *Administrative Report, Volume 1 (Summary), Seventh Census of Canada, 1931* (Ottawa: King's Printer, 1936), 60.

16 N. Keyfitz and H.F.Greenway, "Robert Coats and the Organization of Statistics," *Canadian Journal of Economics and Political Science*, 27, no. 3 (August 1961): 318.

17 *Administrative Report*, 1931 Census, 7.

18 They appeared serially, as and when completed, before being compiled in volumes 12 and 13 in 1942.

19 NA, RG 31, Accession No. 1989–90/133, Box 21, File 1421.

20 House of Commons, *Debates*, 20 April 1931, 726.

21 Ibid., 4 May 1931, 1238.

22 Ibid., 10 February 1932, 95.

23 Coats was authorized to hire academics on a temporary basis to assist with the preparatory work. These included Kenneth W. Taylor, who was paid at the rate of $335 per month.

24 Among the advisers to the other eight delegations, only three were identifiable by their titles as statisticians.

25 NA, RG 31, Accession No. 1989–90/133, Box 19, File 1388, Pt. I, R.H. Coats to Hon. H.H. Stevens, 17 October 1932, enclosing an undated memorandum, "Social and Economic Research – Governmental Machinery in Canada – A Policy Outline."

26 Ibid., 5.

27 Ibid., 15.

28 His list of suggested representatives included the National Council of Women.

29 Ibid., 16–17.

30 Ibid., 18.

31 NA, RG 31, Accession No. 1989–90/133, Box 19, File 1388, Pt. I, H.H. Stevens to R.H. Coats, 24 October 1932.

32 The Economic Council of Canada Act, 1935, 25–26 Geo. V, cap. 19.

33 Ibid., section 6.

34 Ibid., sections 5(1) and 8.

35 House of Commons, *Debates*, 18 March 1935, 1,793.

36 NA, RG 31, Vol. 1408, File 1466, R.H. Coats to R.B. Bennett, 10 June 1935.

37 House of Commons, *Debates*, 24 February 1936, 436–7.

38 Ibid., 27 February 1936, 577.

39 Ibid., 578.

40 MacGregor, "External Forces," 5.

41 Ibid.

42 See below, in this chapter.

43 Order in Council PC 1562, 31 July 1933.

44 House of Commons, *Debates*, 30 January 1934, 84.

45 Larry A. Glassford, *Reaction and Reform: The Politics of the Conservative Party under R.B. Bennett, 1927–1938* (Toronto, Buffalo and London: University of Toronto Press, 1992), 125.

46 *Report of the Committee on Finance and Industry*, Cmd. 3897 (London: His Majesty's Stationery Office, 1931).

47 NA, RG 31, Accession No. 1989–90/133, Box 21, File 1426, Memorandum: "The Relative Completeness of British and Canadian Statistics as regards their Usefulness for the Guidance of Financial and Monetary Policy," undated (but probably April 1932).

48 *Proceedings of the Royal Commission on Banking and Currency*, Addenda, 217–34.

49 Ibid., 3,076–3,080.

50 NA, RG 31, Accession No. 1989–90/133, Box 21, File 1426. An unsigned, undated document that appears to have been written by Herbert Marshall.

51 John Maynard Keynes, *Treatise on Money*, 2 vols. (London: MacMillan, 1930).

52 NA, RG 31, Accession No. 1989–90/133, Box 21, File 1426, W.C. Clark to R.H. Coats, 6 September 1933.

53 *Report of the Royal Commission on Banking and Currency in Canada, 1933* (Ottawa: King's Printer, 1933), para 287.

54 NA, RG 31, Vol. 1405, File 1459, R.H. Coats to J.A.C. Osborne, 14 January 1935.

55 House of Commons, *Debates*, 2 February 1934, 188.

56 In her account of the work of the committee and the royal commission that followed it, Hill, *Canada's Salesman to the World*, 462, quotes an editorial in the Vancouver *Sun* of 20 August 1934 dealing with Stevens and the inquiry, headlined "Statesman or Evangelist?"

57 The Winnipeg *Free Press* was said by Hill to have described Stevens as "accuser, prosecuting attorney, judge and executioner." Ibid., 460.

58 Ibid., 462.

59 NA, RG 31, Vol. 1435, Pamphlet, *Price Spreads and Mass Buying: An Explanation of the Work Done and Results Achieved by the Special Select Committee of the House of Commons*, 27 July 1934.

60 Hill, *Canada's Salesman to the World*, 601 n. 18, notes that in his memoirs, Stevens referred to the pamphlet as "the book that Bennett banned."

61 NA, RG 31, Accession No. 1989–90/133, Box 22, File 1441, Memo of 26 March 1934, Minister's Office to R.H. Coats.

62 *Economic Journal*, (London, UK) 45, (September 1935): 591.

63 Much of the statistical work was done by the accounting firm of Clarkson, Gordon and Company.

64 NA, RG 31, Accession No. 1989–90/133, Box 22, File 1441, R.H. Coats to Professor Gilbert E. Jackson, University of Toronto, 28 February 1934.

65 Ibid., Memo of 5 April 1934.

66 Ibid., Memo of 1 May 1934.

67 This paper, "Live Stock – the Problem," bears no date and can only be attributed to Grindlay by Coats's handwritten annotation.

68 NA, RG 31, Accession No. 1989–90/133, Box 22, File 1441, R.H. Coats to H.H. Stevens, 9 July 1934.

69 Ibid., R.H. Coats to Lester B. Pearson, 19 October 1934.

70 Ibid., Lester B. Pearson to R.H. Coats, 20 October 1934.

71 *Report of the Royal Commission on Price Spreads*, (Ottawa: King's Printer, 1935), 272.

72 Ibid., 273.

73 Ibid., 137.

74 The Dominion Trade and Industry Commission Act, 1935, 25–26 Geo. V, cap. 59.

75 Ibid.

76 Later in the decade, it became possible to put this work on a permanent basis.

77 Herbert Marshall was Coats's candidate for this position.

78 NA, RG 31, Accession No. 1989–90/133, Box 20, File 1405, Pt. III, Updated memorandum: "Economic Investigation by the Dominion Trade and Industry Commission," with covering letter of 2 August 1935.

79 PC 1908, 14 August 1937.

80 *Report of the Royal Commission on Dominion-Provincial Relations*, Book 1 (Ottawa: King's Printer, 3 May 1940), 14–15.

81 NA, RG 31, Vol. 1410, File 1507, "Proposed Outline of Independent Research for the Royal Commission on Dominion Provincial Relations," 1. This eleven page document is unsigned and undated, but a pencilled note on its cover in Coats's handwriting indicates that it came from Skelton.

82 Ibid., 1, 2.

83 Ibid., 2. In 1935 MacGregor had developed historical compilations of national income for the Bank of Nova Scotia, following pioneer work of his own.

84 NA, RG 31, Vol. 1410, File 1507, "Proposed Outline of Independent Research," 5.

85 *Report of the Royal Commission on Dominion-Provincial Relations*, Book 1, 18.

86 NA, RG 31, Vol. 1410, File 1507, R.H. Coats to R.A.C. Henry, 13 July 1938.

87 Exhibit 139, "Memo re Constitution and Administrative Machinery of the Dominion Bureau of Statistics," pages 3,835–51 of the Evidence.

88 Ibid., letter from R.H. Coats to Major J.G. Parmelee, 10 January 1938, accompanying Exhibit 139. Some fields of statistics, like those of municipal and provincial finance, may have been "brought under review" but with results that were by no means satisfactory. Others, like highway transportation, had scarcely been touched.

89 *Report of the Royal Commission on Dominion-Provincial Relations*, Book 1, 13.

90 Ibid., Book 2, 181.

91 Ibid.

92 Ibid., 171.

93 Ibid., 137.

94 Ibid., 140.

95 Ibid., 84.

96 Ibid.

97 D.C. MacGregor, J.B. Rutherford, G.E. Britnell, and J.J. Deutsch, *National Income: A Study Prepared for the Royal Commission on Dominion-Provincial Relations* (Ottawa: King's Printer, 1939). Rutherford was chief of the bureau's Agricultural Statistics Branch, and generous reference was made to the assistance rendered by such bureau officers as Herbert Marshall, A.C. Steedman, A. Cohen, M.C. MacLean, O.A. Lemieux, and A.H. LeNeveu.

98 Ibid., 11.

99 Ibid., 13.

100 But see chapter 9, below.

101 NA, RG 31, Vol. 1410, File 1507, R.H. Coats to Alex Skelton, 18 February 1939. Coats was referring to the "income produced" and "income paid out" methods.

102 Dominion/provincial conferences had been organized on provincial financial statistics in 1933, and on municipal statistics in 1937.

103 In 1944 Lowther succeeded the veteran J.R. Munro as chief of the Public Finance Statistics Branch.

104 By 1948 a further thirteen clerks had been assigned to this work. See *Annual Report of the Dominion Statistician for the year ended March 31, 1948* (Ottawa, 1948).

105 R.H. Coats, "Statistics Comes of Age:" Presidential Address delivered at a joint meeting of the Canadian Political Science Association and the Canadian Historical Association, 26 May 1936, *Canadian Journal of Economics and Political Science*, 2, no. 3 (August 1936): 271.

106 Ibid., 285.

107 Ibid., 286.

108 Ibid., 284, 285.

109 Ibid., 285.

110 However, his friend Georges Vanier, who was at that time High Commissioner for Canada in London, paid him the compliment all statisticians crave: "Until I read your address, I really didn't think it was possible to infuse such life and lightness into Statistics." NA, RG 31, Vol. 1408, File 1474, Georges Vanier to R.H. Coats, 18 September 1936.

111 Ibid., R.H. Coats to V.W. Bladen, 8 September 1936.

112 NA, RG 31, Accession No. 1989–90/133, Box 3, File 317, Pt. III, Memorandum, J.B. Rutherford to R.H. Coats, "Re Organization of Canadian Social Science Research Council," 26 March 1938.

113 Ibid., R.H. Coats to Professor H.A. Innis, 7 April 1938.

114 See note 6, above.

115 MacGregor, Part I, "Position of Statistics in the Universities," 2.

116 Ibid., Part III, "Limitations of the work of the DBS from the Standpoint of Economic Research," 1.

117 Ibid., 2.

118 Ibid., Part IV, "Personnel, " 1.

119 Ibid. MacGregor no doubt had in mind people like Nathan Keyfitz, C.D. Blyth, A.L. Neal, J.B. Rutherford, and C.F. Wilson.

120 Ibid., 2.

121 See chapter 13, below.

Chapter Eight

1 Resolution 11 of the conference. This was the first official use of the term "Commonwealth."

2 *League of Nations, Conference on International Co-operation in Statistics, August 14 and 15, 1919*, (London: Harrison and Sons, 1919), 39.

3 Ibid.

4 *British Empire Statistical Conference, 1920*, Minutes Day 18, Discussion with Sir Eric Drummond, Secretary, League of Nations.

5 This organization, founded in 1913, had been prevented by the war from beginning operations but was currently preparing to do so.

6 League of Nations, A.10–EFS 74, *International Statistics Commission (Paris – October, 1920) Report with Annexes* (Geneva, August 1921), 7. Archival records show no evidence of the bureau's dealings with the International Bureau of Commercial Statistics. In any case its functions were taken over by the League of Nations in 1935. The Dominion statistician's annual reports between the wars refer intermittently to the submission of data to the International Institute of Commerce, but this organization ceased operation in the mid-1940s. Canada is currently a member of the Customs Co-operation Council established in Brussels in 1950 with aims similar to those of the older organizations.

7 Ibid., 20.

8 Ibid.

9 Ibid., 22.

10 Ibid., 25.

11 Ibid., 30.

12 J.W. Nixon, *A History of the International Statistical Institute, 1885–1960*, (The Hague: International Statistical Institute, 1960), 31.

13 This was not a League of Nations conference, but it requested the league to take action on its recommendations.

14 See Article IV of the *Statutes of the Institute* (1887), quoted in Nixon, *A History*, 139. In the following year Coats was admitted to the institute as a full member, to be followed by Cudmore in 1929, who attended the Warsaw session of the same year.

15 Members were appointed in their personal capacities rather than as delegates of their countries.

16 The titles included *Statistics of the Gainfully-Occupied Population* (No. 1); *Minimum List of Commodities of International Trade Statistics* (No. 2); *Timber Statistics* (No. 3); *Statistics Relating to Capital Formation* (No. 4); *Housing Statistics* (No. 5); *Indices of Industrial Production* (No. 6). A number of studies that were interrupted by the outbreak of war in 1939 were subsequently completed and published under the auspices of the United Nations. See chapter 12, note 54, below.

17 Nixon, *A History*, 33, 34.

18 Ibid., 34.

19 NA, RG 31, Accession No. 1989–90/133, Box 15, File 904, Albert Thomas, director, International Labour Office, to the minister of Labour, Canada, 2 October 1920.

20 Meeker, at the time, had the title of chief of the Scientific Division. He had served as United States commissioner of Labour Statistics from 1913 to 1920.

21 NA, RG 31, Accession No. 1989–90/133, Box 15, File 904, R.H. Coats to Albert Thomas, undated, hand-written draft.

22 Ibid., Albert Thomas to R.H. Coats, 18 October 1920.

23 Ibid., Albert Thomas to the minister of Labour, Canada, 10 August 1923.

24 A complete statement of Coats's position was published as "Classification Problems in Statistics," *International Labour Review*, 11, no. 4 (April 1925): 509–25.

25 International Labour Office, *Report of the Second International Conference of Labour Statisticians, held at Geneva, 20–25 April, 1925*, Studies and Reports, Series N (Statistics), no. 8, Resolution 4 (Geneva, 1925).

26 Ibid., *Report of the Third International Conference of Labour Statisticians, held at Geneva, 18 to 23 October 1926*, Studies and Reports, Series N (Statistics) No. 12, Resolution 3 (Geneva, 1926).

27 NA, RG 31, Vol. 1422.

28 NA, RG 31, Accession No. 1989–90/133, Box 4, File 335.

29 NA, RG 31, Vol. 1422.

30 NA, RG 31, Vol. 1410, File 1493, Pt. 1, Memo of 23 December 1936, T.W. Grindlay to R.H. Coats.

31 NA, RG 31, Vol. 1422.

32 *Report and Resolutions Adopted by the Second Conference of Government Officers Engaged in Dealing with Statistics in the British Commonwealth of Nations* (Ottawa: King's Printer, 1935), para 22.

33 NA, RG 31, Accession No. 1989–90/133, Box 4, File 335.

34 Ibid.

35 *British Empire Statistical Conference, 1920, Report and Resolutions*, Cmd. 648, (London: His Majesty's Stationery Office, 1920).

36 Godfrey contracted double pneumonia *en route* to the conference and was unable to take part in its proceedings.

37 Flux, the senior British delegate, had a Canadian connection, having served as William Dow Professor of Political Economy at McGill University from 1901 to 1908.

38 Coats served on five of them: trade statistics, census, labour statistics, financial statistics, and prices and index numbers.

39 Fifteen years later, the next conference reported that the recommendations had "since exercised a considerable influence upon official statistics throughout the British Commonwealth and elsewhere." *Conference of British Commonwealth Statisticians, 1935, Report and Resolutions* (Otawa: King's Printer, 1935).

40 *British Empire Statistical Conference 1920*, Minutes, Day 5, 14 et seq.

41 Ibid., *Report and Resolutions*, 19.

42 Ibid., Minutes, Day 7, 28.

43 Ibid., Day 19, 12. Writing many years later to a UK official whom he had met at one of the imperial conferences, Coats recalled that, as a consequence of the fragmentation and jealousies among the UK delegates in 1920, "we had actually at one stage to re-form the Conference, because the population fellows wouldn't attend a meeting presided over by a Board of Trade man – Flux, who had been appointed the General Chairman of the Conference on opening." NA, RG 31, Vol. 1405, File 1454, R.H. Coats to Sir George Schuster, 5 November 1934.

44 British Empire Statistical Conference, 1920, Minutes, Day 19, 13.

45 See ibid., *Report and Resolutions*, 12–16.

46 PC 1732, 25 August 1920.

47 NA, RG 31, Accession No. 1989–90/133, Box 19, File 1380, Imperial Economic Conference Document (23)–4, "British Empire Statistics," Dispatch from the Governor-General of Australia to the Rt. Hon. the Secretary of State for the Colonies, 9 August 1920.

48 From *Journal of the Royal Statistical Society* 83 (London 1920): 131.

49 Ibid.

50 Ibid., vol. 84 (London 1921): 611.

51 NA, RG 31, Accession No. 1989–90/133, Box 19, File 1380, Imperial Economic Conference Document (23)–4, "British Empire Statistics." The reservations of the Dominions spared the UK government the embarrassment of making its own position explicit.

52 The Board of Trade had put a similar suggestion before the Dominions royal commission in 1914.

53 Coats was present at the meeting, and these comments are taken from his "Memorandum re: Agenda of Imperial Economic Conference: Part II – British Empire Statistics." Subsequently, Hon. George P. Graham, minister of Railways and Canals, who had been a delegate, told the minister of Trade and Commerce that "the service and advice given by Mr R.H. Coats were very highly appreciated. Even side by side with the flower of the British Civil Service, Canada's advisory delegation shone." NA, RG 32, Vol. 49, R.H. Coats Personnel File, letter of 3 December 1923.

54 Cudmore served as an economic adviser to the Canadian government delegation to this conference.

55 O. Mary Hill provided a fascinating account of this conference in *Canada's Salesman to the World*, chapter 24, "Ottawa Plays Host to the Empire."

56 For the bureau, on which the burden of organizing the statistical conference would mainly fall, this would undoubtedly have been a relief because, for many months prior to the date of the economic conference, it was heavily involved in providing statistical support to the various preparatory committees.

57 Coats's particular friend and ally on the principle of centralization in 1920, George

Knibbs of Australia, had died later in the decade. The Australian delegate in 1935 was Roland Wilson, who had the distinction of being the youngest man at the conference. In April 1986, as Sir Roland Wilson, he was fêted in Canberra on the occasion of the fiftieth anniversary of his appointment as Commonwealth statistician.

58 *Report and Resolutions Adopted by the Second Conference of Government Officers Engaged in Dealing with Statistics in the British Commonwealth of Nations* (Ottawa: King's Printer, 1935), paras. 83 and 84.

59 Ibid., 43, resolution 107.

60 Ibid., 8.

61 Ibid., 44, para. 78.

62 Ibid., 45, para. 80.

63 NA, RG 31, Accession No. 1989–90/133, Box 16, File 1318, Sir Francis Floud to O.D. Skelton, 16 April 1935.

64 Ibid., J.G. Parmelee to R.H. Coats, 28 May 1935.

65 Ibid., R.H. Coats to J.G. Parmelee, 31 May 1935.

66 Ibid., J.G. Parmelee to R.H. Coats, 15 August 1935.

67 Ibid., S.A. Cudmore to R.H. Coats, 1 December 1937.

68 Ibid., 1 October 1937.

69 Ibid., R.H. Coats to E.A. Pickering, Prime Minister's Office, 2 June 1938.

70 Ibid., Sir Francis Floud to O.D. Skelton, 7 October 1938.

Chapter Nine

1 The *Canada Year Book* of 1941, writing about the First World War, commented on "the amateurishness and the piecemeal character of the statistics then available." Introduction, xliii.

2 The board's first secretary was Professor K.W. Taylor, well known to the bureau for his work on international trade. Donald Gordon, the banker, was chairman from 1941, and Walter E. Duffett, a future Dominion statistician, joined the board's Research and Statistics Division from Sun Life of Canada.

3 The cost of living index increased by less than fifteen percent.

4 The board apparently took it for granted that the bureau would be willing to report "illegal price increases" encountered during the field collection work, but it was set straight in a 25 November 1941 letter from Coats: "If this voluntary service [price reporting] laid [respondents] open to special observation and possible prosecution, they would almost certainly object on grounds of discrimination and our modus operandi would disintegrate." NA, RG 31, Vol. 1413, File 1527, Pt. II.

5 Later, local "cost of living representatives" were hired to collect prices data, laying the foundation for the network of regional offices that developed at war's end.

See A.B. Mackay, "The Regional Operations of Statistics Canada: Its Origin and Early Development" (mimeograph), July 1983, 8.

6 These records were eventually microfilmed and used to furnish proof of birthdate for old age and other kinds of pension entitlements.

7 "Wartime Activities of the Bureau of Statistics," Cat. No. 11–D–61 (1943), 19.

8 Ibid., 19–20. The emphasis is in the original.

9 N.L. McKellar joined the bureau in 1942 to take charge.

10 Not only were insured workers covered but also uninsured workers in the same establishments.

11 *Canada Year Book*, 1943–44, xlviii.

12 There was probably more regulation of agricultural production and marketing than anywhere else in the economy.

13 For example, a Food Requirements Committee was set up in October 1942 to coordinate domestic and external demands on Canadian food production.

14 NA, RG 31, Vol. 1410, File 1490, S.A. Cudmore to under secretary of state of External Affairs, 30 July 1943.

15 See below, in this chapter.

16 Cat. No. 67–D–52.

17 NA, RG 31, Vol. 1413, File 1527, Pt. IV.

18 Order in Council PC 4428, 18 August 1942.

19 NA, RG 31, Vol. 1414, File 1527–X, Undated memo (probably February or March 1943), "Effects of the Order in Council Establishing the Directorate of Government Office Economies Control (PC 4428) upon the Work of the Dominion Bureau of Statistics."

20 NA, RG 31, Vol. 1414, File 1527, Part 24.

21 Ibid., File 1527–X, memo, "Effects of the Order in Council."

22 Ibid., John Thompson to S.A. Cudmore, 9 November 1942.

23 NA, RG 31, Vol. 1416, File 1549, S.A. Cudmore to Hon. J.A. MacKinnon, 5 March 1943.

24 NA, RG 31, Vol. 1418, File: Miscellaneous Subjects Material – No Definite Category, letter of 23 September 1940.

25 Ibid.

26 NA, RG 31, Vol. 1417, File on Census Material, Memorandum of 27 November 1939 to R.H. Coats: "The Necessity of Taking the Eighth Decennial Census of Canada in 1941." Author not identified but probably S.A. Cudmore.

27 The costs of the 1941 census, which were spread over the four fiscal years from 1940–41 to 1943–44, were about $3.5 million. During these years the government's total budgetary expenditures increased from $1,885 million in 1940–41 to $5,246 million in 1943–44.

28 By contrast, the heavy immigration of the 1920s had shrunk to a trickle. It was stressed that "internal migration rather than assimilation of immigrants is today a

major population problem." *Administrative Report of the Dominion Statistician, Eighth Census of Canada, 1941* (Ottawa: King's Printer, 1945) 3.

29 Ten percent samples from the completed population schedules were also used to compile, with the least possible delay, preliminary information on occupations, earnings, and employment for the Department of Finance, and on the population of working age for the National Selective Service and branches of the armed forces. See *Administrative Report,* 1941 Census, 61–9.

30 Ibid., 32.

31 Public notice of 2 June 1941, *The Eighth Decennial Census of Canada*, issued by authority of the minister of Trade and Commerce, Hon. James A. MacKinnon, MP.

32 *Administrative Report*, 1941 Census, 50.

33 Ibid., 75.

34 In 1947 she returned to the UK after completing the census monograph associated with her name.

35 *Canada Gazette,* 6 July 1946.

36 NA, RG 31, Vol. 1420, File: League of Nations (*sic*) Pt. III, letter of 26 October 1939.

37 NA, RG 31, Accession No. 1989–90/133, Box 9, File 876, minutes of the 14 November 1939 meeting of the Committee on National Income.

38 Ibid., minutes of the 27 June 1940 meeting of the Committee on National Income.

39 The preface (p. 4), signed by Coats, promised that "other parts dealing with the operating accounts of industrial and service groups, geographical distribution by industries, and capital formation and consumers' outlay, will be issued as opportunity permits."

40 NA, RG 31, Accession No. 1989–90/133, Box 9, File 876, Undated memorandum, "Part I, National Income of Canada," furnished in response to Smith's written request of 17 April 1941.

41 Sydney B. Smith, *National Income of Canada, 1919–1938, Part I* (Ottawa, 1941), Catalogue No. 13–502 B, 46.

42 NA, RG 31, Accession No. 1989–90/133, Box 9, File 876, Undated memorandum, "Part I, National Income of Canada."

43 Ibid., "Some Comments on the Dominion Bureau of Statistics Report on National Income, Part I," J.J. Deutsch to S.A. Cudmore, 28 April 1941.

44 Ibid.

45 Ibid.

46 Ibid., Minutes of Meeting, National Income Committee, 16 June 1941.

47 Ibid.

48 Ibid., Memorandum of 22 July 1941, S.A. Cudmore to R.H. Coats, "Re National Income Statistics."

49 NA, RG 19, Vol. 445, File 111–1R, R.B. Bryce, "Memorandum on Conversation with Mr Bangs of the Bureau," 19 March 1942.

50 Ibid., S.A. Cudmore to L.D. Wilgress, deputy minister, Department of Trade and Commerce, 16 June 1942.

51 Ibid., R.B. Bryce to R.G. Bangs, 7 May 1942.

52 Ibid., Memorandum of 23 January 1942 by S.A. Cudmore, "Note on Present Position of National Income Investigation."

53 Ibid., J.J. Deutsch and R.B. Bryce, "Memorandum on National Income Statistics."

54 Ibid., R.B. Bryce, "Memorandum for Dr Clark," 7 March 1942.

55 The meeting was formally a subcommittee of the Advisory Committee on Economic Policy.

56 NA, RG 19, Vol. 445, File 111–1R, R.B. Bryce, "Draft Notes on National Income for Dr Clark in Reference to Meeting on April 9, 1942."

57 Ibid., R.B. Bryce, "Notes on meeting on National Income Statistics, April 9, 1942."

58 Ibid.

59 *Canada Year Book*, 1943–44, 798.

60 Ibid., 1945, 906.

61 Ibid., 1946, 872–8.

62 In 1912 he had been a founding member of the association.

63 His presidential addresses to these associations were "Statistics Comes of Age," *Canadian Journal of Economics and Political Science*, no. 3 (August 1936), and "Science and Society," *Journal of the American Statistical Association* 34, no. 205 (March 1939).

64 NA, RG 32 C2, Vol. 66, File 68, "Retirement Speech," 24 January 1942.

65 A photographic memento of the occasion, including portraits of key staff members, was prepared by Nathan Keyfitz and presented to Coats. It is presently held by the Statistics Canada library.

66 NA, RG 32 C2, Vol. 66, File 68, "Retirement Speech," 24 January 1942.

67 NA, RG 32, Vol. 49 (R.H. Coats Personnel File), R.H. Coats to L.D. Wilgress, deputy minister, Department of Trade and Commerce, 18 July 1941.

68 There is no definitive version of this document, which is not in the archives and of which the few extant copies in Statistics Canada's library and elsewhere vary in the number of appendices they contain.

69 Coats, "Valedictory Report," 18.5.

70 Ibid.

71 Ibid., 3–7.

72 Coats noted in his "Valedictory Report" (p. 7) that "in only one Province, namely Québec, has a Provincial Bureau of Statistics been established, though approaches have been made in Alberta and British Columbia."

73 This wording was adopted almost verbatim in the 1948 revision of the Statistics Act.

74 Coats, "Valedictory Report," 11.

75 Ibid., 19.

76 N.a., *The Dominion Bureau of Statistics: Its Origin, Constitution.*

77 R.H. Coats and M.C. Maclean, *The American-born in Canada: A Statistical Interpretation* (Toronto: Ryerson Press, 1943). It was one of the few statistical publications in a contemporary series, "The Relations of Canada and the United States," funded by the Division of Economics and History of the Carnegie Endowment for International Peace.

78 *Canadian Historical Review* 27, no. 2 (June 1946).

79 His presidential address, "Cephalus: A Prologue", in *Transactions of the Royal Society of Canada*, 3d series, section 2, vol. 28 (1944) was a somewhat highbrow departure from his usual earthy style.

80 NA, RG 32, Vol. 49 (R.H. Coats Personnel File), R.H. Coats to S.S. Swettenham et al, 26 July 1957. Swettenham had started as a messenger in the old Census and Statistics Office and, in 1975, attended the official opening of the R.H. Coats Building.

81 R.H. Coats to N. Keyfitz, 21 December 1959. A copy of the letter is in the author's personal archive.

82 N. Keyfitz and H.F.Greenway, "Robert Coats and the Organization of Statistics," *Canadian Journal of Economics and Political Science*, 27, no. 3 (August 1961): 318. Greenway was still with the bureau at this time, but Keyfitz had become a professor in the Department of Political Economy at the University of Toronto.

83 Knibbs, later Sir George Knibbs, served from 1906 to 1921. See Colin Forster and Cameron Hazelhurst, "Australian Statisticians and the Development of Official Statistics," *Yearbook Australia*, 1988.

84 *Minutes of Proceedings of the Royal Society of Canada*, 1960, 100.

CHAPTER TEN

1 A.L. Neal, one of Cudmore's closest advisors, commented on "a marked tendency towards the breakdown of centralized statistics in Canada." See NA, RG 31, Vol. 1416, File 1550, "Growth of Wartime Statistics Needs," 11 December 1942.

2 Advisory Committee on Reconstruction, *Report*, Ottawa, 24 September 1943, 10, 11.

3 *Employment and Income with special reference to the Initial Period of Reconstruction* (Ottawa: King's Printer, April 1945).

4 *Report of the Department of Trade and Commerce for the Year Ended March 31, 1945*, (Ottawa: King's Printer, 1945), 36.

5 NA, RG 31, Accession No. 1989–90/133, Box 9, File 876, R.B. Bryce, "Memorandum for Dr Clark," 7 March 1942.

6 Order In Council, PC 608, 23 January 1943.

7 NA, RG 31, Vol. 1416, File 1550.

8 Ibid., File 1553.

9 Stone was at this time with the Central Statistical Office in London, which had been established in the previous year at Churchill's insistence to provide leadership and coordination of the decentralized system of statistics then prevailing in the UK, and specifically to develop national income and expenditure accounts as a basis for war finance.

10 NA, RG 19 E 2(f), Vol. 3440, File N–7–3, "Report of Canadian Representatives at Post-War Economic Talks Held in London between 23 October and 9 November 1942," section 4.

11 Goldberg, *The Development of National Accounts in Canada*, 38. Writing so soon after the interdepartmental disagreements of the early war years, Goldberg had no option but to publicly represent these developments as an unremarkable transition from the bureau's earlier work on national income.

12 NA, RG 19, Vol. 4457, File 111–1R, "Content of National Income and Expenditure," Ottawa, 25 September 1944.

13 Edward F. Denison, "Report on the Tripartite Discussions of National Income Measurement," in vol. 10, part 1 of Conference on Research in Income and Wealth, *Studies in Income and Wealth* (New York: National Bureau of Economic Research, 1947), 4–21. The conference was a continuing forum of the long-established National Bureau of Economic Research, and during the postwar years the Dominion Bureau of Statistics became an important contributor to its deliberations.

14 This was not the senior committee that had been established earlier in the year but a technical group chaired by Herbert Marshall.

15 Alex Skelton, "Obituary," *Canadian Journal of Economics and Political Science*, 11, no. 3 (August 1945): 478–9.

16 Almost half a century later, Isbister told me that the early national accounts had been a collection of pigeon-holes with nothing in many of them (taped interview, 20 February 1992).

17 R.H. Coats, "The Place of Statistics in National Administration," *Transactions of the Royal Society of Canada*, section 2 (1929): 88.

18 R.H. Coats, "Science and Society", 16.

19 A full statement of the system was provided in *Classification of Industries (used in the Dominion Bureau of Statistics)*, (Ottawa, 1928), Cat. No. 12–501 H.

20 Most notably at the British Empire Statistical Conference, London, 1920.

21 NA, RG 31, Vol. 1434, An unsigned memo to Cudmore, "The Problem of Classification," 11 January 1944. It would almost certainly have been written by A.L. Neal.

22 Taped interview with N.L. McKellar in 1989.

23 On the recommendation of Herbert Marshall, who had succeeded Cudmore as Dominion statistician late in 1945 and had become an active participant in the work of the newly established United Nations Statistical Commission.

24 As with the industrial classification project, there was a basis of prior work by the League of Nations Committee of Statistical Experts on which to build.

25 This superseded the criterion of *stage of production* used in earlier classifications,

which resulted in the broad categories of "crude," "simply transformed," and "more elaborately transformed."

26 In the 1921 census, information had been published only on a narrow range of principal occupations within industries.

27 N. Keyfitz and H.L. Robinson, "The Canadian Sample for Labour Force and other Population Data," *Population Studies* (Cambridge, UK) 2 (1948–49): 428.

28 A.B. MacKay, a retired regional director, provided a good nontechnical account of these difficulties in "*The Regional Operations of Statistics Canada: Its Origin and Early Development*" (mimeograph, July 1983).

29 Ibid, 28.

30 NA, RG 32, Vol. 592, Herbert Marshall Personal File 24–25 Vol. 1, Memorandum of 30 April 1942, H. Marshall to S.A. Cudmore.

31 Ibid.

32 Cudmore and Herbert Marshall, together with M.W. Mackenzie, the deputy minister, and Finlay Sim, the departmental secretary, had met with Messrs Bland and Jackson of the Civil Service Commission.

33 The provision of technical assistance in these areas by other bureau officers was inspired by the success of Cudmore's own contribution in pre–war Palestine.

Chapter Eleven

1 In 1944, when the Central Research and Development Staff was set up, there had been an Interdepartmental Standing Committee on Statistics, but this had apparently lapsed.

2 NA, RG 31, Vol. 1430, File: "National Accounts, 1949–56," Herbert Marshall to Hon. C.D. Howe, 12 September 1949.

3 A Dominion/provincial conference had been called in January 1941 to consider the recommendations of the Rowell–Sirois Commission but broke down in the face of opposition from some provinces. Subsequently the Dominion assumed for the duration of the war exclusive powers to levy income and corporation taxes.

4 NA, RG 31, Vol. 1434.

5 He served in this capacity until the appointment of Fraser Harris in 1948.

6 A telling indication of this confidence was that the Bank of Canada was no longer making its own estimates of national income.

7 NA, RG 31, Vol. 1434, "Memorandum re: Bureau of Statistics Reorganization," Dominion Statistician, Ottawa, 24 January 1946.

8 Ibid. Specifically, it was stated that the only other person in Canada who had worked on national income at the same level was Professor MacGregor of the University of Toronto, and that "we would not exchange Isbister for him."

9 Ibid. This rather general reference to international work no doubt encompassed Isbister's service as Canadian representative on the Sub–Committee on National Income Statistics of the League of Nations Committee of Statistical Experts, which

was convened in 1945 to complete a prewar study dealing with national income and social accounts. See chapter 12, note 54, below.

10 Ibid.

11 Ibid., "Memorandum on Reorganization of Central Staff," undated and unsigned but probably written by Herbert Marshall in late 1945.

12 In his mid-1945 discussions with senior Trade and Commerce management and the Civil Service Commission on restructuring the bureau, Cudmore had insisted on this as a *sine qua non.*

13 The two areas of statistics had been traditionally combined in the British and US statistical systems, as they had been in the Canadian Department of Labour before the establishment of the Dominion Bureau of Statistics. A decade or so later, they again split apart.

14 Blyth was in effect "director in waiting," since he continued also to hold the position of acting chief of the Statistics and Research Branch of the Foreign Exchange Control Board until that body was disbanded in December 1951.

15 NA, RG 31, Vol. 1434, "Memorandum re: Bureau of Statistics Reorganization."

16 Mahoney later returned as director, serving until the early 1960s. In 1958 the division was renamed the Business Finance Division.

17 Isbister's subsequent career in the public service was an illustrious one. He eventually served as deputy minister in several departments before retiring in the mid-1970s.

18 NA, RG 31, Vol. 1435, File: Status of the Dominion Statistician, unsigned and undated memorandum, "Staff Situation in the Dominion Bureau of Statistics." Emphasis is from the original.

19 Ibid.

20 Ibid., H. Marshall to M.W. Mackenzie, 29 April 1947.

21 House of Commons, *Debates*, 29 August 1946, 5614.

22 Ibid., 5615.

23 On the very next day, a supplementary estimate of $196,718 was put forward to cover the costs of an index of deaths. Ibid., 30 August 1946, 5622.

24 *Annual Report of the Dominion Statistician*, 1947–48, 6–9. This, incidentally, was the first separate report by the Dominion statistician since that for 1926–27. In the intervening years, the bureau's reports had been part of the overall Trade and Commerce reports.

25 *Annual Report of the Dominion Bureau of Statistics for the Fiscal Year Ended March 31, 1951* (Ottawa, 1951), 11. This change in the titling of the report prevailed through the 1950s and 1960s.

26 NA. RG 31, Vol. 1434, "Memorandum on Reorganization of Central Staff."

27 Ibid.

28 House of Commons, *Debates*, 14 July 1955, 6170.

29 NA, RG 31, Vol. 1435, File: Status of the Dominion Statistician, H. Marshall to M.W. Mackenzie, deputy minister, Trade and Commerce, 23 February 1951.

30 Ibid., 15 July 1948.

31 Ibid., 30 December 1948.

32 Ibid., 23 February 1951.

33 Ibid.

34 Ibid., M.W. MacKenzie to H. Marshall, 16 March 1951.

35 House of Commons, *Debates*, 3 June 1948, 4,755.

36 Ibid., 4,756.

37 G.S. Wrong, the original chief of transportation statistics and still in office, had made a second career of writing memoranda on these difficulties.

38 House of Commons, *Debates*, 3 June 1948, 4,756.

39 The bureau was also planning to use sampling again in the 1951 census.

40 The Statistics Act, 1948, 11–12 Geo. VI, cap. 45.

41 See chapter 13, below.

42 In 1947 the director of the division, J.H. Lowther, was awarded the Gold Medal of the Professional Institute of the Civil Service for his work in developing a system of uniform accounting for all levels of government.

43 The largest of these, the Québec Bureau of Statistics, had been founded in 1913 and thus predated the Dominion bureau. Ontario had a Bureau of Statistics and Research, set up in 1943 as a branch of the Treasury Department. Alberta had a Bureau of Statistics, and British Columbia a Bureau of Economics and Statistics.

44 NA, RG 31, Vol. 1425, R.M. Putnam to H. Marshall, 19 September 1947.

45 NA, RG 31, Vol. 1425.

46 One of their representatives was stationed in the bureau on a continuing basis.

47 Some work was also done for other departments of government, although the bureau had long since given up on Coats's ambition during the early 1920s to provide a centralized service for all departments.

48 *Annual Report of the Dominion Statistician for the Year Ended March 31, 1949* (Ottawa, 1949), 41.

49 *Annual Report of the Dominion Bureau of Statistics for the Fiscal Year Ended March 31, 1956* (Ottawa, 1956), 7.

50 NA, RG 31, Vol. 1423, File – Atlas of Canada, 1946–54, Part II (*sic*), R Ziola, "Electronic Data Processing Machines, Report No. 1," 17 February 1956. His remarks were prophetic of the difficulties that later beset the bureau.

51 Ibid., H. Marshall, Memorandum to Directors, 28 March 1956.

52 Ibid.

53 Ibid.

54 Ibid., Memo of 12 April 1956, S.A. Goldberg to H. Marshall.

55 Named after Anthony Tunney, an Irish immigrant who operated a dairy business there until his death in 1915. Joan Tremblay, a bureau colleague, provided the author with a copy of an article on the history of the pasture and its colourful owners written by Tunney's granddaughter, Evelyn Tunney, which appeared in the Toronto *Globe and Mail* of 14 July 1956.

56 The bureau's wartime responsibilities generated paper as never before. Many retired employees recall the collapse of the shelving that supported an enormous quantity of national registration records, loss of life and limb being only narrowly averted.

57 Corolyn Cox, "Name in the News," *Saturday Night,* 58, no. 19 (16 January 1943):2.

58 Austin F. Cross, *Evening Citizen*, Ottawa, Friday, September 26 1952, 21.

59 *Dominion Bureau of Statistics: History, Function, Organization* (Ottawa: Dominion Bureau of Statistics, 1952), appendix E. What was described as the "Ground Floor" was in fact the basement.

60 The cold war also led to rumours that the building would have a bomb shelter and could be converted for use as a military hospital.

61 Dominion Bureau of Statistics press release of 26 September 1952: "The New Building for the Dominion Bureau of Statistics."

62 See, for example, appendix E, *Dominion Bureau of Statistics: History, Function.*

63 House of Commons, *Debates*, 14 July 1955, 6,174.

64 Ibid. When the bureau eventually came to be mainly housed in climate-controlled highrises, there was a good deal of nostalgic recollection of the ability to open windows in the 1952 building.

65 House of Commons, *Debates*, 4 July 1956, 5,651.

66 Ibid., 9 August 1956, 7,307.

67 By 1962 the bureau's staff had grown to more than 1,800, and by the end of the 1960s it exceeded 3,000.

68 The census and other social statistics divisions moved to Temporary Buildings Nos. 5 and 8 on Carling Avenue.

Chapter Twelve

1 The first issue of what became an annual publication, now catalogued as 13–201.

2 *Annual Report of the Dominion Statistician*, 1948–49, 15.

3 *Annual Report of the Dominion Bureau of Statistics for the Fiscal Year Ended March 31, 1952* (Ottawa, 1952), 38.

4 *Inter-Industry Flow of Goods and Services, Canada, 1949*, Reference paper No. 72, Cat. No. 13–510 (Ottawa: Queen's Printer, 1956), Preface.

5 These data were benchmarked against annual totals from the corporation tax returns of the Department of National Revenue (Taxation) with which the bureau developed, for the first time, a constructive working relationship. This began when the bureau was permitted to conduct a sample survey of tax returns back to 1926 for the purposes of the historic national accounts series. The responsible officers were Mark Sprott of National Revenue and Frank Emmerson of the bureau. National Revenue later initiated the annual publication of *Taxation Statistics*. Emmerson's work laid the basis for the eventual development of a comprehensive program of corporate financial statistics.

6 NG, RG 31, Vol. 1410, File 1507, R.A.C. Henry to R.H. Coats, 13 July 1938.

7 Catalogue No. 98–1941 M8 (Ottawa: King's Printer, 1946). Prepared by a Census Research Group consisting of E. Charles, N. Keyfitz, and H. Roseborough.

8 *The Future Population of Canada*, 1.

9 NA, RG 20, Vol. 994, File 12:72, Vol. 1, M.W. MacKenzie to O. Master, 6 March 1946.

10 Ibid., H. Marshall to O. Master, 13 March 1946.

11 "Memorandum on the Projection of Population Statistics, 1954" (unpublished), Introduction.

12 E.g., *Population Projections for Canada and the Provinces, 1972–2001*, (Ottawa: Statistics Canada, 1972) Cat. No. 91–514.

13 *Administrative Report, Vol. 10, Ninth Census of Canada, 1951* (Ottawa: Queen's Printer, 1955).

14 The preface expressed the hope that they "may prove of value to statisticians and demographers in other countries, as well as to Canadian census officials engaged in the planning of future censuses" (Ibid., 5). The report was twice the length of its 1941 counterpart.

15 The United States Bureau of the Census, although technologically ahead of its Canadian counterpart in using UNIVAC 1 – the first computer designed for mass data processing – to process its 1950 census, nevertheless used an input system based on the manual preparation of punched cards, which turned out to be slow and expensive. By the time of the 1960 census, it had developed, together with the National Bureau of Standards, an electronic device for "reading" the questionnaires, known as FOSDIC (Film Optical Sensing Device for Input to Computers). FOSDIC was used by Canada in 1971.

16 Bélisle, whose inventive genius had served Canadian censuses since 1911, did not retire until 1950 and would thus have been involved in this decision, as also would his long-time supervisor and colleague A.E. Thornton, who retired in 1949.

17 *Administrative Report*, 1951 Census, 104.

18 Ibid., 84–93.

19 *Administrative Report of the 1956 Census*, Bulletin 3–10, Census of Canada 1956 (Ottawa: Queen's Printer, 1958), 10–5.

20 Ibid.

21 NA, RG 31, Vol. 1417, S.A. Cudmore to R.H. Coats, "The Quinquennial Census," 24 April 1935.

22 NA, RG 20, Vol. 994, File 12–71, Vol. I, undated, unattributed memorandum, "Quinquennial Census," (probably late 1953), 6.

23 Ibid., unattributed "Memorandum re Quinquennial Census," 12 July 1954.

24 Ibid., M.W. Sharp to R.B. Bryce, 7 January 1954.

25 Ibid., R.B. Bryce to H. Marshall, 14 January 1954.

26 Ibid., K.W. Taylor to M.W. Sharp, 16 February 1954.

27 Order in Council PC 3109, 8 July 1948.

28 *Report of the Royal Commission on Prices,* vol. 1 (Ottawa: King's Printer, 1949), 42–43.

29 Ibid., 40.

30 Ibid.

31 *The Consumer Price Index, January 1949-August 1952* (Ottawa: Dominion Bureau of Statistics, 1952) Cat. No. 62–502.

32 The previous index had assumed that home ownership costs moved proportionally with those of rental costs.

33 Four decades later, the same misperception is still common.

34 House of Commons, *Debates*, 5 April 1955, 2,740.

35 Walter, L. Gordon, *A Political Memoir*, (Halifax, NS: Goodread Biographies, Formac Publishing, 1983), 59.

36 Ibid., 60.

37 Order in Council PC 1955–909, 17 June 1955.

38 See Royal Commission on Canada's Economic Prospects, W^{m}. C. Hood, *Financing of Economic Activity in Canada*, 30 July 1958, including a presentation of National Transactions Accounts by L.M. Read, S.J. Handfield-Jones, and F.W. Emmerson, (Ottawa: Queen's Printer, 1959).

39 *Financial Flow Accounts, 1962–67, A Preliminary Report* (Ottawa: Dominion Bureau of Statistics, May 1969), Cat. No. 13–530.

40 *Annual Report of the Dominion Bureau of Statistics for the Fiscal Year Ended March 31, 1950* (Ottawa, 1950), 7.

41 Ibid., 9.

42 *Report of the Dominion Bureau of Statistics for the Fiscal Year Ended March 31, 1954* (Ottawa, 1954), 9.

43 *Report of the Dominion Statistician for the Fiscal Year Ended March 31 1948*, 12. This section handled all printing work other than the yearbook and handbook, which were printed by the Department of Public Printing and Stationery.

44 Part of the miscellany collected by the author from former colleagues.

45 *Annual Report of the Dominion Statistician, 1948–49*, 5.

46 *Annual Report of the Dominion Bureau of Statistics*, 1951–52, 7.

47 See, for instance a 1933 report by a "Committee of Enquiry on Printing and Stationery" and a 1938 Report by a "Committee on Publications," NA, RG 31, Vol. 1410, File 1492.

48 NA, RG 31, Vol. 1431, File: Publications 1950–56, John J. Deutsch to Herbert Marshall, 12 January 1956. The "new building" referred to was the Printing Office being built at that time in Hull.

49 Ibid.

50 Ibid., H. Marshall to J.J. Deutsch, March 1956.

51 NA, RG 31, Vol. 1431, File: Publications, 1950–56.

52 ECOSOC res. 8(II), 22 June 1946.

53 At that time, the principle of geographical representation was first being introduced. When Canada was passed over for membership, Marshall complained to W.R. Leonard, acting director of the U.N. Statistics Office: "I thought that appointments were to be made on the basis of statistical competence, and not on the basis of geographic or political representation." NA, RG 31, Vol. 1432, letter of 11 October 1949.

54 Published as No. 7 in the *League of Nations Series, Studies and Reports on Statistical Methods*. C.D. Blyth contributed to a related study of balance of payments statistics, which was published as No. 9.

55 A.H. LeNeveu in 1949 and Herbert Marshall in 1954.

56 The list was originally developed by a Frenchman, Jacques Bertillon, for the ISI during the late nineteenth century. Bertillon had a better-known brother, Alphonse, who developed the system for identification by fingerprints.

57 Largely through the interest and initiative of Simon Goldberg, the association became a major showcase for the bureau's research work in this area. The bureau also became an active participant in the work of a parallel but older forum, the continuing Conferences on Research in Income and Wealth, organized by the US National Bureau of Economic Research, Inc.

58 Assistant director for Statistical Standards, US Bureau of the Budget. He was elected president of the ISI in 1947, serving until 1953.

59 *Statutes of the Institute*, (Rome, 1887), article 1, paras. 2 and 4.

60 *Statutes of the Institute*, (The Hague, 1948). The institute was nevertheless granted consultative status by the Economic and Social Council of the UN.

61 The office of president eluded Canadians until 1987, when Dr Ivan P. Fellegi, chief statistician of Canada, was elected for a two-year term.

62 This meeting immediately preceded the first United Nations International Seminar on Statistical Organization. Both events were held in the bureau's new premises in Tunney's Pasture.

63 At the request of the department, Spanish-language versions of the Canada handbook were frequently prepared.

64 *Report of Proceedings, Conference of British Commonwealth Statisticians*, Canberra, Australia, 12–23 November 1951 (Canberra: Commonwealth Government Printer, 1952).

65 NA, RG 32, Vol. 547.

66 Ibid., Isabel McWhinney, a longstanding officer of the Prices and Labour Division, wrote the testimonial.

67 See p. 405, no. 68.

68 Many years later, Simon Goldberg remarked to me that Marshall had the knack of always being able to say the right thing at the right time.

69 M.C. Urquhart and K.A.H. Buckley, eds., *Historical Statistics of Canada* (Cambridge: Cambridge University Press; Toronto: Macmillan, 1965), Section F, 142–86.

70 NA, RG 31, Vol. 1434 contains Marshall's draft material.

Chapter Thirteen

1 NA, RG 32, Vol. 547, reported in 31 August 1956 memo, M.W. Sharp to W.F. Bull, deputy minister, Department of Trade and Commerce.

2 See, for example, the report for the fiscal year ended 31 March 1956, "General Activities," 7.

3 Order in Council PC 1960–1269.

4 The Civil Service Commission's longstanding position was that bureau staff were not directly involved in the making of government policy and could not claim parity with those who were.

5 When the Statistical Society of London, later the Royal Statistical Society, was formed in the 1830s, it adopted a wheat sheaf badge and the motto *Aliis exterendum* (Let others do the threshing). The badge remains, but the motto was eventually dropped. See also the epigraph.

6 Such as D.H. Fullerton, C.L. Barber, J.A. Sawyer, G. Rosenbluth, A.E. Safarian, and A.S. Rubinoff.

7 NA, RG 31, Vol. 1448, File 4000, Pt. 3, undated memorandum to file by S.A. Goldberg.

8 Bureau publicity releases at the time of the opening of the new building in Tunney's Pasture made much of the efficacy of its office layouts for improved clerical productivity.

9 NA, RG 31, Vol. 1448, File 4000, Pt. 1.

10 Ibid.

11 Ibid.

12 Ibid., "Organization of the Dominion Bureau of Statistics," 24 October 1961, unsigned but probably written by S.A. Goldberg.

13 NA, RG 31, Vol. 1448, File 4000, Pt. 2.

14 Ibid.

15 Ibid., Professor E.F. Beach, "Report on the Bureau of Statistics, Economic Analyses and Statistics," 16 November 1961.

16 *Report of the Royal Commission on Government Organization,* Vol. 3 (Ottawa: Queen's Printer, 1962), 40.

17 Ibid., 45.

18 This illustration subsequently became an almost mandatory reference in the bureau's correspondence with central agencies on the subject of staffing.

19 *Report of the Royal Commission on Government Organization*, 45, 49.

20 The Office of Statistical Standards in the US Bureau of the Budget had a similar responsibility.

21 NA, RG 31, Vol. 1439, File 1400–2.

22 NA, RG 31, Vol. 1524, File 145, memo from Dominion statistician to directors, 3 January 1963.

23 NA, RG 31, Vol. 1448, File 4000, Pt. 2.

24 Treasury Board Management Improvement Policy Statement, M1–II–66, dated 12 September 1966 (T13659860).

25 NA, RG 31. Vol. 1444, File 2000–1, memo to file, 14 December 1964.

26 NA, RG 31, Vol. 1443, File 2000–1, "Report by the Dominion Statistician on Classification Structure," 6 February 1964.

27 Glassco Commission *Report*, Vol. 3, 35.

28 NA, RG 31, Vol. 1443, File 2000–1, "Report by the Dominion Statistician on Classification Structure," 1.

29 NA, RG 31, Vol. 1444, File: Appraisals – Senior Professionals.

30 See the bureau's annual reports for the years in question.

31 NA, RG 31, Vol. 1448, File 4000, Pt. 2, "Organization of the Dominion Bureau of Statistics," 24 October 1961.

32 Three of them in fact had the rank of assistant Dominion statistician.

33 *Report of the Dominion Bureau of Statistics for the Fiscal Year Ended March 31, 1967*, (Ottawa, 1967) 7.

34 V.R. Berlinguette was the first bureau director to take the Civil Service Commission's new course for senior officers.

35 Only six years later, yet a further administrative layer was added with the interposition of six assistant chief statisticians between the directors general and the chief statistician of Canada.

36 The work of this division had earlier been known as "Public Finance."

37 Formerly the Industry Division.

38 Later integrated with the work of Central Classifications.

39 Dominion Bureau of Statistics, "Brief to the Special Committee on Science Policy, Senate of Canada," December 1968.

40 *Report of the Senate Special Committee on Science Policy*, Vol. 1, *A Critical Review: Past and Present*, (Ottawa: Queen's Printer, 1970), 164.

41 Volumes 2 and 3 of the committee's report.

42 *To Know and to be Known – Report of the Task Force on Government Information*, Vol. 1, (Ottawa: Queen's Printer, 1969), Preface, ii.

43 Ibid., Vol. 2, 250.

44 Ibid., 249.

45 *Image*, report of a Statistics Canada Study Group (Ottawa, June 1972).

46 *Strengthening the Statistical System*, report of a Statistics Canada Reorganization Task Force (Ottawa, January 1973; revised July 1973), 2.

47 I.P. Fellegi, G.B. Gray, and R. Platek, "The Redesign of the Canadian Labour Force Survey," *Journal of the American Statistical Association*, 62, no. 318 (June 1967): 421–53.

48 Both this and the IBM 360/30 were "third generation" computers with solid state circuits.

49 Some members of the staff, as it was constituted at this time, achieved great distinction later in their careers. Ivan Fellegi became chief statistician of Canada,

and Tim Holt was appointed director of the Central Statistical Office and head of the Government Statistical Service of the UK. Ruth Hubbard was appointed president of the Public Service Commission of Canada, and Richard Platek was awarded the Knight's Cross of the Order of Merit by the government of Poland for services to international statistics.

50 Theoretically, the estimates projected for particular years in successive program forecasts could have been used for monitoring the consistency of departmental plans, but there is no evidence that the Treasury Board Secretariat followed this practice.

51 Statistics Act, 1971, 19–20 Eliz. II, cap. 15. It came into force on 1 May 1971.

52 House of Commons, *Debates*, 16 December 1970, 2,116.

53 Ibid., 2,117.

54 In wording similar to that of the acts of 1918 and 1948, the new act stated (section 3) that "there shall continue to be a statistics bureau under the Minister, to be known as..."

Chapter Fourteen

1 The narrative of this section draws heavily on the administrative reports of the three censuses.

2 These appointments were traditionally within the gift of the minister, but candidates were required to satisfy the bureau's skill requirements.

3 Statutory authority for the conduct of mid-decade censuses was obtained in the 1971 revision of the Statistics Act.

4 Appendix A of the *Census of Canada, 1971 Vol. 6, Pt. 1, Administrative Report* (Ottawa: Queen's Printer, 1976) provided a history of the questions included in past censuses of population and housing (whether and when included) and an explanation of their purpose.

5 See *Administrative Report*, 1971 Census, appendix C.

6 In 1971 household and family data were also included.

7 This is a conceptually integrated framework describing the structure and functioning of the economy as a whole with interrelated subsystems covering income and expenditure accounts, the balance of international payments, input-output tables, indexes of real domestic product by industry, financial flow accounts, and productivity studies.

8 As explained in an earlier chapter, these historically preceded the income and expenditure accounts.

9 See John W. Kendrick, *Productivity Trends in the United States*, National Bureau of Economic Research Study, No. 71, General Series (Princeton, NJ: Princeton University Press, 1961). When the US Bureau of Labor Statistics later adopted this approach, it was referred to more modestly as "multi-factor productivity."

10 NA, RG 31, Vol. 1458, "Productivity Study Group, 1962–63."

11 Edward F. Denison, assisted by Jean-Pierre Poullier, *Why Growth Rates Differ: Post War Experience in Nine Western Countries*, (Washington, DC: Brookings Institution, 1967).

12 Dorothy Walters, *Canadian Income Levels and Growth: An International Perspective*, Staff Study No. 23 (Ottawa: Economic Council of Canada, 1968).

13 CALURA operations, although housed in bureau premises, were initially segregated by chicken-wire barriers. In the organizational restructuring of 1967, the CALURA Division was integrated into a new Financial Statistics Branch.

14 House of Commons, *Debates*, 19 July 1958, 2,463.

15 Ibid.

16 *Statistics of Unemployment in Canada*, memorandum prepared by the Dominion Bureau of Statistics and the Economics and Research Branch, Department of Labour (Ottawa, 1958).

17 For June 1958 the labour force survey figure was 320,000 persons, while the NES figure was 526,600.

18 Dominion Bureau of Statistics/Department of Labour, *Statistics of Unemployment in Canada*, 20.

19 House of Commons, *Debates*, 24 March 1960, 2,387.

20 Catalogue No. 71–001.

21 M.C. Urquhart and K.A.H. Buckley, eds., *Historical Statistics of Canada*, (Cambridge: University Press, and Toronto: MacMillan, 1965).

22 House of Commons, Debates, 6 April 1966, 3,915.

23 Ibid., reply to Question 2449, 30 January 1967, 12,401.

24 Figures are taken from ibid., answers to Question 284, 5 July 1967, 2,265–6, and Question 1659, 14 April 1969, 7,458.

25 Ibid., reply to Question 284, 5 July 1967, 2,265–6.

26 Ibid., reply to Question 1,659, 14 April 1969, 7,458.

27 Statistics Canada, *Strengthening the Statistical System*, Report of a Statistics Canada Reorganisation Task Force, January 1973 (revised July 1973), 4.

EPILOGUE

1 C.A. Moser et al., *Statistics Canada Methodology Review*, March 1980, 11.

2 Price Waterhouse Associates, *Statistics Canada Organization Study*, February 1980, 14.

3 See n.a., *75 Years and Counting – A History of Statistics Canada* (Ottawa: Statistics Canada, 1993), 78–83.

4 *Report of the Auditor General of Canada to The House of Commons, Fiscal Year Ended 31 March 1983* (Ottawa: Minister of Supply and Services, 1983), Statistics Canada – Synopsis, para. 16.2, 487.

5 *Management of Government – Major Surveys, A Study Team Report to the Task Force on Program Review* (Ottawa: Minister of Supply and Services Canada, 1985), 66.

Index